4 Symbols

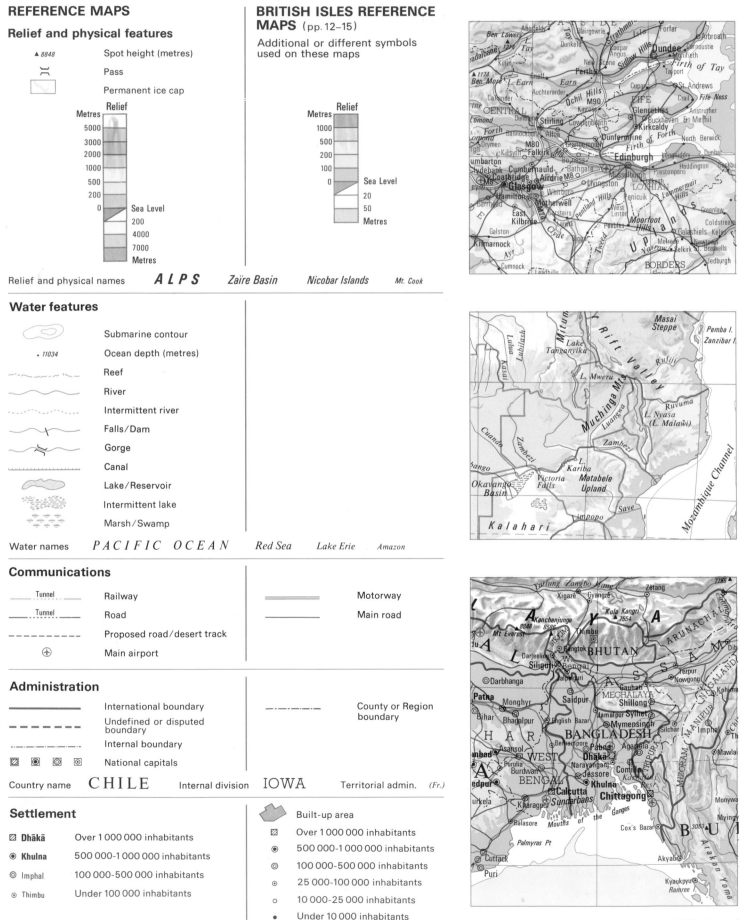

REFERENCE MAPS
Relief and physical features

▲ 8848   Spot height (metres)

⊃⊂   Pass

Permanent ice cap

Relief

Metres	
5000	
3000	
2000	
1000	
500	
200	
0	Sea Level
200	
4000	
7000	
Metres	

Relief and physical names   *ALPS*   *Zaïre Basin*   *Nicobar Islands*   *Mt. Cook*

Water features

Submarine contour

. 11034   Ocean depth (metres)

Reef

River

Intermittent river

Falls/Dam

Gorge

Canal

Lake/Reservoir

Intermittent lake

Marsh/Swamp

Water names   *PACIFIC OCEAN*   *Red Sea*   *Lake Erie*   *Amazon*

Communications

Tunnel ⸺ Railway

Tunnel ⸺ Road

– – – – – Proposed road/desert track

⊕ Main airport

Administration

⸻ International boundary

– – – Undefined or disputed boundary

·–·–· Internal boundary

National capitals

Country name   CHILE

Settlement

☑ **Dhākā**   Over 1 000 000 inhabitants

◉ **Khulna**   500 000-1 000 000 inhabitants

◎ Imphal   100 000-500 000 inhabitants

○ Thimbu   Under 100 000 inhabitants

BRITISH ISLES REFERENCE MAPS (pp. 12–15)

Additional or different symbols used on these maps

Relief

Metres	
1000	
500	
200	
100	
0	Sea Level
	20
	50
	Metres

Motorway

Main road

County or Region boundary

Internal division   IOWA   Territorial admin.   (Fr.)

Built-up area

☑ Over 1 000 000 inhabitants

◉ 500 000-1 000 000 inhabitants

◎ 100 000-500 000 inhabitants

◎ 25 000-100 000 inhabitants

○ 10 000-25 000 inhabitants

• Under 10 000 inhabitants

© Collins ◇ Longman Atlases

To draw a map of the world, or of a part of the world, the real area has to be reduced in size, or scaled down, to fit onto the map sheet or atlas page. The **scale** of any map therefore tells us precisely how much the real area has been reduced in size.

To use a map to work out the size of areas or distances on the real ground, we need to refer to the scale of that particular map. Map scales can be shown in several ways:

As a **linear scale** — a horizontal line is marked off in units which show how the real ground distances are represented on the map, as in the example below.

```
0    1    2    3    4    5 km
```

As a **statement of scale** — the linear scale above would be written as *1 cm to 1 km.* This means that 1 cm on the map represents 1 km on the real ground.

As a **representative fraction** — for example the scale shown above would be *1:100 000.* This means that every 1 unit of measurement on the map represents 100 000 units on the real ground.

As the scale becomes smaller the amount of real ground that can be fitted onto the map becomes larger. But in making the scale smaller, the accuracy of the map, and the detail it can show, have to be reduced.

The four examples on this page show what happens when the map scale is made smaller. As the scale decreases from the top to the bottom of the page, the details shown on the maps become less precise and more generalised.

On Map A, at a scale of *1:2 000 000,* the Isle of Wight is shown as a county of England, and detail of roads, the location of towns and relief is clearly shown. It is possible to distinguish bays and inlets around the coast.

On Map B, at a scale of *1:4 000 000,* a larger area of the south of England is shown. Thus the coastline of the Isle of Wight has been generalised, and there are few details about the island other than its name.

On Map C, at a scale of *1:16 000 000,* it is possible to show the whole of England and part of the mainland of Europe. The coastline of the Isle of Wight is very generalised, and the island is no longer named.

On Map D, at a scale of *1:85 000 000,* all of Europe can be shown, but the Isle of Wight is represented only by a small dot. At this small scale it is impossible to show any detail of the actual shape of the island, but its location is marked.

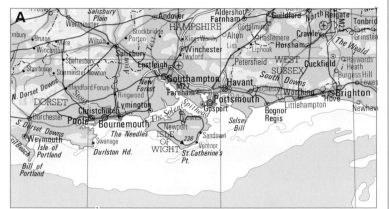

The scale of this map is 1:2 000 000 or 1cm represents 20 km

The scale of this map is 1:4 000 000 or 1cm represents 40 km

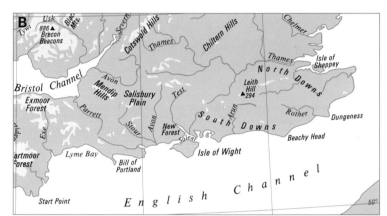

The scale of this map is 1:16 000 000 or 1cm represents 160 km

The scale of this map is 1:85 000 000 or 1cm represents 850 km

6 Latitude and Longitude

Lines of latitude and longitude are imaginary lines drawn around a globe or on maps of the whole, or part of the world. Like the grid lines on Ordnance Survey maps they can be used to locate a place accurately.

LATITUDE

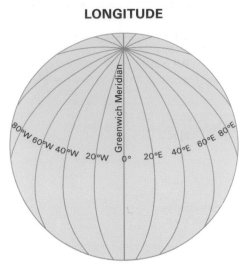

LONGITUDE

THE EARTH'S GRID SYSTEM

Lines of **latitude** (or *parallels*) are drawn parallel to the Equator. They are numbered in **degrees** either *north* or *south* of the Equator.
The Equator is numbered 0°, the North Pole 90°N and the South Pole 90°S.

Other important lines of latitude are the Tropic of Cancer (23½°N) and the Tropic of Capricorn (23½°S), the Arctic Circle (66½°N) and the Antarctic Circle (66½°S).

Lines of **longitude** (or *meridians*) are drawn from the North Pole to the South Pole. The prime meridian, numbered 0°, runs through the Greenwich Observatory in London and is called the Greenwich Meridian. Lines of longitude are numbered in **degrees** either *east* or *west* of the Greenwich Meridian. The 180° line of longitude, exactly opposite the Greenwich Meridian on the other side of the globe, is the International Date Line.

When lines of latitude and longitude are drawn on a globe or map they form a grid, with the parallels and meridians meeting at right angles. By using a combination of a place's latitude and longitude that place can be accurately located on the globe or map.

To be really accurate each degree of latitude and longitude can be divided into smaller units called **minutes**. There are 60 minutes in one degree. For example the location of Moscow is 55° 45' north of the Equator, and 37° 42' east of the Greenwich Meridian — this latitude and longitude reference is usually shortened to 55 45N 37 42E.

THE HEMISPHERES

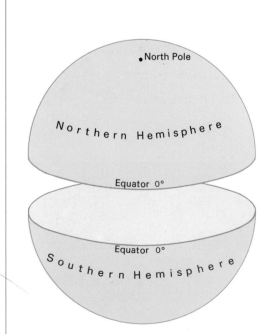

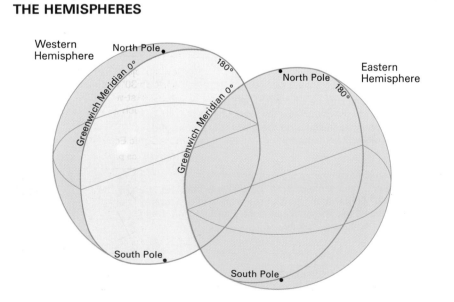

By splitting the globe along the line of the Equator the earth can be divided into two halves, called the Northern and Southern **hemispheres**. If the globe is divided into two from the North Pole to the South Pole, along the 0° and 180° lines of longitude, the halves are called the Eastern Hemisphere and the Western Hemisphere.

An atlas map of the world shows the whole world on the flat surface of the page. Yet in reality the earth is actually a sphere. This means that a system has to be used to turn the round surface of the earth into a flat map of the world, or part of the world. This cannot be done without some distortion — on a map some parts of the world have been stretched, other parts have been compressed. A system for turning the globe into a flat map is called a **projection**.

There are many different projections, each of which distort different things to achieve a flat map. Correct area, correct shape, correct distances or correct directions can be achieved by a projection; but, by achieving any one of these things the others have to be distorted. When choosing the projection to use for a particular map it is important to think which of these things it is most important to have correct.

The projections below illustrate the main types of projections, and include some of those used in this atlas.

PROJECTION GROUPS

Cylindrical Projection

Cylindrical projections are constructed by projecting the surface of the globe on to a cylinder just touching the globe.

Conic Projection

Conic projections are constructed by projecting part of the globe on to a cone which just touches a circle on the globe.

Azimuthal Projection

Azimuthal projections are constructed by projecting part of the globe on to a plane which touches the globe only at one point.

EXAMPLES OF PROJECTIONS

Mercator Conformal Cylindrical
World

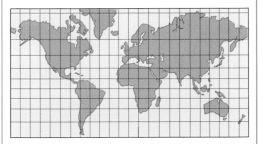

The Mercator projection avoids distorting the shape but makes the areas near the poles larger than they should be.
This projection is used for navigation as directions can be plotted as straight lines.

Winkel Equal Area
World pp. 120-121

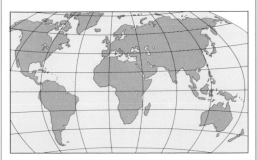

Equal area projections such as Winkel are useful for world maps where it is important to show the correct relative sizes of areas.

Conic Equal Area
Europe pp. 32-33

Conic projections are best suited for areas between 30° and 60° north and south with longer east-west extent than north-south extent, such as Europe.

Bonne Conic Equal Area
North America p. 79

The Bonne projection is a special kind of conic projection best suited for areas with a greater north-south than east-west extent such as North America.

Lambert Azimuthal Equal Area
Africa p. 94

Lambert's projection is useful for areas which have similar east-west, north-south dimensions such as Africa.

Azimuthal Equidistant
Antarctica p. 128

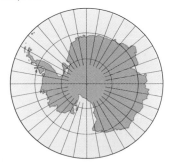

This projection is a good choice for showing travel routes from a central point as points on the map are in constant relative position and distance from the centre.

Scale 1:4 000 000

0   50   100   150 km

Conic Projection

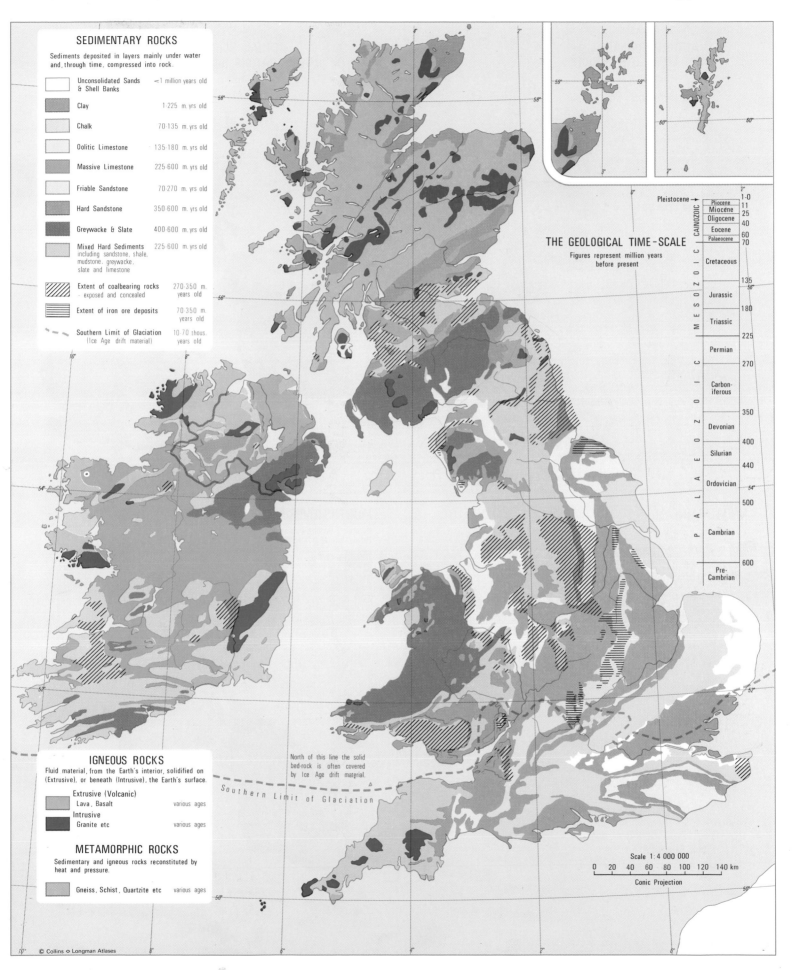

SEDIMENTARY ROCKS

Sediments deposited in layers mainly under water and, through time, compressed into rock.

	Unconsolidated Sands & Shell Banks	<1 million years old
	Clay	1-225 m. yrs old
	Chalk	70-135 m. yrs old
	Oolitic Limestone	135-180 m. yrs old
	Massive Limestone	225-600 m. yrs old
	Friable Sandstone	70-270 m. yrs old
	Hard Sandstone	350-600 m. yrs old
	Greywacke & Slate	400-600 m. yrs old
	Mixed Hard Sediments including sandstone, shale, mudstone, greywacke, slate and limestone	225-600 m. yrs old
	Extent of coalbearing rocks - exposed and concealed	270-350 m. years old
	Extent of iron ore deposits	70-350 m. years old
	Southern Limit of Glaciation (Ice Age drift material)	10-70 thous. years old

THE GEOLOGICAL TIME-SCALE

Figures represent million years before present

CAINOZOIC		Pleistocene →	1·0
		Pliocene	11
		Miocene	25
		Oligocene	40
		Eocene	60
		Palaeocene	70
MESOZOIC		Cretaceous	135
		Jurassic	180
		Triassic	225
PALAEOZOIC		Permian	270
		Carbon-iferous	350
		Devonian	400
		Silurian	440
		Ordovician	500
		Cambrian	600
		Pre-Cambrian	

North of this line the solid bed-rock is often covered by Ice Age drift material.

Southern Limit of Glaciation

IGNEOUS ROCKS

Fluid material, from the Earth's interior, solidified on (Extrusive), or beneath (Intrusive), the Earth's surface.

	Extrusive (Volcanic) Lava, Basalt	various ages
	Intrusive Granite etc	various ages

METAMORPHIC ROCKS

Sedimentary and igneous rocks reconstituted by heat and pressure.

	Gneiss, Schist, Quartzite etc	various ages

Scale 1:4 000 000

0 20 40 60 80 100 120 140 km

Conic Projection

© Collins ◇ Longman Atlases

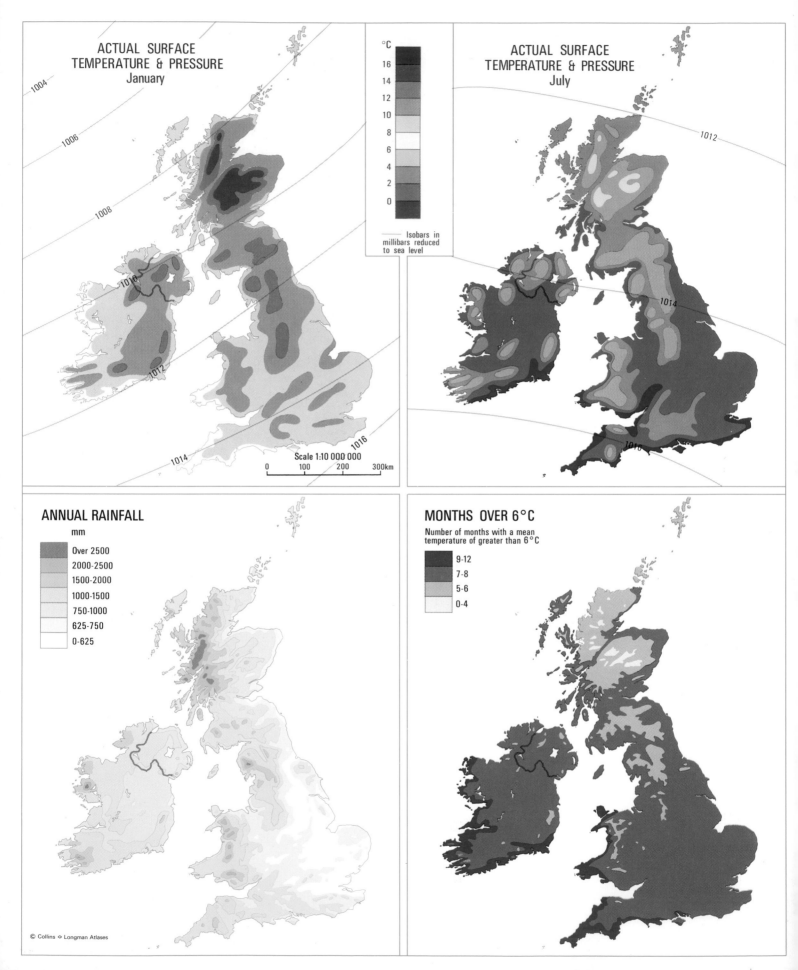

ACTUAL SURFACE
TEMPERATURE & PRESSURE
January

1004
1006
1008
1010
1012
1014
1016

°C
16
14
12
10
8
6
4
2
0

Isobars in
millibars reduced
to sea level

Scale 1:10 000 000
0   100   200   300km

ACTUAL SURFACE
TEMPERATURE & PRESSURE
July

1012
1014
1016

ANNUAL RAINFALL

mm

Over 2500
2000-2500
1500-2000
1000-1500
750-1000
625-750
0-625

MONTHS OVER 6°C

Number of months with a mean
temperature of greater than 6°C

9-12
7-8
5-6
0-4

© Collins ◇ Longman Atlases

WEATHER MAP

H Anticyclone
L Depression

~~1012~~ Pressure in millibars
Cold front
Warm front
Occluded front

Note : Data supplied by Meteorological Office

WEATHER SATELLITE PHOTOGRAPH

CLIMATIC GRAPHS

Height in metres above sea level.

Mean monthly temperature.

Average monthly rainfall.

ABERDEEN 14m
Rain mm — Temp. °C

BELFAST 19m
Rain mm — Temp. °C

BIRMINGHAM 157m
Rain mm — Temp. °C

CARDIFF 16m
Rain mm — Temp. °C

FORT WILLIAM 52m
Rain mm — Temp. °C

GLASGOW 55m
Rain mm — Temp. °C

HOLYHEAD 5m
Rain mm — Temp. °C

MARGATE 16m
Rain mm — Temp. °C

NORWICH 28m
Rain mm — Temp. °C

PENZANCE 17m
Rain mm — Temp. °C

SOUTHAMPTON 20m
Rain mm — Temp. °C

STORNOWAY 16m
Rain mm — Temp. °C

TYNEMOUTH 15m
Rain mm — Temp. °C

YORK 17m
Rain mm — Temp. °C

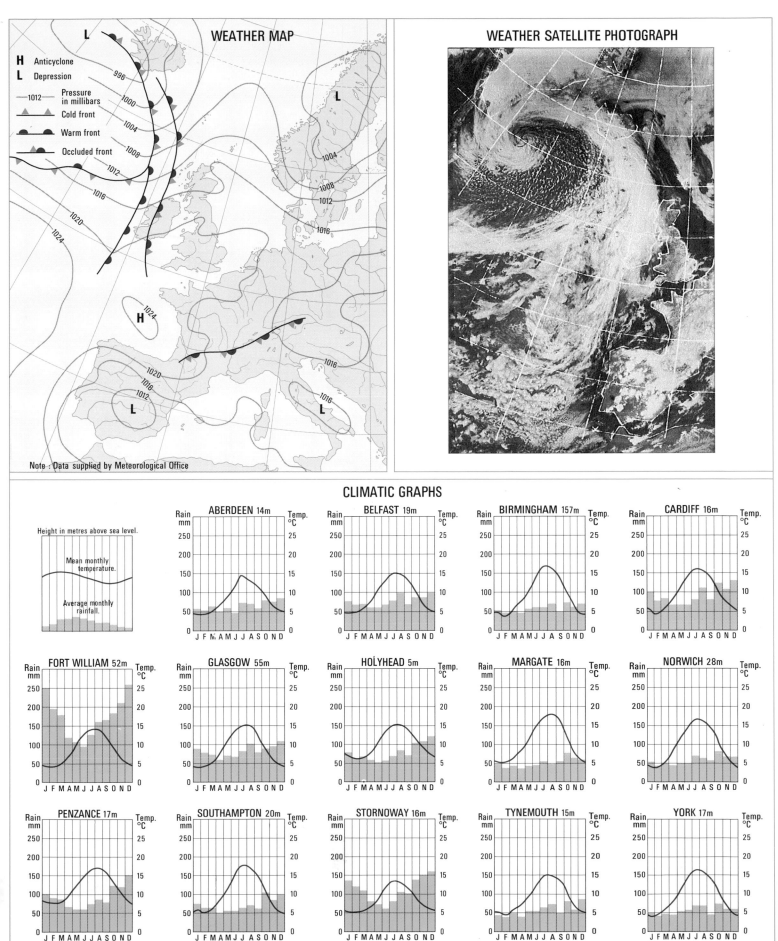

© Collins ◇ Longman Atlases

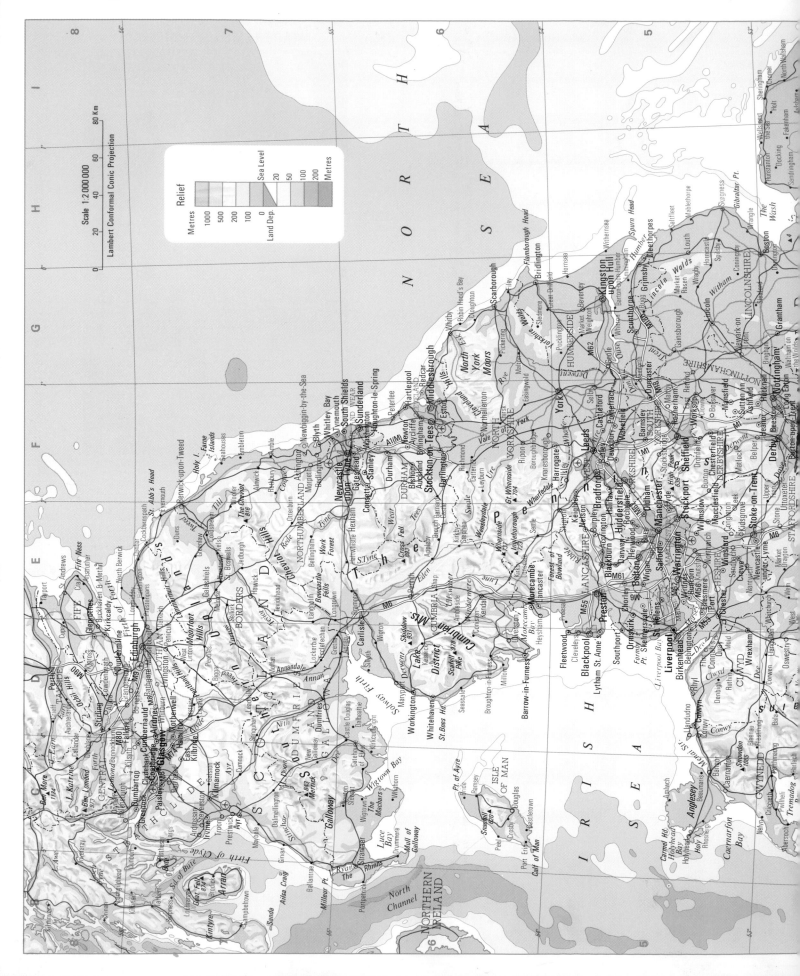

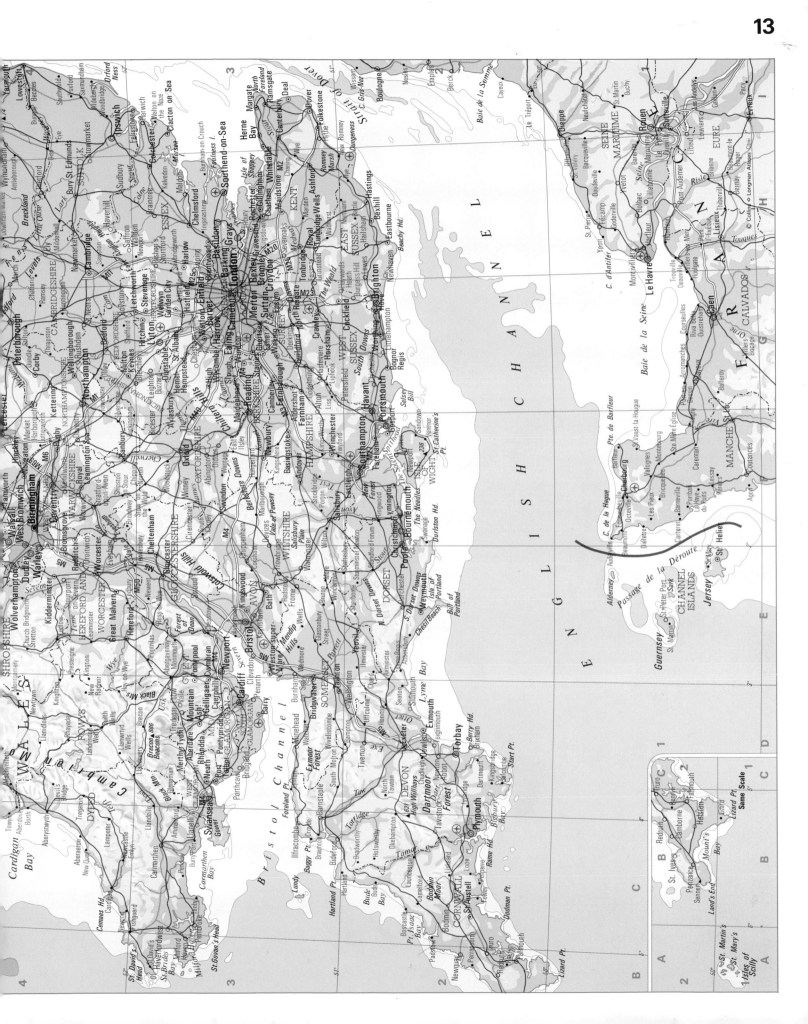

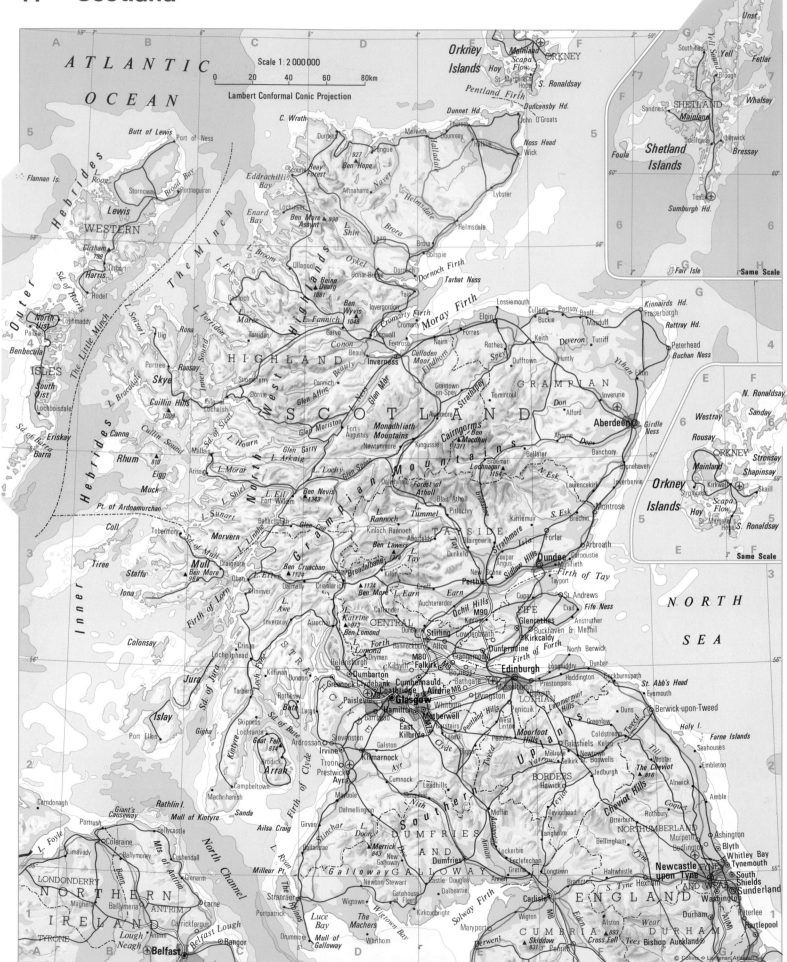

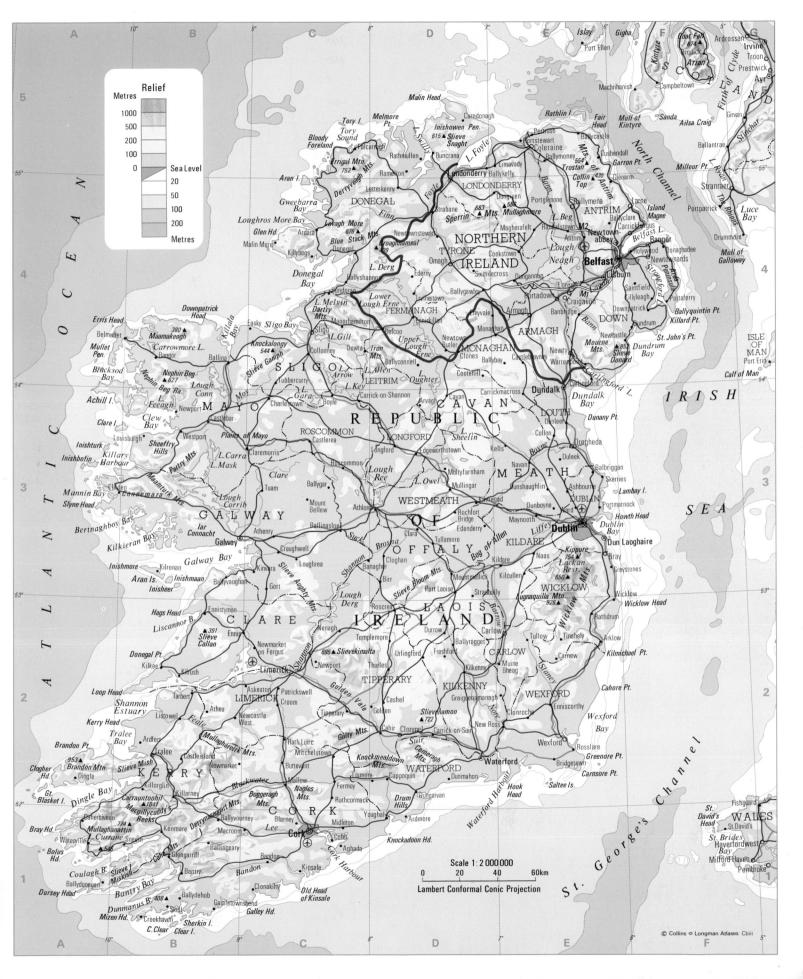

Relief
Metres
1000
500
200
100
0
Sea Level
20
50
100
200
Metres

Scale 1: 2 000 000

0   20   40   60km

Lambert Conformal Conic Projection

© Collins ◊ Longman Atlases Cbiii

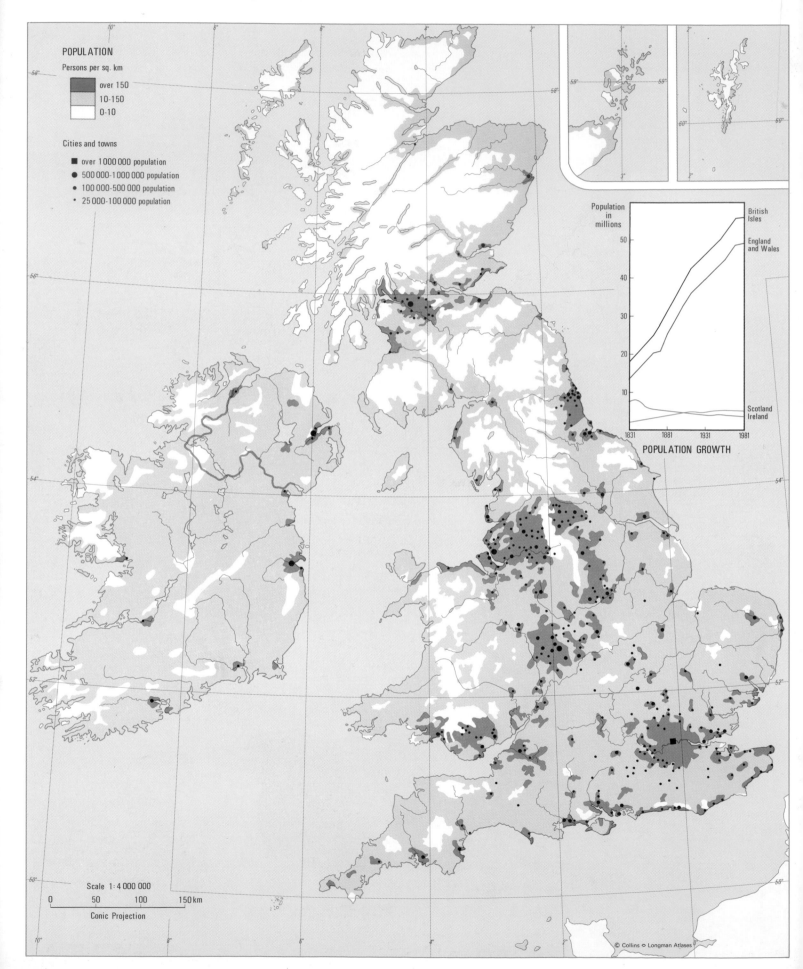

POPULATION

Persons per sq. km

- over 150
- 10-150
- 0-10

Cities and towns

- ■ over 1 000 000 population
- ● 500 000-1 000 000 population
- ● 100 000-500 000 population
- · 25 000-100 000 population

Population
in
millions

British
Isles

England
and Wales

Scotland
Ireland

POPULATION GROWTH

Scale 1 : 4 000 000

0   50   100   150 km

Conic Projection

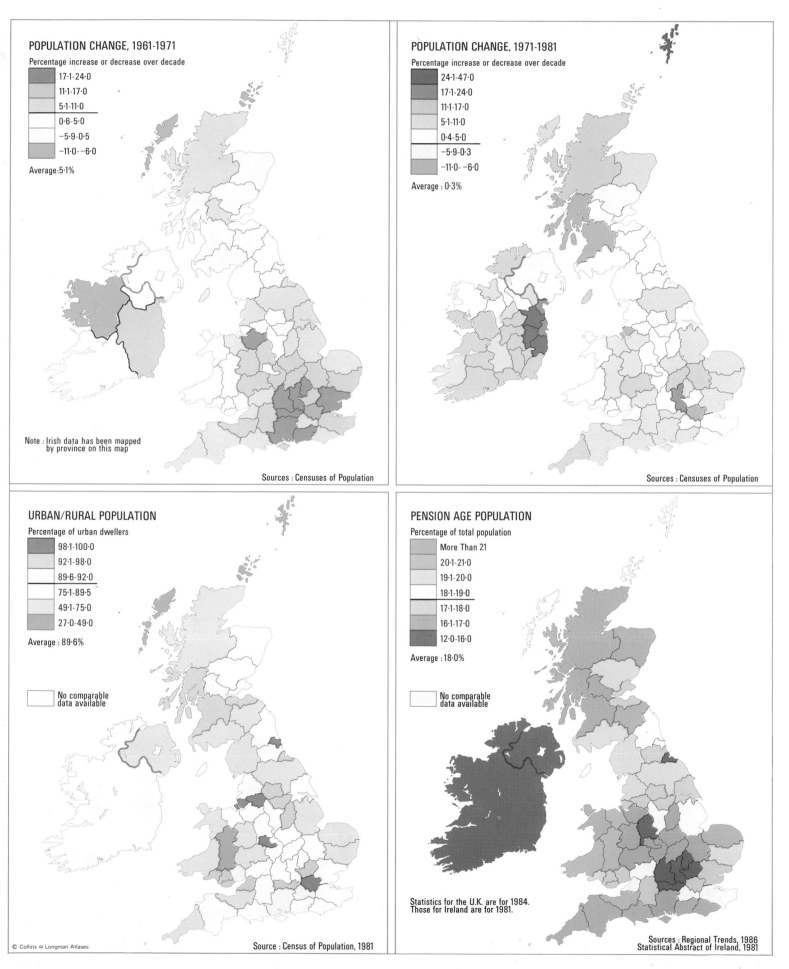

POPULATION CHANGE, 1961-1971

Percentage increase or decrease over decade

- 17·1-24·0
- 11·1-17·0
- 5·1-11·0
- 0·6-5·0
- −5·9-0·5
- −11·0--6·0

Average: 5·1%

Note : Irish data has been mapped by province on this map

Sources : Censuses of Population

POPULATION CHANGE, 1971-1981

Percentage increase or decrease over decade

- 24·1-47·0
- 17·1-24·0
- 11·1-17·0
- 5·1-11·0
- 0·4-5·0
- −5·9-0·3
- −11·0--6·0

Average : 0·3%

Sources : Censuses of Population

URBAN/RURAL POPULATION

Percentage of urban dwellers

- 98·1-100·0
- 92·1-98·0
- 89·6-92·0
- 75·1-89·5
- 49·1-75·0
- 27·0-49·0

Average : 89·6%

No comparable data available

© Collins ◇ Longman Atlases

Source : Census of Population, 1981

PENSION AGE POPULATION

Percentage of total population

- More Than 21
- 20·1-21·0
- 19·1-20·0
- 18·1-19·0
- 17·1-18·0
- 16·1-17·0
- 12·0-16·0

Average : 18·0%

No comparable data available

Statistics for the U.K. are for 1984.
Those for Ireland are for 1981.

Sources : Regional Trends, 1986
Statistical Abstract of Ireland, 1981

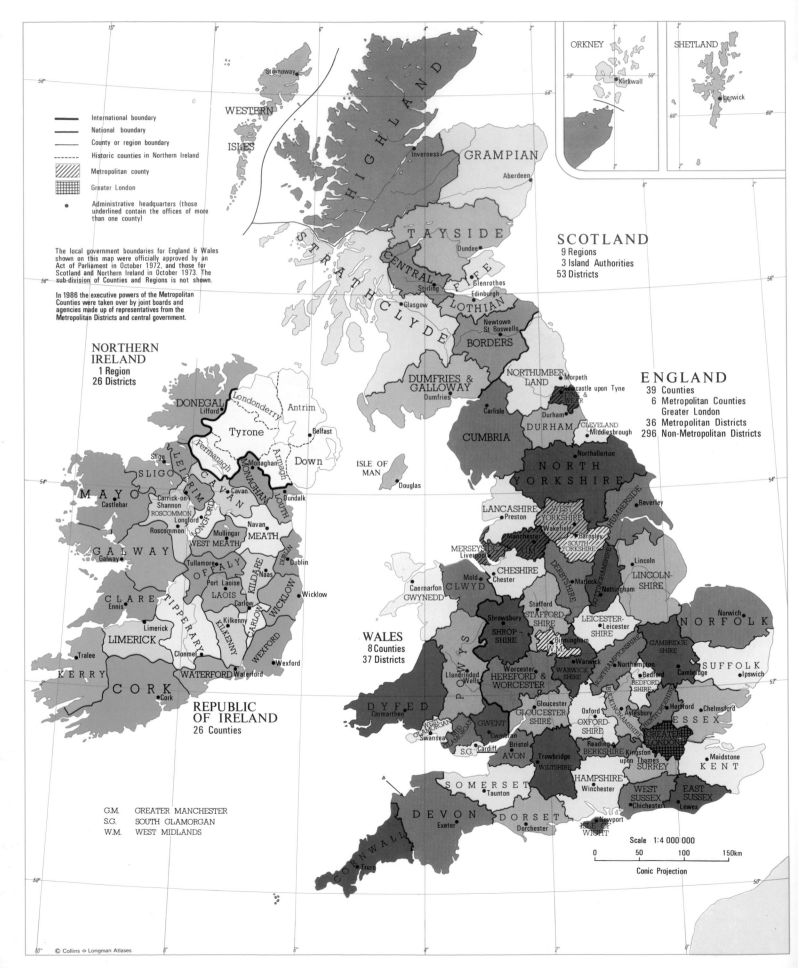

ORKNEY

Kirkwall

SHETLAND

Lerwick

Administrative headquarters (those underlined contain the offices of more than one county)

International boundary
National boundary
County or region boundary
Historic counties in Northern Ireland
Metropolitan county
Greater London

The local government boundaries for England & Wales shown on this map were officially approved by an Act of Parliament in October 1972, and those for Scotland and Northern Ireland in October 1973. The sub-division of Counties and Regions is not shown.

In 1986 the executive powers of the Metropolitan Counties were taken over by joint boards and agencies made up of representatives from the Metropolitan Districts and central government.

NORTHERN IRELAND
1 Region
26 Districts

SCOTLAND
9 Regions
3 Island Authorities
53 Districts

ENGLAND
39 Counties
6 Metropolitan Counties
Greater London
36 Metropolitan Districts
296 Non-Metropolitan Districts

WALES
8 Counties
37 Districts

REPUBLIC OF IRELAND
26 Counties

WESTERN ISLES
Stornoway

HIGHLAND
Inverness

GRAMPIAN
Aberdeen

TAYSIDE
Dundee

CENTRAL
Stirling

FIFE
Glenrothes

LOTHIAN
Edinburgh

STRATHCLYDE
Glasgow

BORDERS
Newtown St Boswells

DUMFRIES & GALLOWAY
Dumfries

NORTHUMBERLAND
Morpeth
Newcastle upon Tyne
TYNE & WEAR

Carlisle

DURHAM
Durham

CLEVELAND
Middlesbrough

CUMBRIA

ISLE OF MAN
Douglas

NORTH YORKSHIRE
Northallerton

HUMBERSIDE
Beverley

LANCASHIRE
Preston

WEST YORKSHIRE
Wakefield
Barnsley

SOUTH YORKSHIRE

MERSEYSIDE
Liverpool

G.M.
Manchester

CHESHIRE
Chester

DERBYSHIRE
Matlock

NOTTINGHAMSHIRE
Nottingham

Lincoln

LINCOLNSHIRE

DONEGAL
Lifford

Londonderry

Antrim

Tyrone

Belfast

Fermanagh

Armagh

Down

Monaghan

SLIGO
Sligo

LEITRIM

CAVAN
Cavan

MONAGHAN

LOUTH
Dundalk

MAYO
Castlebar

Carrick-on-Shannon

ROSCOMMON
Roscommon

LONGFORD
Longford

Mullingar

WEST MEATH

MEATH
Navan

GALWAY
Galway

OFFALY
Tullamore

Port Laoise

LAOIS

KILDARE
Naas

DUBLIN
Dublin

CLARE
Ennis

TIPPERARY

KILKENNY
Kilkenny

CARLOW
Carlow

WICKLOW
Wicklow

LIMERICK
Limerick

WEXFORD
Wexford

KERRY
Tralee

Clonmel

WATERFORD
Waterford

CORK
Cork

GWYNEDD
Caernarfon

CLWYD
Mold
Chester

POWYS
Llandrindod Wells

SHROPSHIRE
Shrewsbury

STAFFORDSHIRE
Stafford

WEST MIDLANDS
Birmingham
W.M.

WARWICKSHIRE
Warwick

LEICESTERSHIRE
Leicester

NORTHAMPTONSHIRE
Northampton

CAMBRIDGESHIRE
Cambridge

NORFOLK
Norwich

SUFFOLK
Ipswich

HEREFORD & WORCESTER
Worcester

GLOUCESTERSHIRE
Gloucester

OXFORDSHIRE
Oxford

BUCKINGHAMSHIRE
Aylesbury

BEDFORDSHIRE
Bedford

HERTFORDSHIRE
Hertford

Chelmsford

ESSEX

DYFED
Carmarthen

WEST GLAMORGAN
Swansea

MID GLAMORGAN

GWENT
Cwmbran

S.G.
Cardiff

AVON
Bristol

WILTSHIRE
Trowbridge

BERKSHIRE
Reading

GREATER LONDON
Kingston upon Thames

SURREY

KENT
Maidstone

SOMERSET
Taunton

HAMPSHIRE
Winchester

WEST SUSSEX
Chichester

EAST SUSSEX
Lewes

DEVON
Exeter

DORSET
Dorchester

ISLE OF WIGHT
Newport

CORNWALL
Truro

WALES

G.M.   GREATER MANCHESTER
S.G.   SOUTH GLAMORGAN
W.M.   WEST MIDLANDS

Scale 1:4 000 000
0   50   100   150km

Conic Projection

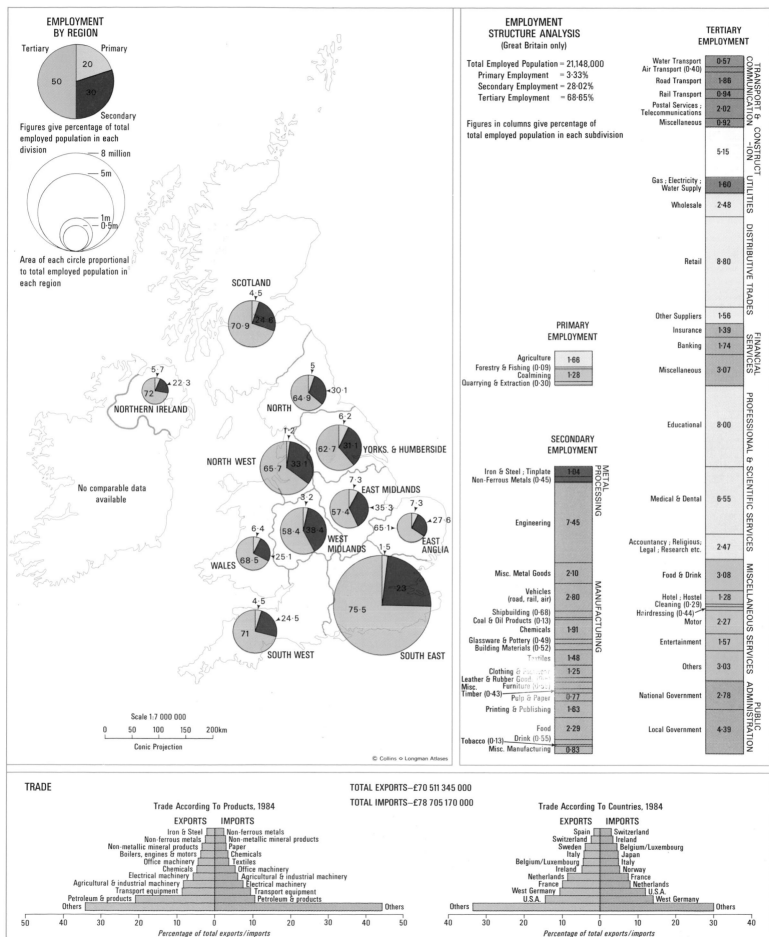

EMPLOYMENT BY REGION

Tertiary · Primary
50 · 20
30
Secondary

Figures give percentage of total employed population in each division

8 million
5m
1m
0·5m

Area of each circle proportional to total employed population in each region

No comparable data available

SCOTLAND 4·5 / 70·9 / 24·6

NORTHERN IRELAND 5·7 / 72 / 22·3

NORTH 5 / 64·9 / 30·1

YORKS. & HUMBERSIDE 6·2 / 62·7 / 31·1

NORTH WEST 1·2 / 65·7 / 33·1

EAST MIDLANDS 7·3 / 57·4 / 35·3

WEST MIDLANDS 3·2 / 58·4 / 38·4

EAST ANGLIA 7·3 / 65·1 / 27·6

WALES 6·4 / 68·5 / 25·1

SOUTH WEST 4·5 / 71 / 24·5

SOUTH EAST 1·5 / 75·5 / 23

Scale 1:7 000 000
0   50   100   150   200km

Conic Projection

© Collins ◇ Longman Atlases

EMPLOYMENT STRUCTURE ANALYSIS
(Great Britain only)

Total Employed Population = 21,148,000
Primary Employment = 3·33%
Secondary Employment = 28·02%
Tertiary Employment = 68·65%

Figures in columns give percentage of total employed population in each subdivision

PRIMARY EMPLOYMENT

Agriculture	1·66
Forestry & Fishing (0·09)	
Coalmining	1·28
Quarrying & Extraction (0·30)	

SECONDARY EMPLOYMENT

METAL PROCESSING

Iron & Steel ; Tinplate / Non-Ferrous Metals (0·45) — 1·04
Engineering — 7·45

MANUFACTURING

Misc. Metal Goods — 2·10
Vehicles (road, rail, air) — 2·80
Shipbuilding (0·68)
Coal & Oil Products (0·13)
Chemicals — 1·91
Glassware & Pottery (0·49)
Building Materials (0·52)
Textiles — 1·48
Clothing & Footwear — 1·25
Leather & Rubber Goods
Misc. Furniture (0·05)
Timber (0·43) / Pulp & Paper — 0·77
Printing & Publishing — 1·63
Food — 2·29
Tobacco (0·13) / Drink (0·55)
Misc. Manufacturing — 0·83

TERTIARY EMPLOYMENT

TRANSPORT & COMMUNICATION

Water Transport	0·57
Air Transport (0·40)	
Road Transport	1·86
Rail Transport	0·94
Postal Services ; Telecommunications	2·02
Miscellaneous	0·92

CONSTRUCTION — 5·15

UTILITIES

Gas ; Electricity ; Water Supply — 1·60

DISTRIBUTIVE TRADES

Wholesale — 2·48
Retail — 8·80
Other Suppliers — 1·56

FINANCIAL SERVICES

Insurance — 1·39
Banking — 1·74
Miscellaneous — 3·07

PROFESSIONAL & SCIENTIFIC SERVICES

Educational — 8·00
Medical & Dental — 6·55
Accountancy ; Religious ; Legal ; Research etc. — 2·47

MISCELLANEOUS SERVICES

Food & Drink — 3·08
Hotel ; Hostel — 1·28
Cleaning (0·29)
Hairdressing (0·44)
Motor — 2·27
Entertainment — 1·57
Others — 3·03

PUBLIC ADMINISTRATION

National Government — 2·78
Local Government — 4·39

TRADE

TOTAL EXPORTS—£70 511 345 000
TOTAL IMPORTS—£78 705 170 000

Trade According To Products, 1984

EXPORTS — IMPORTS

EXPORTS:
Iron & Steel
Non-ferrous metals
Non-metallic mineral products
Boilers, engines & motors
Office machinery
Chemicals
Electrical machinery
Agricultural & industrial machinery
Transport equipment
Petroleum & products
Others

IMPORTS:
Non-ferrous metals
Non-metallic mineral products
Paper
Chemicals
Textiles
Office machinery
Agricultural & industrial machinery
Electrical machinery
Transport equipment
Petroleum & products
Others

50 40 30 20 10 0 10 20 30 40 50
Percentage of total exports/imports

Trade According To Countries, 1984

EXPORTS — IMPORTS

EXPORTS:
Spain
Switzerland
Sweden
Italy
Belgium/Luxembourg
Ireland
Netherlands
France
West Germany
U.S.A.
Others

IMPORTS:
Switzerland
Ireland
Belgium/Luxembourg
Japan
Italy
Norway
France
Netherlands
U.S.A.
West Germany
Others

40 30 20 10 0 10 20 30 40
Percentage of total exports/imports

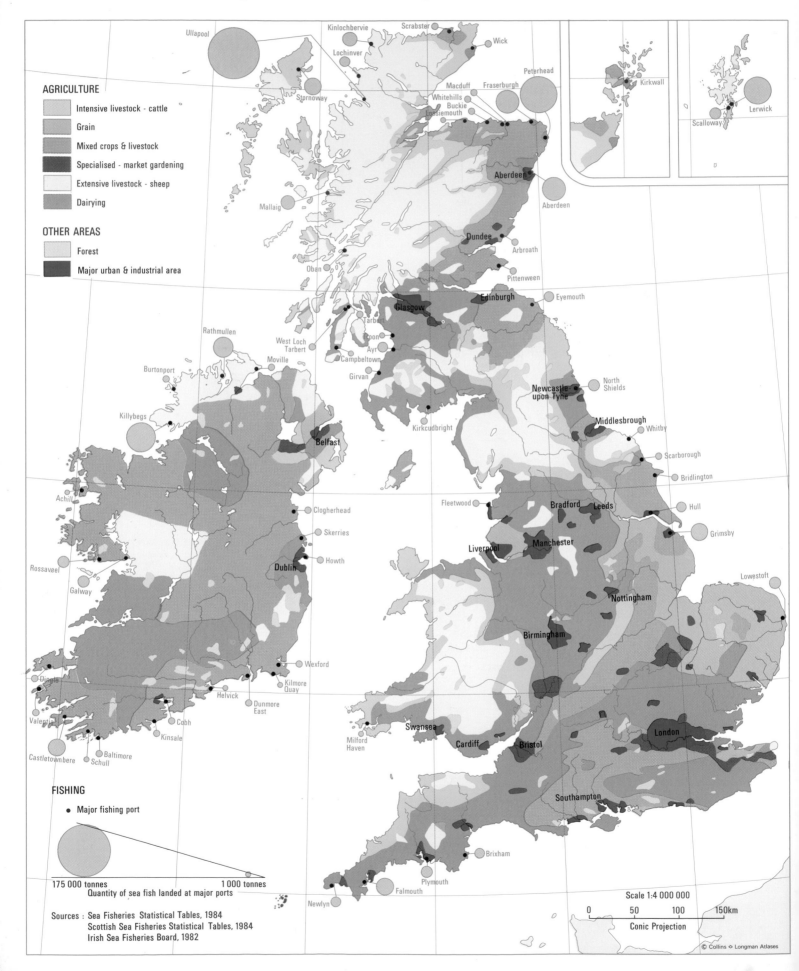

AGRICULTURE

- Intensive livestock - cattle
- Grain
- Mixed crops & livestock
- Specialised - market gardening
- Extensive livestock - sheep
- Dairying

OTHER AREAS

- Forest
- Major urban & industrial area

FISHING

- • Major fishing port

175 000 tonnes   1 000 tonnes
Quantity of sea fish landed at major ports

Sources : Sea Fisheries Statistical Tables, 1984
Scottish Sea Fisheries Statistical Tables, 1984
Irish Sea Fisheries Board, 1982

Scale 1:4 000 000

0   50   100   150km

Conic Projection

© Collins ◇ Longman Atlases

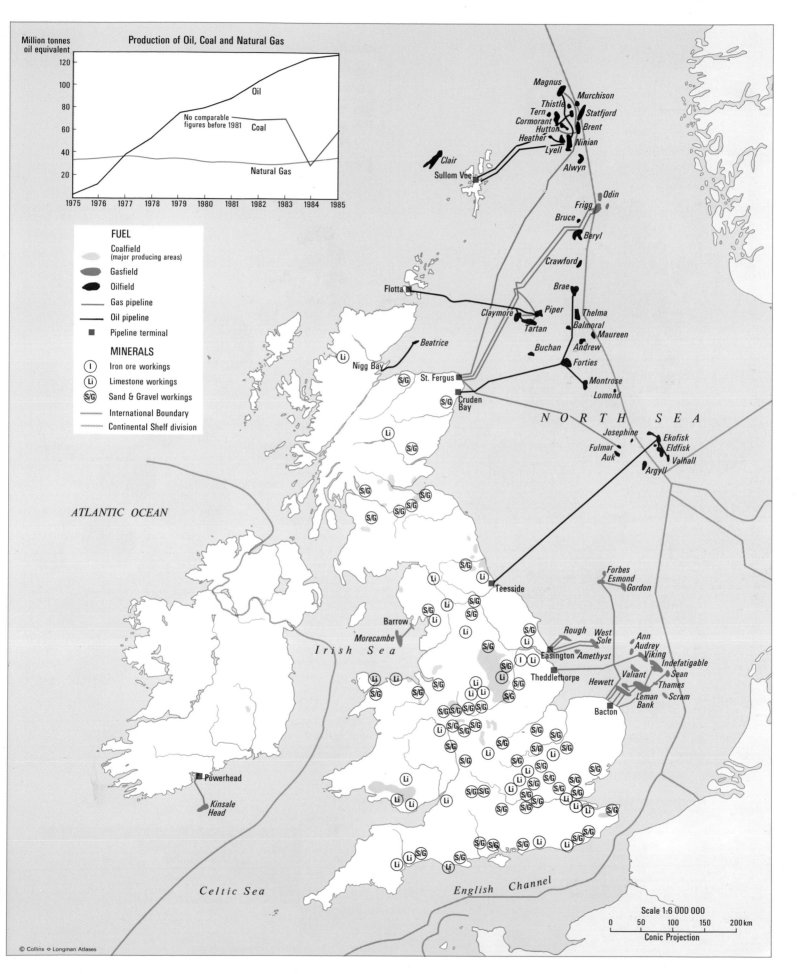

Production of Oil, Coal and Natural Gas

Million tonnes oil equivalent

Oil

No comparable figures before 1981

Coal

Natural Gas

1975 1976 1977 1978 1979 1980 1981 1982 1983 1984 1985

FUEL

Coalfield (major producing areas)

Gasfield

Oilfield

Gas pipeline

Oil pipeline

Pipeline terminal

MINERALS

(I) Iron ore workings

(Li) Limestone workings

(S/G) Sand & Gravel workings

International Boundary

Continental Shelf division

ATLANTIC OCEAN

NORTH SEA

Irish Sea

Celtic Sea

English Channel

Magnus
Murchison
Thistle
Tern
Statfjord
Cormorant
Brent
Hutton
Heather
Ninian
Lyell
Alwyn
Clair
Sullom Voe
Odin
Frigg
Bruce
Beryl
Crawford
Brae
Flotta
Piper
Thelma
Claymore
Balmoral
Tartan
Maureen
Buchan
Andrew
Beatrice
Forties
Nigg Bay
Montrose
St. Fergus
Lomond
Cruden Bay
Josephine
Ekofisk
Fulmar
Eldfisk
Auk
Valhall
Argyll
Teesside
Forbes
Esmond
Gordon
Barrow
Rough
West Sole
Morecambe
Ann
Audrey
Viking
Easington
Amethyst
Indefatigable
Theddlethorpe
Sean
Valiant
Thames
Hewett
Scram
Leman Bank
Bacton
Powerhead
Kinsale Head

Scale 1:6 000 000

0 50 100 150 200 km

Conic Projection

© Collins ◇ Longman Atlases

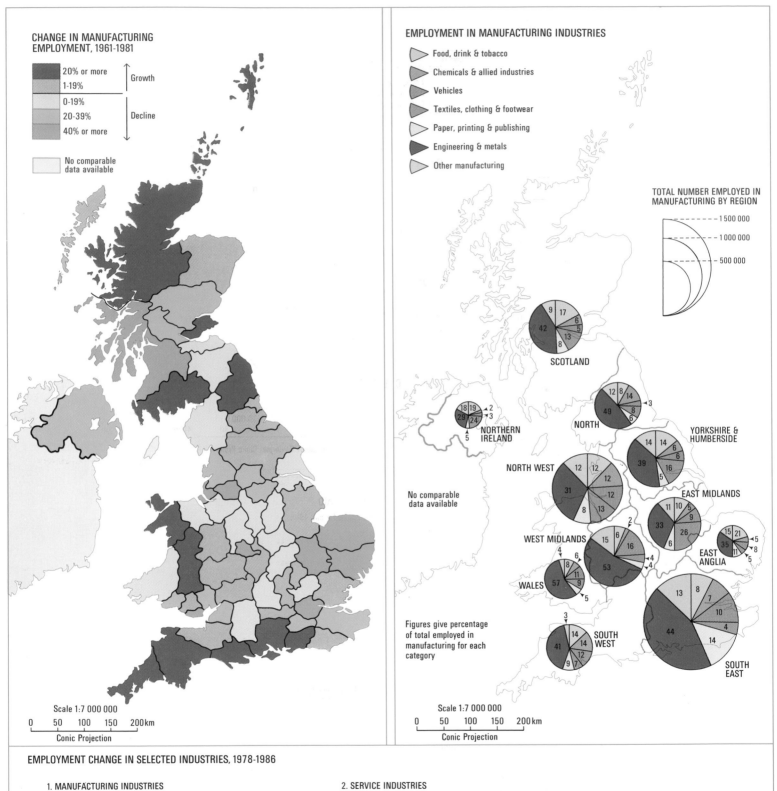

CHANGE IN MANUFACTURING
EMPLOYMENT, 1961-1981

20% or more	Growth
1-19%	
0-19%	Decline
20-39%	
40% or more	

No comparable
data available

Scale 1:7 000 000

0 50 100 150 200km

Conic Projection

EMPLOYMENT IN MANUFACTURING INDUSTRIES

- Food, drink & tobacco
- Chemicals & allied industries
- Vehicles
- Textiles, clothing & footwear
- Paper, printing & publishing
- Engineering & metals
- Other manufacturing

TOTAL NUMBER EMPLOYED IN
MANUFACTURING BY REGION

- 1 500 000
- 1 000 000
- 500 000

SCOTLAND
9 17 6 5 42 13 8

NORTHERN IRELAND
18 19 2 29 24 3 5

NORTH
12 8 14 49 8 6 3

YORKSHIRE &
HUMBERSIDE
14 14 6 39 16 5

NORTH WEST
12 12 31 12 8 13

EAST MIDLANDS
11 10 5 33 9 26 6

EAST ANGLIA
15 21 5 35 11 8 5

WEST MIDLANDS
15 2 16 53 4 4

WALES
4 6 8 11 57 9 5

SOUTH WEST
3 14 14 41 12 9 7

SOUTH EAST
13 8 7 10 44 14 4

No comparable
data available

Figures give percentage
of total employed in
manufacturing for each
category

Scale 1:7 000 000

0 50 100 150 200km

Conic Projection

EMPLOYMENT CHANGE IN SELECTED INDUSTRIES, 1978-1986

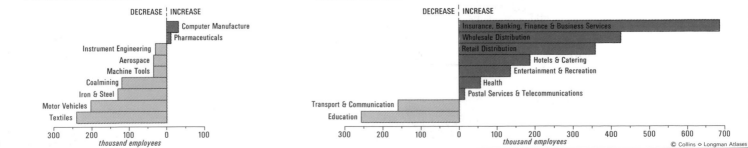

1. MANUFACTURING INDUSTRIES

DECREASE | INCREASE

- Computer Manufacture
- Pharmaceuticals
- Instrument Engineering
- Aerospace
- Machine Tools
- Coalmining
- Iron & Steel
- Motor Vehicles
- Textiles

300 200 100 0 100
thousand employees

2. SERVICE INDUSTRIES

DECREASE | INCREASE

- Insurance, Banking, Finance & Business Services
- Wholesale Distribution
- Retail Distribution
- Hotels & Catering
- Entertainment & Recreation
- Health
- Postal Services & Telecommunications
- Transport & Communication
- Education

300 200 100 0 100 200 300 400 500 600 700
thousand employees

© Collins ○ Longman Atlases

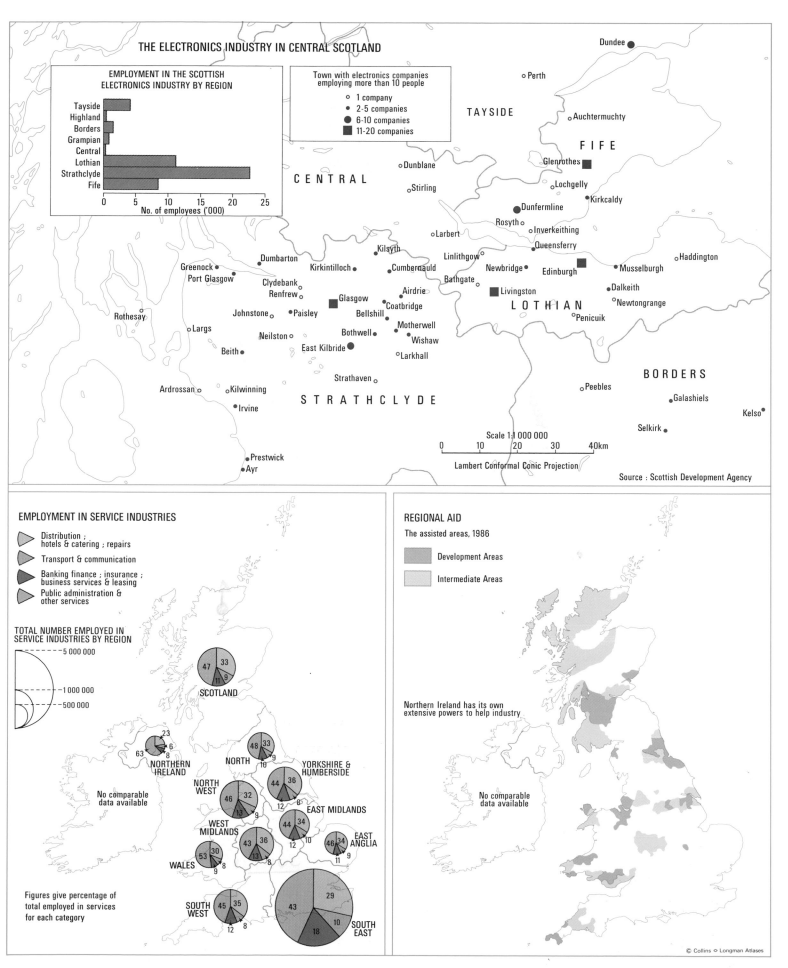

THE ELECTRONICS INDUSTRY IN CENTRAL SCOTLAND

EMPLOYMENT IN THE SCOTTISH ELECTRONICS INDUSTRY BY REGION

Tayside
Highland
Borders
Grampian
Central
Lothian
Strathclyde
Fife

No. of employees ('000)
0   5   10   15   20   25

Town with electronics companies employing more than 10 people
○ 1 company
• 2-5 companies
● 6-10 companies
■ 11-20 companies

Dundee
Perth
Auchtermuchty
TAYSIDE
FIFE
Glenrothes
Dunblane
Lochgelly
Stirling
Kirkcaldy
Dunfermline
CENTRAL
Rosyth
Inverkeithing
Larbert
Queensferry
Kilsyth
Linlithgow
Newbridge
Haddington
Greenock
Dumbarton
Kirkintilloch
Cumbernauld
Edinburgh
Musselburgh
Port Glasgow
Clydebank
Airdrie
Bathgate
Renfrew
Glasgow
Coatbridge
Livingston
Dalkeith
Johnstone
Paisley
Bellshill
LOTHIAN
Newtongrange
Motherwell
Rothesay
Neilston
Bothwell
Penicuik
Largs
Wishaw
Beith
East Kilbride
Larkhall
BORDERS
Ardrossan
Kilwinning
Strathaven
Peebles
Galashiels
Irvine
STRATHCLYDE
Selkirk
Kelso

Scale 1:1 000 000
0   10   20   30   40km
Lambert Conformal Conic Projection

Source : Scottish Development Agency

EMPLOYMENT IN SERVICE INDUSTRIES

◢ Distribution ; hotels & catering ; repairs
◢ Transport & communication
◢ Banking finance ; insurance ; business services & leasing
◢ Public administration & other services

TOTAL NUMBER EMPLOYED IN SERVICE INDUSTRIES BY REGION
5 000 000
1 000 000
500 000

SCOTLAND 47 33 11 9

NORTHERN IRELAND 63 23 6 8

No comparable data available

NORTH 48 33 9 10

YORKSHIRE & HUMBERSIDE 44 36 12 8

NORTH WEST 46 32 13 9

EAST MIDLANDS 44 34 12 10

WEST MIDLANDS 43 36 13 8

EAST ANGLIA 46 34 11 9

WALES 53 30 9 8

SOUTH WEST 45 35 12 8

SOUTH EAST 43 29 18 10

Figures give percentage of total employed in services for each category

REGIONAL AID

The assisted areas, 1986

■ Development Areas
□ Intermediate Areas

Northern Ireland has its own extensive powers to help industry

No comparable data available

© Collins ◇ Longman Atlases

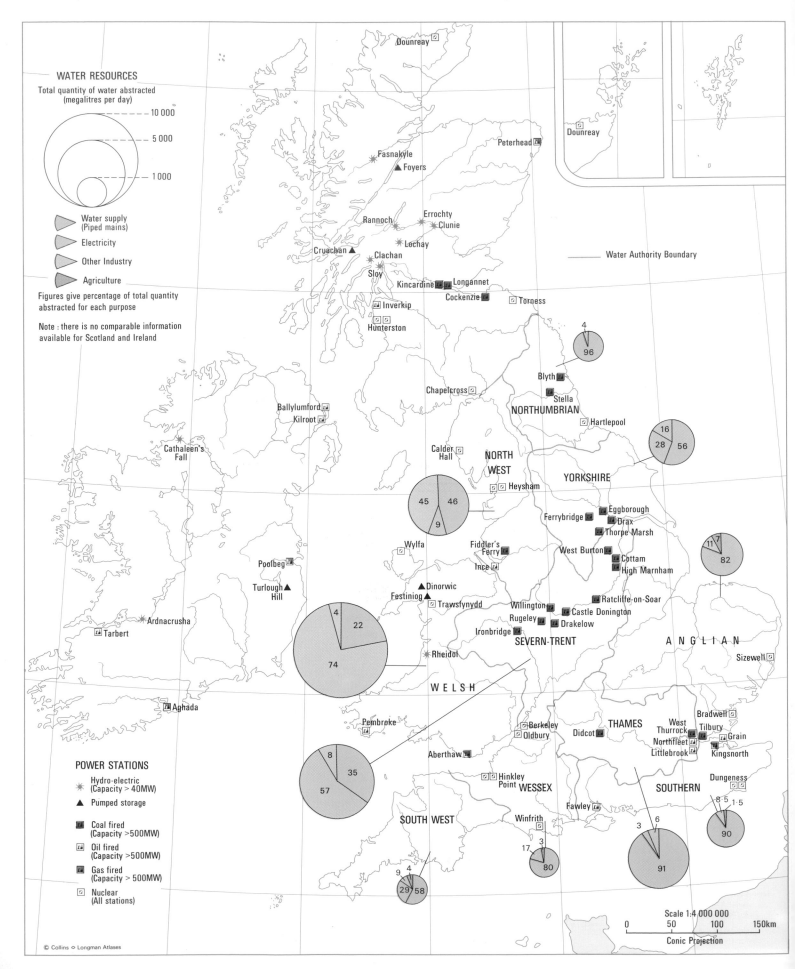

WATER RESOURCES

Total quantity of water abstracted
(megalitres per day)

— 10 000
— 5 000
— 1 000

Water supply
(Piped mains)

Electricity

Other Industry

Agriculture

Figures give percentage of total quantity
abstracted for each purpose

Note : there is no comparable information
available for Scotland and Ireland

Water Authority Boundary

POWER STATIONS

✳ Hydro-electric
(Capacity > 40MW)

▲ Pumped storage

▪ Coal fired
(Capacity >500MW)

▫ Oil fired
(Capacity >500MW)

▪ Gas fired
(Capacity > 500MW)

▫ Nuclear
(All stations)

Scale 1:4 000 000

0   50   100   150km

Conic Projection

© Collins ◇ Longman Atlases

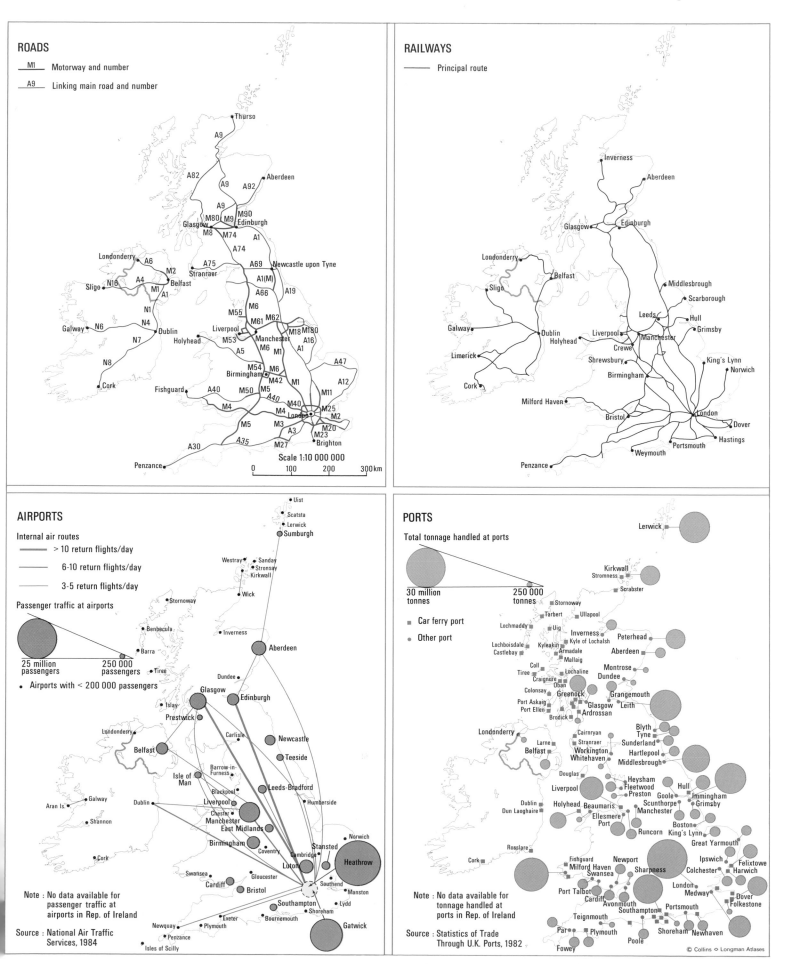

ROADS

M1 — Motorway and number

A9 — Linking main road and number

Scale 1:10 000 000
0   100   200   300 km

RAILWAYS

— Principal route

AIRPORTS

Internal air routes

— > 10 return flights/day

— 6-10 return flights/day

— 3-5 return flights/day

Passenger traffic at airports

25 million passengers — 250 000 passengers

• Airports with < 200 000 passengers

Note : No data available for passenger traffic at airports in Rep. of Ireland

Source : National Air Traffic Services, 1984

PORTS

Total tonnage handled at ports

30 million tonnes — 250 000 tonnes

■ Car ferry port

● Other port

Note : No data available for tonnage handled at ports in Rep. of Ireland

Source : Statistics of Trade Through U.K. Ports, 1982

© Collins ◇ Longman Atlases

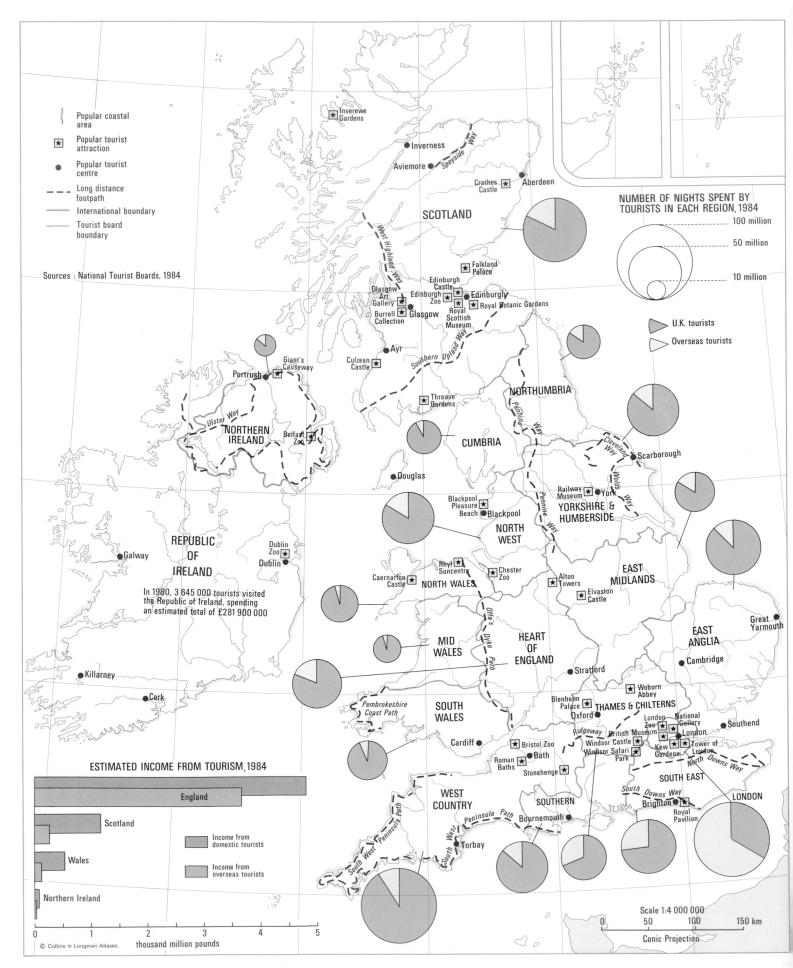

Popular coastal area

☒ Popular tourist attraction

● Popular tourist centre

- - - Long distance footpath

— International boundary

═══ Tourist board boundary

Sources : National Tourist Boards, 1984

NUMBER OF NIGHTS SPENT BY TOURISTS IN EACH REGION, 1984

100 million
50 million
10 million

◤ U.K. tourists
◺ Overseas tourists

Inverewe Gardens

● Inverness

Aviemore
Speyside Way

Crathes ☒ Castle
● Aberdeen

SCOTLAND

☒ Falkland Palace

Edinburgh Castle
Glasgow ☒ Art Gallery
Edinburgh ☒ Zoo ☒ ● Edinburgh
Burrell ☒ Royal Botanic Gardens
Collection ☒ ☒ Royal
☒ Glasgow Scottish Museum

West Highland Way

● Ayr

Culzean ☒ Castle

Southern Upland Way

NORTHUMBRIA

Giant's Causeway

Portrush ☒ ●

Ulster Way

NORTHERN IRELAND

Belfast ☒ Zoo

☒ Threave Gardens

CUMBRIA

Pennine Way

● Douglas

Pennine Way

Cleveland Way

● Scarborough

Railway ☒ Museum ☒ York
Wolds Way

YORKSHIRE & HUMBERSIDE

Blackpool ☒ Pleasure Beach ● Blackpool

NORTH WEST

REPUBLIC OF IRELAND

In 1980, 3 645 000 tourists visited the Republic of Ireland, spending an estimated total of £281 900 000

● Galway

Dublin ☒ Zoo
Dublin ●

Rhyl ☒ Suncentre
Caernarfon ☒ Castle
NORTH WALES

☒ Chester Zoo

Alton ☒ Towers

☒ Elvaston Castle

EAST MIDLANDS

EAST ANGLIA

Great ● Yarmouth

● Killarney

● Cork

MID WALES

Offa's Dyke Path

HEART OF ENGLAND

● Stratford

● Cambridge

☒ Woburn Abbey

Blenheim ☒ **THAMES & CHILTERNS**
Palace Oxford ●
London ☒ ☒ National
Ridgeway ☒ British Museum Gallery
☒ ☒ ● London
Windsor Castle ☒ Kew ☒ Tower of
Windsor Safari ☒ Gardens London
Park **SOUTH EAST**
North Downs Way

● Southend

Pembrokeshire Coast Path

SOUTH WALES

● Cardiff

☒ Bristol Zoo
Roman ☒ ● Bath
Baths
☒ Stonehenge

WEST COUNTRY

South West Peninsula Path

South West Peninsula Path

SOUTHERN

● Bournemouth

South Downs Way

Brighton ● ☒
☒ Royal
Pavilion

LONDON

● Torbay

ESTIMATED INCOME FROM TOURISM, 1984

England

Scotland

Wales

Northern Ireland

☒ Income from domestic tourists
☒ Income from overseas tourists

0   1   2   3   4   5
thousand million pounds

© Collins ○ Longman Atlases

Scale 1:4 000 000

0   50   100   150 km

Conic Projection

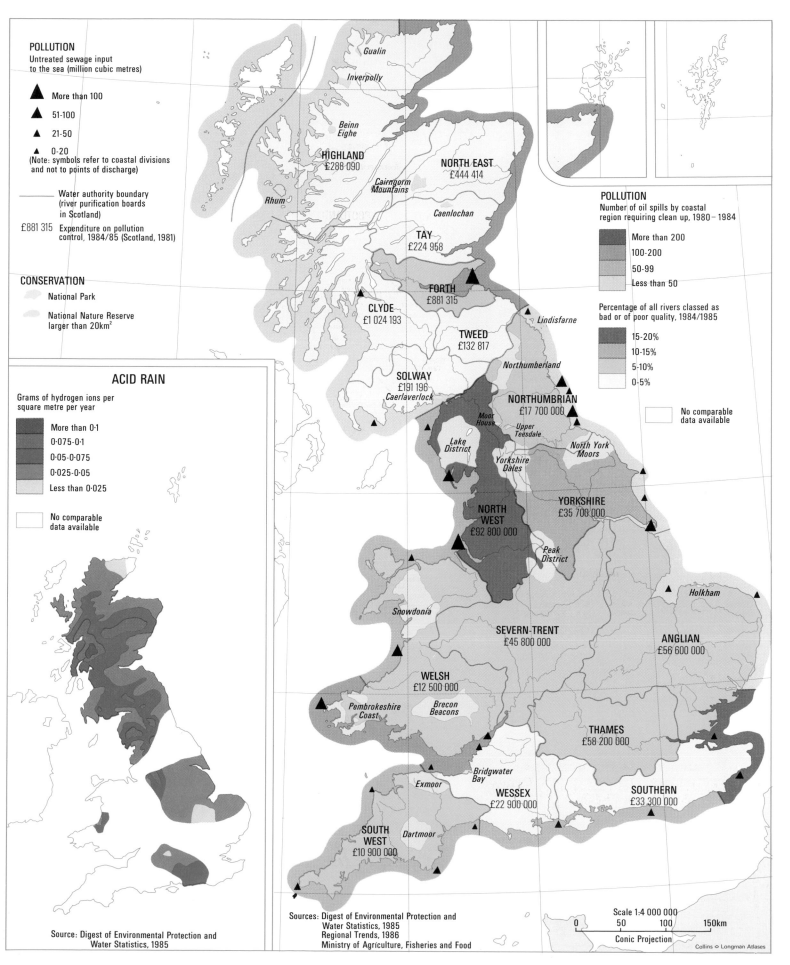

POLLUTION

Untreated sewage input to the sea (million cubic metres)

▲ More than 100

▲ 51-100

▲ 21-50

▲ 0-20

(Note: symbols refer to coastal divisions and not to points of discharge)

—— Water authority boundary (river purification boards in Scotland)

£881 315 Expenditure on pollution control, 1984/85 (Scotland, 1981)

CONSERVATION

National Park

National Nature Reserve larger than 20km²

ACID RAIN

Grams of hydrogen ions per square metre per year

More than 0·1

0·075-0·1

0·05-0·075

0·025-0·05

Less than 0·025

No comparable data available

POLLUTION

Number of oil spills by coastal region requiring clean up, 1980 – 1984

More than 200

100-200

50-99

Less than 50

Percentage of all rivers classed as bad or of poor quality, 1984/1985

15-20%

10-15%

5-10%

0-5%

No comparable data available

Gualin

Inverpolly

Beinn Eighe

HIGHLAND £288 090

Rhum

Cairngorm Mountains

Caenlochan

NORTH EAST £444 414

TAY £224 958

CLYDE £1 024 193

FORTH £881 315

Lindisfarne

TWEED £132 817

Northumberland

SOLWAY £191 196
Caerlaverock

NORTHUMBRIAN £17 700 000

Moor House

Upper Teesdale

Lake District

North York Moors

Yorkshire Dales

NORTH WEST £92 800 000

YORKSHIRE £35 700 000

Peak District

Snowdonia

Holkham

SEVERN-TRENT £45 800 000

ANGLIAN £56 600 000

WELSH £12 500 000

Brecon Beacons

Pembrokeshire Coast

THAMES £58 200 000

Bridgwater Bay

Exmoor

WESSEX £22 900 000

SOUTHERN £33 300 000

SOUTH WEST £10 900 000

Dartmoor

Scale 1:4 000 000

0   50   100   150km

Conic Projection

Sources: Digest of Environmental Protection and Water Statistics, 1985
Regional Trends, 1986
Ministry of Agriculture, Fisheries and Food

Source: Digest of Environmental Protection and Water Statistics, 1985

Collins ◇ Longman Atlases

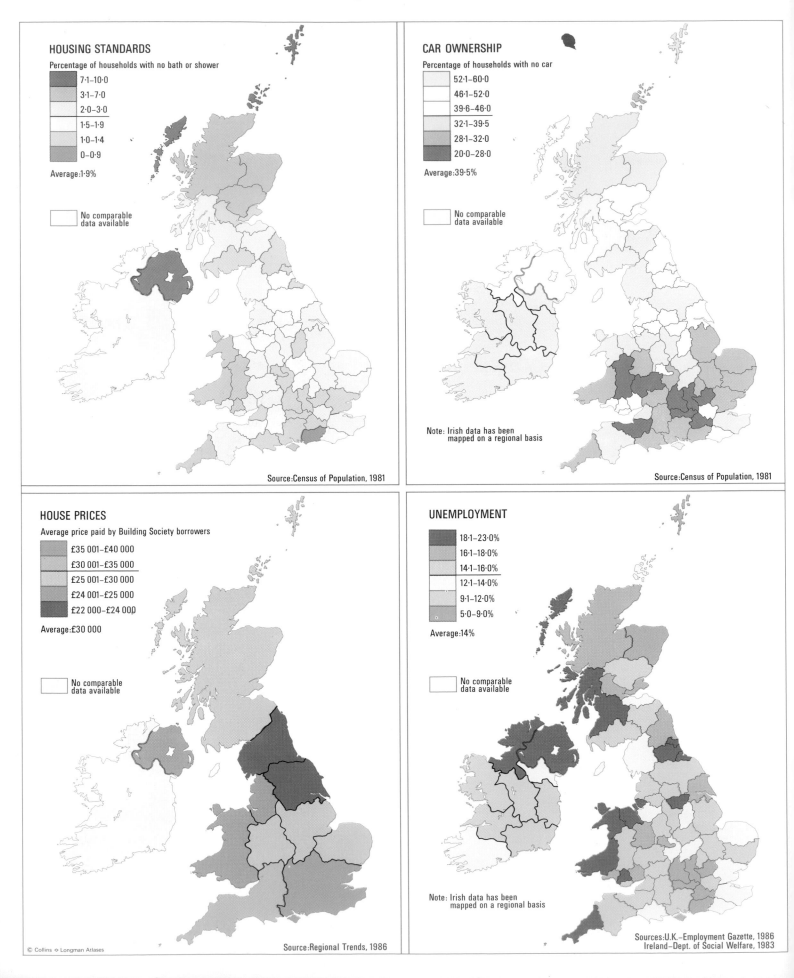

HOUSING STANDARDS

Percentage of households with no bath or shower

- 7·1–10·0
- 3·1–7·0
- 2·0–3·0
- 1·5–1·9
- 1·0–1·4
- 0–0·9

Average:1·9%

No comparable data available

Source:Census of Population, 1981

CAR OWNERSHIP

Percentage of households with no car

- 52·1–60·0
- 46·1–52·0
- 39·6–46·0
- 32·1–39·5
- 28·1–32·0
- 20·0–28·0

Average:39·5%

No comparable data available

Note: Irish data has been mapped on a regional basis

Source:Census of Population, 1981

HOUSE PRICES

Average price paid by Building Society borrowers

- £35 001–£40 000
- £30 001–£35 000
- £25 001–£30 000
- £24 001–£25 000
- £22 000–£24 000

Average:£30 000

No comparable data available

© Collins ◇ Longman Atlases

Source:Regional Trends, 1986

UNEMPLOYMENT

- 18·1–23·0%
- 16·1–18·0%
- 14·1–16·0%
- 12·1–14·0%
- 9·1–12·0%
- 5·0–9·0%

Average:14%

No comparable data available

Note: Irish data has been mapped on a regional basis

Sources:U.K.–Employment Gazette, 1986
Ireland–Dept. of Social Welfare, 1983

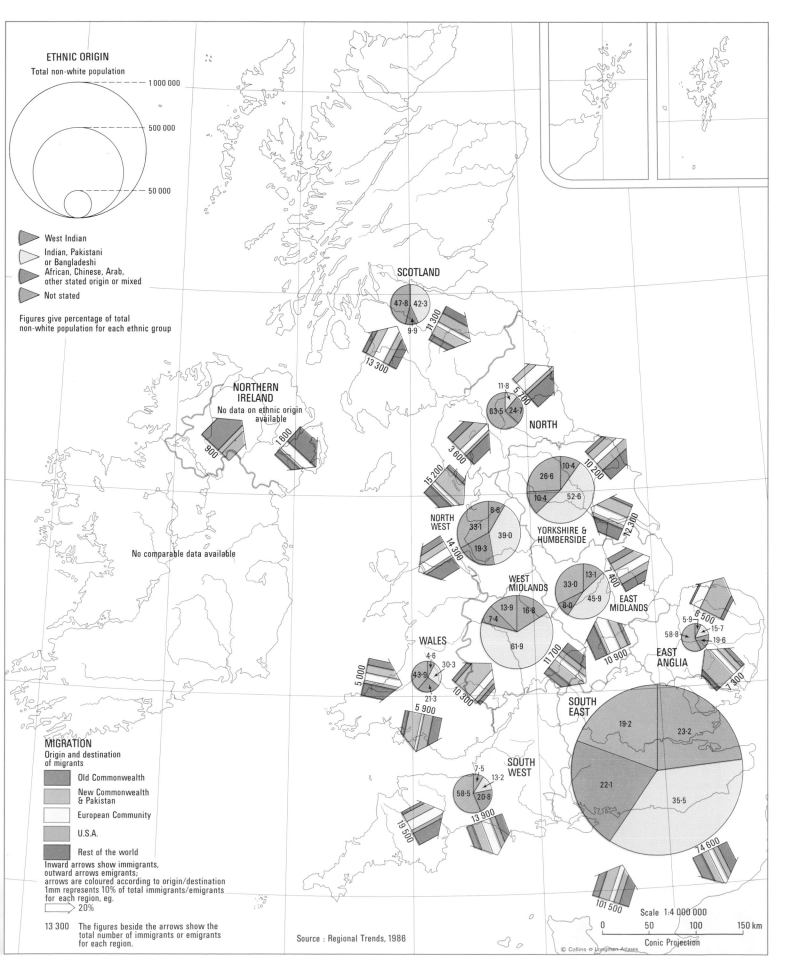

ETHNIC ORIGIN
Total non-white population

1 000 000

500 000

50 000

West Indian

Indian, Pakistani
or Bangladeshi

African, Chinese, Arab,
other stated origin or mixed

Not stated

Figures give percentage of total
non-white population for each ethnic group

SCOTLAND
47·8 42·3
9·9
11 300
13 300

NORTHERN
IRELAND
No data on ethnic origin
available
900   1 600

No comparable data available

11·8 5 700
63·5 24·7
NORTH
3 600
10·4 10 200
26·6
15 200
10·4 52·6
12 300
YORKSHIRE &
HUMBERSIDE

NORTH
WEST
8·8
33·1
39·0
19·3
14 300

13·1 7 400
33·0
8·0 45·9
EAST
MIDLANDS
10 900

WEST
MIDLANDS
13·9 16·8
7·4
61·9
11 700

8 500
5·9 15·7
58·8
19·6
EAST
ANGLIA
7 300

WALES
4·6
30·3
43·9
21·3
5 000
10 300
5 900

SOUTH
EAST
19·2   23·2
22·1   35·5
74 600

SOUTH
WEST
7·5
13·2
58·5
20·8
13 900
19 500
101 500

MIGRATION
Origin and destination
of migrants

Old Commonwealth

New Commonwealth
& Pakistan

European Community

U.S.A.

Rest of the world

Inward arrows show immigrants,
outward arrows emigrants;
arrows are coloured according to origin/destination
1mm represents 10% of total immigrants/emigrants
for each region, eg.
20%

13 300   The figures beside the arrows show the
total number of immigrants or emigrants
for each region.

Source : Regional Trends, 1986

Scale 1:4 000 000
0   50   100   150 km
Conic Projection

© Collins ◇ Longman Atlases

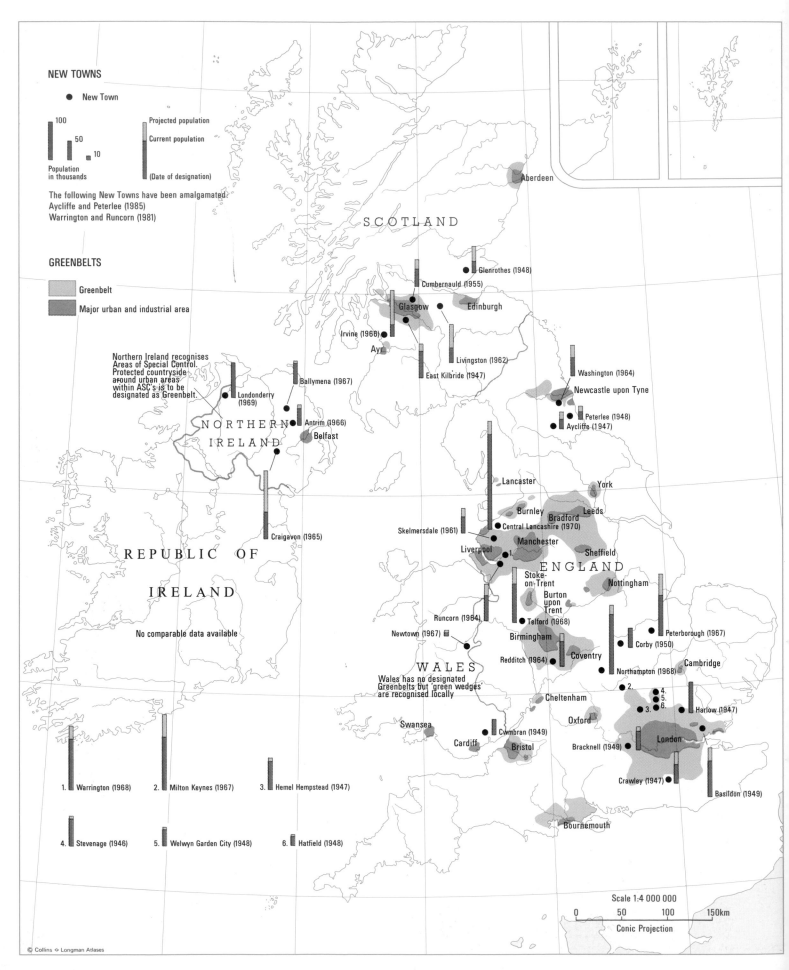

NEW TOWNS

● New Town

100
50
10
Population
in thousands

Projected population
Current population

(Date of designation)

The following New Towns have been amalgamated:
Aycliffe and Peterlee (1985)
Warrington and Runcorn (1981)

GREENBELTS

Greenbelt

Major urban and industrial area

Northern Ireland recognises
Areas of Special Control.
Protected countryside
around urban areas
within ASC's is to be
designated as Greenbelt.

SCOTLAND

Aberdeen

Glenrothes (1948)
Cumbernauld (1955)
Glasgow
Edinburgh
Irvine (1966)
Ayr
Livingston (1962)
East Kilbride (1947)
Washington (1964)
Newcastle upon Tyne
Peterlee (1948)
Aycliffe (1947)

Ballymena (1967)
Londonderry (1969)
Antrim (1966)
Belfast

NORTHERN
IRELAND

Craigavon (1965)

REPUBLIC OF

IRELAND

No comparable data available

Lancaster
York
Burnley
Bradford
Leeds
Central Lancashire (1970)
Skelmersdale (1961)
Liverpool
Manchester
Sheffield
1.
Stoke-on-Trent
ENGLAND
Burton upon Trent
Nottingham
Runcorn (1964)
Newtown (1967)
Telford (1968)
Peterborough (1967)
Birmingham
Corby (1950)
Redditch (1964)
Coventry
Cambridge
Northampton (1968)
WALES
2.
4.
5.
6.
Wales has no designated
Greenbelts but 'green wedges'
are recognised locally
Cheltenham
3.
Harlow (1947)
Oxford
Swansea
Cwmbran (1949)
London
Cardiff
Bristol
Bracknell (1949)
Crawley (1947)
Bournemouth
Basildon (1949)

1. Warrington (1968)   2. Milton Keynes (1967)   3. Hemel Hempstead (1947)

4. Stevenage (1946)   5. Welwyn Garden City (1948)   6. Hatfield (1948)

Scale 1:4 000 000
0   50   100   150km
Conic Projection

© Collins ◇ Longman Atlases

ARCTIC

North Cape

NORWEGIAN SEA

ATLANTIC OCEAN

Relief
Metres
5000
3000
2000
1000
500
200
0 Sea Level
Land Dep.
200
4000
7000
Metres

Arctic Circle

NORTH SEA

Vesterålen
Lofoten
Vestfjorden
▲2123
Kebnekaise
Lapta
Muonio
Torne
Inari
Kemi
Storavan
Skellefte
Lule
Ume
Indals
Storsjön
Ljusnan
Näsijärvi
Oulujärvi
Kallave
L. Peipus
Pst
Gulf of Bothnia
Frohavet
Åland Is.
Saaremaa
Gulf of Riga
Gulf of Finland

Faroe Is.

Shetland Is.

Orkney Is.
Hebrides
Moray Firth
Ben Nevis
1343▲
Grampian
Mountains
Firth of Forth
Southern
Uplands
The Pennines
Malin Head
Galway Bay
Irish Sea
Shannon
Wicklow Mts.
Snowdon
1085▲
Cambrian Mts.
Cape Clear
St. George's Channel
Celtic Sea
Land's End
Isles of Scilly
Trent
The Wash
The Fens
Thames
Severn

Dovrefjell
Glittertind ▲2470
Jotunheimen
Sognefjorden
Hardangerfjorden
Mjösa
Glåma
Klar
Dal
Göta
Vänern
Vättern
Gotland
Öland
Lindesnes
Oslofjorden
Otra
Skagerrak
Limfjorden
Kattegat
Jutland
Zealand
Funen
Bornholm
Neman
BALTIC SEA

English Channel
Channel Is.
Str. of Dover
Frisian Is.
IJsselmeer
Kiel Canal
Elbe
Oder
Weser
Maas
Rhine
Ardennes
Mosel
Taunus
Harz Mts.
Spree
Ore Mts.
Sudeten Mts.
Silesian Plateau
Vistula
Warta
Bug
Neman
NORTH EU

Brittany

Bay of Biscay

Scale 1:16 000 000
0 200 400 600 800 km
Conic Projection

Seine
Marne
Loire
Loire
Vienne
Saône
Allier
Gironde
Garonne
Dordogne
Mont Dore
▲1886
Massif
Central
Cevennes
Rhône
Vosges
Jura Mts.
L. Geneva
Rhône
Mt. Blanc
▲4807
Black Forest
Constance
Inn
Danube
Brenner Pass
Gross Glockner
▲3798
Mt. Rosa
▲4634
ALPS
Dolomites
Adige
Po
Durance
Bohemian Forest
Gerlachovka
▲2663
Carpathian
Morava
Tisza
Drava
Hungarian Plain
Sava
Danube
Mures
Transylvanian
Iron Gate

C. Finisterre
Cantabrian Mts.
Douro
Iberian Mts.
Douro
Tagus
Gulf of Gascony
Ebro
Pyrénées
Pico de Aneto ▲3404
Gulf of Lions
Ebro Delta
C. Creus
Balearic Is.
Minorca
Majorca
Ibiza
C. de la Nao
C. Palos
Ligurian Sea
Arno
G. of Genoa
Corsica
Str. of Bonifacio
Sardinia
Tyrrhenian Sea
Tibero
Apennines
▲2914 Mt. Corno
1277▲
Vesuvius
ADRIATIC SEA
Dinaric Alps
Drina
Durmitor ▲2522
L. Shkoder
Morava
Danube
Balka
Rhodope
Struma
Mesala ▲2925
Adria

Iberian Peninsula
C. Roca
Guadiana
Sierra Morena
Guadalquivir
Mulhacén
3482▲
Sierra Nevada
Gulf of Cadiz
C. St. Vincent
Str. of Gibraltar
Rif Mts.
Sebou
Oum er Rbia
Toubkal ▲4165
High Atlas
Tell Atlas
Cheliff
Chott ech Chergui
Saharan Atlas
Mejerda
C. Bon
MEDITERRANE

Sicily
Mt. Etna ▲3340
C. Spartivento
C. Passero
Stromboli 926▲
G. of Taranto
Str. of Otranto
Corfu
Ionian Islands
Mt. Olympus ▲2911
Pindus Mts.
Killini ▲2376
Ionian Sea
C. Matapan

© Collins ◊ Longman Atlases

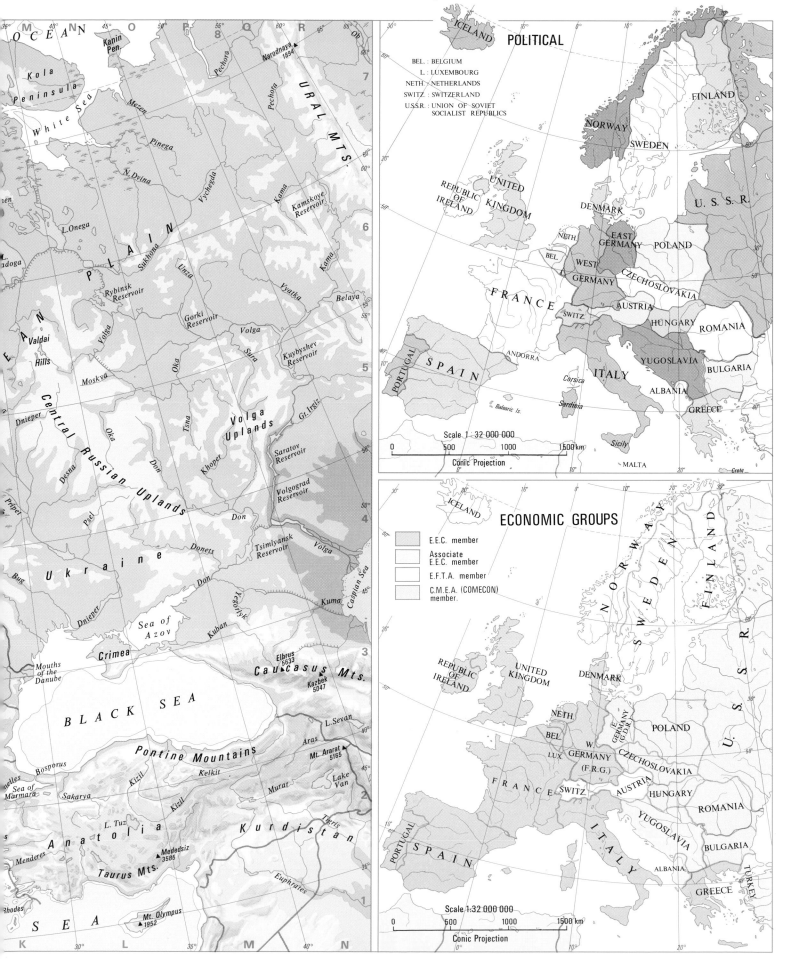

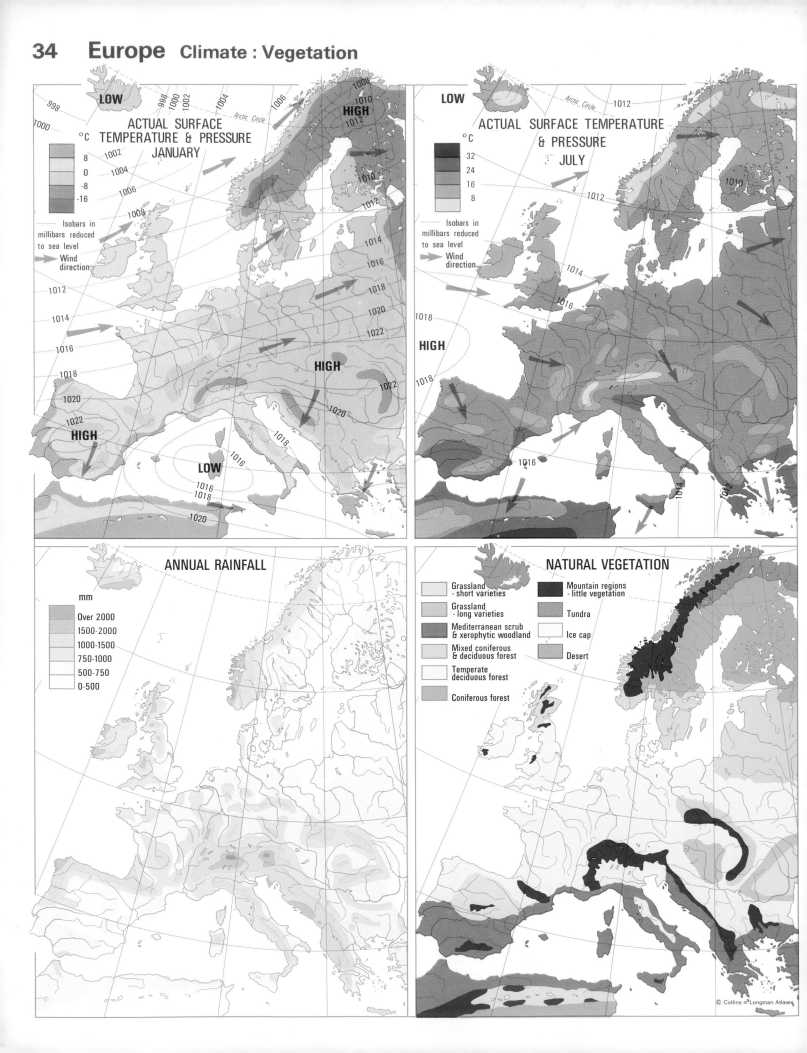

ACTUAL SURFACE TEMPERATURE & PRESSURE JANUARY

°C
8
0
-8
-16

— Isobars in millibars reduced to sea level
→ Wind direction

LOW
HIGH
HIGH
HIGH
LOW

ACTUAL SURFACE TEMPERATURE & PRESSURE JULY

°C
32
24
16
8

— Isobars in millibars reduced to sea level
→ Wind direction

LOW
HIGH

ANNUAL RAINFALL

mm
Over 2000
1500-2000
1000-1500
750-1000
500-750
0-500

NATURAL VEGETATION

Grassland - short varieties
Grassland - long varieties
Mediterranean scrub & xerophytic woodland
Mixed coniferous & deciduous forest
Temperate deciduous forest
Coniferous forest
Mountain regions - little vegetation
Tundra
Ice cap
Desert

© Collins ∘ Longman Atlases

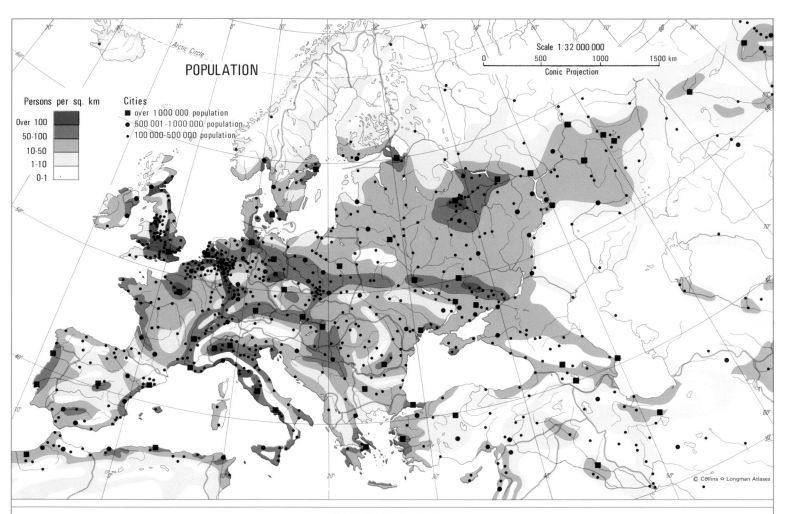

POPULATION

Persons per sq. km

Over 100
50-100
10-50
1-10
0-1

Cities
■ over 1 000 000 population
● 500 001 - 1 000 000 population
• 100 000 - 500 000 population

Scale 1:32 000 000
0   500   1000   1500 km
Conic Projection

© Collins ◇ Longman Atlases

POPULATION STATISTICS

COUNTRY	TOTAL POPULATION	% URBAN POPULA-TION	LIFE EXPECTATION AT BIRTH		% OF TOTAL POPULATION BY AGE GROUP				
			MALE	FEMALE	0-14	15-34	35-54	55-74	75+
ALBANIA	2 841 000	33.8	68.00	71.50	na	na	na	na	na
AUSTRIA	7 549 000	54.9	69.18	76.59	20.0	30.4	24.2	19.2	6.2
BELGIUM	9 856 000	94.6	68.60	75.08	20.0	31.1	24.2	18.9	5.8
BULGARIA	8 939 000	64.6	68.68	73.91	22.1	28.8	26.4	18.7	4.0
CZECHOSLOVAKIA	15 415 000	66.7	67.00	74.34	24.3	30.8	23.2	17.4	4.3
DENMARK	5 114 000	82.6	71.40	77.40	19.7	30.2	24.9	19.3	5.9
EAST GERMANY	16 699 000	76.6	69.09	75.10	19.3	31.1	25.8	17.4	6.4
FINLAND	4 863 000	59.9	69.53	77.77	20.0	33.4	24.6	17.8	4.2
FRANCE	54 652 000	73.4	70.41	78.47	21.8	31.3	23.5	17.3	6.1
GREECE	9 840 000	na	70.13	73.64	22.4	28.4	26.5	17.7	5.0
HUNGARY	10 690 000	54.3	66.14	73.68	22.0	28.8	25.4	19.1	4.7
ICELAND	237 000	88.7	73.91	79.45	26.9	34.9	20.3	13.7	4.2
IRELAND, REPUBLIC OF	3 508 000	55.6	68.77	73.52	30.6	31.0	19.1	15.5	3.8
ITALY	56 559 000	na	69.69	75.91	21.4	29.6	25.4	18.6	5.0
LUXEMBOURG	365 000	77.8	66.80	72.80	19.0	31.2	26.8	18.2	4.8
NETHERLANDS	14 362 000	88.4	72.70	79.30	21.8	34.0	23.3	16.3	4.6
NORWAY	4 129 000	70.7	72.64	79.41	21.3	30.4	22.0	20.2	6.1
POLAND	36 571 000	59.3	67.24	75.20	24.7	33.7	23.0	15.0	3.6
PORTUGAL	10 099 000	29.7	65.09	72.86	25.9	32.1	22.3	16.2	3.5
ROMANIA	22 553 000	48.5	67.42	72.18	27.0	28.8	25.0	15.9	3.3
SPAIN	38 228 000	91.4	70.41	76.21	25.6	29.8	23.7	16.7	4.2
SWEDEN	8 329 000	82.7	73.05	79.08	19.2	28.4	24.2	21.6	6.6
SWITZERLAND	6 505 000	57.1	72.00	78.70	19.0	30.8	26.3	18.2	5.7
U.S.S.R.	272 500 000	64.1	64.00	74.00	na	na	na	na	na
UNITED KINGDOM	55 610 000	89.6	69.86	75.80	20.2	30.1	23.6	20.1	6.0
WEST GERMANY	61 421 000	na	70.18	76.85	16.9	30.7	27.0	19.2	6.2
YUGOSLAVIA	22 855 000	na	67.72	73.15	24.4	32.8	25.9	13.8	3.1

Source : U.N. Demographic Yearbook 1983   Figures are the latest available census figures or estimates.

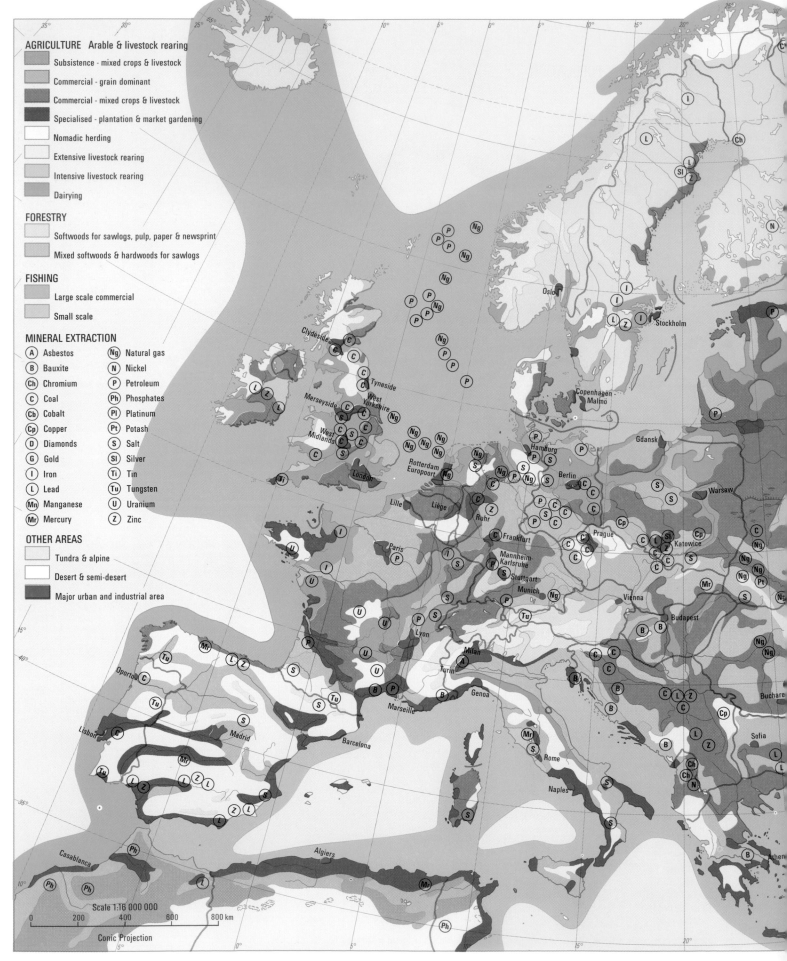

AGRICULTURE Arable & livestock rearing

- Subsistence - mixed crops & livestock
- Commercial - grain dominant
- Commercial - mixed crops & livestock
- Specialised - plantation & market gardening
- Nomadic herding
- Extensive livestock rearing
- Intensive livestock rearing
- Dairying

FORESTRY

- Softwoods for sawlogs, pulp, paper & newsprint
- Mixed softwoods & hardwoods for sawlogs

FISHING

- Large scale commercial
- Small scale

MINERAL EXTRACTION

- (A) Asbestos
- (B) Bauxite
- (Ch) Chromium
- (C) Coal
- (Cb) Cobalt
- (Cp) Copper
- (D) Diamonds
- (G) Gold
- (I) Iron
- (L) Lead
- (Mn) Manganese
- (Mr) Mercury

- (Ng) Natural gas
- (N) Nickel
- (P) Petroleum
- (Ph) Phosphates
- (Pl) Platinum
- (Pt) Potash
- (S) Salt
- (Sl) Silver
- (Ti) Tin
- (Tu) Tungsten
- (U) Uranium
- (Z) Zinc

OTHER AREAS

- Tundra & alpine
- Desert & semi-desert
- Major urban and industrial area

Scale 1:16 000 000

0   200   400   600   800 km

Conic Projection

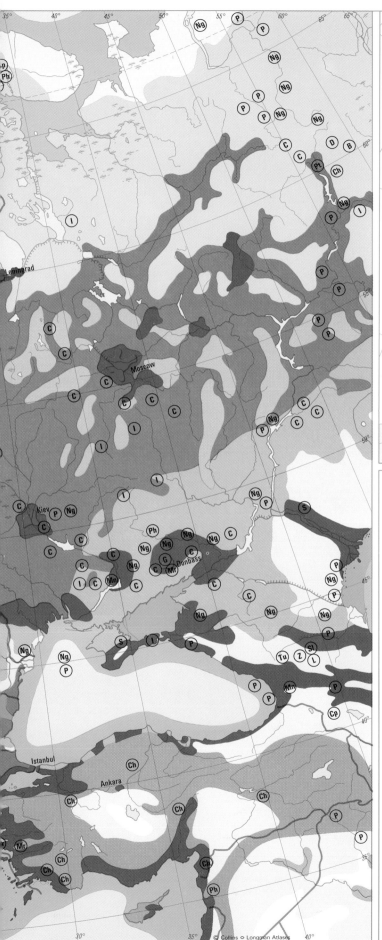

ENERGY PRODUCTION

Production of energy
Thousand metric tons of coal equivalent

- 500 001-2 500 000
- 100 001-500 000
- 50 001-100 000
- 20 001-50 000
- 5 001-20 000
- 0-5000

Scale 1:32 000 000

0   500   1000   1500 km

ENERGY PRODUCTION STATISTICS

Figures in thousand metric tons of coal equivalent for 1982

COUNTRY	TOTAL	SOLIDS mainly coal	LIQUIDS mainly petroleum	GAS	ELEC-TRICITY
ALBANIA	6 689	800	5 089	529	271
AUSTRIA	8 884	1 385	1 876	1 825	3 798
BELGIUM	8 637	6 539	na	42	2 056
BULGARIA	18 441	16 211	436	97	1 697
CZECHOSLOVAKIA	66 265	64 176	134	776	1 179
DENMARK	2 454	0	2 451	na	3
EAST GERMANY	89 855	84 231	80	3 992	1 552
FINLAND	3 990	450	na	na	3 540
FRANCE	55 885	20 595	3 460	19 440	21 390
GREECE	7 153	5 225	1 490	na	438
HUNGARY	22 934	10 036	4 102	8 776	20
ICELAND	398	na	na	na	398
IRELAND, REPUBLIC OF	4 162	1 382	na	2 632	148
ITALY	28 878	454	2 810	19 019	6 595
LUXEMBOURG	61	na	na	na	61
NETHERLANDS	92 046	0	14 605	76 961	480
NORWAY	83 102	472	35 728	35 488	11 432
POLAND	171 080	164 639	418	5 703	320
PORTUGAL	1 034	190	na	na	844
ROMANIA	92 606	17 331	17 859	55 958	1 458
SPAIN	25 558	18 804	2 226	1	4 527
SWEDEN	11 697	27	20	na	11 650
SWITZERLAND	6 311	na	na	na	6 311
U.S.S.R.	2 013 473	495 618	892 263	594 193	31 399
UNITED KINGDOM	311 328	103 261	154 404	47 561	6 102
WEST GERMANY	163 702	127 475	6 190	19 801	10 236
YUGOSLAVIA	35 005	22 901	6 326	2 381	3 397

Source : UN Statistical Yearbook 1982

AGRICULTURE & SOILS

Heath and dune - poorest sandy soils.

Dairying on fertile alluvial soils.

Extensive livestock farming with fodder crops on poor sandy soils.

Livestock farming with cereals on fertile clay soils.

Intensive dairying and pig farming with cereals and sugar beet on fertile clay soils.

Scale 1:2 000 000

0   20   40   60   80 km

Conic Projection

© Collins Longman Atlases

ZUIDER ZEE SCHEME

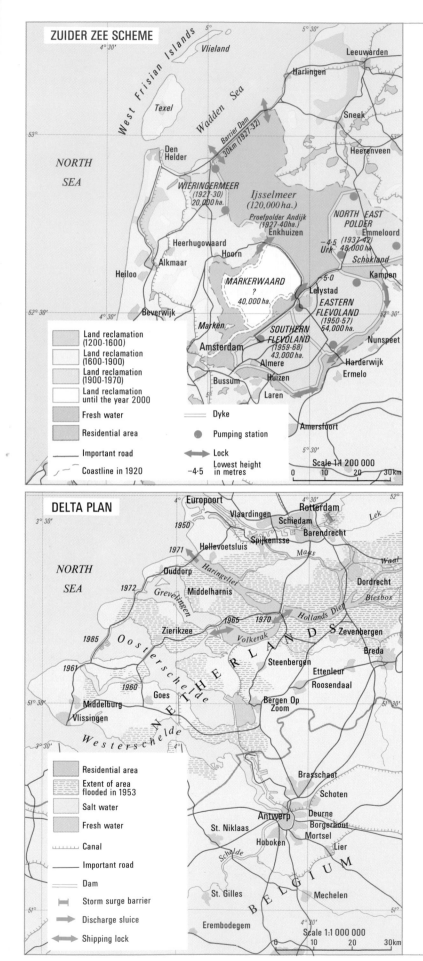

West Frisian Islands

Vlieland

Leeuwarden

Harlingen

Texel

Wadden Sea

Sneek

Den Helder

Barrier Dam
30km (1927-32)

Heerenveen

NORTH SEA

WIERINGERMEER
(1927-30)
20,000 ha.

Ijsselmeer
(120,000 ha.)

Proefpolder Andijk
(1927-40 ha.)

Enkhuizen

NORTH EAST POLDER
(1937-42)
-4·5   48,000 ha

Emmeloord

Urk

Schokland

Heerhugowaard

Hoorn

Kampen

Alkmaar

-5·0

Schokland

Heiloo

MARKERWAARD
?
40,000 ha.

Lelystad

EASTERN
FLEVOLAND
(1950-57)
54,000 ha.

Beverwijk

Marken

Nunspeet

SOUTHERN
FLEVOLAND
(1959-68)
43,000 ha.

Amsterdam

Harderwijk

Almere

Ermelo

Bussum

Huizen

Laren

Amersfoort

Land reclamation (1200-1600)	
Land reclamation (1600-1900)	
Land reclamation (1900-1970)	
Land reclamation until the year 2000	
Fresh water	Dyke
Residential area	● Pumping station
Important road	◄► Lock
Coastline in 1920	-4·5 Lowest height in metres

Scale 1:1 200 000

0   10   20   30km

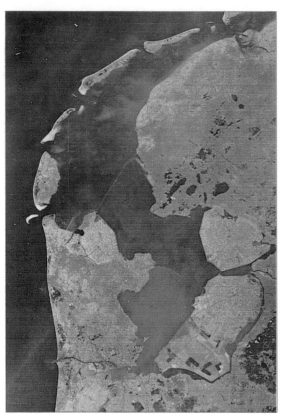

Satellite view of the Zuider Zee Scheme

DELTA PLAN

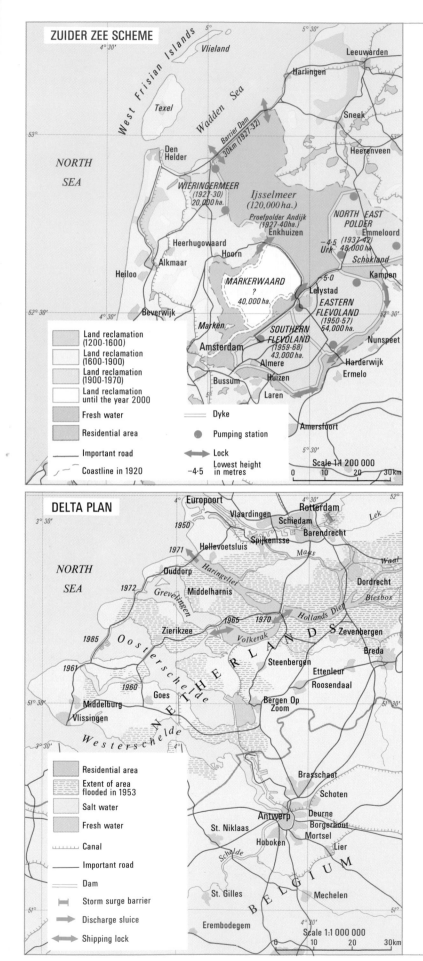

Europoort

Rotterdam

Lek

Vlaardingen

Schiedam

1950

Barendrecht

Hellevoetsluis

Spijkenisse

Maas

Waal

1971

Ouddorp

Haringvliet

Dordrecht

NORTH SEA

Grevelingen

Middelharnis

Biesbos

1972

1965   1970

Hollands Diep

1985

Oosterschelde

Volkerak

Zevenbergen

Zierikzee

NETHERLANDS

Breda

1961

Steenbergen

1960

Goes

Bergen Op Zoom

Roosendaal

Ettenleur

Middelburg

Westerschelde

Vlissingen

Brasschaat

Residential area	
Extent of area flooded in 1953	
Salt water	
Fresh water	
Canal	
Important road	
Dam	
Storm surge barrier	
Discharge sluice	
Shipping lock	

Schoten

Antwerp

Deurne

St. Niklaas

Borgerhout

Hoboken

Mortsel

Schelde

Lier

BELGIUM

St. Gilles

Mechelen

Erembodegem

Scale 1:1 000 000

0   10   20   30km

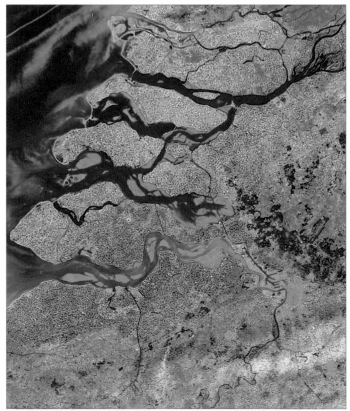

Satellite view of the Delta Plan

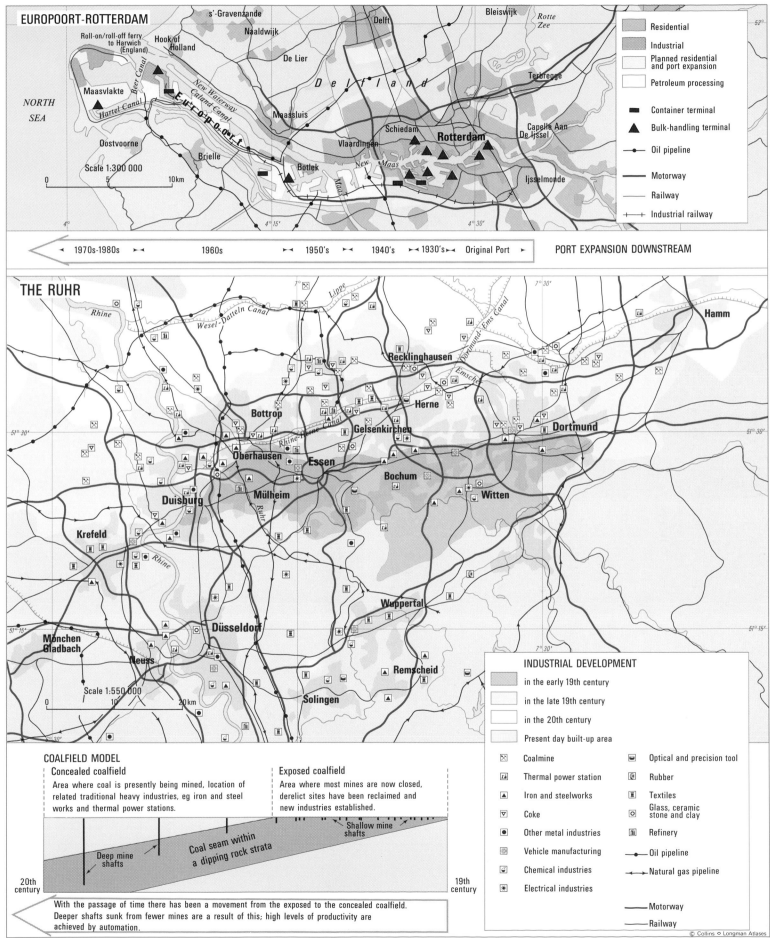

EUROPOORT-ROTTERDAM

s'-Gravenzande
Naaldwijk
De Lier
Delft
Bleiswijk
Rotte Zee
Hook of Holland
Roll-on/roll-off ferry to Harwich (England)
Maasvlakte
Beer Canal
Caland Canal
New Waterway
Hartel Canal
NORTH SEA
EUROPOORT
Oostvoorne
Brielle
Botlek
Maassluis
Vlaardingen
Schiedam
Rotterdam
Delfland
Terbregge
Capelle Aan De Ijssel
New Maas
Ijsselmonde

Scale 1:300 000
0   5   10km

Legend:
- Residential
- Industrial
- Planned residential and port expansion
- Petroleum processing
- Container terminal
- Bulk-handling terminal
- Oil pipeline
- Motorway
- Railway
- Industrial railway

PORT EXPANSION DOWNSTREAM
1970s-1980s | 1960s | 1950's | 1940's | 1930's | Original Port

THE RUHR

Rhine
Lippe
Wesel-Datteln Canal
Dortmund-Ems Canal
Hamm
Recklinghausen
Emscher
Herne
Dortmund
Bottrop
Rhine-Herne Canal
Gelsenkirchen
Oberhausen
Essen
Bochum
Witten
Duisburg
Mülheim
Ruhr
Krefeld
Rhine
Wuppertal
Mönchen Gladbach
Düsseldorf
Neuss
Remscheid
Solingen

Scale 1:550 000
0   10   20km

COALFIELD MODEL

Concealed coalfield
Area where coal is presently being mined, location of related traditional heavy industries, eg iron and steel works and thermal power stations.

Exposed coalfield
Area where most mines are now closed, derelict sites have been reclaimed and new industries established.

Deep mine shafts
Coal seam within a dipping rock strata
Shallow mine shafts
20th century
19th century

With the passage of time there has been a movement from the exposed to the concealed coalfield. Deeper shafts sunk from fewer mines are a result of this; high levels of productivity are achieved by automation.

INDUSTRIAL DEVELOPMENT

- in the early 19th century
- in the late 19th century
- in the 20th century
- Present day built-up area

- Coalmine
- Thermal power station
- Iron and steelworks
- Coke
- Other metal industries
- Vehicle manufacturing
- Chemical industries
- Electrical industries
- Optical and precision tool
- Rubber
- Textiles
- Glass, ceramic stone and clay
- Refinery
- Oil pipeline
- Natural gas pipeline
- Motorway
- Railway

© Collins ◇ Longman Atlases

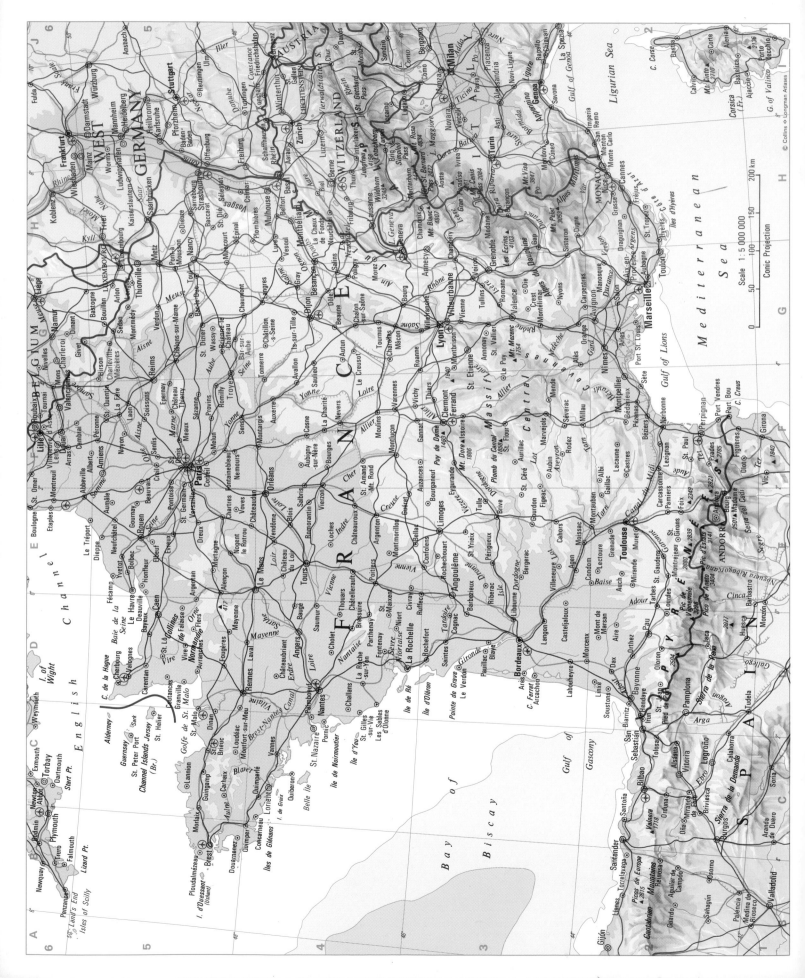

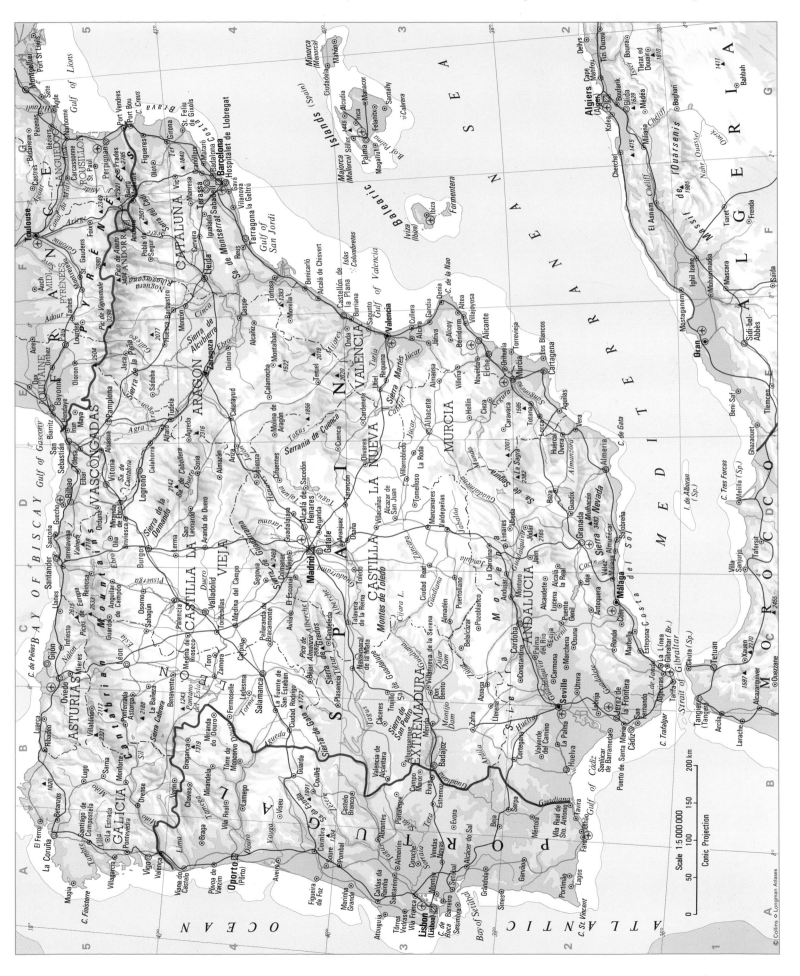

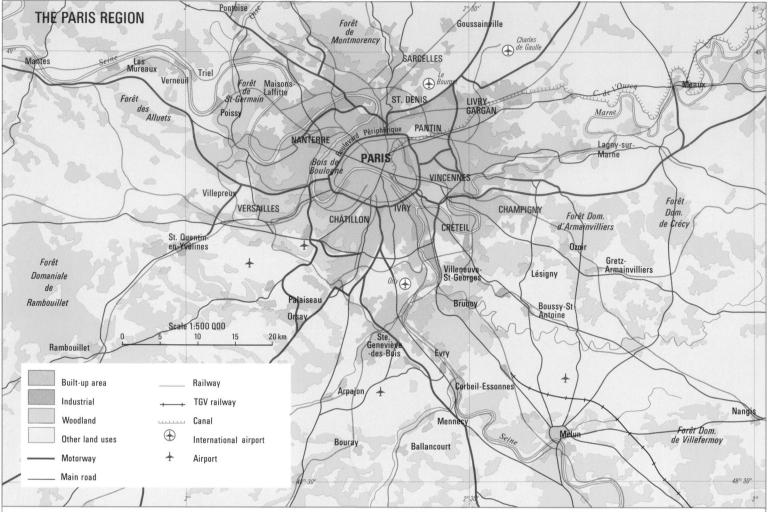

THE PARIS REGION

Pontoise
Oise
Goussainville
Forêt de Montmorency
Charles de Gaulle
Mantes
Seine
Les Mureaux
Triel
Verneuil
SARCELLES
Le Bourget
Meaux
C. de l'Ourcq
Forêt de St-Germain
Maisons-Laffitte
ST. DENIS
LIVRY GARGAN
Marne
Forêt des Alluets
Poissy
PANTIN
Lagny-sur-Marne
NANTERRE
Boulevard Périphérique
PARIS
Villepreux
Bois de Boulogne
VINCENNES
VERSAILLES
IVRY
CHAMPIGNY
Forêt Dom. d'Armainvilliers
Forêt Dom. de Crécy
CHÂTILLON
CRÉTEIL
St. Quentin-en-Yvélines
Ozoir
Gretz-Armainvilliers
Forêt Domaniale de Rambouillet
Orly
Villeneuve-St-Georges
Lésigny
Palaiseau
Brunoy
Boussy-St-Antoine
Orsay
Ste. Geneviève-des-Bois
Evry
Rambouillet
Arpajon
Corbeil-Essonnes
Nangis
Mennecy
Melun
Bouray
Ballancourt
Seine
Forêt Dom. de Villefermoy

Scale 1:500 000
0   5   10   15   20 km

Legend
Built-up area		Railway	
Industrial		TGV railway	
Woodland		Canal	
Other land uses		International airport ⊕	
Motorway		Airport ✈	
Main road			

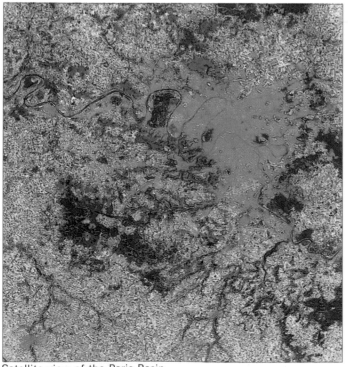

Satellite view of the Paris Basin

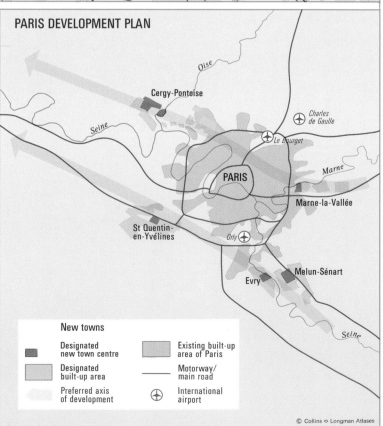

PARIS DEVELOPMENT PLAN

Oise
Cergy-Pontoise
Seine
Charles de Gaulle
Le Bourget
PARIS
Marne
Marne-la-Vallée
St Quentin-en-Yvélines
Orly
Evry
Melun-Sénart
Seine

New towns
■ Designated new town centre		Existing built-up area of Paris	
Designated built-up area		Motorway/main road	
Preferred axis of development		International airport ⊕	

© Collins ○ Longman Atlases

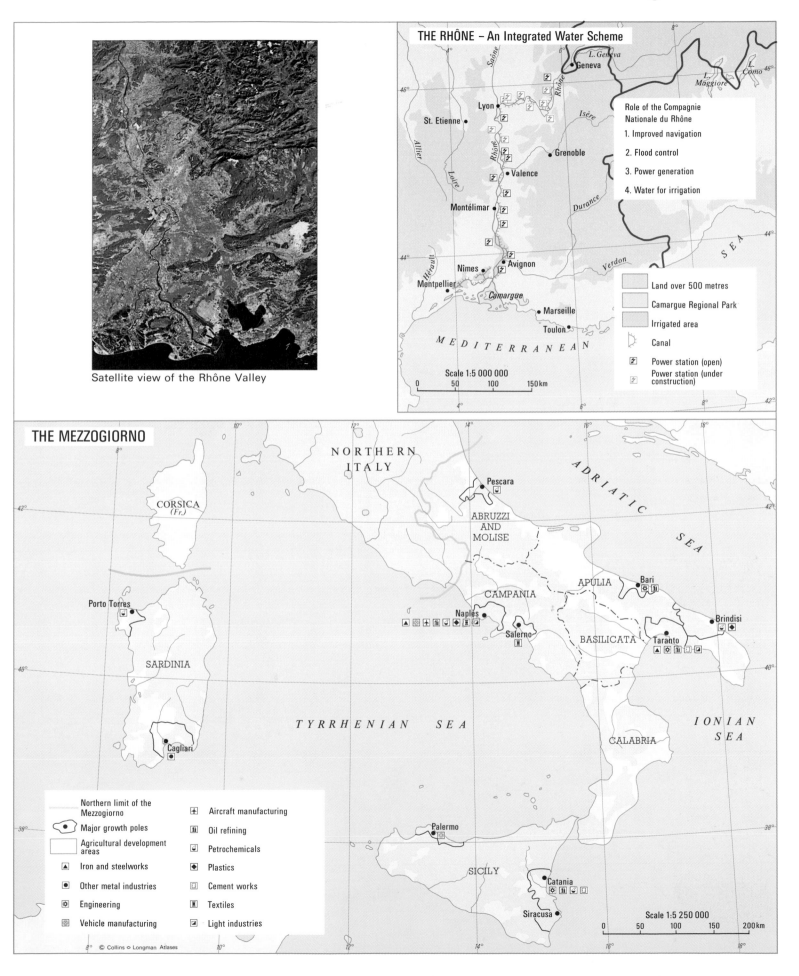

Satellite view of the Rhône Valley

THE RHÔNE – An Integrated Water Scheme

Saône
L. Geneva
Geneva
L. Como
L. Maggiore
Rhône
Lyon
St. Etienne
Isère
Grenoble
Rhône
Allier
Loire
Valence
Durance
Montélimar
Hérault
Nîmes
Avignon
Verdon
Montpellier
Camargue
Marseille
Toulon
SEA
MEDITERRANEAN

Role of the Compagnie Nationale du Rhône

1. Improved navigation
2. Flood control
3. Power generation
4. Water for irrigation

Land over 500 metres
Camargue Regional Park
Irrigated area
Canal
Power station (open)
Power station (under construction)

Scale 1:5 000 000
0   50   100   150km

THE MEZZOGIORNO

NORTHERN ITALY

CORSICA (Fr.)

ADRIATIC SEA

Pescara

ABRUZZI AND MOLISE

Porto Torres

APULIA
Bari

CAMPANIA
Naples
Salerno
BASILICATA
Taranto
Brindisi

SARDINIA

TYRRHENIAN SEA

CALABRIA

IONIAN SEA

Cagliari

Palermo

SICILY
Catania

Siracusa

Northern limit of the Mezzogiorno
Major growth poles
Agricultural development areas
▲ Iron and steelworks
▣ Other metal industries
✚ Engineering
◉ Vehicle manufacturing

⊞ Aircraft manufacturing
🏭 Oil refining
⎌ Petrochemicals
◆ Plastics
▢ Cement works
▤ Textiles
◪ Light industries

Scale 1:5 250 000
0   50   100   150   200km

Scale 1:5 250 000

0   50   100   150   200 km

Conic Projection

© Collins ○ Longman Atlases

© Wm Collins Sons & Co Ltd C/L bi

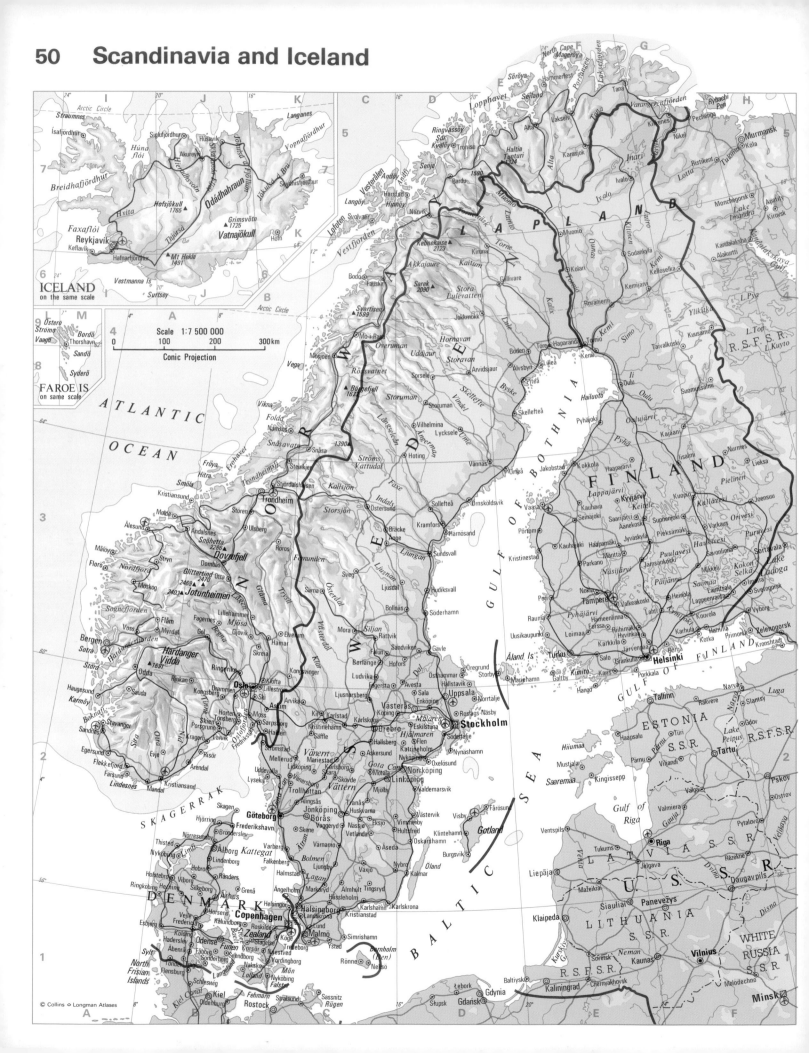

50 Scandinavia and Iceland

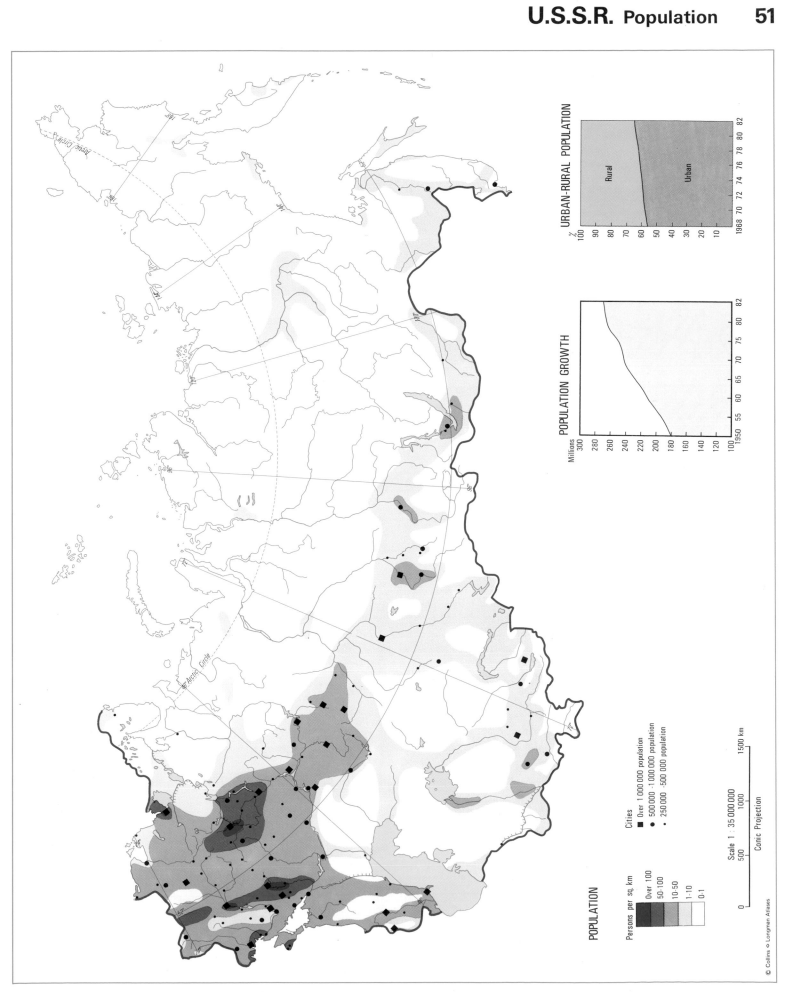

URBAN-RURAL POPULATION

Rural

Urban

POPULATION GROWTH

Millions

POPULATION

Persons per sq. km

Over 100
50-100
10-50
1-10
0-1

Cities

■ Over 1 000 000 population
● 500 000 - 1 000 000 population
● 250 000 - 500 000 population

Scale 1 : 35 000 000

0   500   1000   1500 km

Conic Projection

© Collins ○ Longman Atlases

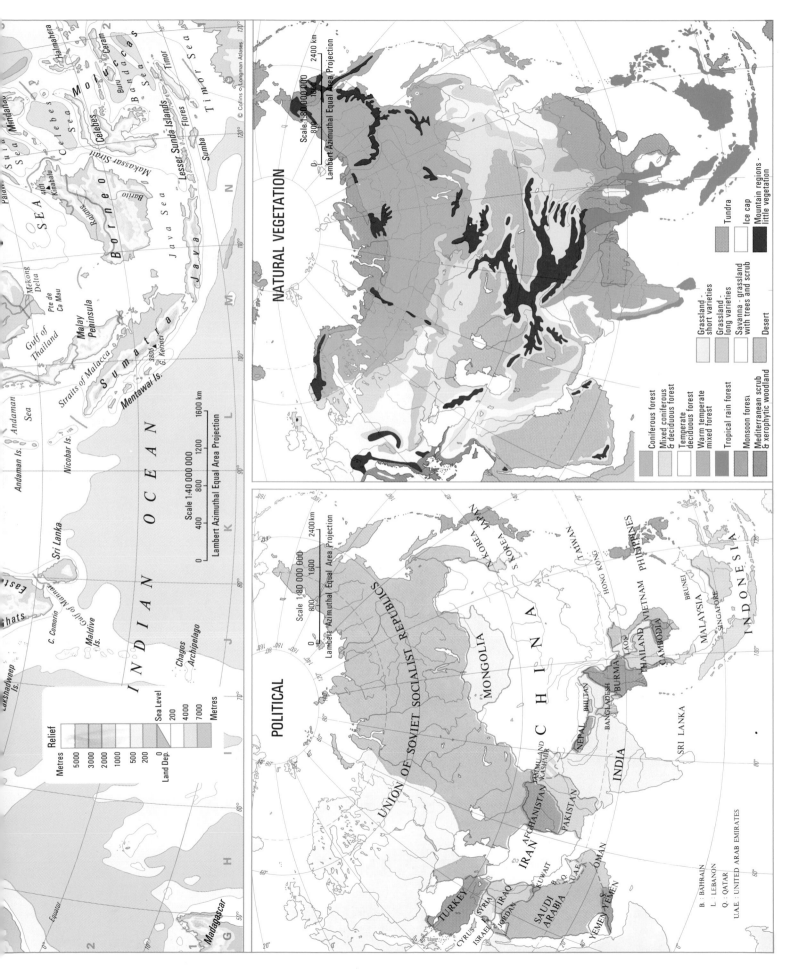

NATURAL VEGETATION

Coniferous forest

Mixed coniferous & deciduous forest

Temperate deciduous forest

Warm temperate mixed forest

Tropical rain forest

Monsoon forest

Mediterranean scrub & xerophytic woodland

Grassland - short varieties

Grassland - long varieties

Savanna - grassland with trees and scrub

Desert

Tundra

Ice cap

Mountain regions - little vegetation

Scale 1:80 000 000

Lambert Azimuthal Equal Area Projection

0   800   1600   2400 km

POLITICAL

Scale 1:80 000 000

Lambert Azimuthal Equal Area Projection

0   800   1600   2400 km

UNION OF SOVIET SOCIALIST REPUBLICS

MONGOLIA

C H I N A

N.KOREA

S.KOREA

JAPAN

TAIWAN

HONG KONG

PHILIPPINES

VIETNAM

THAILAND

CAMBODIA

LAOS

BURMA

BRUNEI

MALAYSIA

SINGAPORE

I N D O N E S I A

BHUTAN

BANGLADESH

NEPAL

INDIA

SRI LANKA

PAKISTAN

AFGHANISTAN

JAMMU AND KASHMIR

IRAN

TURKEY

SYRIA

IRAQ

KUWAIT

CYPRUS

ISRAEL

JORDAN

SAUDI ARABIA

Q.

U.A.E.

OMAN

YEMEN

YEMEN

B : BAHRAIN

L : LEBANON

Q : QATAR

U.A.E. : UNITED ARAB EMIRATES

Left map (relief)

SEA

Molucca Sea

Halmahera

Celebes

Sula

Mindanao

Buru

Ceram

Banda Sea

Moluccas

Timor

Timor Sea

Celebes Sea

Borneo

Palu

Kinabalu 4101 ▲

Makassar Strait

Bartoo

Barito Region

Java Sea

Lesser Sunda Islands

Flores

Sumba

Sumbawa

Bali

Java

Java Sea

Mekong Delta

Pte de Ca Mau

Malay Peninsula

Gulf of Thailand

Straits of Malacca

Sumatra

Mentawai Is.

G. Kerinci 3805 ▲

Andaman Is.

Andaman Sea

Nicobar Is.

I N D I A N   O C E A N

Sri Lanka

C. Comorin

Gulf of Mannar

Lakshadweep Is.

Maldive Is.

Chagos Archipelago

Eastern Ghats

Madagascar

Equator

Scale 1:40 000 000

Lambert Azimuthal Equal Area Projection

0   400   800   1200   1600 km

Relief

Metres

5000

3000

2000

1000

500

200

Sea Level

200

4000

7000

Metres

Land Dep.

© Collins o Longman Atlases

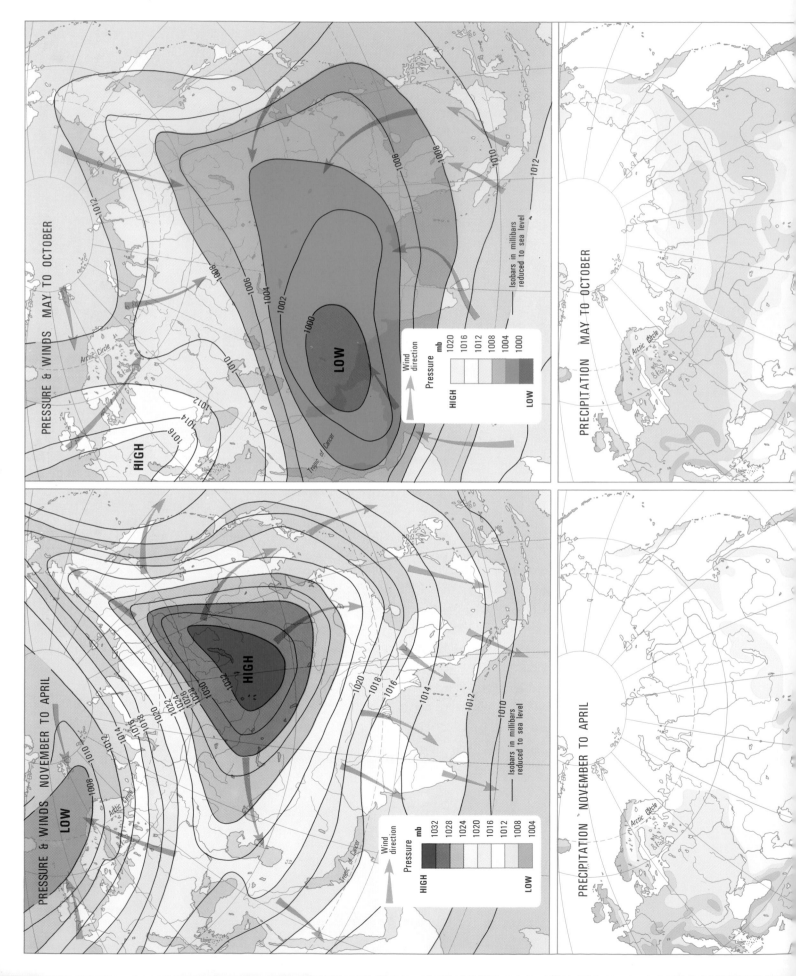

PRESSURE & WINDS MAY TO OCTOBER

PRESSURE & WINDS NOVEMBER TO APRIL

PRECIPITATION MAY TO OCTOBER

PRECIPITATION NOVEMBER TO APRIL

Isobars in millibars reduced to sea level

Wind direction

Pressure

mb
1020
1016
1012
1008
1004
1000

HIGH

LOW

Isobars in millibars reduced to sea level

Wind direction

Pressure

mb
1032
1028
1024
1020
1016
1012
1008
1004

HIGH

LOW

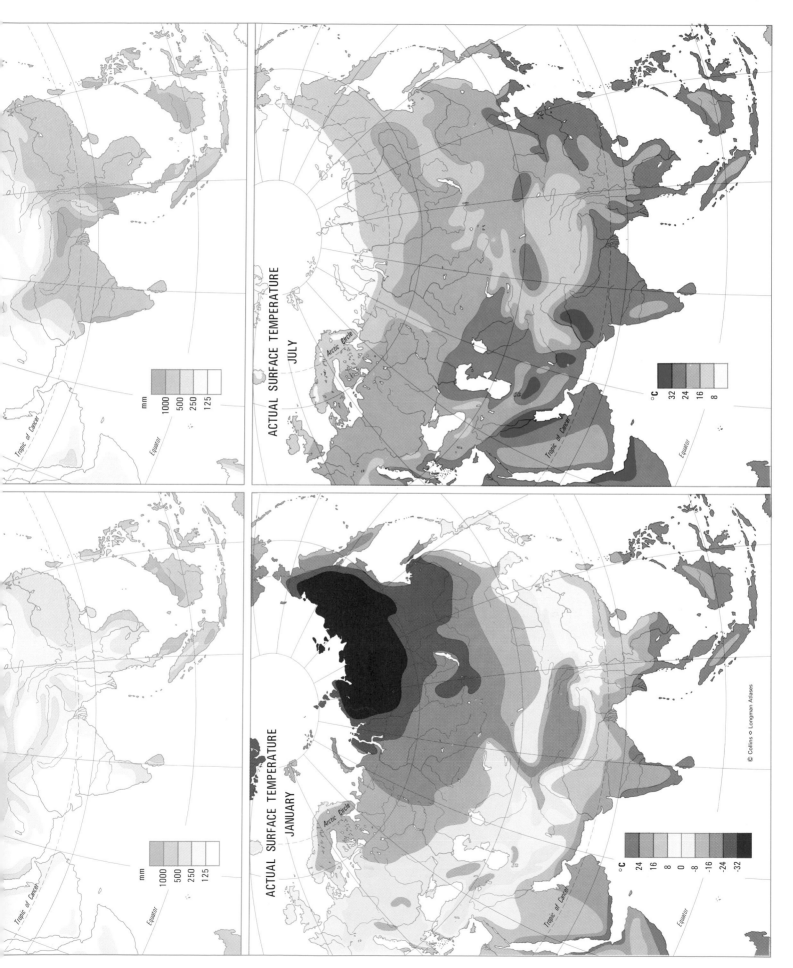

ACTUAL SURFACE TEMPERATURE
JULY

mm
1000
500
250
125

°C
32
24
16
8

ACTUAL SURFACE TEMPERATURE
JANUARY

mm
1000
500
250
125

°C
24
16
8
0
-8
-16
-24
-32

Arctic Circle

Tropic of Cancer

Equator

© Collins ◇ Longman Atlases

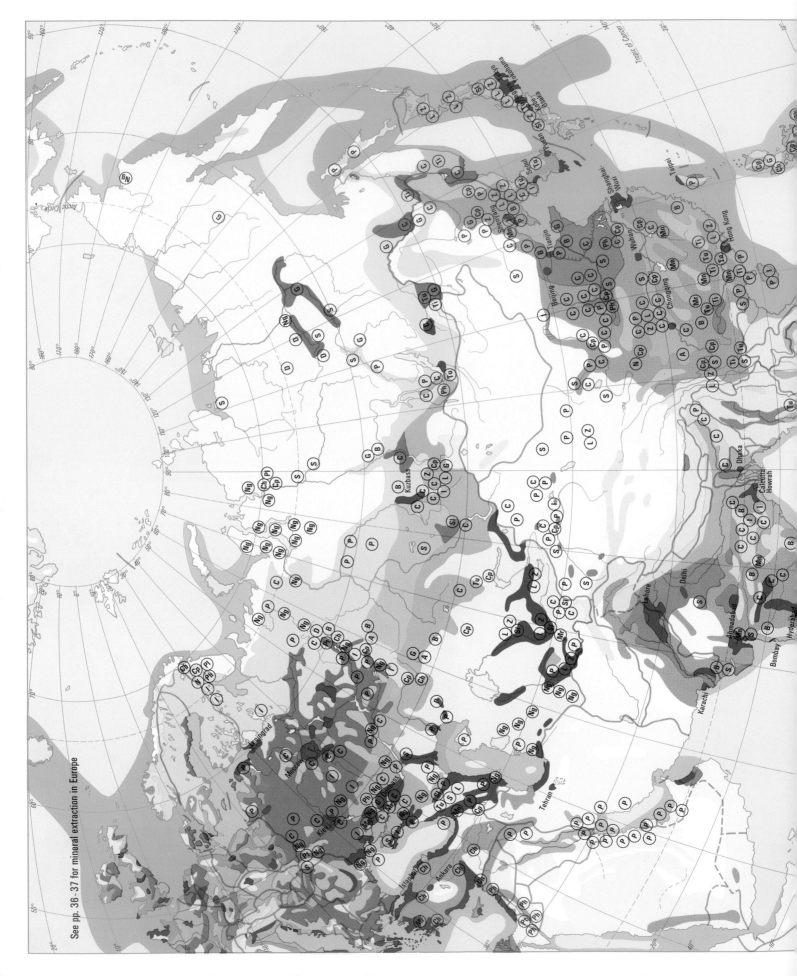

See pp. 36-37 for mineral extraction in Europe

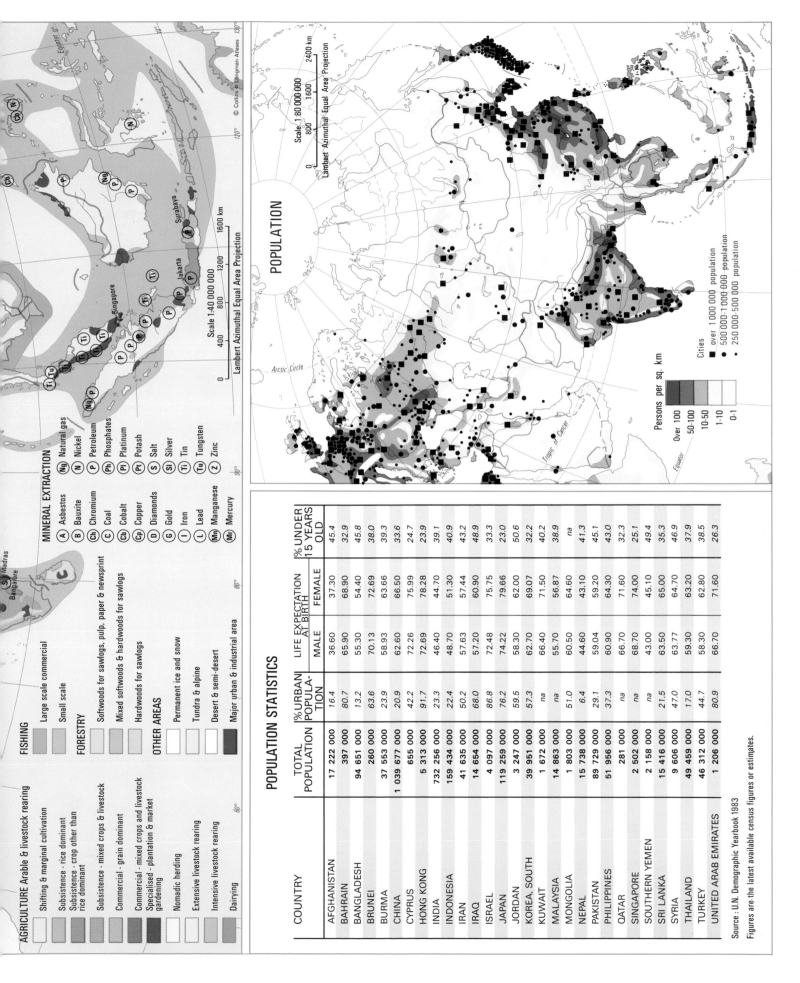

AGRICULTURE Arable & livestock rearing

- Shifting & marginal cultivation
- Subsistence - rice dominant
- Subsistence - crop other than rice dominant
- Subsistence - mixed crops & livestock
- Commercial - grain dominant
- Commercial - mixed crops and livestock
- Specialised - plantation & market gardening
- Nomadic herding
- Extensive livestock rearing
- Intensive livestock rearing
- Dairying

FISHING

- Large scale commercial
- Small scale

FORESTRY

- Softwoods for sawlogs, pulp, paper & newsprint
- Mixed softwoods & hardwoods for sawlogs
- Hardwoods for sawlogs

OTHER AREAS

- Permanent ice and snow
- Tundra & alpine
- Desert & semi-desert
- Major urban & industrial area

MINERAL EXTRACTION

- (A) Asbestos
- (B) Bauxite
- (Ch) Chromium
- (C) Coal
- (Cb) Cobalt
- (Cp) Copper
- (D) Diamonds
- (G) Gold
- (I) Iron
- (L) Lead
- (Mn) Manganese
- (Mr) Mercury
- (Ng) Natural gas
- (N) Nickel
- (P) Petroleum
- (Ph) Phosphates
- (Pl) Platinum
- (Pt) Potash
- (S) Salt
- (Si) Silver
- (Ti) Tin
- (Tu) Tungsten
- (Z) Zinc

Scale 1:40 000 000

Lambert Azimuthal Equal Area Projection

POPULATION

Scale 1:80 000 000

Lambert Azimuthal Equal Area Projection

Cities
- ■ over 1 000 000 population
- ● 500 000-1 000 000 population
- • 250 000-500 000 population

Persons per sq. km
- Over 100
- 50-100
- 10-50
- 1-10
- 0-1

POPULATION STATISTICS

COUNTRY	TOTAL POPULATION	% URBAN POPULA-TION	LIFE EXPECTATION AT BIRTH MALE	LIFE EXPECTATION AT BIRTH FEMALE	% UNDER 15 YEARS OLD
AFGHANISTAN	17 222 000	16.4	36.60	37.30	45.4
BAHRAIN	397 000	80.7	65.90	68.90	32.9
BANGLADESH	94 651 000	13.2	55.30	54.40	45.8
BRUNEI	260 000	63.6	70.13	72.69	38.0
BURMA	37 553 000	23.9	58.93	63.66	39.3
CHINA	1 039 677 000	20.9	62.60	66.50	33.6
CYPRUS	655 000	42.2	72.26	75.99	24.7
HONG KONG	5 313 000	91.7	72.69	78.28	23.9
INDIA	732 256 000	23.3	46.40	44.70	39.1
INDONESIA	159 434 000	22.4	48.70	51.30	40.9
IRAN	41 635 000	50.2	57.63	57.44	43.2
IRAQ	14 654 000	68.0	57.20	60.90	48.9
ISRAEL	4 097 000	86.8	72.48	75.75	33.3
JAPAN	119 259 000	76.2	74.22	79.66	23.0
JORDAN	3 247 000	59.5	58.30	62.00	50.6
KOREA, SOUTH	39 951 000	57.3	62.70	69.07	32.2
KUWAIT	1 672 000	na	66.40	71.50	40.2
MALAYSIA	14 863 000	na	55.70	56.87	38.9
MONGOLIA	1 803 000	51.0	60.50	64.60	na
NEPAL	15 738 000	6.4	44.60	43.10	41.3
PAKISTAN	89 729 000	29.1	59.04	59.20	45.1
PHILIPPINES	51 956 000	37.3	60.90	64.30	43.0
QATAR	281 000	na	66.70	71.60	32.3
SINGAPORE	2 502 000	na	68.70	74.00	25.1
SOUTHERN YEMEN	2 158 000	na	43.00	45.10	49.4
SRI LANKA	15 416 000	21.5	63.50	65.00	35.3
SYRIA	9 606 000	47.0	63.77	64.70	46.9
THAILAND	49 459 000	17.0	59.30	63.20	37.9
TURKEY	46 312 000	44.7	58.30	62.80	38.5
UNITED ARAB EMIRATES	1 206 000	80.9	66.70	71.60	26.3

Source : U.N. Demographic Yearbook 1983

Figures are the latest available census figures or estimates.

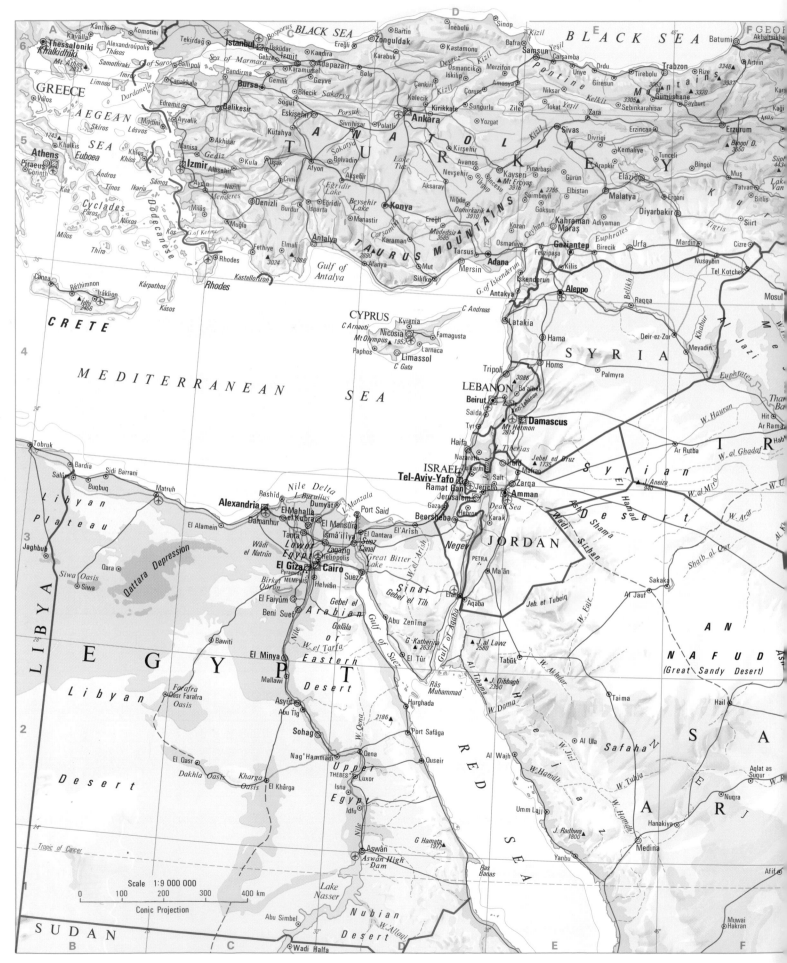

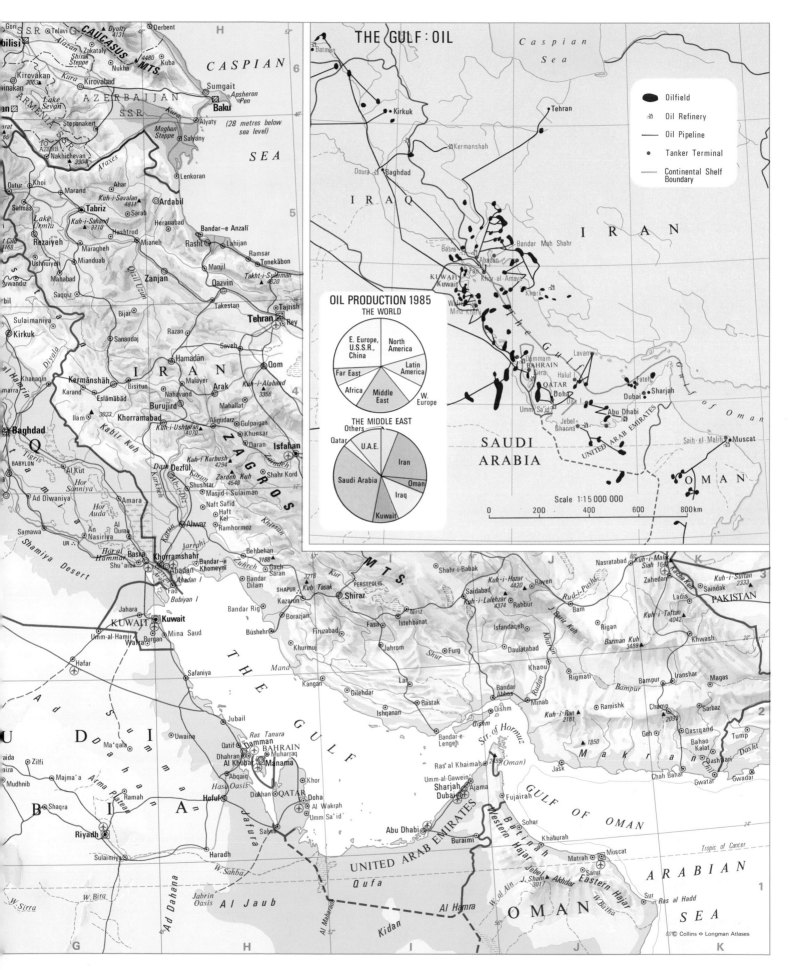

THE GULF: OIL

Oilfield
Oil Refinery
Oil Pipeline
Tanker Terminal
Continental Shelf Boundary

OIL PRODUCTION 1985

THE WORLD

E. Europe, U.S.S.R., China
North America
Far East
Latin America
Africa
Middle East
W. Europe

THE MIDDLE EAST

Others
Qatar
U.A.E.
Iran
Saudi Arabia
Oman
Iraq
Kuwait

Scale 1:15 000 000

0   200   400   600   800km

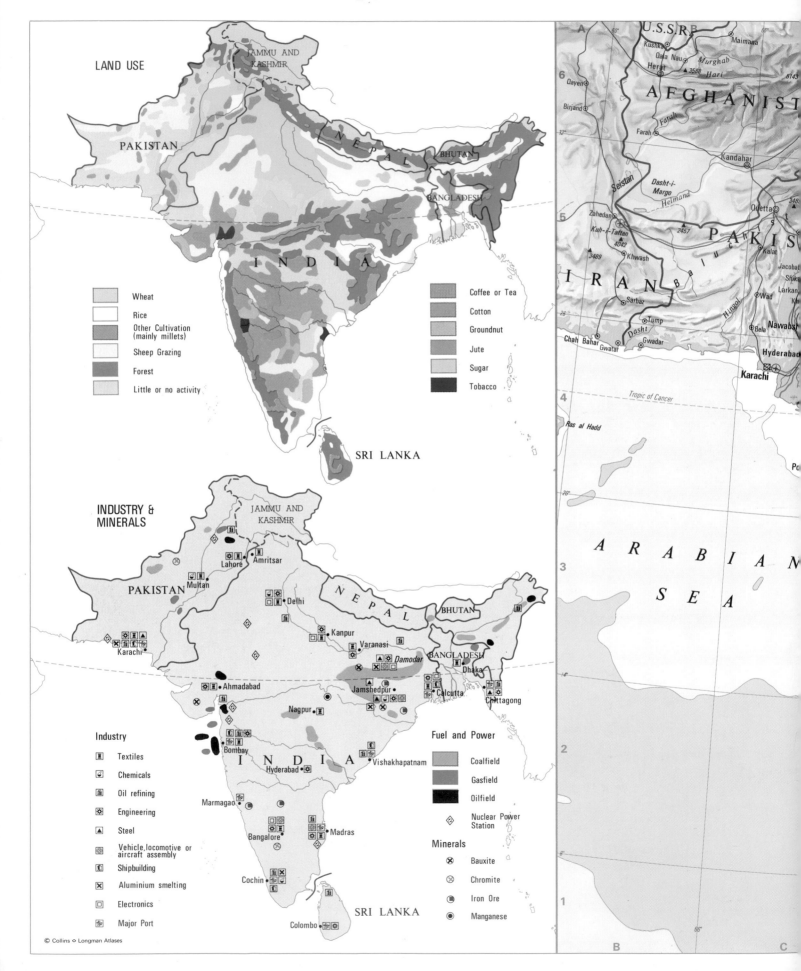

LAND USE

JAMMU AND KASHMIR

PAKISTAN

NEPAL

BHUTAN

BANGLADESH

INDIA

Wheat

Rice

Other Cultivation (mainly millets)

Sheep Grazing

Forest

Little or no activity

Coffee or Tea

Cotton

Groundnut

Jute

Sugar

Tobacco

SRI LANKA

INDUSTRY & MINERALS

JAMMU AND KASHMIR

PAKISTAN

Lahore
Amritsar
Multan
Delhi
Kanpur
Varanasi
Damodar
Jamshedpur
Ahmadabad
Nagpur
Bombay
Hyderabad
Vishakhapatnam
Marmagao
Bangalore
Madras
Cochin

NEPAL

BHUTAN

BANGLADESH
Dhaka
Calcutta
Chittagong

Karachi

INDIA

SRI LANKA
Colombo

Industry

▥ Textiles

◩ Chemicals

▣ Oil refining

✳ Engineering

▲ Steel

◉ Vehicle, locomotive or aircraft assembly

▤ Shipbuilding

✕ Aluminium smelting

▢ Electronics

✚ Major Port

Fuel and Power

Coalfield

Gasfield

Oilfield

◈ Nuclear Power Station

Minerals

⊗ Bauxite

⊘ Chromite

◐ Iron Ore

◉ Manganese

© Collins ◇ Longman Atlases

U.S.S.R.

Kushka
Qala Nau
Murghab
Hari
Qayen
Birjand
Herat
3588
Farah
AFGHANISTAN

Zahedan
Kuh-i-Taftan
4042
Khwash
3489
Sarbaz

IRAN

Seistan
Dasht-i-Margo
Helmand
Kandahar

Dasht
Tump
Chah Bahar
Gwatar
Gwadar
Hingol
Bela

Quetta
Kalat
Jacobabad
Larkana
Wad
Nawabshah

PAKISTAN

Baluchistan

Hyderabad

Karachi

Tropic of Cancer

Ras al Hadd

ARABIAN

SEA

A B I A

S E A

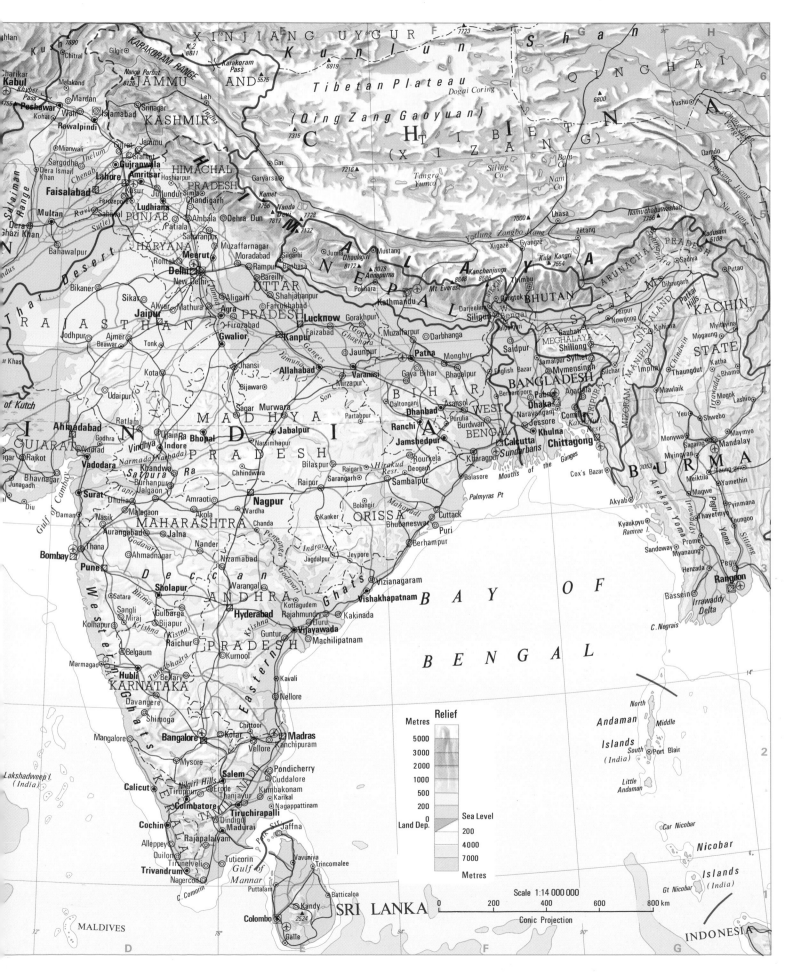

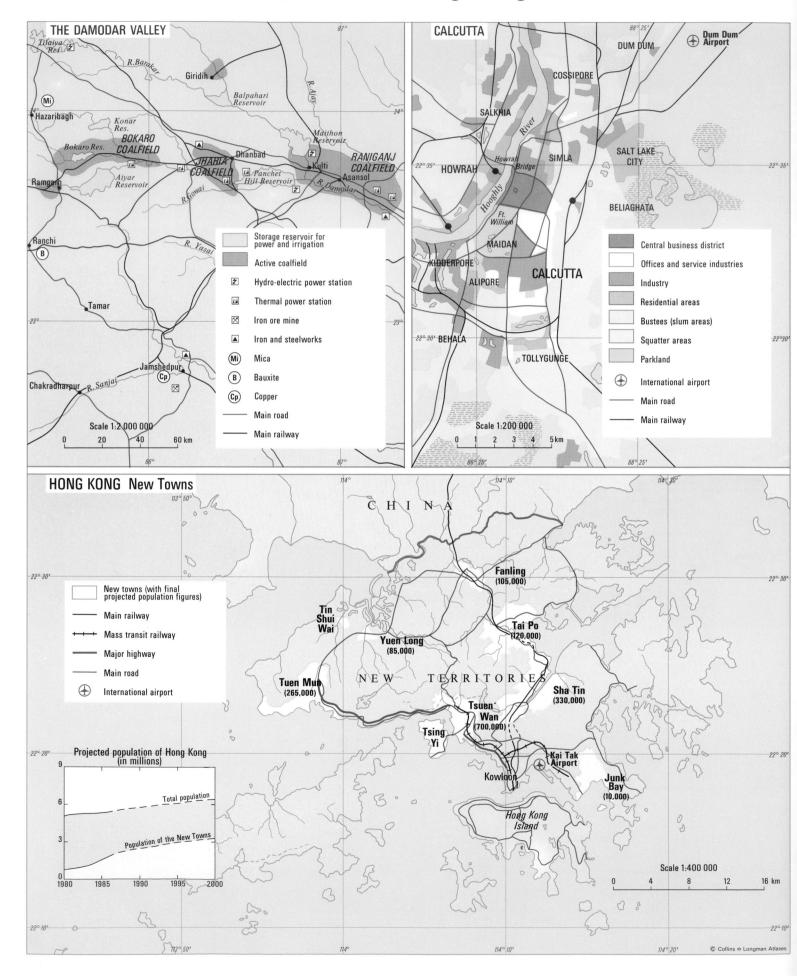

THE DAMODAR VALLEY

Tilaiya Res.
Giridih
R. Barakar
R. Alay
Balpahari Reservoir
(Mi)
Hazaribagh
Konar Res.
BOKARO COALFIELD
Bokaro Res.
Maithon Reservoir
Dhanbad
JHARIA COALFIELD
Kulti
RANIGANJ COALFIELD
Aiyar Reservoir
Panchet Hill Reservoir
Asansol
R. Gowai
Ramgarh
R. Damodar
R. Yasai
Ranchi
(B)
Tamar
Chakradharpur
R. Sanjai
Jamshedpur
(Cp)

Storage reservoir for power and irrigation
Active coalfield
Hydro-electric power station
Thermal power station
Iron ore mine
Iron and steelworks
(Mi) Mica
(B) Bauxite
(Cp) Copper
Main road
Main railway

Scale 1:2 000 000
0   20   40   60 km

CALCUTTA

Dum Dum Airport
DUM DUM
COSSIPORE
SALKHIA
Howrah River
SIMLA
SALT LAKE CITY
HOWRAH
Howrah Bridge
Hooghly
BELIAGHATA
Ft. William
KIDDERPORE
MAIDAN
CALCUTTA
ALIPORE
BEHALA
TOLLYGUNGE

Central business district
Offices and service industries
Industry
Residential areas
Bustees (slum areas)
Squatter areas
Parkland
International airport
Main road
Main railway

Scale 1:200 000
0   1   2   3   4   5km

HONG KONG New Towns

CHINA
Fanling (105,000)
Tin Shui Wai
Tai Po (120,000)
Yuen Long (85,000)
NEW   TERRITORIES
Tuen Mun (265,000)
Sha Tin (330,000)
Tsuen Wan (700,000)
Tsing Yi
Kai Tak Airport
Kowloon
Junk Bay (10,000)
Hong Kong Island

New towns (with final projected population figures)
Main railway
Mass transit railway
Major highway
Main road
International airport

Projected population of Hong Kong (in millions)
Total population
Population of the New Towns
1980   1985   1990   1995   2000

Scale 1:400 000
0   4   8   12   16 km

© Collins ○ Longman Atlases

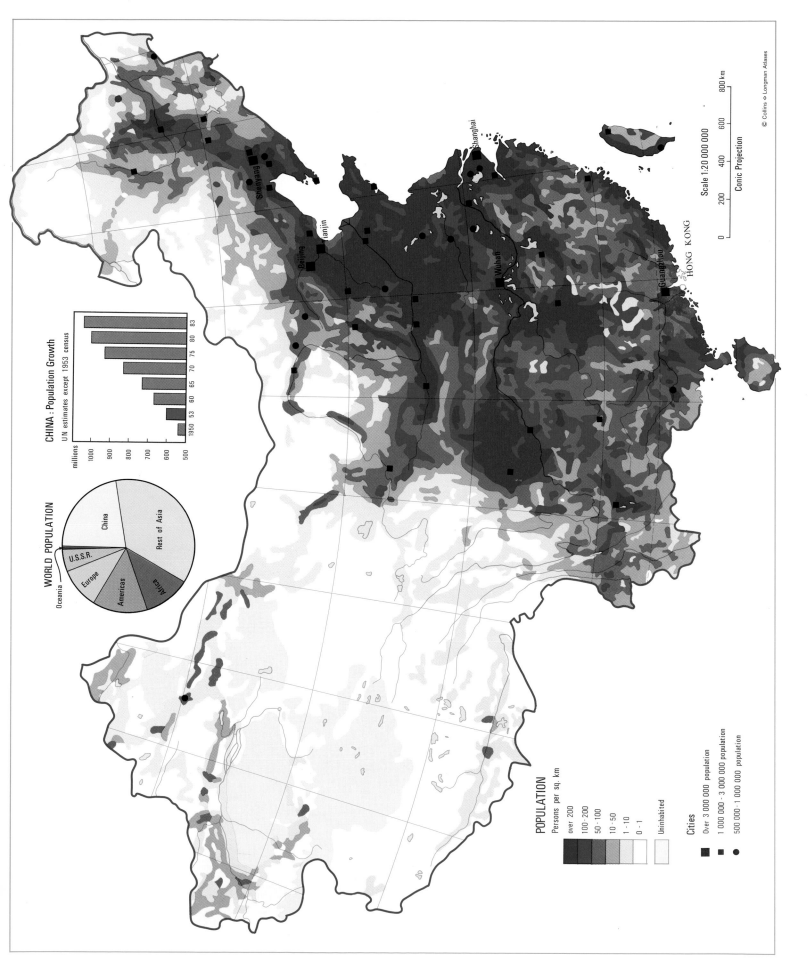

Scale 1:20 000 000

0 200 400 600 800 km

Conic Projection

CHINA : Population Growth
UN estimates except 1953 census

millions
1000
900
800
700
600
500

1950 53 60 65 70 75 80 83

WORLD POPULATION

Oceania
U.S.S.R.
Europe
Americas
Africa
China
Rest of Asia

Shenyang
Shanghai
Tianjin
Beijing
Wuhan
Guangzhou
HONG KONG

POPULATION
Persons per sq. km

over 200
100 - 200
50 - 100
10 - 50
1 - 10
0 - 1
Uninhabited

Cities

■ Over 3 000 000 population
■ 1 000 000 - 3 000 000 population
● 500 000 - 1 000 000 population

CHINA
Gejiu Mengzi Guiping Xi Jiang E Mei Xian
Nanning Wuzhou Guangzhou Chao an
D Guiping Fashan Shantou
Ha Giang Dao Bang Yulin Maoming Kowloon
Phong Saly Bac Can Pingxiang Lang Son Mon Cai Beihai Macau HONG KONG Gaox
Dien Bien Phu Thai Son Tay Bac Ninh Zhanjiang (Port.)
Lagkang Nguyen Hanoi Hai Duong
B. Houei Sai Son La Back Nam Dinh Haiphong Haikou
BURMA Muang Chiang Rai Luang Xieng Ninh Binh Gulf of Hainan
Ramree I. Chiang Mai Prabang Thanh Hoa Tongking
Sandoway M. Lampang Khouang Vinh Dongfang Yacheng Ya Xian
Pyinmana M.Nan Nong Khai Vinh Mei Xian

SOUTH

CHINA

SEA

INDIAN

OCEAN

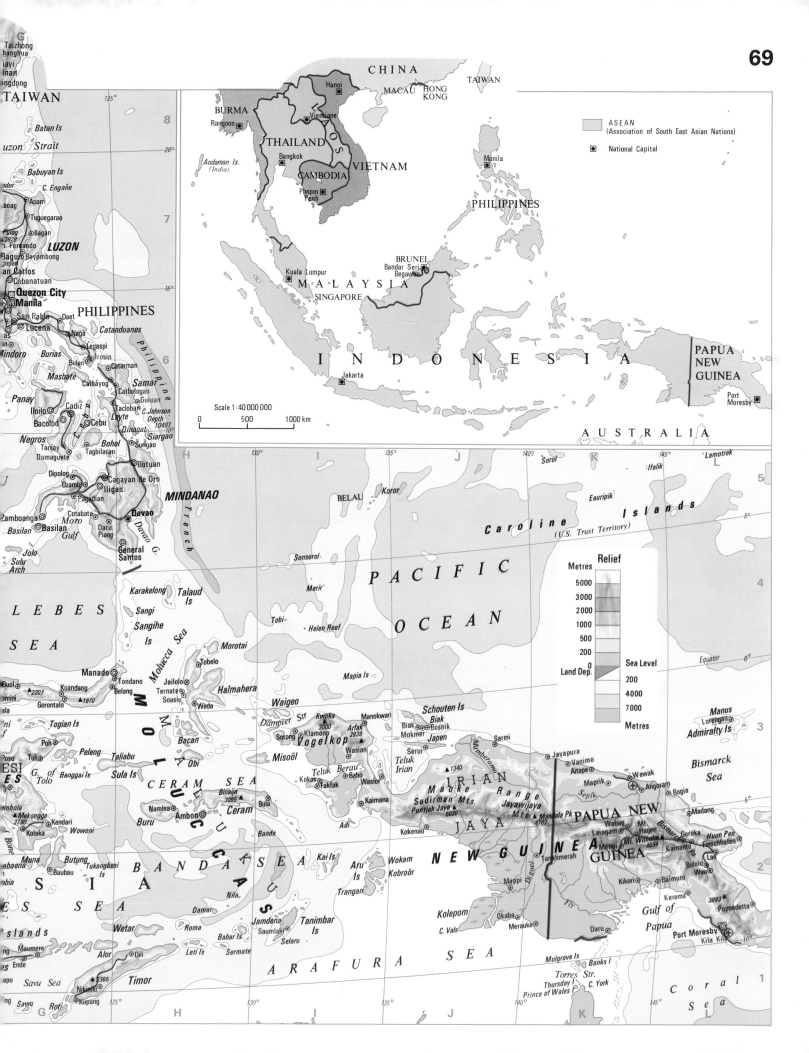

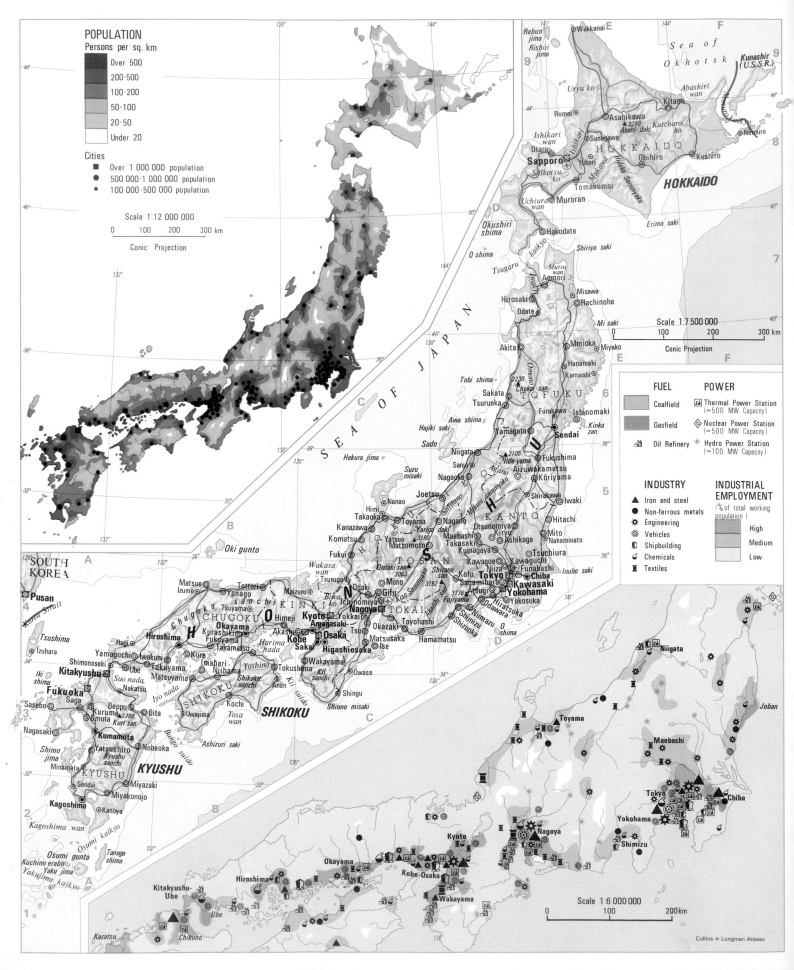

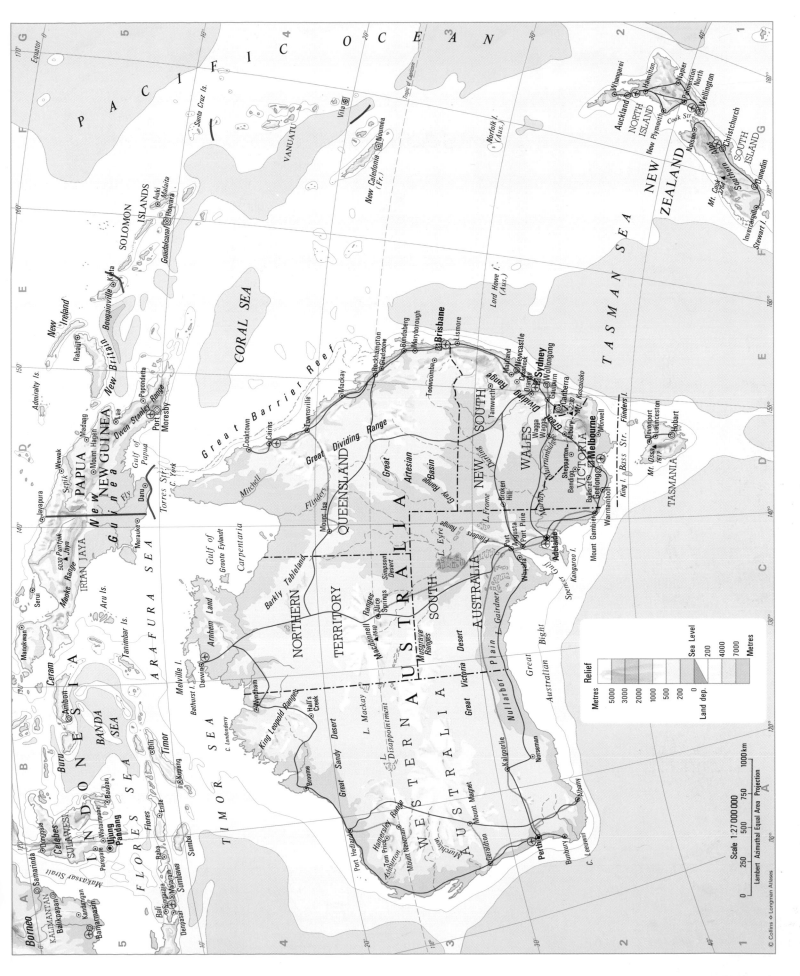

Relief

Metres								Sea Level				Metres
5000	3000	2000	1000	500	200	0		200	4000	7000		

Land dep.

Scale 1:27 000 000

Lambert Azimuthal Equal Area Projection

© Collins • Longman Atlases

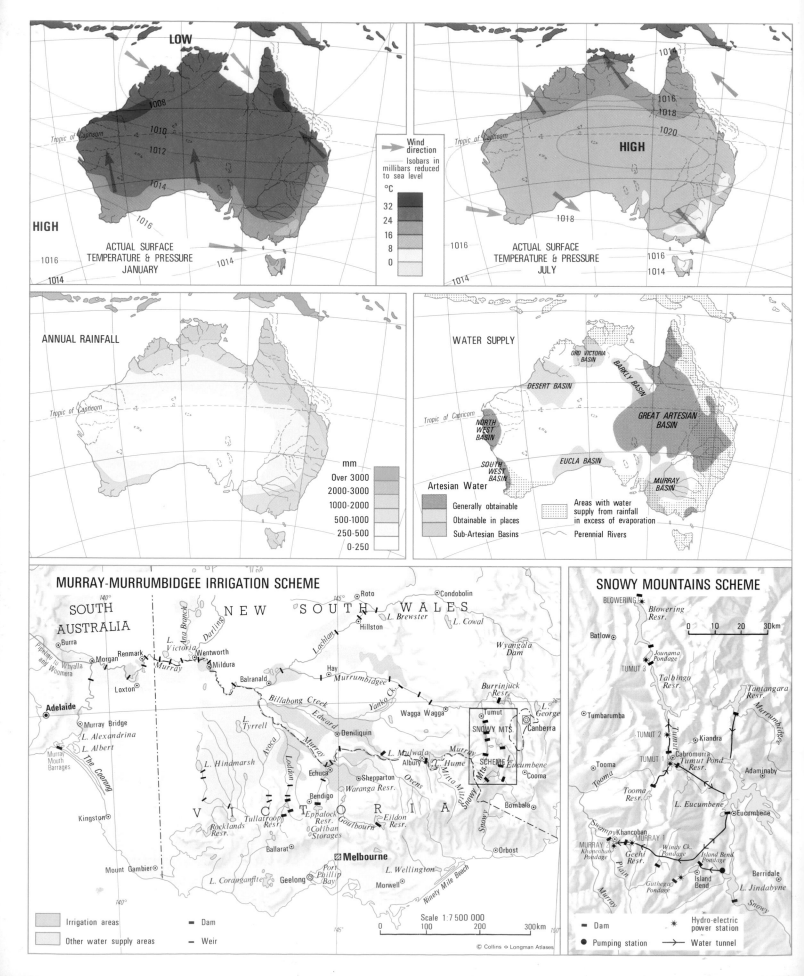

LOW

1008
1010
1012
1014
1016

HIGH

1016
1014

Tropic of Capricorn

ACTUAL SURFACE
TEMPERATURE & PRESSURE
JANUARY

1014
1016
1018
1020

HIGH

1018
1016
1014

Tropic of Capricorn

ACTUAL SURFACE
TEMPERATURE & PRESSURE
JULY

→ Wind
  direction

── Isobars in
    millibars reduced
    to sea level

°C
32
24
16
8
0

ANNUAL RAINFALL

Tropic of Capricorn

mm
Over 3000
2000-3000
1000-2000
500-1000
250-500
0-250

WATER SUPPLY

ORD VICTORIA BASIN
BARKLY BASIN
DESERT BASIN
GREAT ARTESIAN BASIN
NORTH WEST BASIN
SOUTH WEST BASIN
EUCLA BASIN
MURRAY BASIN

Tropic of Capricorn

Artesian Water

Generally obtainable

Obtainable in places

Sub-Artesian Basins

Areas with water
supply from rainfall
in excess of evaporation

Perennial Rivers

MURRAY-MURRUMBIDGEE IRRIGATION SCHEME

SOUTH AUSTRALIA

N E W   S O U T H   W A L E S

Roto
Condobolin
Hillston
L. Brewster
L. Cowal
Wyangala Dam
Burra
L. Ana Branch
Darling
L. Victoria
Renmark
Wentworth
Mildura
Morgan
Murray
Loxton
Balranald
Hay
Lachlan
Murrumbidgee
Burrinjuck Resr.
Pipeline to Whyalla and Woomera
Billabong Creek
Yanko Ck.
Wagga Wagga
L. George
Adelaide
Murray Bridge
L. Alexandrina
L. Albert
Edward
Deniliquin
Murray
Canberra
SNOWY MTS.
Murray Mouth Barrages
The Coorong
L. Tyrrell
Avoca
L. Mulwala
Albury
Hume
Eucumbene
Cooma
L. Hindmarsh
Loddon
Echuca
Shepparton
Waranga Resr.
Ovens
Mitta Mitta
SCHEME
Snowy
Kingston
Bendigo
V I C T O R I A
Bombala
Eppalock Resr.
Coliban Storages
Goulburn
Eildon Resr.
Snowy
Rocklands Resr.
Tullaroop Resr.
Ballarat
Orbost
Mount Gambier
L. Coranganite
Geelong
Port Phillip Bay
Morwell
Melbourne
L. Wellington
Ninety Mile Beach

Irrigation areas
Other water supply areas
── Dam
── Weir

Scale 1:7 500 000
0   100   200   300km

© Collins ◇ Longman Atlases

SNOWY MOUNTAINS SCHEME

BLOWERING
Blowering Resr.
Batlow
Jounama Pondage
TUMUT 3
Talbinga Resr.
Tantangara Resr.
Tumbarumba
Murrumbidgee
TUMUT 2
Kiandra
TUMUT 1
Cabramurra
Tumut Pond Resr.
Adaminaby
Tooma
Tooma Resr.
L. Eucumbene
Eucumbene
Swampy Khancoban
MURRAY 1
MURRAY 2
Khancoban Pondage
Windy Ck. Pondage
Geehi Resr.
Island Bend Pondage
Berridale
Murray
Guthega Pondage
Island Bend
L. Jindabyne
Snowy
Plain

0   10   20   30km

── Dam
● Pumping station
✳ Hydro-electric power station
→ Water tunnel

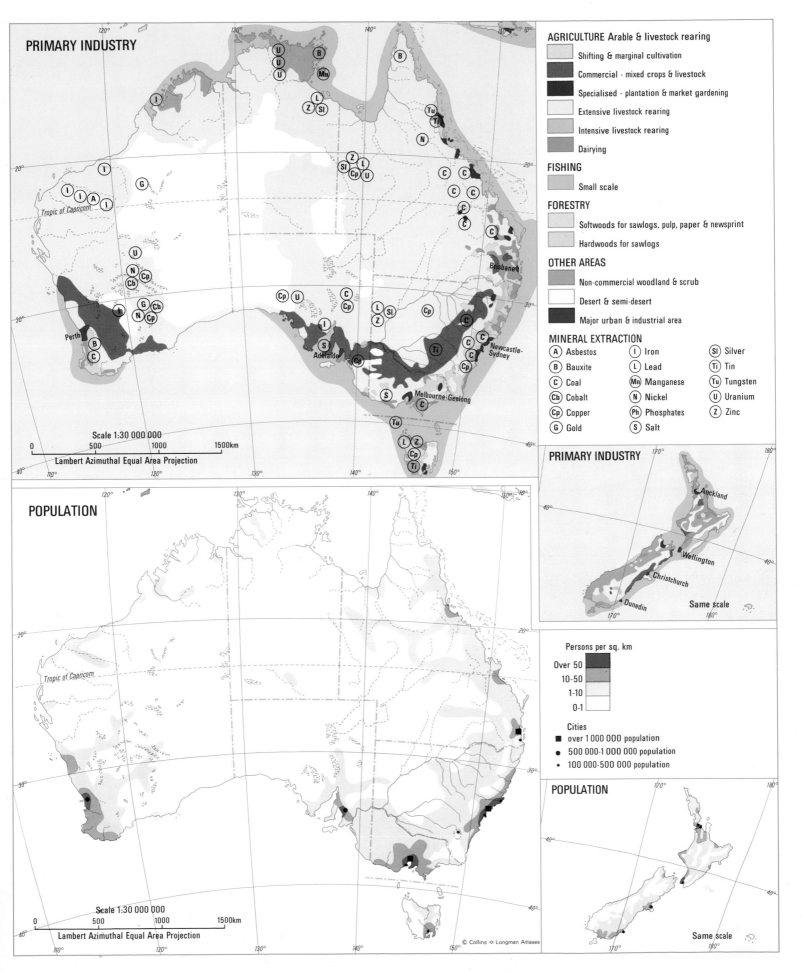

PRIMARY INDUSTRY

AGRICULTURE Arable & livestock rearing

- Shifting & marginal cultivation
- Commercial - mixed crops & livestock
- Specialised - plantation & market gardening
- Extensive livestock rearing
- Intensive livestock rearing
- Dairying

FISHING

- Small scale

FORESTRY

- Softwoods for sawlogs, pulp, paper & newsprint
- Hardwoods for sawlogs

OTHER AREAS

- Non-commercial woodland & scrub
- Desert & semi-desert
- Major urban & industrial area

MINERAL EXTRACTION

Ⓐ Asbestos	Ⓘ Iron	Ⓢⓛ Silver
Ⓑ Bauxite	Ⓛ Lead	Ⓣⓘ Tin
Ⓒ Coal	Ⓜⓝ Manganese	Ⓣⓤ Tungsten
Ⓒⓑ Cobalt	Ⓝ Nickel	Ⓤ Uranium
Ⓒⓟ Copper	Ⓟⓗ Phosphates	Ⓩ Zinc
Ⓖ Gold	Ⓢ Salt	

Scale 1:30 000 000

0   500   1000   1500km

Lambert Azimuthal Equal Area Projection

Perth

Adelaide

Brisbane

Newcastle-Sydney

Melbourne-Geelong

PRIMARY INDUSTRY

Auckland

Wellington

Christchurch

Dunedin

Same scale

POPULATION

Persons per sq. km

- Over 50
- 10-50
- 1-10
- 0-1

Cities

- ■ over 1 000 000 population
- ● 500 000-1 000 000 population
- • 100 000-500 000 population

POPULATION

Tropic of Capricorn

Scale 1:30 000 000

0   500   1000   1500km

Lambert Azimuthal Equal Area Projection

© Collins ◇ Longman Atlases

Same scale

The 34 countries surrounding the Pacific Ocean and the 23 island states scattered across it have become a region of great economic and political importance. Approximately 2.4 billion people live in the region – more than half of the world's population. The region produces half of the world's total wealth (GNP) and has an abundance of natural resources, including 21% of the world's oil resources, 63% of its wool, 67% of its cotton, 87% of its natural rubber and 94% of its natural silk.

The graphs on these two pages show the importance of the trade between the major countries in the region. (The graphs show the trade between countries as a percentage of total trade for each selected country).

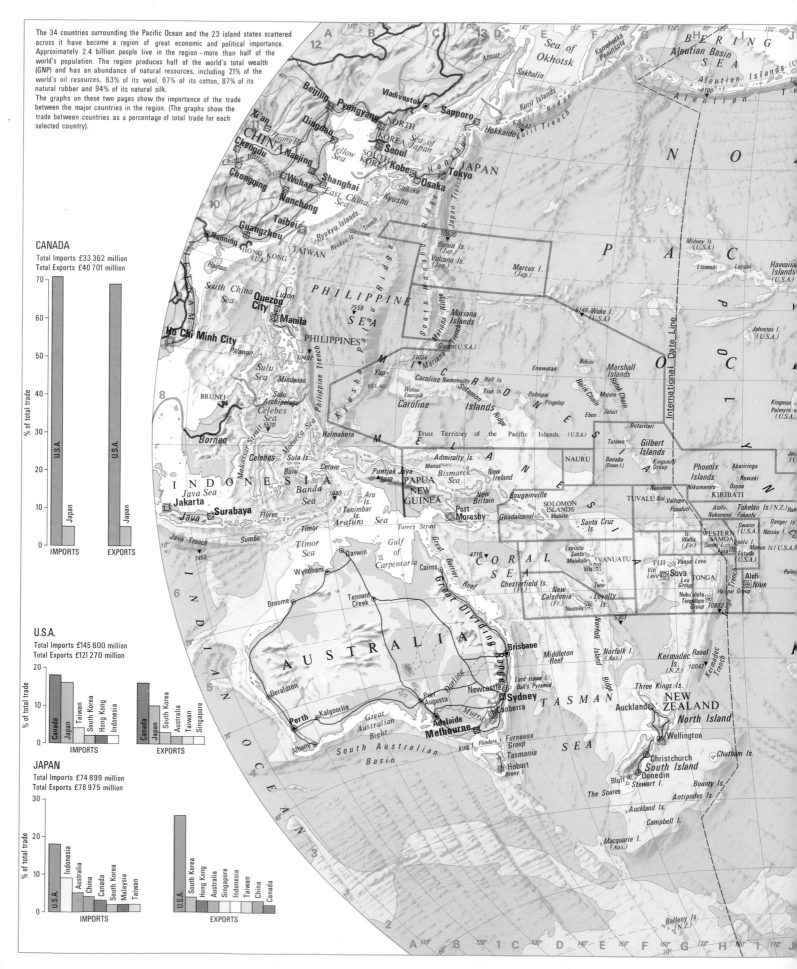

CANADA
Total Imports £33 362 million
Total Exports £40 701 million

U.S.A.
Total Imports £145 600 million
Total Exports £121 270 million

JAPAN
Total Imports £74 899 million
Total Exports £78 975 million

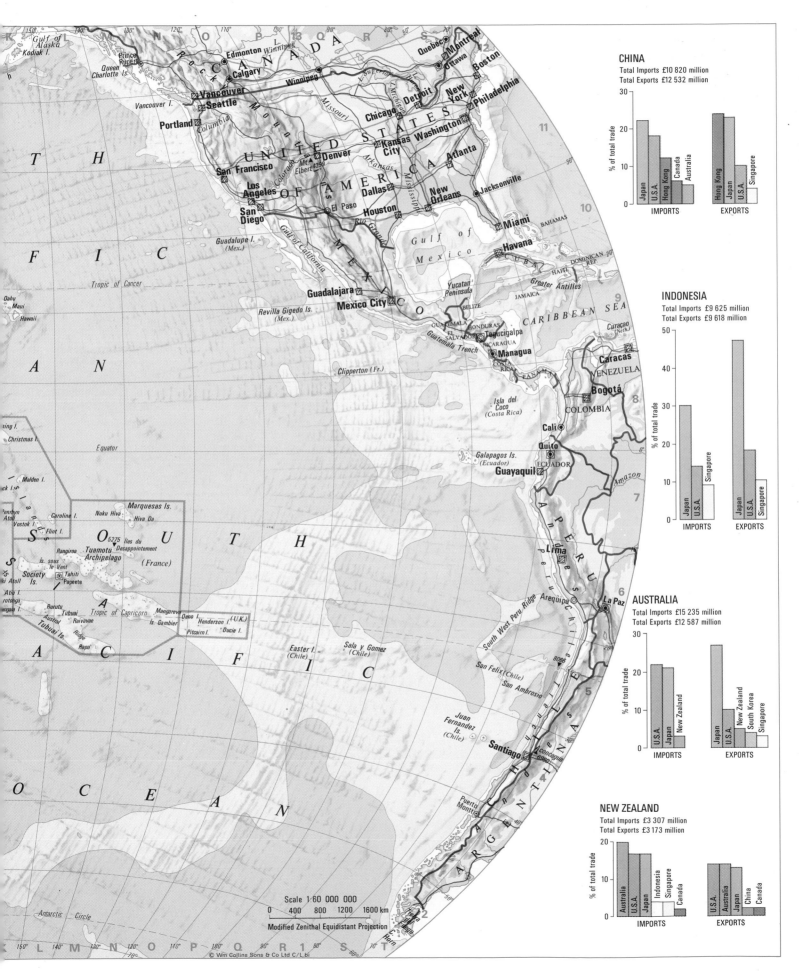

CHINA
Total Imports £10 820 million
Total Exports £12 532 million

% of total trade

IMPORTS — Japan, U.S.A., Hong Kong, Canada, Australia
EXPORTS — Hong Kong, Japan, U.S.A., Singapore

INDONESIA
Total Imports £9 625 million
Total Exports £9 618 million

% of total trade

IMPORTS — Japan, U.S.A., Singapore
EXPORTS — Japan, U.S.A., Singapore

AUSTRALIA
Total Imports £15 235 million
Total Exports £12 587 million

% of total trade

IMPORTS — U.S.A., Japan, New Zealand
EXPORTS — Japan, U.S.A., New Zealand, South Korea, Singapore

NEW ZEALAND
Total Imports £3 307 million
Total Exports £3 173 million

% of total trade

IMPORTS — Australia, U.S.A., Japan, Indonesia, Singapore, Canada
EXPORTS — U.S.A., Australia, Japan, China, Canada

Scale 1 60 000 000
0   400   800   1200   1600 km
Modified Zenithal Equidistant Projection

© Wm Collins Sons & Co Ltd C/L bi

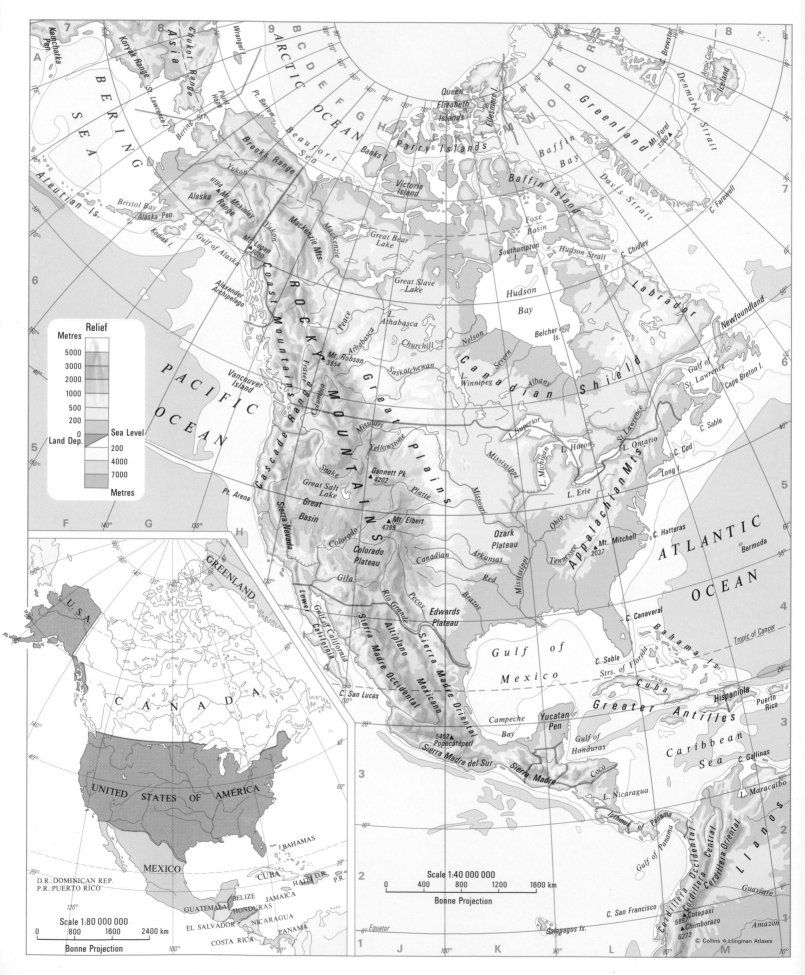

Relief
Metres
5000
3000
2000
1000
500
200
0   Sea Level
Land Dep.
200
4000
7000
Metres

Scale 1:40 000 000
0   400   800   1200   1600 km
Bonne Projection

Scale 1:80 000 000
0   800   1600   2400 km
Bonne Projection

D.R.:DOMINICAN REP.
P.R.:PUERTO RICO

© Collins ◇ Longman Atlases

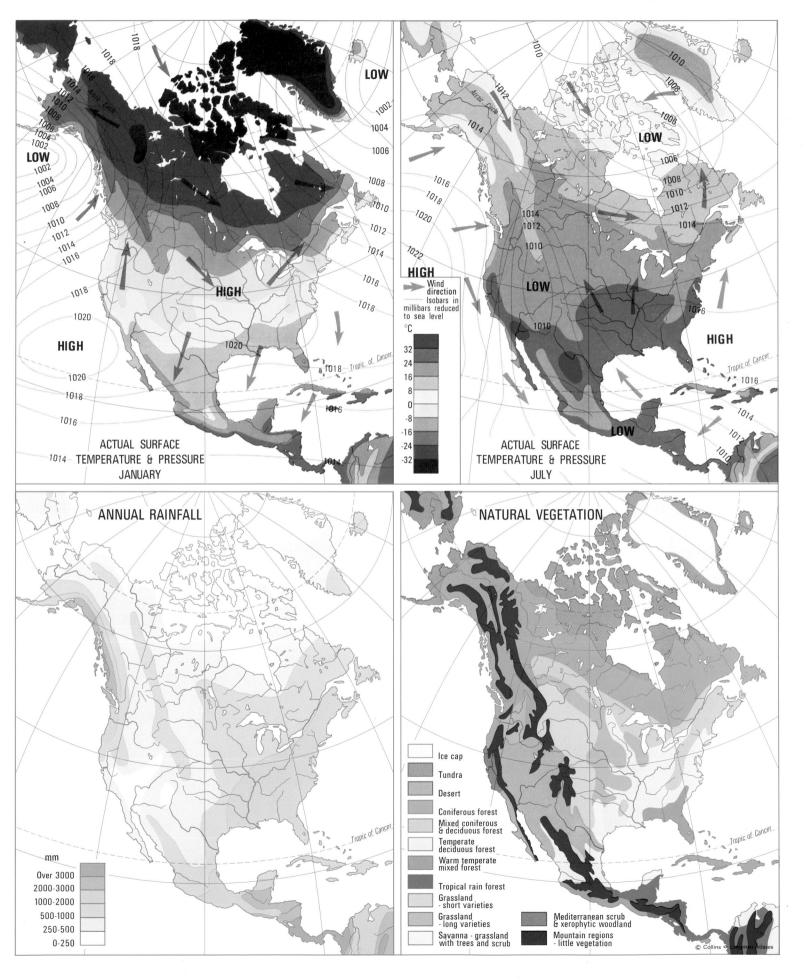

ACTUAL SURFACE
TEMPERATURE & PRESSURE
JANUARY

ACTUAL SURFACE
TEMPERATURE & PRESSURE
JULY

LOW

HIGH

HIGH

LOW

HIGH

LOW

LOW

HIGH

LOW

→ Wind
direction
Isobars in
millibars reduced
to sea level

°C

32
24
16
8
0
-8
-16
-24
-32

Tropic of Cancer

ANNUAL RAINFALL

NATURAL VEGETATION

mm

Over 3000
2000-3000
1000-2000
500-1000
250-500
0-250

Ice cap
Tundra
Desert
Coniferous forest
Mixed coniferous
& deciduous forest
Temperate
deciduous forest
Warm temperate
mixed forest
Tropical rain forest
Grassland
- short varieties
Grassland
- long varieties
Savanna - grassland
with trees and scrub

Mediterranean scrub
& xerophytic woodland
Mountain regions
- little vegetation

© Collins Longman Atlases

POPULATION DISTRIBUTION

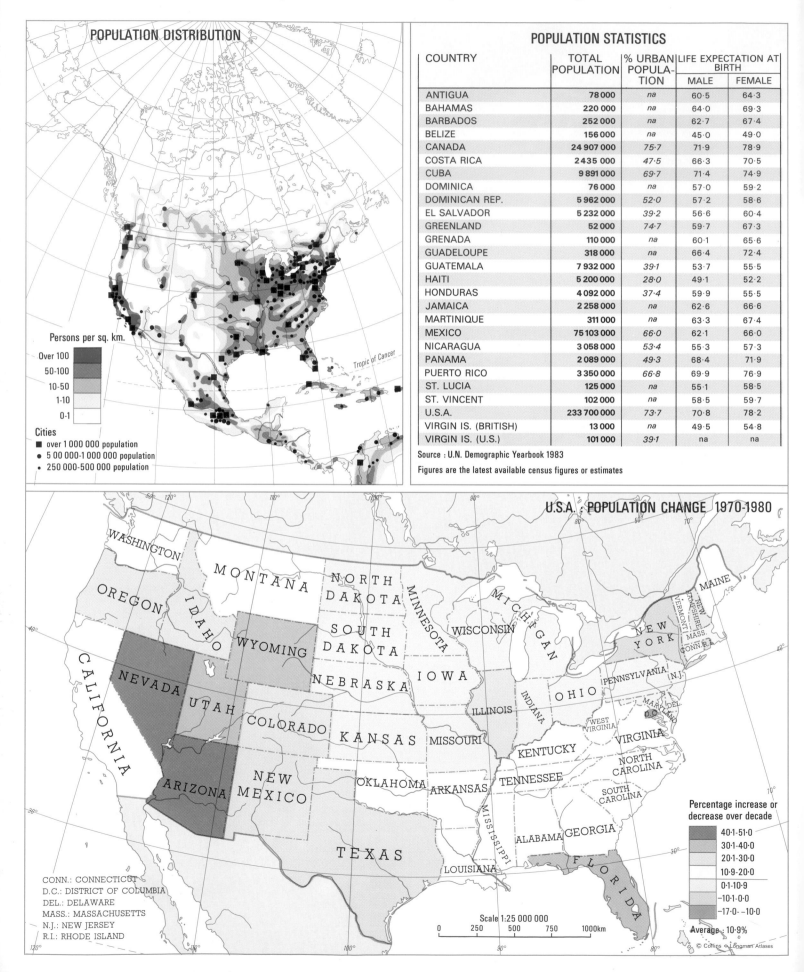

Persons per sq. km.

	Over 100
	50-100
	10-50
	1-10
	0-1

Cities
- ■ over 1 000 000 population
- ● 5 00 000-1 000 000 population
- • 250 000-500 000 population

Tropic of Cancer

POPULATION STATISTICS

COUNTRY	TOTAL POPULATION	% URBAN POPULA-TION	LIFE EXPECTATION AT BIRTH MALE	LIFE EXPECTATION AT BIRTH FEMALE
ANTIGUA	78 000	na	60·5	64·3
BAHAMAS	220 000	na	64·0	69·3
BARBADOS	252 000	na	62·7	67·4
BELIZE	156 000	na	45·0	49·0
CANADA	24 907 000	75·7	71·9	78·9
COSTA RICA	2 435 000	47·5	66·3	70·5
CUBA	9 891 000	69·7	71·4	74·9
DOMINICA	76 000	na	57·0	59·2
DOMINICAN REP.	5 962 000	52·0	57·2	58·6
EL SALVADOR	5 232 000	39·2	56·6	60·4
GREENLAND	52 000	74·7	59·7	67·3
GRENADA	110 000	na	60·1	65·6
GUADELOUPE	318 000	na	66·4	72·4
GUATEMALA	7 932 000	39·1	53·7	55·5
HAITI	5 200 000	28·0	49·1	52·2
HONDURAS	4 092 000	37·4	59·9	55·5
JAMAICA	2 258 000	na	62·6	66·6
MARTINIQUE	311 000	na	63·3	67·4
MEXICO	75 103 000	66·0	62·1	66·0
NICARAGUA	3 058 000	53·4	55·3	57·3
PANAMA	2 089 000	49·3	68·4	71·9
PUERTO RICO	3 350 000	66·8	69·9	76·9
ST. LUCIA	125 000	na	55·1	58·5
ST. VINCENT	102 000	na	58·5	59·7
U.S.A.	233 700 000	73·7	70·8	78·2
VIRGIN IS. (BRITISH)	13 000	na	49·5	54·8
VIRGIN IS. (U.S.)	101 000	39·1	na	na

Source : U.N. Demographic Yearbook 1983

Figures are the latest available census figures or estimates

U.S.A. : POPULATION CHANGE 1970-1980

Percentage increase or decrease over decade

	40·1-51·0
	30·1-40·0
	20·1-30·0
	10·9-20·0
	0·1-10·9
	-10·1-0·0
	-17·0--10·0

Average : 10·9%

CONN.: CONNECTICUT
D.C.: DISTRICT OF COLUMBIA
DEL.: DELAWARE
MASS.: MASSACHUSETTS
N.J.: NEW JERSEY
R.I.: RHODE ISLAND

Scale 1:25 000 000
0   250   500   750   1000km

© Collins · Longman Atlases

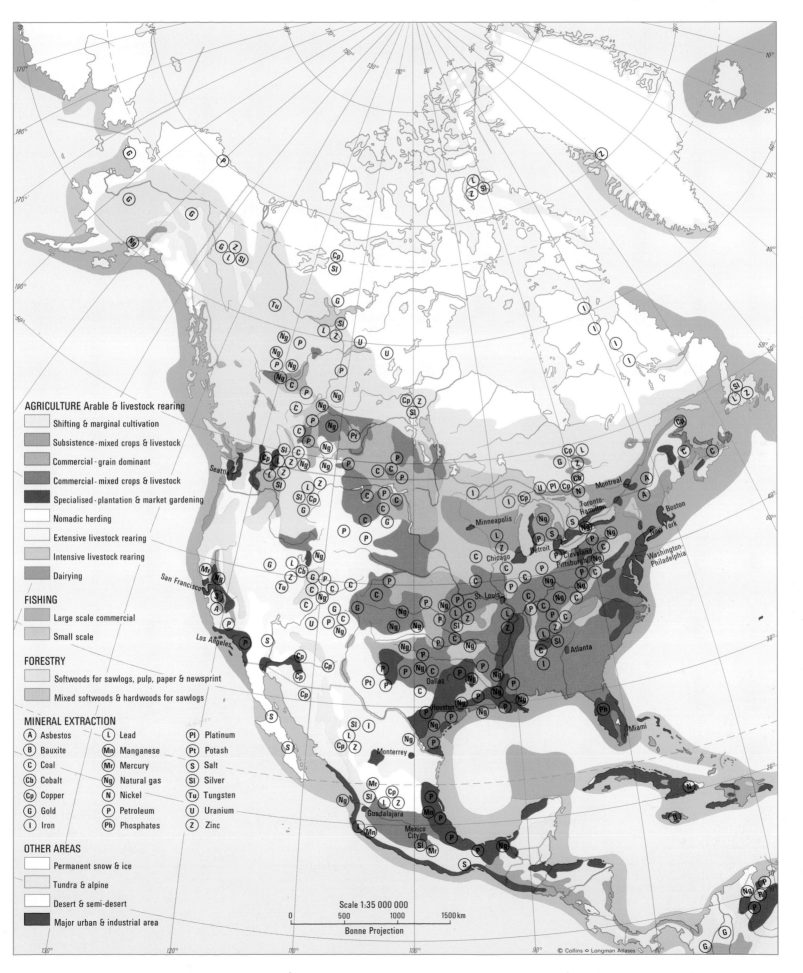

AGRICULTURE Arable & livestock rearing

Shifting & marginal cultivation

Subsistence - mixed crops & livestock

Commercial - grain dominant

Commercial - mixed crops & livestock

Specialised - plantation & market gardening

Nomadic herding

Extensive livestock rearing

Intensive livestock rearing

Dairying

FISHING

Large scale commercial

Small scale

FORESTRY

Softwoods for sawlogs, pulp, paper & newsprint

Mixed softwoods & hardwoods for sawlogs

MINERAL EXTRACTION

(A)	Asbestos	(L)	Lead	(Pl)	Platinum
(B)	Bauxite	(Mn)	Manganese	(Pt)	Potash
(C)	Coal	(Mr)	Mercury	(S)	Salt
(Cb)	Cobalt	(Ng)	Natural gas	(Sl)	Silver
(Cp)	Copper	(N)	Nickel	(Tu)	Tungsten
(G)	Gold	(P)	Petroleum	(U)	Uranium
(I)	Iron	(Ph)	Phosphates	(Z)	Zinc

OTHER AREAS

Permanent snow & ice

Tundra & alpine

Desert & semi-desert

Major urban & industrial area

Scale 1:35 000 000

0   500   1000   1500 km

Bonne Projection

© Collins ◇ Longman Atlases

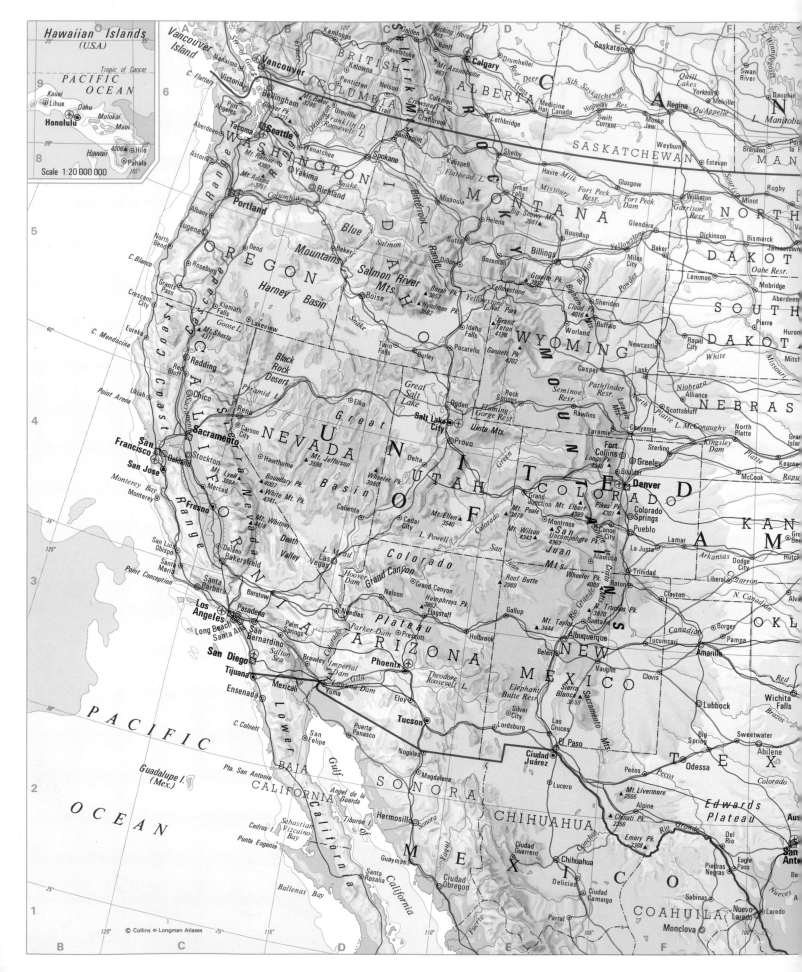

Hawaiian Islands
(U.S.A.)

Tropic of Cancer

PACIFIC
OCEAN

Kauai ⊙ Lihue
Oahu
Honolulu
Molokai
Maui
Hawaii 4206 ⊙ Hilo
⊙ Pahala

Scale 1:20 000 000

PACIFIC

OCEAN

Guadalupe I.
(Mex.)

© Collins ○ Longman Atlases

Scale 1:12 000 000

| 0 | 100 | 200 | 300 | 400 | 500 | 600 km |

Bonne Projection

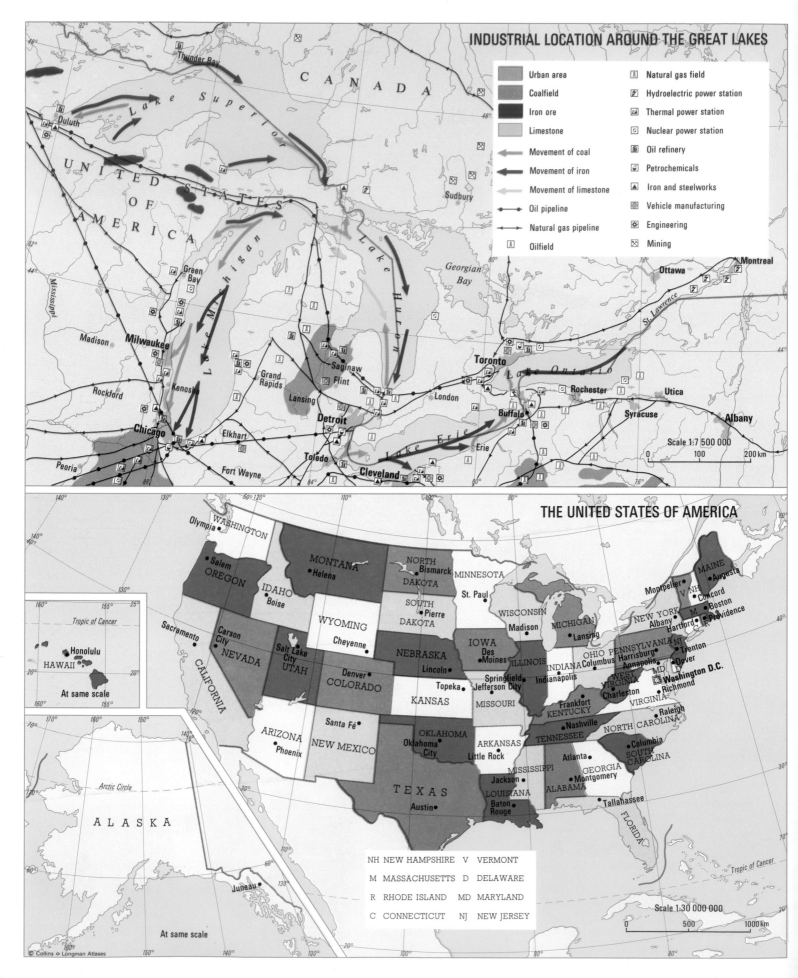

INDUSTRIAL LOCATION AROUND THE GREAT LAKES

Urban area	Natural gas field
Coalfield	Hydroelectric power station
Iron ore	Thermal power station
Limestone	Nuclear power station
Movement of coal	Oil refinery
Movement of iron	Petrochemicals
Movement of limestone	Iron and steelworks
Oil pipeline	Vehicle manufacturing
Natural gas pipeline	Engineering
Oilfield	Mining

Scale 1:7 500 000
0   100   200 km

THE UNITED STATES OF AMERICA

Scale 1:30 000 000
0   500   1000 km

NH	NEW HAMPSHIRE	V	VERMONT
M	MASSACHUSETTS	D	DELAWARE
R	RHODE ISLAND	MD	MARYLAND
C	CONNECTICUT	NJ	NEW JERSEY

© Collins ◇ Longman Atlases

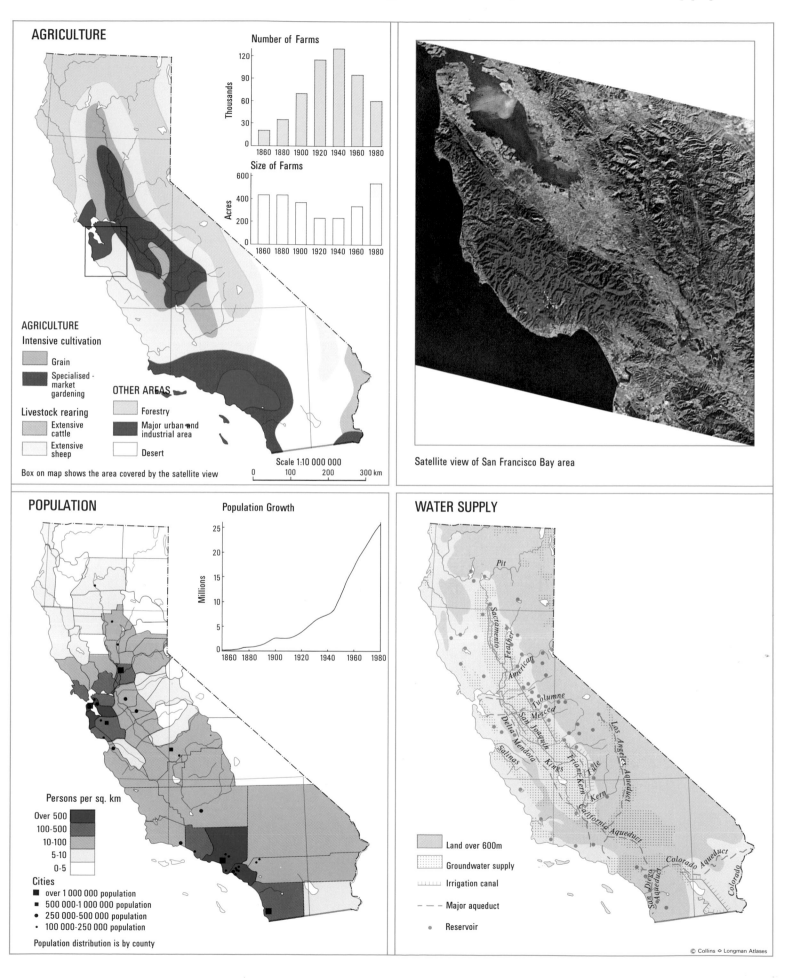

AGRICULTURE

Number of Farms

Thousands

120 90 60 30

1860 1880 1900 1920 1940 1960 1980

Size of Farms

Acres

600 400 200

1860 1880 1900 1920 1940 1960 1980

AGRICULTURE

Intensive cultivation

Grain

Specialised - market gardening

Livestock rearing

Extensive cattle

Extensive sheep

OTHER AREAS

Forestry

Major urban and industrial area

Desert

Box on map shows the area covered by the satellite view

Scale 1:10 000 000

0   100   200   300 km

Satellite view of San Francisco Bay area

POPULATION

Population Growth

Millions

25 20 15 10 5

1860 1880 1900 1920 1940 1960 1980

Persons per sq. km

Over 500

100-500

10-100

5-10

0-5

Cities

■ over 1 000 000 population

■ 500 000-1 000 000 population

● 250 000-500 000 population

• 100 000-250 000 population

Population distribution is by county

WATER SUPPLY

Pit

Feather

Sacramento

American

Tuolumne

Merced

San Joaquin

Delta Mendota

Salinas

Kings

Friant Kern

Tule

Kern

Los Angeles Aqueduct

California Aqueduct

San Diego Aqueduct

Colorado Aqueduct

Colorado

Land over 600m

Groundwater supply

Irrigation canal

Major aqueduct

● Reservoir

© Collins ○ Longman Atlases

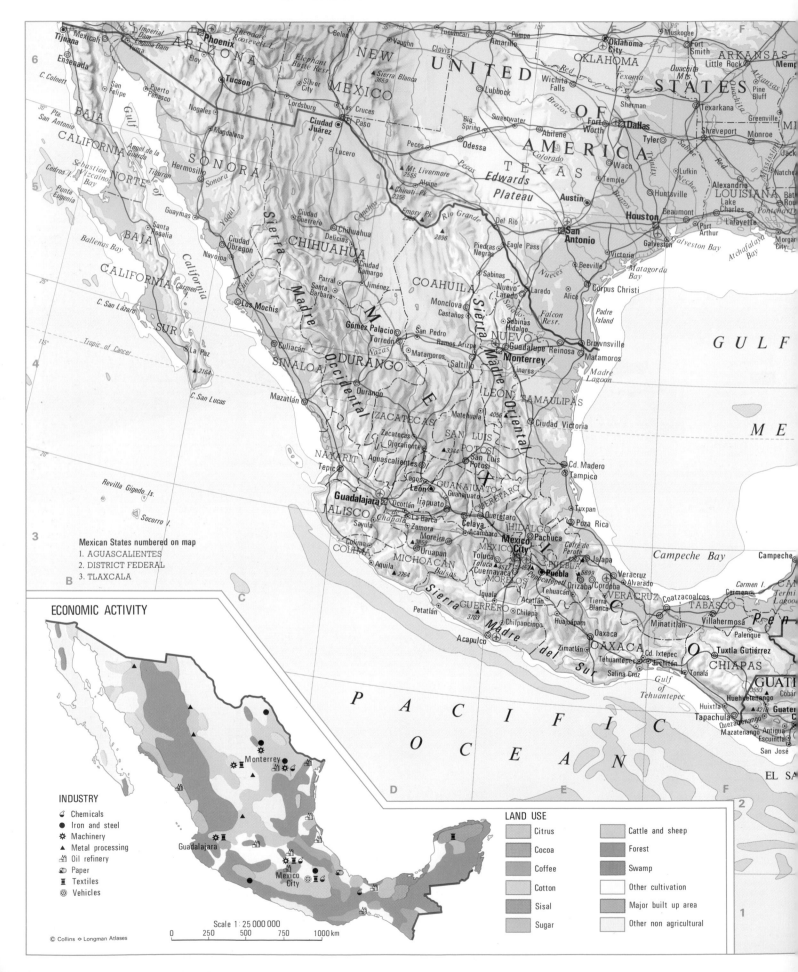

Mexican States numbered on map
1. AGUASCALIENTES
2. DISTRICT FEDERAL
3. TLAXCALA

ECONOMIC ACTIVITY

INDUSTRY
- ⌕ Chemicals
- ● Iron and steel
- ✿ Machinery
- ▲ Metal processing
- ⚒ Oil refinery
- ⬙ Paper
- ▥ Textiles
- ⊛ Vehicles

LAND USE

Citrus	Cattle and sheep
Cocoa	Forest
Coffee	Swamp
Cotton	Other cultivation
Sisal	Major built up area
Sugar	Other non agricultural

Scale 1 : 25 000 000
0   250   500   750   1000 km

© Collins ◇ Longman Atlases

TENNESSEE
Pickwick L.
Tennessee
Tupelo
Tuscaloosa
PPI
dian
ALABAMA
Mobile
Biloxi
Mississippi
Delta
OF

Ashville
Chattanooga
Gadsden
Guntersville L.
Birmingham
Montgomery
Columbus
Albany
Dothan
Pensacola
Panama City
Mobile Bay

Charlotte
Greenville
Fayetteville
SOUTH CAROLINA
Atlanta
Augusta
GEORGIA
Macon
Columbus
Flint
Thomasville
Madison
Lake City
Gainesville
Ocala
Orlando
Tampa
Lakeland
St. Petersburg
Tampa B.
Fort Myers
C. Romano
C. Sable
Key West

NORTH CAROLINA
New Bern
C. Lookout
Wilmington
C. Fear
Florence
Orangeburg
Columbia
Charleston
C. Romain
Savannah
Altamaha
Brunswick
Waycross
Okefenokee Swamp
St. Augustine
Jacksonville
Daytona Beach
Cape Canaveral
West Palm Beach
Fort Lauderdale
Fort Miami
Freeport
Grand Bahama I.
Great Abaco I.

ATLANTIC

OCEAN

Eleuthera I.
New Providence
Nassau
Cat I.
BAHAMAS
San Salvador
Andros I.
Exuma Is.
Rum Cay
Long I.
Gt. Exuma
Samana Cay
Crooked I.
Plana Cays
Acklin's I.
Mayaguana I.
Little Inagua
Great Inagua

Tropic of Cancer

Turks and Caicos Is. (U.K.)
Caicos Is.
Turks Is.

CO
Yucatan Channel
Straits
Havana (La Habana)
Matanzas
Cardenas
Archo. de Sabana
Marianao
Pinar del Rio
Guane
Nueva Gerona
Isle of Pines
Canarreos
Gulf of Batabanó
Archo. de los Canarreos
Cozumel I.
G. Catoche
Pto. Juárez
C. San Antonio
YUCATAN
QUINTANA ROO
atan

of Florida
Florida Keys
Sagua la Grande
Santa Clara
Cienfuegos
Trinidad
Sancti Spiritus
CUBA
Camagüey
Victoria de las Tunas
Ciego de Avila
Morón
Nuevitas
Jardines de la Reina
Little Cayman
Cayman Brac
Grand Cayman
Georgetown
Cayman Is. (U.K.)
Manzanillo
Bayamo
S. Luis
Holguín
Banes
Baracoa
Guantánamo
Sa. Maestra
1971
Santiago de Cuba
C. Cruz

Puerto Rico Trench
8528

CARIBBEAN

Greater
Windward Passage
Tortue
Cap Haitien
Gonaïves
St. Marc
HAITI
Jérémie
Port-au-Prince
2414
Les Cayes
2680
Barahona
Hispaniola
Antilles

Puerto Plata
San Francisco de Macorís
Valverde
Santiago
La Vega
DOMINICAN REP.
Azua
S. Cristóbal
Santo Domingo
S. Pedro
La Romana
Saona
Samana

San Juan
Bayamon
Arecibo
1338
Mayaguez
Mona
Ponce
Caguas
PUERTO RICO (U.S.A.)

SEA

Netherlands Antilles
Aruba
Curaçao
Bonaire
Willemstad

Montego Bay
St. Ann's Bay
Port Antonio
Black River
JAMAICA
Kingston

BELIZE
Chetumal
Corozal
Ambergris Cay
Belize
Belmopan
Turneffe Is.
Punta Gorda
Pto. Cortés
Tela
La Ceiba
S. Pedro Sula
HONDURAS
Sta. Rosa
Comayagua
Tegucigalpa
Juticalpa
2469
San Salvador
Ampala
2400
Choluteca
NICARAGUA
Chinandega
Corinto
León
Managua
Granada
Jinotepe
Rivas
Lake Nicaragua
Liberia
Nicoya Peninsula
Puntarenas
COSTA
RICA
San José
Cartago
3432
Irazú
C. Blanco
G. of Nicoya
Osa Pen.
Pto. Armuelles
Pta. Burica
Coiba I.

Gulf of Honduras
Bay Is.
C. Camarón
Caratasca Lagoon
Mosquitia Plain
C. Gracias á Dios
Pto. Cabezas
Prinzapolca
Rio Grande
Bluefields
Rama
Escondido
San Juan del Norte
S. Juan del Norte
S. Sta. Elena
San Juan
Chirripó
3820
Limón
Chiriqui Lagoon
Gulf of Mosquitos
David
Santiago
Azuero Peninsula
PANAMA
Penonome
Colón
Balboa
Panama City
Gulf of Panama
Archo. de las Perlas
El Real
Gulf of Darien
Turbo

Mosquito Coast

Colombia
Barranquilla
Cartagena
Turbaco
Arjona
Carmen
Sincelejo
Monteria
Magangué
Cerete
Puerto Rey
Montelibano
Sta. Marta
Ciénaga
Cristóbal Colón
5775
Barranca
Valledupar
Sabanalarga
Plato
Magdalena
Cauca
Barrancabermeja
4300
Yarumal
6493
COLOMBIA
Cúcuta
San Cristóbal
Pamplona
Bucaramanga
Piedecuesta
Rubio
Arauca
Meta

VENEZUELA
Guajira Peninsula
Castilletes
Gulf of Venezuela
Paraguaná Pen.
Punto Fijo
Coro
Puerto Cabello
Maracay
Valencia
San Felipe
Barquisimeto
Cabimas
Lagunillas
Maracaibo
Lake Maracaibo
La Concepción
Machiques
Valera
Trujillo
Mérida
6007
Guanare
Barinas
Apure
Arauca

Relief
Metres
5000
3000
2000
1000
500
200
0
Land Dep.
Sea Level
200
4000
7000

Scale 1:12 500 000
0 100 200 300 400 500 600km
Chamberlin Trimetric Projection

Collins ◇ Longman Atlases

Puerto Rico Trench
St. Thomas
Virgin Is. (U.K.)
Anegada
Virgin Gorda
Anguilla (U.K.)
St. Martin (Fr.)
St. Barthelemy (Fr.)
San Juan
Bayamon
Arecibo
1338
Mayaguez
Ponce
Caguas
Vieques
St. Croix
PUERTO RICO (U.S.A.)
Virgin Is. (U.S.A.)
Sint Maarten (Neth.)
Saba (Neth.)
Sint Eustatius (Neth.)
ST. KITTS
NEVIS
Barbuda (U.K.)
ANTIGUA
St. John's
Montserrat (U.K.)
1484
Guadeloupe (Fr.)
Basse-Terre
Marie Galante
Pointe-à-Pitre
Roseau
DOMINICA
Martinique (Fr.)
Fort-de-France
ST. LUCIA
Castries
St. Kingstown
ST. VINCENT AND THE GRENADINES
St. George's
GRENADA
Lesser Antilles
Leeward Islands
Windward Islands
BARBADOS
Bridgetown

Same scale

Lesser Antilles
Bonaire
Los Roques
Orchila
La Blanquilla
Tortuga
Margarita I.
Dragon's Mouth
Port of Spain
TOBAGO
San Fernando
TRINIDAD
Serpent's Mouth
Araya Pen.
Carúpano
Pta. La Cruz
Barcelona
La Guaira
Cumaná
Porlamar
G. of Paria
Paria Pen.
Maturín
Orinoco Delta
Bonaire

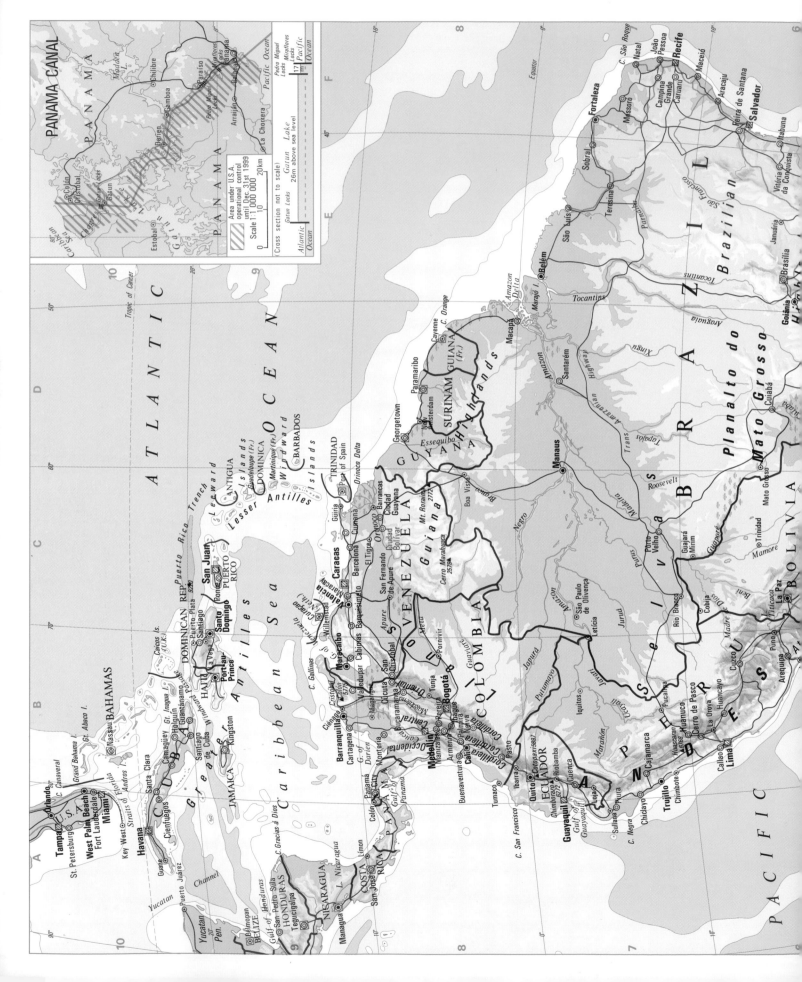

PANAMA CANAL

PANAMA

Pacific Ocean

Atlantic Ocean

Area under U.S.A operational control until Dec. 31st 1999

Scale 1:1 000 000

0   10   20km

Cross section not to scale

Gatun Lake

26m above sea level

Pedro Miguel Locks   Miraflores Locks

17   11

Pacific Ocean

Atlantic Ocean

ATLANTIC OCEAN

Tropic of Cancer

Equator

BAHAMAS

Nassau

Grand Bahama I.

Gt. Abaco I.

Gt. Inagua I.

Caicos Is.

Turks Is. (U.K.)

Key West

Miami

Fort Lauderdale

West Palm Beach

Orlando

C. Canaveral

Tampa

St. Petersburg

U.S.A.

Straits of Florida

Havana

Guane

Cienfuegos

Santa Clara

Camagüey

C U B A

Holguín

Santiago de Cuba

Guantánamo

Great Antilles

JAMAICA

Kingston

Windward Passage

HAITI

Port-au-Prince

DOMINICAN REP.

Santiago

La Vega

Santo Domingo

Puerto Plata

PUERTO RICO

San Juan

Ponce

Caribbean Sea

Lesser Antilles

Leeward Islands

ANTIGUA

Guadeloupe (Fr.)

DOMINICA

Martinique (Fr.)

Windward Islands

BARBADOS

Antilles

TRINIDAD

Port of Spain

Netherl. Antilles

Curaçao

Willemstad

Aruba

G. of Venezuela

C. Gallinas

Maracaibo

L. Maracaibo

Cabimas

Valledupar

Gulf of Darien

Cartagena

Barranquilla

Ciénaga

C. San Francisco

PANAMA

Panamá City

Colón

Gulf of Panamá

Gulf of Honduras

BELIZE

Belmopan

HONDURAS

Tegucigalpa

NICARAGUA

Managua

L. Nicaragua

COSTA RICA

San José

Limón

C. Gracias à Dios

San Pedro Sula

Yucatan Pen.

Puerto Juárez

Yucatan Channel

PACIFIC

São Roque

Natal

João Pessoa

Recife

Maceió

Aracaju

Salvador

Feira de Santana

Ilhéus

Vitória da Conquista

Caruaru

Campina Grande

Mossoró

Fortaleza

Sobral

Teresina

Parnaíba

Piauí

São Luís

Belém

Amazon Delta

Marajó I.

Macapá

Cayenne

GUIANA (Fr.)

SURINAM

Paramaribo

New Amsterdam

Georgetown

GUYANA

Essequibo

GUYANA Highlands

Mt. Roraima 2772

Boa Vista

Brazil

Planalto do Mato Grosso

Brasília

Goiânia

Cuiabá

Mato Grosso

Araguaia

Tocantins

Tocantins

Xingu

Iriri

Tapajós

Trans Amazon Highway

Santarém

Manaus

Negro

Roosevelt

Madeira

Porto Velho

Guajará Mirim

BOLIVIA

Trinidad

Guaporé

Mamoré

Beni

Cobija

Rio Branco

Madre de Dios

Puno

Cuzco

Arequipa

Lago Titicaca

La Paz

P E R U

Callao

Lima

Cerro de Pasco

La Oroya

Huancayo

Huánuco

Huascarán 6768

Chimbote

Trujillo

Cajamarca

Chiclayo

Piura

Sullana

C. Negra

Gulf of Guayaquil

Guayaquil

ECUADOR

Quito

Chimborazo 6272

Cotopaxi 5897

Riobamba

Cuenca

Loja

Ambato

Ibarra

Tumaco

Buenaventura

Cali

Popayán

Pasto

Nariño

Neiva

Palmira

Armenia

Manizales

Medellín

COLOMBIA

Bogotá

Cordillera Occidental

Cordillera Central

Cordillera Oriental

Magdalena

Cauca

Ibagué

Tunja

Bucaramanga

Cúcuta

San Cristóbal

Barrancabermeja

Montería

VENEZUELA

Caracas

Maracay

Valencia

Barquisimeto

San Fernando de Apure

Barcelona

Cumaná

Güiria

El Tigre

Ciudad Bolívar

Ciudad Guayana

Barrancas

Orinoco

Orinoco Delta

Cerro Marahuaca 2579

Guiana

Meta

Apure

Putumayo

Caquetá

Japurá

Juruá

Purus

Iquitos

Pucallpa

Ucayali

Marañón

Leticia

São Paulo de Olivença

Amazon

Amazon

Río Branco

BRAZIL

Junáia

São Francisco

A N D E S

A N D E S

S O U T H

C. San Francisco

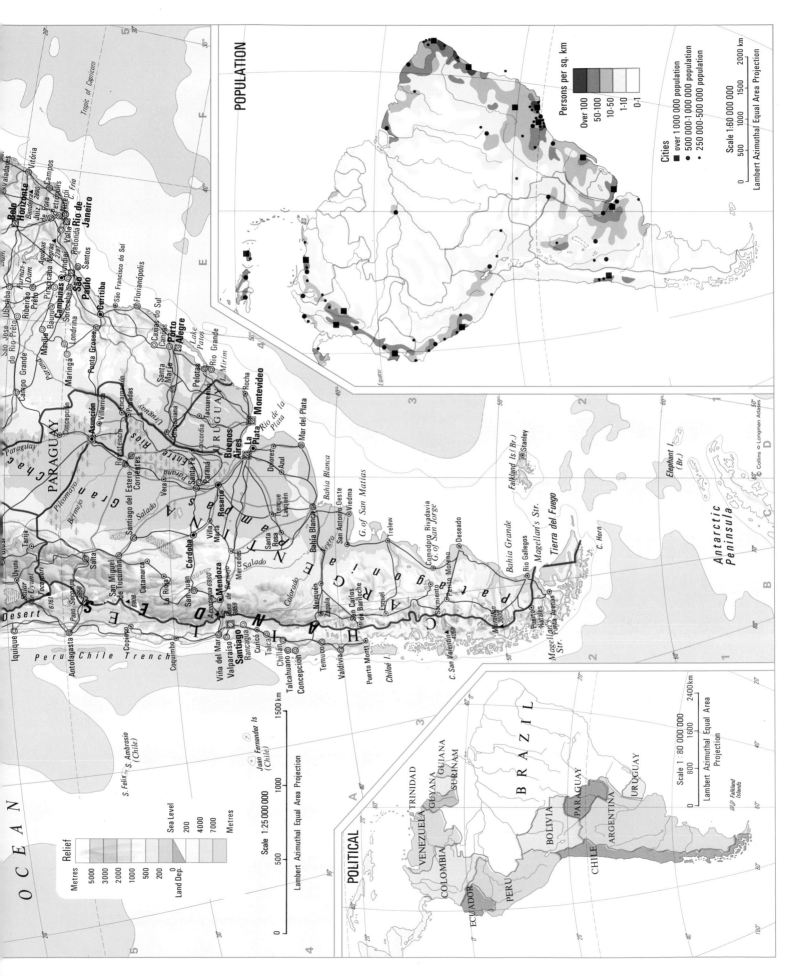

POPULATION

Persons per sq. km

Over 100
50-100
10-50
1-10
0-1

Cities
■ over 1 000 000 population
■ 500 000-1 000 000 population
● 250 000-500 000 population

Scale 1:60 000 000

0 500 1000 1500 2000 km

Lambert Azimuthal Equal Area Projection

© Collins ○ Longman Atlases

O C E A N

Tropic of Capricorn

Belo Horizonte
Rio de Janeiro
São Paulo
Curitiba
Porto Alegre
PARAGUAY
Asunción
Montevideo
Buenos Aires
Rosario
Córdoba
Mendoza
Santiago
Valparaíso
Concepción

A N D E S

P A T A G O N I A

Bahía Blanca
Tierra del Fuego
C. Horn
Falkland Is (Br.)
Stanley
Antarctic Peninsula

Peru-Chile Trench

Relief

Metres
5000
3000
2000
1000
500
200
Sea Level
200
4000
7000
Metres

Land Dep.

Scale 1:25 000 000

0 500 1000 1500 km

Lambert Azimuthal Equal Area Projection

POLITICAL

VENEZUELA
TRINIDAD
GUYANA
GUIANA
SURINAM
COLOMBIA
ECUADOR
PERU
BRAZIL
BOLIVIA
PARAGUAY
CHILE
URUGUAY
ARGENTINA
Falkland Islands

Scale 1:80 000 000

0 800 1600 2400km

Lambert Azimuthal Equal Area Projection

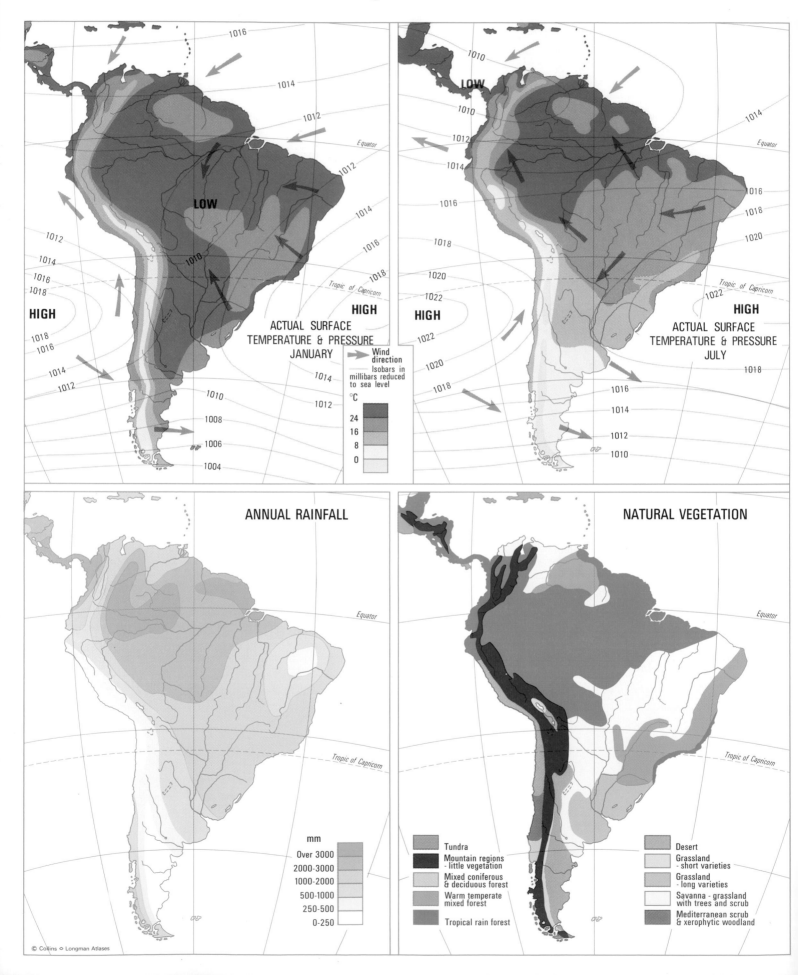

ACTUAL SURFACE
TEMPERATURE & PRESSURE
JANUARY

Wind
direction

Isobars in
millibars reduced
to sea level

°C

24
16
8
0

ACTUAL SURFACE
TEMPERATURE & PRESSURE
JULY

ANNUAL RAINFALL

mm

Over 3000

2000-3000

1000-2000

500-1000

250-500

0-250

NATURAL VEGETATION

Tundra

Mountain regions
- little vegetation

Mixed coniferous
& deciduous forest

Warm temperate
mixed forest

Tropical rain forest

Desert

Grassland
- short varieties

Grassland
- long varieties

Savanna - grassland
with trees and scrub

Mediterranean scrub
& xerophytic woodland

© Collins ○ Longman Atlases

AGRICULTURE Arable & livestock rearing

Shifting & marginal cultivation

Subsistence - rice dominant

Subsistence - crop other than rice dominant

Subsistence - mixed crops & livestock

Commercial - grain dominant

Commercial - mixed crops & livestock

Specialised - plantation & market gardening

Nomadic herding

Extensive livestock rearing

Intensive livestock rearing

Dairying

FISHING

Large scale commercial

Small scale

FORESTRY

Hardwoods for sawlogs

MINERAL EXTRACTION

A	Asbestos	L	Lead	Sl	Silver
B	Bauxite	Mn	Manganese	Ti	Tin
Ch	Chromium	Ng	Natural gas	Tu	Tungsten
Cp	Copper	N	Nickel	U	Uranium
D	Diamonds	P	Petroleum	Z	Zinc
G	Gold	Ph	Phosphates		
I	Iron	S	Salt		

OTHER AREAS

Tundra & alpine

Desert & semi-desert

Major urban & industrial area

Scale 1:35 000 000

0   500   1000   1500km

Lambert Azimuthal Equal Area Projection

ECONOMIC DEVELOPMENT OF AMAZONIA

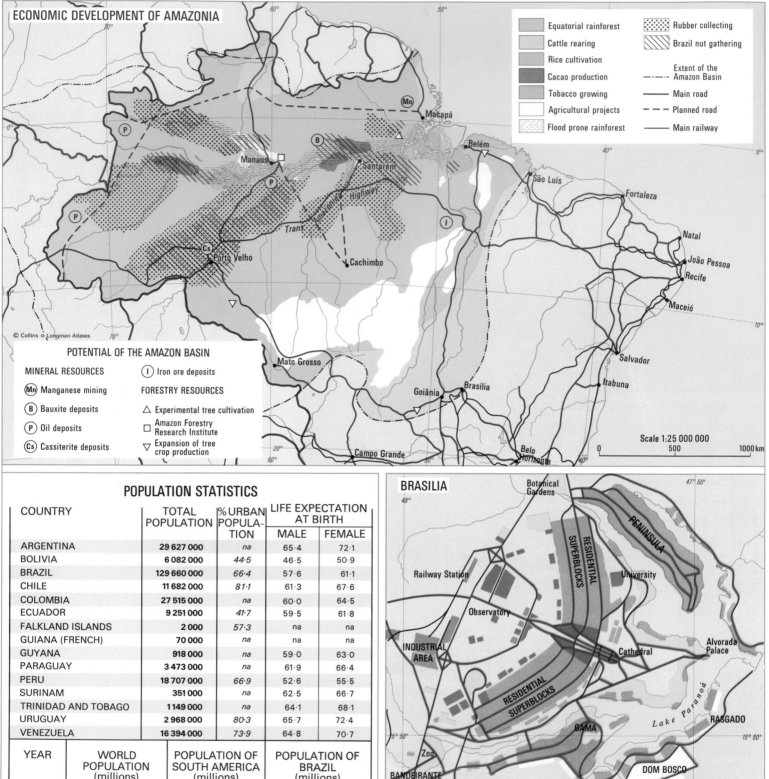

Equatorial rainforest	Rubber collecting
Cattle rearing	Brazil nut gathering
Rice cultivation	
Cacao production	Extent of the Amazon Basin
Tobacco growing	Main road
Agricultural projects	Planned road
Flood prone rainforest	Main railway

POTENTIAL OF THE AMAZON BASIN

MINERAL RESOURCES

(Mn) Manganese mining

(B) Bauxite deposits

(P) Oil deposits

(Cs) Cassiterite deposits

(I) Iron ore deposits

FORESTRY RESOURCES

△ Experimental tree cultivation

□ Amazon Forestry Research Institute

▽ Expansion of tree crop production

Scale 1:25 000 000

0   500   1000 km

© Collins ☉ Longman Atlases

POPULATION STATISTICS

COUNTRY	TOTAL POPULATION	% URBAN POPULATION	LIFE EXPECTATION AT BIRTH	
			MALE	FEMALE
ARGENTINA	29 627 000	na	65·4	72·1
BOLIVIA	6 082 000	44·5	46·5	50·9
BRAZIL	129 660 000	66·4	57·6	61·1
CHILE	11 682 000	81·1	61·3	67·6
COLOMBIA	27 515 000	na	60·0	64·5
ECUADOR	9 251 000	41·7	59·5	61·8
FALKLAND ISLANDS	2 000	57·3	na	na
GUIANA (FRENCH)	70 000	na	na	na
GUYANA	918 000	na	59·0	63·0
PARAGUAY	3 473 000	na	61·9	66·4
PERU	18 707 000	66·9	52·6	55·5
SURINAM	351 000	na	62·5	66·7
TRINIDAD AND TOBAGO	1 149 000	na	64·1	68·1
URUGUAY	2 968 000	80·3	65·7	72·4
VENEZUELA	16 394 000	73·9	64·8	70·7

YEAR	WORLD POPULATION (millions)	POPULATION OF SOUTH AMERICA (millions)	POPULATION OF BRAZIL (millions)
1983	4 685	257	130
1980	4 453	240	121
1970	3 683	191	92
1960	3 014	147	71
1950	2 504	111	52
1940	2 249	90	na
1930	2 015	75	na

Source: U.N. Demographic Yearbook

Figures are the latest available census figures or estimates

BRASILIA

Central business district	Satellite town
Public buildings	Favellas (slum areas)
Government buildings and embassies	
Industry	Main road
Parkland	Main railway
Residential	International airport

Scale 1:150 000

0   1   2   3 km

© Collins ☉ Longman Atlases

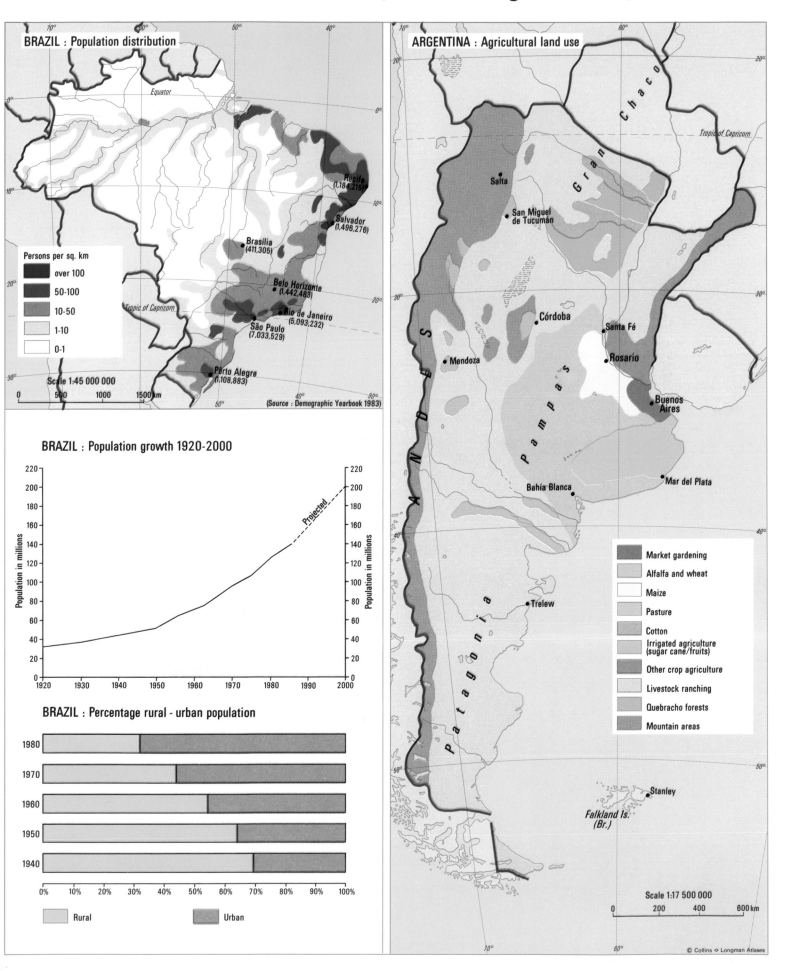

BRAZIL : Population distribution

Persons per sq. km

- over 100
- 50-100
- 10-50
- 1-10
- 0-1

Recife (1,184,216)

Salvador (1,496,276)

Brasília (411,305)

Belo Horizonte (1,442,483)

Rio de Janeiro (5,093,232)

São Paulo (7,033,529)

Pôrto Alegre (1,108,883)

Equator

Tropic of Capricorn

Scale 1:45 000 000

0   500   1000   1500 km

(Source : Demographic Yearbook 1983)

BRAZIL : Population growth 1920-2000

Population in millions

Projected

BRAZIL : Percentage rural - urban population

1980
1970
1960
1950
1940

0% 10% 20% 30% 40% 50% 60% 70% 80% 90% 100%

Rural   Urban

ARGENTINA : Agricultural land use

Salta

San Miguel de Tucumán

Córdoba

Santa Fé

Rosario

Mendoza

Buenos Aires

Bahía Blanca

Mar del Plata

Trelew

Stanley

Falkland Is. (Br.)

Gran Chaco

Tropic of Capricorn

Pampas

Patagonia

- Market gardening
- Alfalfa and wheat
- Maize
- Pasture
- Cotton
- Irrigated agriculture (sugar cane/fruits)
- Other crop agriculture
- Livestock ranching
- Quebracho forests
- Mountain areas

Scale 1:17 500 000

0   200   400   600 km

© Collins ◇ Longman Atlases

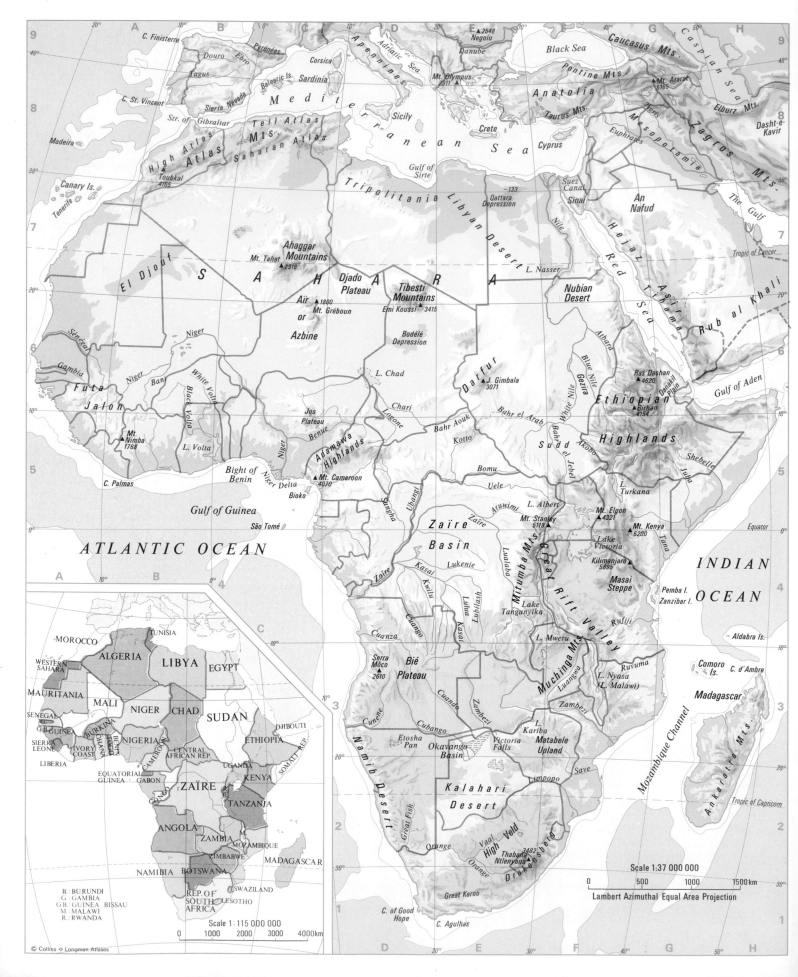

ATLANTIC OCEAN

INDIAN OCEAN

Scale 1:37 000 000

| 0 | 500 | 1000 | 1500km |

Lambert Azimuthal Equal Area Projection

MOROCCO
TUNISIA
WESTERN SAHARA
ALGERIA
LIBYA
EGYPT
MAURITANIA
MALI
NIGER
CHAD
SUDAN
SENEGAL
G.B. GUINEA
BURKINA
DJIBOUTI
SIERRA LEONE
IVORY COAST
GHANA
NIGERIA
CENTRAL AFRICAN REP.
ETHIOPIA
LIBERIA
CAMEROON
SOMALI REP.
EQUATORIAL GUINEA
GABON
UGANDA
KENYA
CONGO
ZAÏRE
TANZANIA
ANGOLA
ZAMBIA
MOZAMBIQUE
ZIMBABWE
MADAGASCAR
NAMIBIA
BOTSWANA
SWAZILAND
REP. OF SOUTH AFRICA
LESOTHO

B : BURUNDI
G : GAMBIA
G.B : GUINEA BISSAU
M : MALAWI
R : RWANDA

Scale 1:115 000 000

| 0 | 1000 | 2000 | 3000 | 4000km |

© Collins ○ Longman Atlases

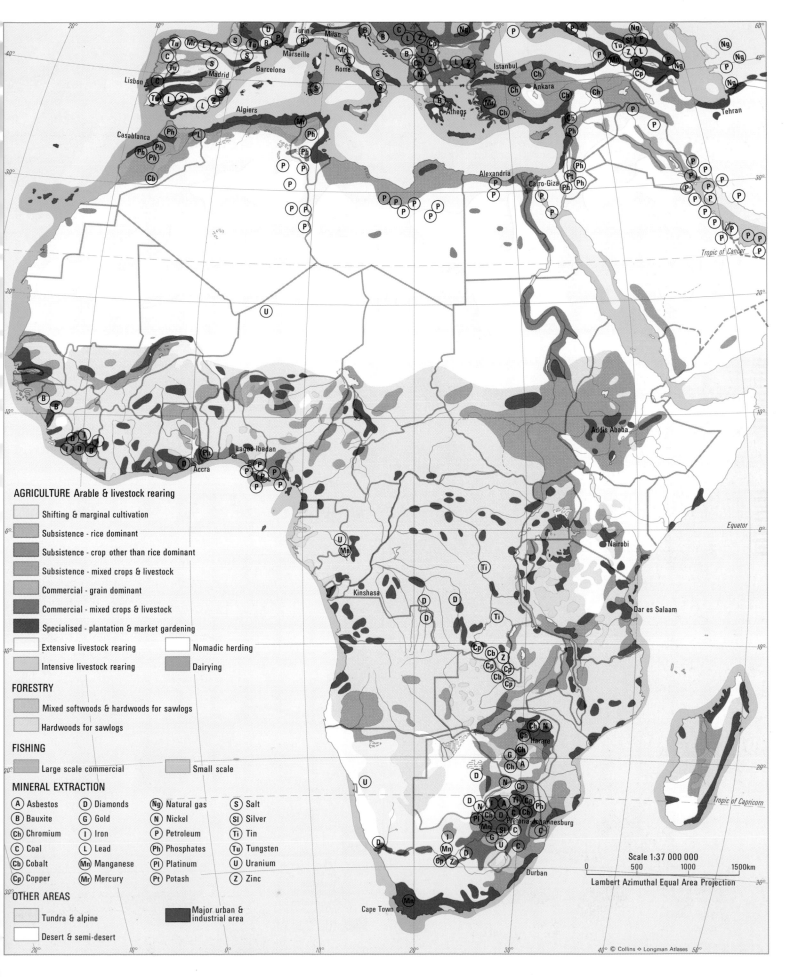

AGRICULTURE Arable & livestock rearing

- Shifting & marginal cultivation
- Subsistence - rice dominant
- Subsistence - crop other than rice dominant
- Subsistence - mixed crops & livestock
- Commercial - grain dominant
- Commercial - mixed crops & livestock
- Specialised - plantation & market gardening
- Extensive livestock rearing
- Nomadic herding
- Intensive livestock rearing
- Dairying

FORESTRY

- Mixed softwoods & hardwoods for sawlogs
- Hardwoods for sawlogs

FISHING

- Large scale commercial
- Small scale

MINERAL EXTRACTION

- (A) Asbestos
- (D) Diamonds
- (Ng) Natural gas
- (S) Salt
- (B) Bauxite
- (G) Gold
- (N) Nickel
- (Sl) Silver
- (Ch) Chromium
- (I) Iron
- (P) Petroleum
- (Ti) Tin
- (C) Coal
- (L) Lead
- (Ph) Phosphates
- (Tu) Tungsten
- (Cb) Cobalt
- (Mn) Manganese
- (Pl) Platinum
- (U) Uranium
- (Cp) Copper
- (Mr) Mercury
- (Pt) Potash
- (Z) Zinc

OTHER AREAS

- Tundra & alpine
- Desert & semi-desert
- Major urban & industrial area

Scale 1:37 000 000

0   500   1000   1500km

Lambert Azimuthal Equal Area Projection

© Collins ◊ Longman Atlases

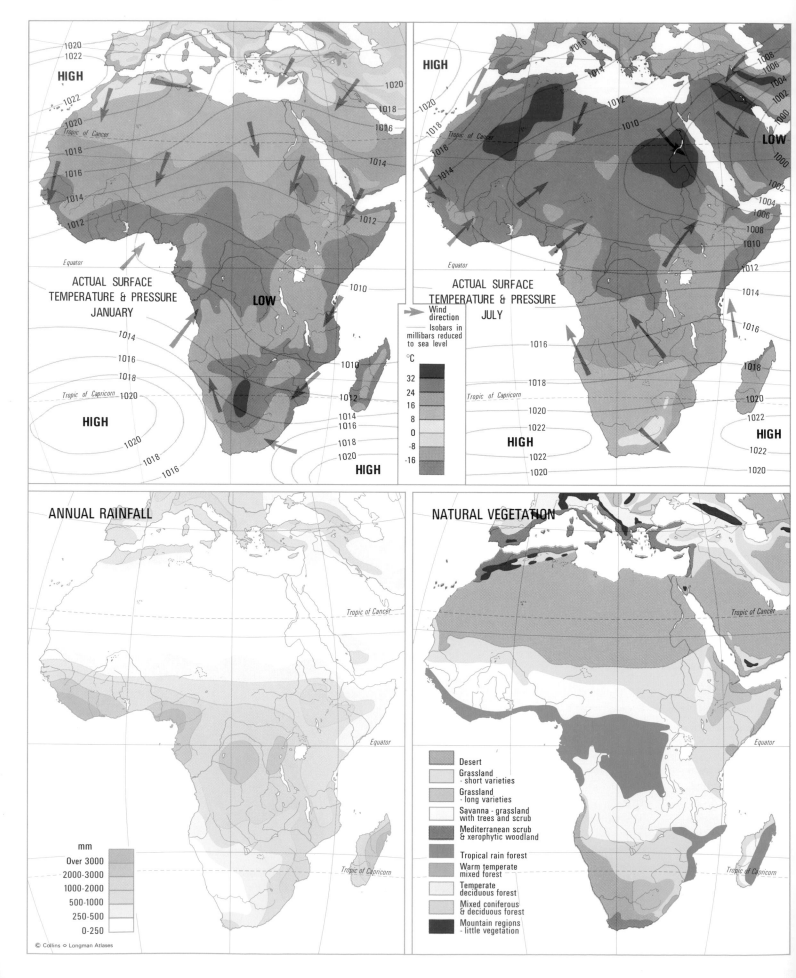

ACTUAL SURFACE
TEMPERATURE & PRESSURE
JANUARY

HIGH

LOW

HIGH

HIGH

ACTUAL SURFACE
TEMPERATURE & PRESSURE
JULY

HIGH

LOW

HIGH

HIGH

Wind
direction
Isobars in
millibars reduced
to sea level

°C
32
24
16
8
0
-8
-16

ANNUAL RAINFALL

mm
Over 3000
2000-3000
1000-2000
500-1000
250-500
0-250

NATURAL VEGETATION

Desert
Grassland
- short varieties
Grassland
- long varieties
Savanna - grassland
with trees and scrub
Mediterranean scrub
& xerophytic woodland
Tropical rain forest
Warm temperate
mixed forest
Temperate
deciduous forest
Mixed coniferous
& deciduous forest
Mountain regions
- little vegetation

© Collins ◇ Longman Atlases

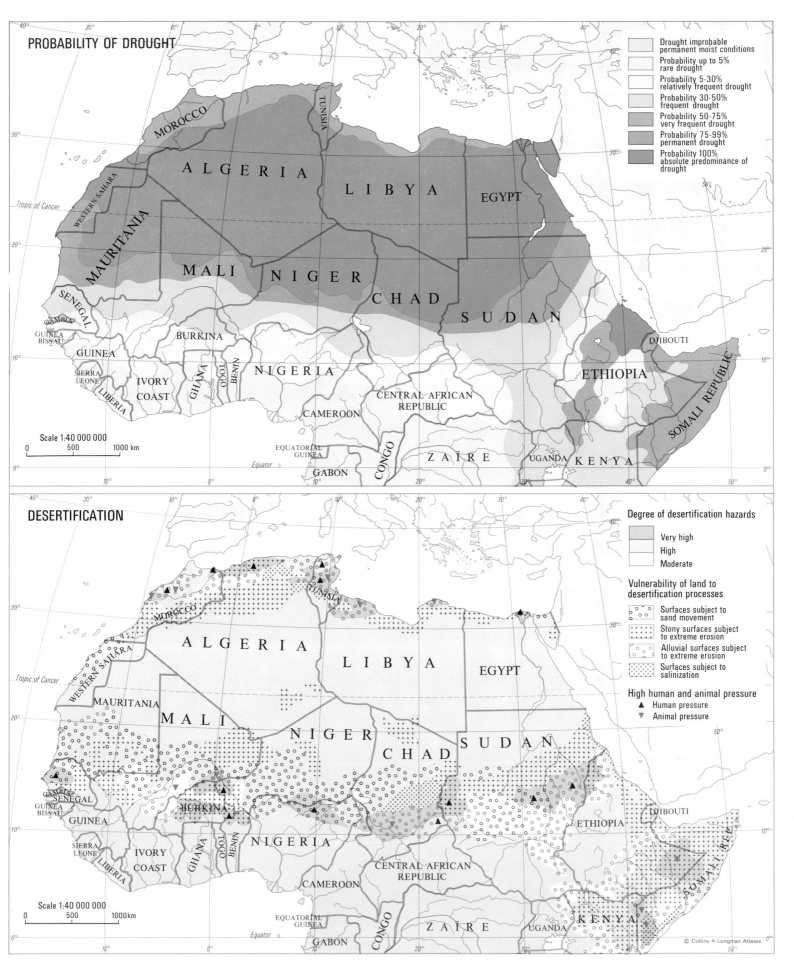

PROBABILITY OF DROUGHT

Drought improbable permanent moist conditions

Probability up to 5% rare drought

Probability 5-30% relatively frequent drought

Probability 30-50% frequent drought

Probability 50-75% very frequent drought

Probability 75-99% permanent drought

Probability 100% absolute predominance of drought

MOROCCO · TUNISIA · ALGERIA · LIBYA · EGYPT · WESTERN SAHARA · MAURITANIA · MALI · NIGER · CHAD · SUDAN · SENEGAL · GAMBIA · GUINEA BISSAU · GUINEA · SIERRA LEONE · LIBERIA · IVORY COAST · GHANA · TOGO · BENIN · BURKINA · NIGERIA · CAMEROON · CENTRAL AFRICAN REPUBLIC · EQUATORIAL GUINEA · GABON · CONGO · ZAÏRE · UGANDA · KENYA · ETHIOPIA · DJIBOUTI · SOMALI REPUBLIC

Tropic of Cancer

Equator

Scale 1:40 000 000

0   500   1000 km

DESERTIFICATION

Degree of desertification hazards

Very high

High

Moderate

Vulnerability of land to desertification processes

Surfaces subject to sand movement

Stony surfaces subject to extreme erosion

Alluvial surfaces subject to extreme erosion

Surfaces subject to salinization

High human and animal pressure

▲ Human pressure

▼ Animal pressure

MOROCCO · TUNISIA · ALGERIA · LIBYA · EGYPT · WESTERN SAHARA · MAURITANIA · MALI · NIGER · CHAD · SUDAN · SENEGAL · GAMBIA · GUINEA BISSAU · GUINEA · SIERRA LEONE · LIBERIA · IVORY COAST · GHANA · TOGO · BENIN · BURKINA · NIGERIA · CAMEROON · CENTRAL AFRICAN REPUBLIC · EQUATORIAL GUINEA · GABON · CONGO · ZAÏRE · UGANDA · KENYA · ETHIOPIA · DJIBOUTI · SOMALI REP.

Tropic of Cancer

Equator

Scale 1:40 000 000

0   500   1000km

© Collins ○ Longman Atlases

POPULATION DISTRIBUTION

Persons per sq. km

- Over 100
- 50-100
- 10-50
- 1-10
- under 1

Tropic of Cancer

Equator

Tropic of Capricorn

POPULATION STATISTICS

COUNTRY	TOTAL POPULATION	% URBAN POPULA-TION	LIFE EXPECTATION AT BIRTH	
			MALE	FEMALE
ALGERIA	20 500 000	52.0	58.5	61.4
ANGOLA	8 339 000	na	38.5	41.6
BOTSWANA	1 007 000	16.1	50.8	54.2
CENTRAL AFRICAN REP.	2 450 000	35.3	33.1	36.1
CONGO	1 651 000	na	43.0	46.1
EGYPT	44 533 000	44.3	51.6	53.8
EQUATORIAL GUINEA	375 000	na	40.4	43.6
ETHIOPIA	33 680 000	14.4	39.3	42.5
GABON	1 127 000	na	25.1	45.1
KENYA	18 784 000	15.5	46.9	51.2
LIBYA	3 342 000	29.8	53.8	57.0
MADAGASCAR	9 400 000	16.3	37.5	38.3
MALAŴI	6 429 000	8.5	40.9	44.2
MAURITANIA	1 719 000	22.8	40.4	43.6
MOROCCO	22 109 000	42.1	53.8	57.0
MOZAMBIQUE	13 311 000	13.2	45.8	49.1
NAMIBIA	1 465 000	na	45.0	47.5
REP. OF SOUTH AFRICA	30 802 000	53.1	49.8	53.2
SOMALI	5 269 000	na	39.3	42.5
SUDAN	20 362 000	20.2	43.9	46.4
TANZANIA	20 378 000	13.8	47.3	50.7
TUNISIA	6 886 000	49.8	57.6	58.6
UGANDA	14 625 000	na	48.3	51.7
WESTERN SAHARA	147 000	45.1	na	na
ZAÏRE	31 151 000	34.2	46.4	49.7
ZAMBIA	6 242 000	40.4	47.7	51.0
ZIMBABWE	7 740 000	23.6	51.3	55.6

Source : U.N. Demographic Yearbook 1983
Figures are the latest available census figures or estimates

CITIES OVER 100 000 - 1963

Tropic of Cancer

Equator

Tropic of Capricorn

Cities
- ■ 1 000 000 - 5 000 000 population
- ● 500 000 - 1 000 000 population
- • 100 000 - 500 000 population

Source : U.N. Demographic Yearbook 1963

CITIES OVER 100 000 - 1983

Tropic of Cancer

Equator

Tropic of Capricorn

Cities
- ■ Over 5 000 000 population
- ■ 1 000 000 - 5 000 000 population
- ● 500 000 - 1 000 000 population
- • 100 000 - 500 000 population

Source : U.N. Demographic Yearbook 1983

© Collins ◊ Longman Atlases

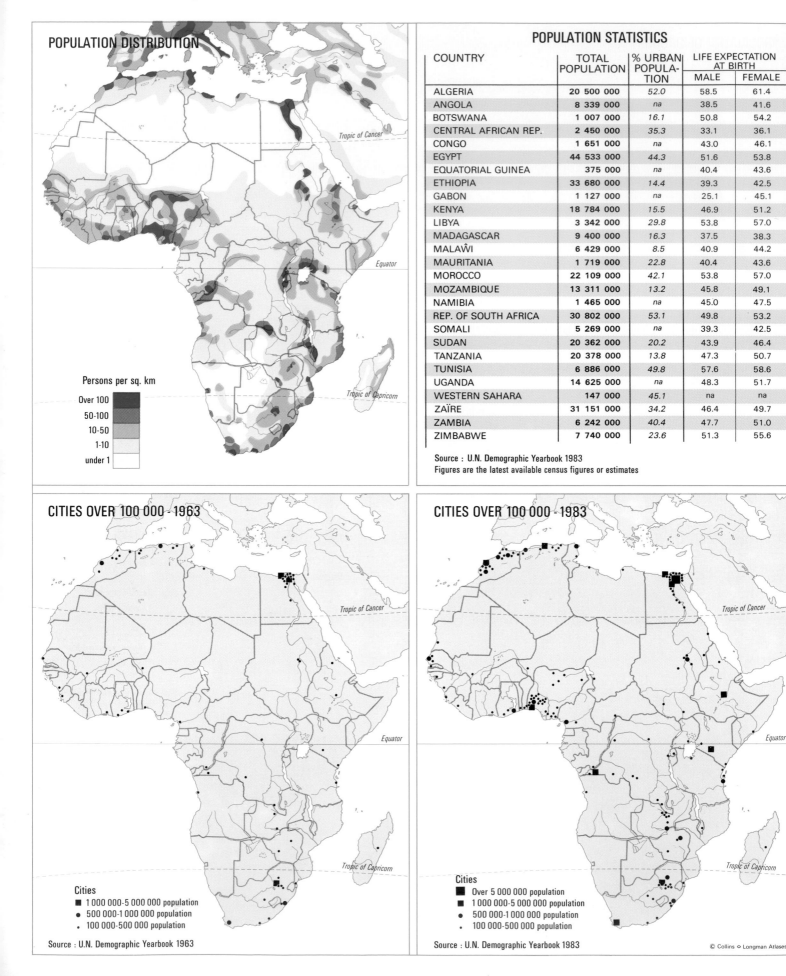

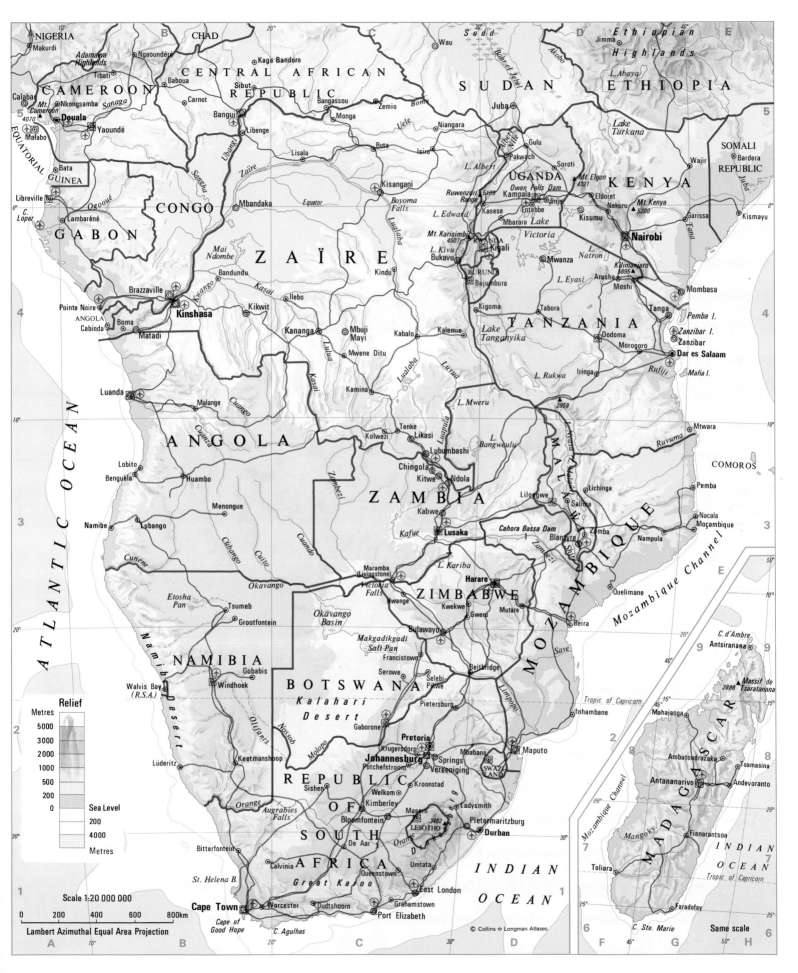

Relief

Metres	
5000	
3000	
2000	
1000	
500	
200	
0	Sea Level
200	
4000	
Metres	

Scale 1:20 000 000

0   200   400   600   800km

Lambert Azimuthal Equal Area Projection

© Collins ○ Longman Atlases

Same scale

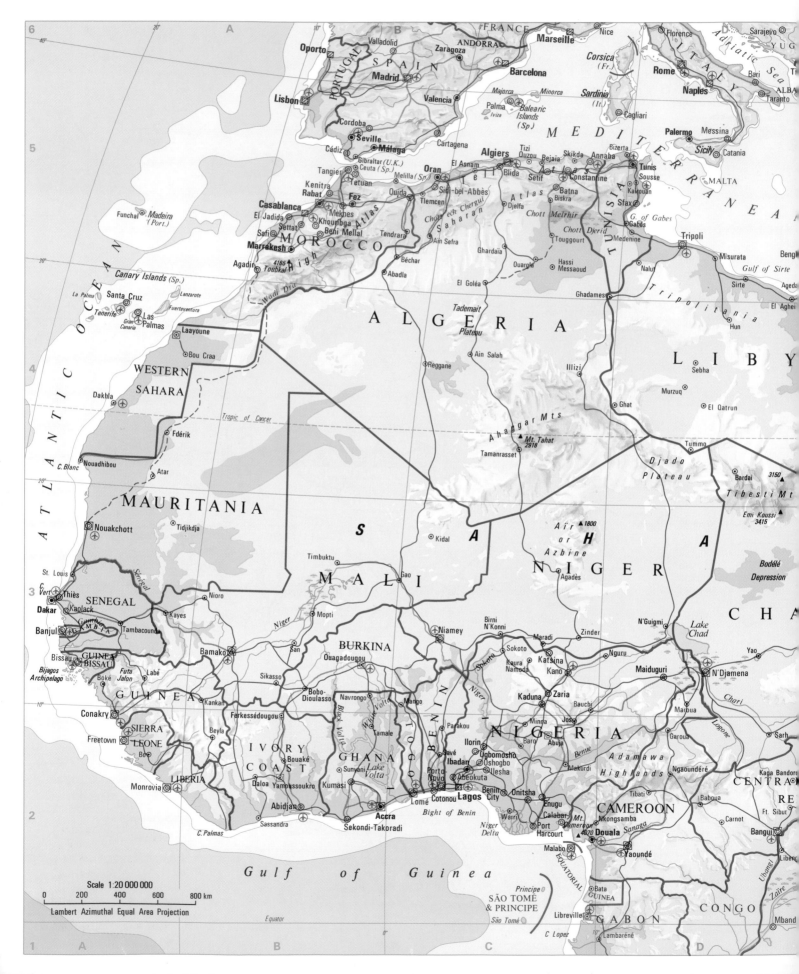

Scale 1:20 000 000

0   200   400   600   800 km

Lambert Azimuthal Equal Area Projection

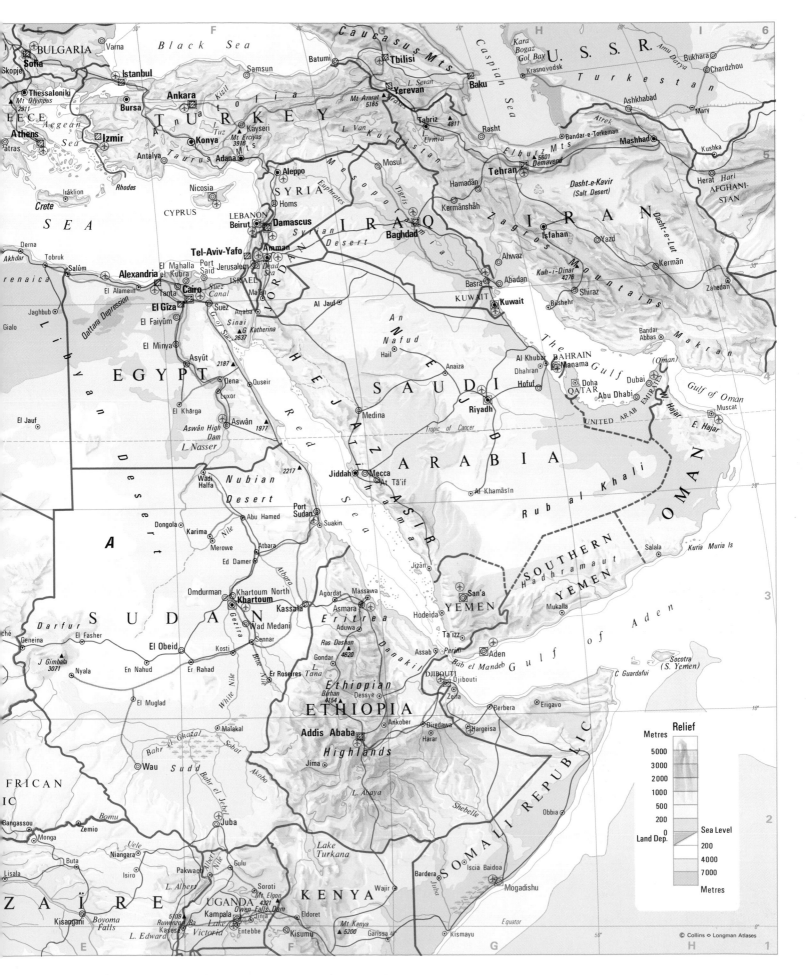

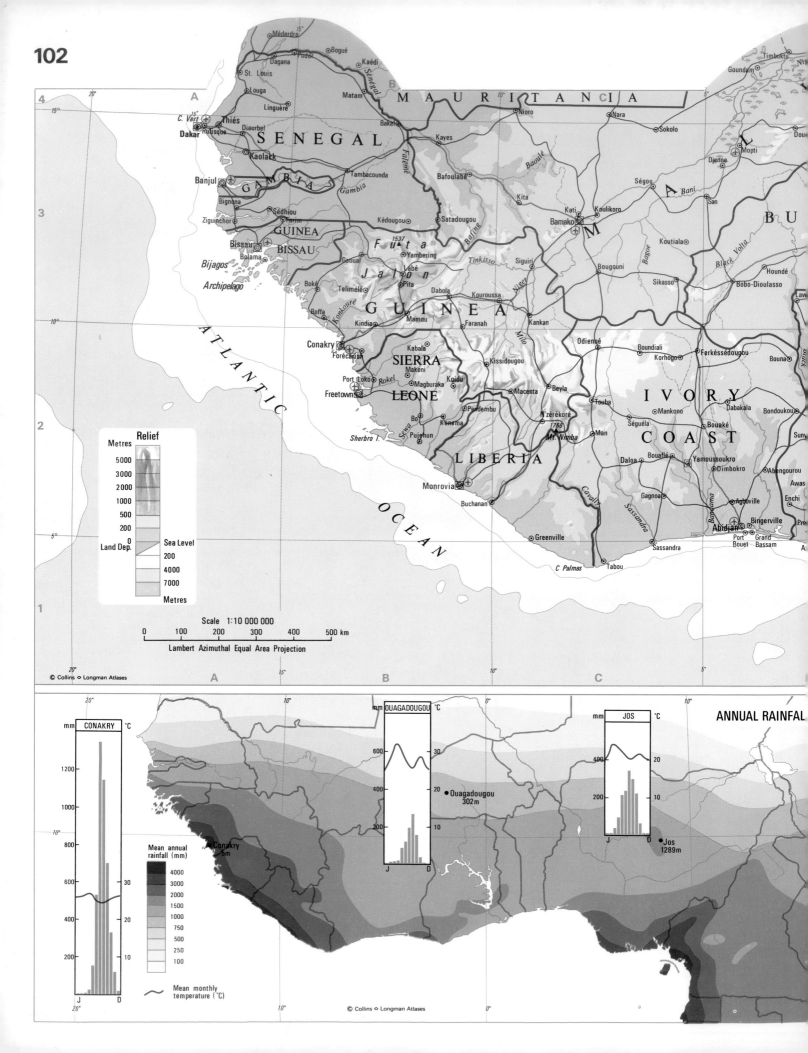

MAURITANIA

Méderdra
Bogué
Dagana
Podor
St. Louis
Louga
C. Vert
Thiès
Dakar
Rufisque
Diourbel
Kaolack

SENEGAL

Kaédi
Matam
Bakel
Kayes

Nioro
Nara
Sokolo

MALI

Timbuktu
Goundam
Mopti
Djenné
Ségou
Bani
San

Banjul
GAMBIA
Bignona
Ziguinchor
Sédhiou
Farim
GUINEA
BISSAU
Bissau
Bolama
Tambacounda
Bafoulabé
Kédougou
Satadougou
Kita
Kati
Koulikoro
Bamako
Ségou
Koutiala

BURKINA

Bijagos
Archipelago
Boké
Telimélé
Futa
Jalon
Gaoual
Yambering
Labé
Pita
Dabola
Siguiri
Bougouni
Sikasso
Bobo-Dioulasso
Houndé
Black Volta

Boffa
Kindia
Mamou
Faranah
Kouroussa
Kankan
Odienné
Boundiali
Korhogo
Ferkéssédougou
Bouna

Conakry
Forécariah
SIERRA
Kabala
Makeni
Kissidougou
IVORY

Port Loko
LEONE
Magburaka
Koidu
Macenta
Beyla
Touba
Mankono
Dabakala
Bouaké
Suny

Freetown
Bo
Pendembu
N'zérékoré
Man
Séguéla
Bouaflé
COAST

Sherbro I.
Pujehun
Kenema
Mt. Wimba
Daloa
Dimbokro
Abengourou

LIBERIA
Gagnoa
Yamoussoukro
Agboville
Bingerville

Monrovia
Buchanan
Abidjan
Port Bouet
Grand Bassam

ATLANTIC

Greenville
Sassandra
Tabou
C. Palmas

OCEAN

Relief

Metres	
5000	
3000	
2000	
1000	
500	
200	
0	**Sea Level**

Land Dep.

200	
4000	
7000	

Metres

Scale 1:10 000 000

0 100 200 300 400 500 km

Lambert Azimuthal Equal Area Projection

© Collins ◇ Longman Atlases

ANNUAL RAINFALL

CONAKRY
mm °C
1200
1000
800
600
400
200
J   D

OUAGADOUGOU
mm °C
600 30
400 20
200 10
J   D
• Ouagadougou
302m

JOS
mm °C
400 20
200 10
J   D
• Jos
1289m

Mean annual
rainfall (mm)

| 4000 |
| 3000 |
| 2000 |
| 1500 |
| 1000 |
| 750 |
| 500 |
| 250 |
| 100 |

• Conakry
6m

Mean monthly
temperature (°C)

© Collins ◇ Longman Atlases

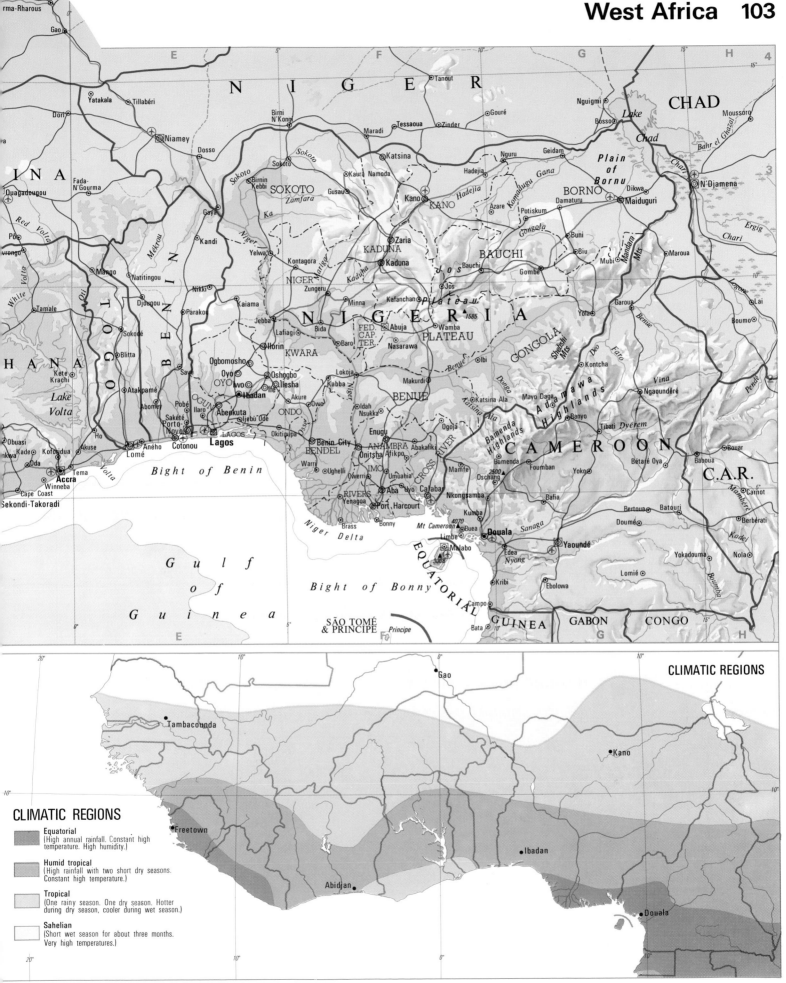

CLIMATIC REGIONS

Equatorial
(High annual rainfall. Constant high temperature. High humidity.)

Humid tropical
(High rainfall with two short dry seasons. Constant high temperature.)

Tropical
(One rainy season. One dry season. Hotter during dry season, cooler during wet season.)

Sahelian
(Short wet season for about three months. Very high temperatures.)

CLIMATIC REGIONS

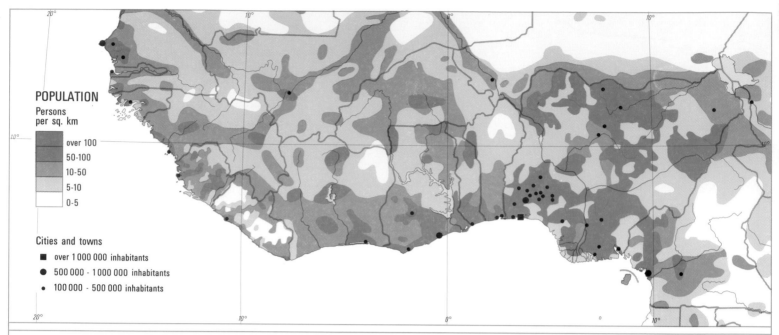

POPULATION

Persons
per sq. km

- over 100
- 50-100
- 10-50
- 5-10
- 0-5

Cities and towns

- ■ over 1 000 000 inhabitants
- ● 500 000 - 1 000 000 inhabitants
- • 100 000 - 500 000 inhabitants

POPULATION STATISTICS

COUNTRY	TOTAL POPULATION	% URBAN POPULA-TION	LIFE EXPECTATION AT BIRTH		% OF TOTAL POPULATION BY AGE GROUP				
			MALE	FEMALE	0-14	15-34	35-54	55-74	75+
BENIN	3 720 000	39.4	39.0	42.1	48.8	28.0	14.1	6.5	2.6
BURKINA	6 607 000	6.4	32.1	31.1	45.4	30.3	16.3	6.5	1.5
CAMEROON	9 165 000	28.0	44.4	47.6	39.3	32.3	16.8	← 11.6 →	
CHAD	4 789 000	18.4	29.0	35.0	37.4	35.9	21.7	← 5 →	
GAMBIA	618 000	18.2	32.0	35.0	41.9	34.7	17.4	5.5	0.5
GHANA	12 700 000	31.4	48.3	51.7	na	na	na	na	na
GUINEA	5 177 000	na	36.7	39.8	na	na	na	na	na
GUINEA BISSAU	863 000	na	39.4	42.6	44.3	31.1	15.8	6.6	2.2
IVORY COAST	9 161 000	32.0	43.4	46.6	44.6	33.7	16.2	4.7	0.8
LIBERIA	2 057 000	29.1	45.8	44.0	40.9	33.7	17.5	6.6	1.3
MALI	7 528 000	17.7	46.9	49.7	44.1	17.6	← 38.3 →		
NIGER	5 772 000	na	39.0	42.1	43.0	na	na	na	na
NIGERIA	89 022 000	na	37.2	36.7	na	na	na	na	na
SENEGAL	6 316 000	34.3	39.7	42.9	43.2	31.9	16.4	6.9	1.6
SIERRA LEONE	3 472 000	na	30.6	33.5	40.6	31.5	17.9	7.4	2.6
TOGO	2 756 000	15.2	31.6	38.5	na	na	na	na	na

(Source: UN Demographic Yearbook 1983)

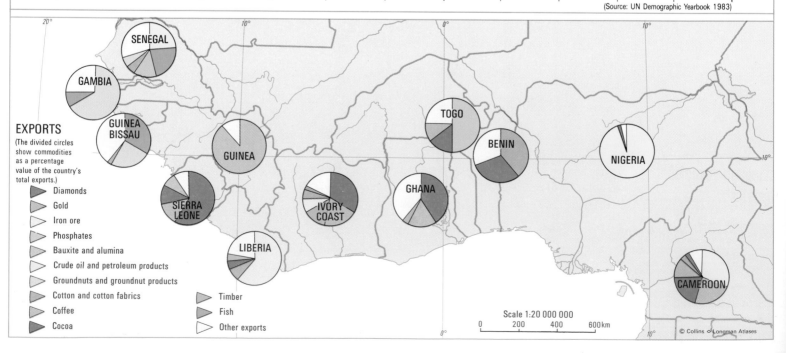

EXPORTS

(The divided circles show commodities as a percentage value of the country's total exports.)

- Diamonds
- Gold
- Iron ore
- Phosphates
- Bauxite and alumina
- Crude oil and petroleum products
- Groundnuts and groundnut products
- Cotton and cotton fabrics
- Coffee
- Cocoa
- Timber
- Fish
- Other exports

Scale 1:20 000 000
0   200   400   600km

© Collins ‑ Longman Atlases

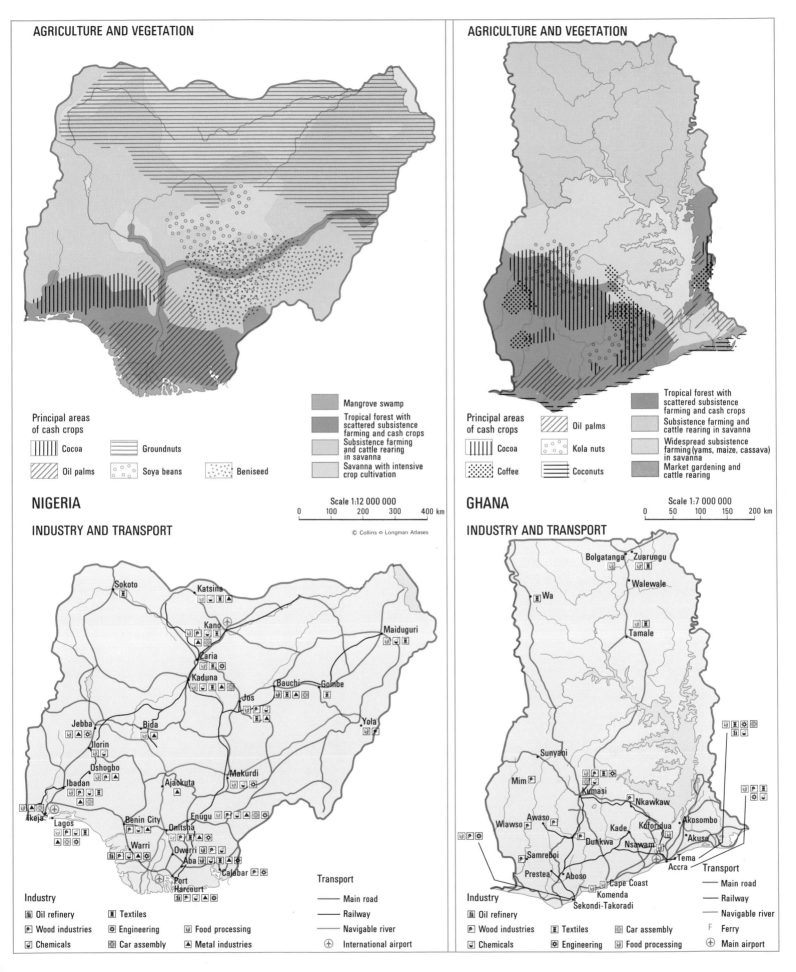

AGRICULTURE AND VEGETATION

Principal areas of cash crops

	Cocoa
	Groundnuts
	Oil palms
	Soya beans
	Beniseed

Mangrove swamp

Tropical forest with scattered subsistence farming and cash crops

Subsistence farming and cattle rearing in savanna

Savanna with intensive crop cultivation

NIGERIA

INDUSTRY AND TRANSPORT

Scale 1:12 000 000

0   100   200   300   400 km

© Collins ◇ Longman Atlases

Sokoto
Katsina
Kano
Zaria
Kaduna
Bauchi   Gombe
Jos
Maiduguri
Yola
Jebba
Bida
Ilorin
Oshogbo
Makurdi
Ibadan
Ajaokuta
Ikeja
Lagos
Benin City
Onitsha
Enugu
Warri
Owerri
Aba   Calabar
Port Harcourt

Industry

	Oil refinery		Textiles
	Wood industries		Engineering
	Chemicals		Car assembly
			Food processing
			Metal industries

Transport

— Main road
— Railway
— Navigable river
✈ International airport

AGRICULTURE AND VEGETATION

Principal areas of cash crops

	Cocoa
	Coffee
	Oil palms
	Kola nuts
	Coconuts

Tropical forest with scattered subsistence farming and cash crops

Subsistence farming and cattle rearing in savanna

Widespread subsistence farming (yams, maize, cassava) in savanna

Market gardening and cattle rearing

GHANA

INDUSTRY AND TRANSPORT

Scale 1:7 000 000

0   50   100   150   200 km

Bolgatanga   Zuarungu
Walewale
Wa
Tamale
Sunyani
Mim
Kumasi
Nkawkaw
Awaso
Wiawso
Kade   Koforidua   Akosombo
Dunkwa   Akuse
Samreboi   Nsawam   Tema
Prestea   Aboso   Accra
Cape Coast
Komenda
Sekondi-Takoradi

Transport

— Main road
— Railway
— Navigable river
F Ferry
✈ Main airport

Industry

	Oil refinery		Textiles
	Wood industries		Engineering
	Chemicals		Car assembly
			Food processing

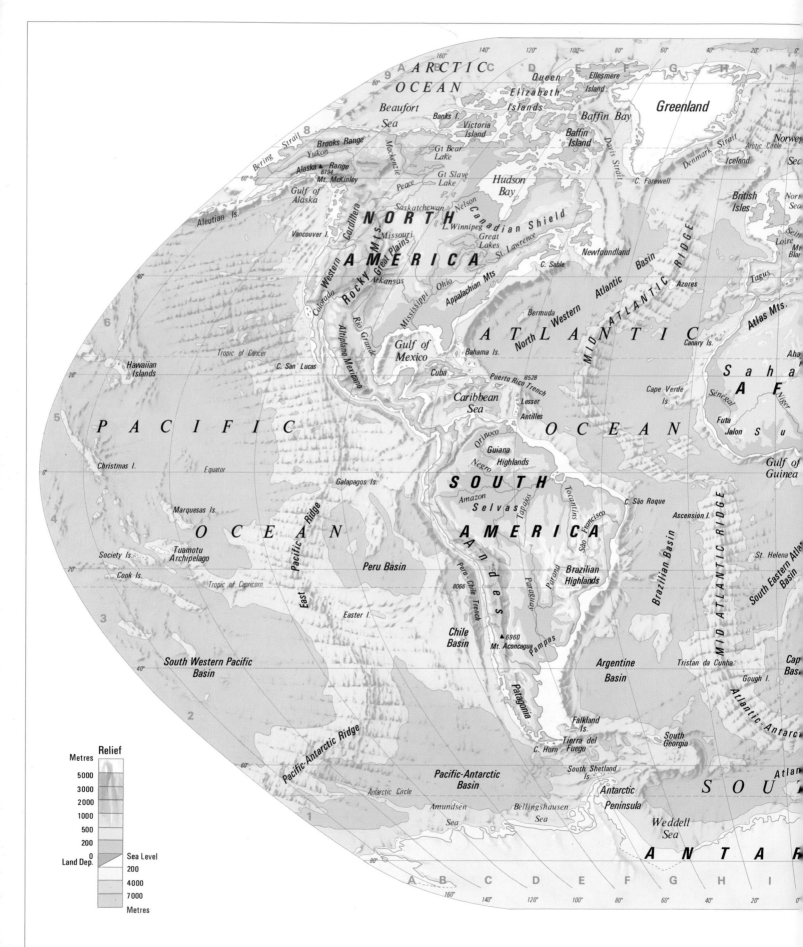

ARCTIC OCEAN

Queen Elizabeth Islands
Ellesmere Island
Greenland
Beaufort Sea
Banks I.
Baffin Bay
Baffin Island
Brooks Range
Gt Bear Lake
Davis Strait
Denmark Strait
Iceland
Arctic Circle
Norwe
Yukon
Victoria Island
Mackenzie
Alaska Range 6194
Mt. McKinley
Peace
Gt Slave Lake
Hudson Bay
C. Farewell
British Isles
Nor
Gulf of Alaska
Sea
Aleutian Is.
Vancouver I.
Saskatchewan
Nelson
Canadian Shield
Newfoundland
NORTH
Western Cordillera
Rocky Mts.
Missouri
L. Winnipeg
Great Lakes
St. Lawrence
Loire
AMERICA
Great Plains
Arkansas
Ohio
Appalachian Mts
C. Sable
Atlantic
Basin
Azores
Tagus
Colorado
Mississippi
Bermuda
North
Western
MID ATLANTIC RIDGE
Atlas Mts.
Rio Grande
Gulf of Mexico
Bahama Is.
A T L A N T I C
Canary Is.
Saha
Tropic of Cancer
C. San Lucas
Cuba
Puerto Rico Trench 8528
A F
Hawaiian Islands
Caribbean Sea
Lesser
Cape Verde Is.
Sénégal
Niger
Altiplano Mexicano
Antilles
O C E A N
Futa Jalon
Su
Aha
P A C I F I C
Orinoco
Guiana Highlands
Gulf of Guinea
Christmas I.
Equator
Negro
Galapagos Is.
SOUTH
C. São Roque
Marquesas Is.
East Pacific Ridge
Amazon
Selvas
Tapajos
Tocantins
Brazilian Basin
Ascension I.
O C E A N
AMERICA
São Francisco
St. Helena
Society Is.
Tuamotu Archipelago
Peru Basin
Andes
South Eastern Atla Basin
Cook Is.
Tropic of Capricorn
Peru Chile Trench
Paraguay
Paraná
Brazilian Highlands
MID ATLANTIC RIDGE
Easter I.
8066
Brazilian Basin
Chile Basin
6960
Mt. Aconcagua
Pampas
Argentine Basin
Tristan da Cunha
Cap Bas
South Western Pacific Basin
Patagonia
Gough I.
Atlantic-Antarc
Pacific-Antarctic Ridge
Falkland Is.
South Georgia
Tierra del Fuego
C. Horn
South Shetland
Atlan
Antarctic Circle
Pacific-Antarctic Basin
Antarctic Peninsula
SOU
Amundsen Sea
Bellingshausen Sea
Weddell Sea
ANTAR

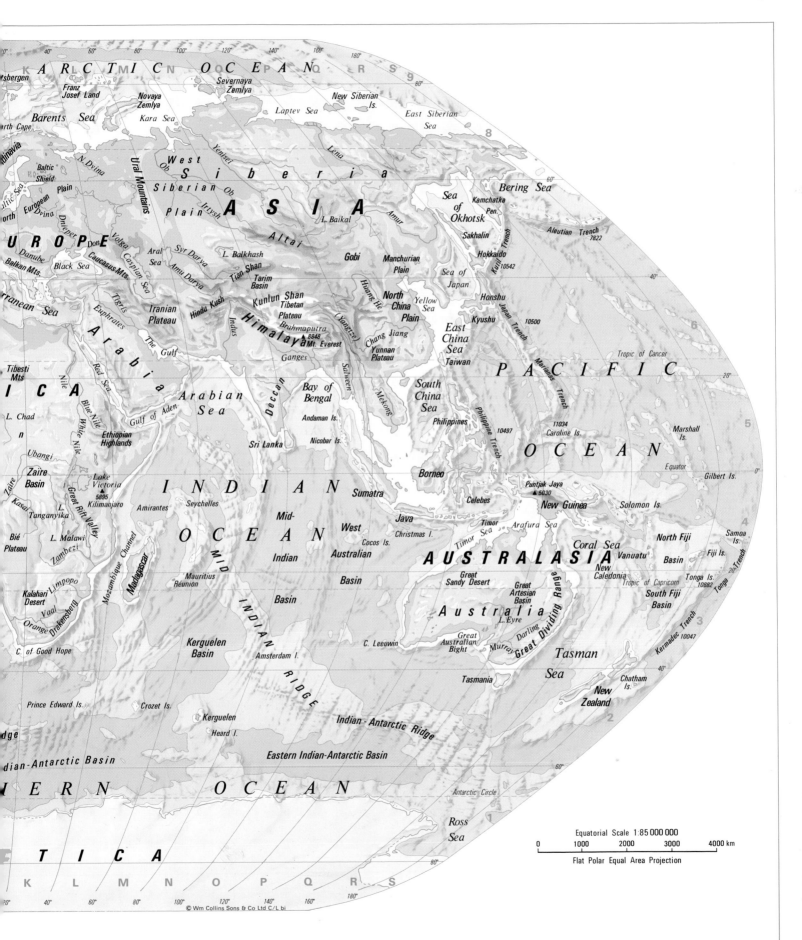

K A R C T M I C N O C E A N Q R S 9

Franz Josef Land
sbergen
Novaya Zemlya
Severnaya Zemlya
New Siberian Is.
Barents Sea
Kara Sea
Laptev Sea
East Siberian Sea
North Cape
8

Bering Sea

inavia
Baltic Shield
N. Dvina
West Ob
Siberian Plain
ASIA
L. Baikal
Amur
Sea of Okhotsk
Kamchatka Pen.
Aleutian Trench 7822

tic Sea
Ural Mountains
Yenisei
Ob
Irtysh
Altai
Kuril Trench 10542
Sakhalin
Hokkaido

North European Plain
Dvina
Volga
Aral Sea
Syr Darya
L. Balkhash
Tian Shan
Gobi
Manchurian Plain
Sea of Japan
Honshu
Japan Trench 10500

UROPE
Don
Caspian Sea
Amu Darya
Tarim Basin
Hwang He
North China Plain
Kyushu

Danube
Caucasus Mts.
Kunlun Shan
Tibetan Plateau
(Yangtze)
Yellow Sea
Balkan Mts.
Black Sea
Iranian Plateau
Hindu Kush
Himalaya
Brahmaputra
8848 Mt. Everest
Chang Jiang
East China Sea

rranean Sea
Tigris
Euphrates
Indus
Ganges
Salween
Yunnan Plateau
Taiwan

ICA
Arabia
Red Sea
The Gulf
Deccan
Bay of Bengal
Mekong
South China Sea
PACIFIC

Tibesti Mts
Nile
Gulf of Aden
Arabian Sea
Andaman Is.
Marianas Trench
Tropic of Cancer

L. Chad
Blue Nile
White Nile
Ethiopian Highlands
Sri Lanka
Nicobar Is.
Philippines
11034
Marshall Is.

Ubangi
Zaire
Lake Victoria
5895 Kilimanjaro
Amirantes
Seychelles
INDIAN
Sumatra
Philippine Trench 10497
Caroline Is.
OCEAN

Zaire Basin
Kasai
L. Tanganyika
Borneo
Equator
Gilbert Is.

Bié Plateau
L. Malawi
Zambezi
OCEAN
Mid-
West
Java
Celebes
Puntjak Jaya 5030
New Guinea
Solomon Is.

Kalahari Desert
Mozambique Channel
Madagascar
Indian
Australian
Christmas I.
Timor Sea
Arafura Sea
North Fiji
Samoa Is.

Vaal
Mauritius
Réunion
Basin
Cocos Is.
AUSTRALASIA
Coral Sea
Vanuatu
Basin
Fiji Is.

Orange Drakensberg
Basin
Great Sandy Desert
Great Artesian Basin
New Caledonia
Tropic of Capricorn
South Fiji Basin
Tonga Is. 10882

C. of Good Hope
Kerguelen Basin
MID INDIAN RIDGE
Australia
L. Eyre
Great Dividing Range
Tonga Trench

Prince Edward Is.
Crozet Is.
Amsterdam I.
C. Leeuwin
Great Australian Bight
Murray
Darling
Tasman
Chatham Is.
Kermadec Trench 10047

dge
Kerguelen
Heard I.
Indian - Antarctic Ridge
Tasmania
Sea
New Zealand

dian-Antarctic Basin
Eastern Indian-Antarctic Basin

ERN OCEAN
Antarctic Circle

Ross Sea

TICA

K L M N O P Q R S

Equatorial Scale 1:85 000 000

0   1000   2000   3000   4000 km

Flat Polar Equal Area Projection

ARCTIC OCEAN

GREENLAND

Godthåb

ICELAND

Reykjavik

U.S.A.
ALASKA

Arctic Circle

C A N A D A

UNITED DEM
KINGDOM
REP. OF
IRELAND Dublin London Ams
Brussels B.
Paris Be
FRANC

Edmonton

Vancouver Winnipeg

Seattle

Ottawa Montreal
Chicago Detroit Toronto
UNITED STATES Pittsburgh Boston
San Francisco New York
OF AMERICA St. Louis Philadelphia
Washington

A T L A N T I C

O C E A N

PORTUGAL Madrid
Lisbon SPAIN

Algiers
Rabat MOROCCO

Los Angeles

Dallas

Houston

Bermuda
(U.K.)

Canary Is.
(Sp.) ALGERI

El Aaiún
WESTERN
SAHARA

Tropic of Cancer

Hawaiian Is.
(U.S.A.)

Monterrey

Miami
Nassau
BAHAMAS

Guadalajara

Havana CUBA

MAURITANIA

Nouakchott

MALI

Mexico City

MEXICO

Guatemala City

JAMAICA HAITI DOMINICAN
BELIZE REP.
Belmopan PUERTO
GUAT HONDURAS Kingston RICO
EL SALVADOR Tegucigalpa ANTIGUA
Managua DOMINICA
NICARAGUA ST. LUCIA

Dakar SENEGAL
GAMBIA Bamako Niam
Bissau GUINEA BURKINA
G.B. Ouagadou
Conakry IVORY Bni
SIERRA LEONE Yamoussoukro COAST
Monrovia Accra Porto Novo Mala
LIBERIA Lama EQUAT
Porto Novo GUI
Lib

P A C I F I C

Caracas

Managua
COSTA San José
RICA Panama
PANAMA VENEZUELA

TRINIDAD
& TOBAGO

Georgetown
Paramaribo SURINAM
Cayenne
GUYANA (Fr.)

KIRIBATI

Bogotá
COLOMBIA

Equator

Galapagos Is.
(Ec.)

Quito
ECUADOR

O C E A N

Marquesas Is.
(Fr.)

BRAZIL

Recife

Ascension I.
(U.K.)

A T L A N T I C

PERU

Samoa
(U.S.A.)

Cook Is.
(N.Z.)

Tuamotu Archipelago

Society Is.
(Fr.)

Lima

La Paz
BOLIVIA
Sucre

Brasília

Belo Horizonte

St. Helena
(U.K.)

O C E A N

Tropic of Capricorn

Easter I.
(Chile)

PARAGUAY
Asunción

Rio de Janeiro
São Paulo

CHILE ARGENTINA URUGUAY

Santiago Buenos Montevideo
Aires

Tristan da Cunha (U.K.)

Gough I. (U.K.)

A. : ANDORRA
ALB. : ALBANIA
AUS. : AUSTRIA
B. : BELGIUM
BANGLA. : BANGLADESH
BULG. : BULGARIA
CAM. : CAMBODIA
CZECH. : CZECHOSLOVAKIA
E. GER. : EAST GERMANY
G.B. : GUINEA BISSAU
GUAT. : GUATEMALA
HUNG. : HUNGARY
L. : LUXEMBOURG
LEB. : LEBANON
M. : MONACO
NETH. : NETHERLANDS
S. : SWITZERLAND
S.M. : SAN MARINO
T. : TURKEY (in Europe)
U.A.E. : UNITED ARAB EMIRATES
W. GER. : WEST GERMANY
YUGO. : YUGOSLAVIA

Falkland Is.
(U.K.)

South Georgia
(U.K.)

Chilean Claim Argentinian Claim

Antarctic Circle

BRITISH ANTARCTIC TERRITORY

NORWEGI

Anta

© Wm Collins Sons & Co Ltd C7L bi

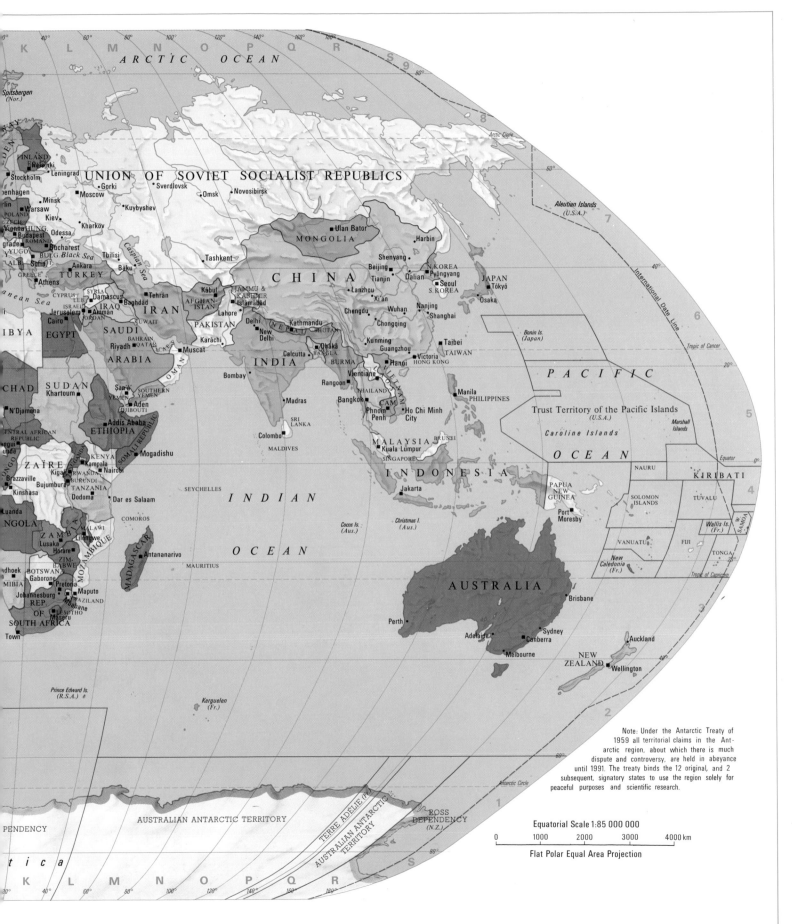

ARCTIC OCEAN

Spitsbergen (Nor.)

FINLAND
Helsinki

UNION OF SOVIET SOCIALIST REPUBLICS

Stockholm · Leningrad · Gorki · Sverdlovsk · Omsk · Novosibirsk
·enhagen · Moscow
lin · Minsk · Kuybyshev
POLAND · Warsaw · Kiev · Kharkov
CZECH Vienna HUNG. · Odessa
·grade · Budapest ROMANIA · Bucharest
YUGO · Sofia Black Sea Tbilisi
ALB. BULG. Ankara · Baku
GREECE TURKEY · Caspian Sea
Athens
·anean Sea CYPRUS SYRIA · Damascus
ISRAEL LEB. Baghdad
Jerusalem JORDAN · Amman · Tehran
Cairo · KUWAIT IRAN
SAUDI BAHRAIN QATAR
·IBYA EGYPT · Riyadh
ARABIA OMAN · Muscat
CHAD SUDAN · Şan'ā' SOUTHERN
Khartoum YEMEN
N'Djamena YEMEN · Aden
DJIBOUTI
·NTRAL AFRICAN Addis Ababa
REPUBLIC ETHIOPIA SOMALI REPUBLIC
·ngui
·undo ZAÏRE KENYA · Mogadishu
·ongo Kigali Kampala
Brazzaville RWANDA Nairobi
Kinshasa BURUNDI
Bujumbura TANZANIA
Dodoma Dar es Salaam
·uanda
NGOLA MALAWI
ZAMBIA Lilongwe
Lusaka MOZAMBIQUE
Harare
·dhoek BOTSWANA ZIM-
MIBIA Gaborone BABWE Pretoria
Johannesburg SWAZILAND Maputo
REP. LESOTHO Maseru
OF
SOUTH AFRICA
·Town

Ulan Bator
MONGOLIA
Harbin
Shenyang
Beijing N KOREA
Tianjin Dalian Pyongyang
Tashkent Lanzhou S. KOREA Seoul JAPAN
Kābul Xi'an Tōkyō
JAMMU & Islāmābād Chengdu Wuhan Nanjing Osaka
KASHMIR Chongqing Shanghai
AFGHAN- Lahore
ISTAN Delhi Kathmandu Kunming Guangzhou
PAKISTAN New NEPAL BHUTAN Taibei
Delhi Dhākā TAIWAN
Karāchi Calcutta BANGLA. Victoria
INDIA BURMA Hanoi HONG KONG
Bombay Rangoon
Vientiane
Madras THAILAND Manila
Bangkok CAM. PHILIPPINES
SRI Phnom Ho Chi Minh
Colombo LANKA Penh City
MALDIVES
MALAYSIA BRUNEI
Kuala Lumpur
SINGAPORE
INDONESIA

CHINA

Aleutian Islands (U.S.A.)

International Date Line

Bonin Is. (Japan)

PACIFIC

Trust Territory of the Pacific Islands (U.S.A.)
Caroline Islands Marshall Islands

OCEAN

NAURU KIRIBATI

PAPUA SOLOMON TUVALU
NEW ISLANDS
GUINEA Wallis Is.
Port (Fr.) W SAMOA
Moresby VANUATU FIJI TONGA
New
Caledonia (Fr.)

INDIAN OCEAN
SEYCHELLES
COMOROS
MADAGASCAR
Antananarivo
MAURITIUS
Cocos Is. (Aus.)
Christmas I. (Aus.)
Jakarta

AUSTRALIA
Brisbane
Perth
Adelaide Sydney
Canberra
Melbourne
Auckland
NEW
ZEALAND Wellington

Prince Edward Is. (R.S.A.)

Kerguelen (Fr.)

Note: Under the Antarctic Treaty of 1959 all territorial claims in the Antarctic region, about which there is much dispute and controversy, are held in abeyance until 1991. The treaty binds the 12 original, and 2 subsequent, signatory states to use the region solely for peaceful purposes and scientific research.

PENDENCY

AUSTRALIAN ANTARCTIC TERRITORY
TERRE ADÉLIE (Fr.)
AUSTRALIAN ANTARCTIC TERRITORY
ROSS
DEPENDENCY
(N.Z.)

·tica

Equatorial Scale 1:85 000 000
0 1000 2000 3000 4000 km
Flat Polar Equal Area Projection

Arctic Circle

Tropic of Cancer

Equator

Tropic of Capricorn

Antarctic Circle

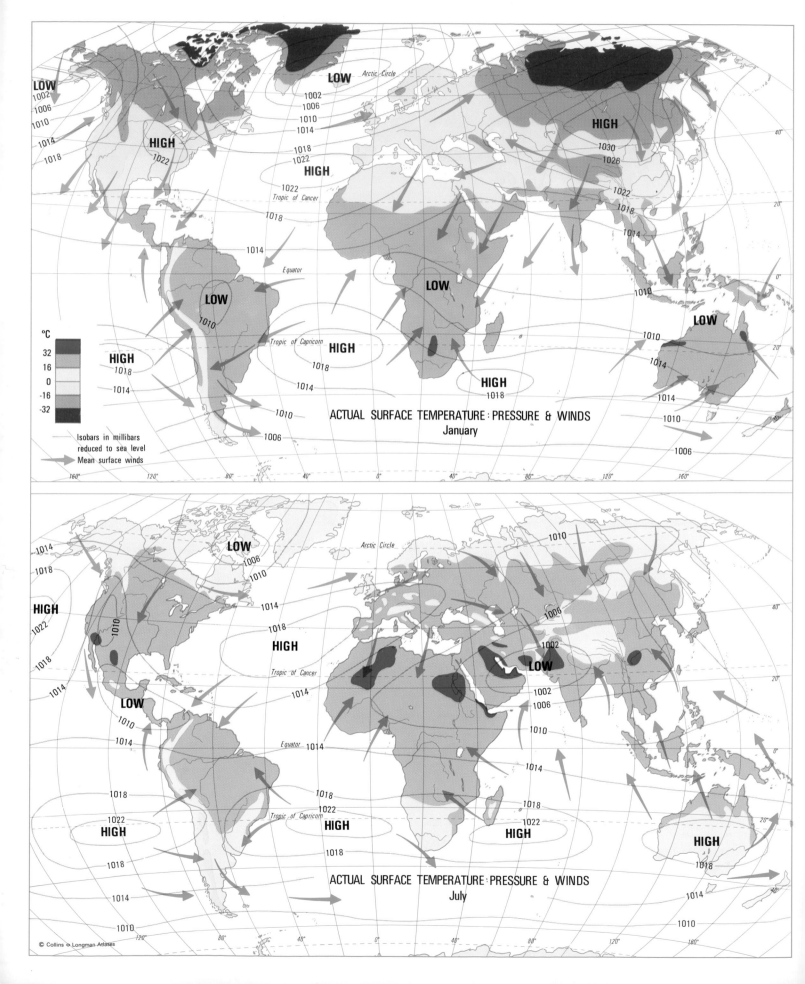

ACTUAL SURFACE TEMPERATURE : PRESSURE & WINDS
January

°C

32
16
0
-16
-32

Isobars in millibars
reduced to sea level
Mean surface winds

ACTUAL SURFACE TEMPERATURE : PRESSURE & WINDS
July

© Collins ◇ Longman Atlases

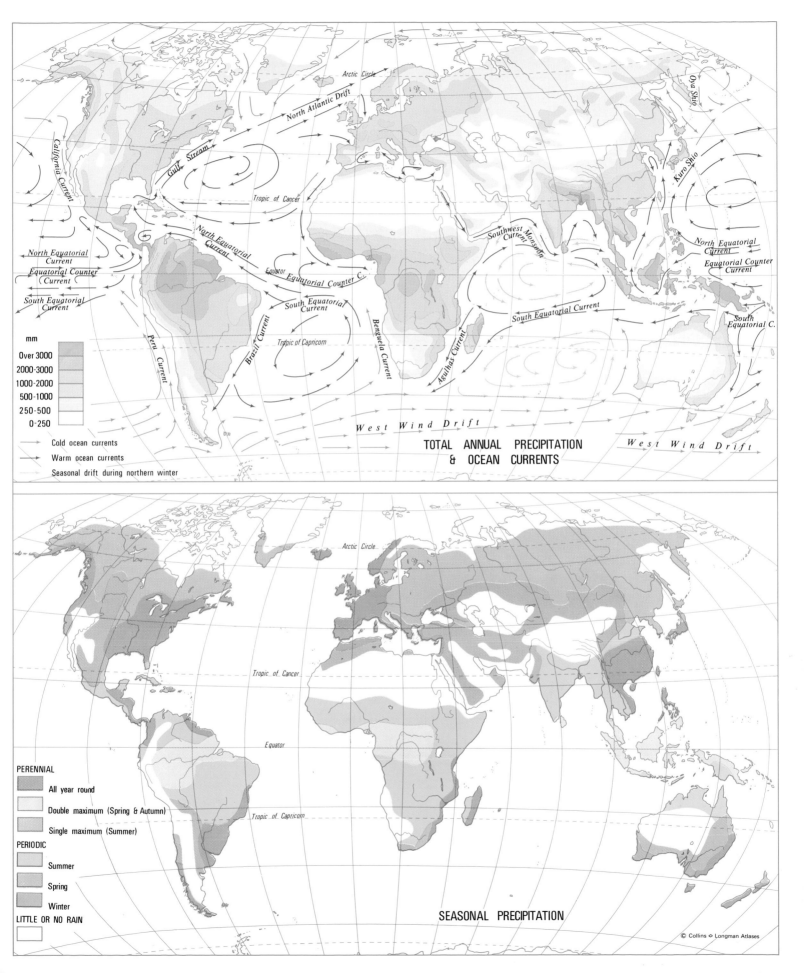

TOTAL ANNUAL PRECIPITATION & OCEAN CURRENTS

mm

- Over 3000
- 2000-3000
- 1000-2000
- 500-1000
- 250-500
- 0-250

→ Cold ocean currents
→ Warm ocean currents
→ Seasonal drift during northern winter

SEASONAL PRECIPITATION

PERENNIAL
- All year round
- Double maximum (Spring & Autumn)
- Single maximum (Summer)

PERIODIC
- Summer
- Spring
- Winter

LITTLE OR NO RAIN

© Collins ◇ Longman Atlases

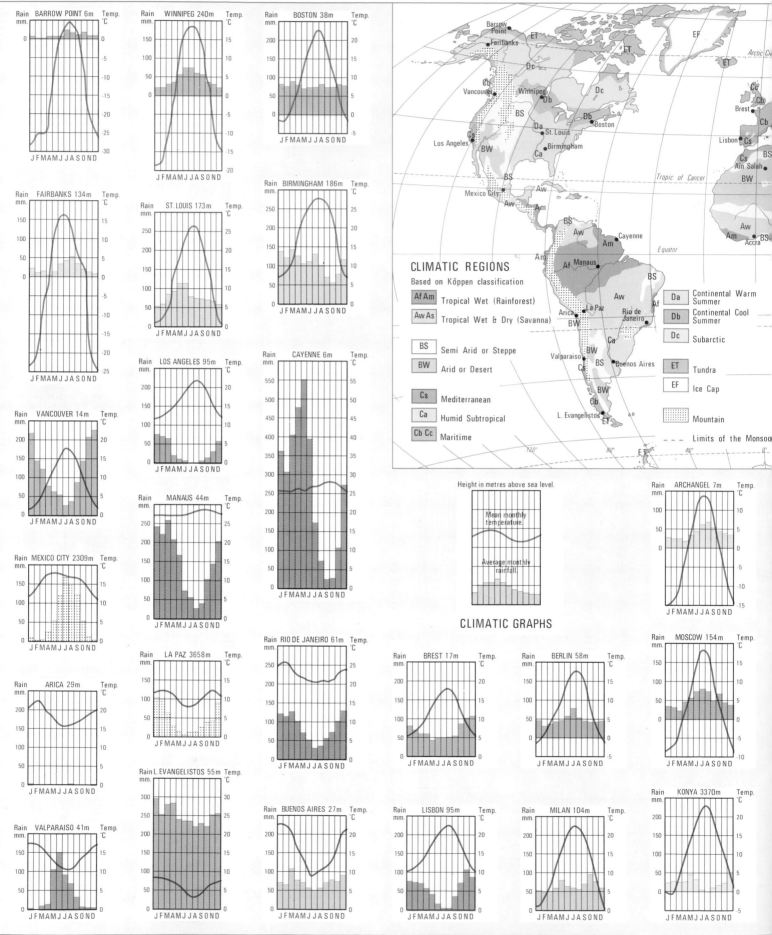

CLIMATIC REGIONS

Based on Köppen classification

Af Am — Tropical Wet (Rainforest)

Aw As — Tropical Wet & Dry (Savanna)

BS — Semi Arid or Steppe

BW — Arid or Desert

Cs — Mediterranean

Ca — Humid Subtropical

Cb Cc — Maritime

Da — Continental Warm Summer

Db — Continental Cool Summer

Dc — Subarctic

ET — Tundra

EF — Ice Cap

Mountain

Limits of the Monsoon

Height in metres above sea level.

Mean monthly temperature.

Average monthly rainfall.

CLIMATIC GRAPHS

BARROW POINT 6m
FAIRBANKS 134m
VANCOUVER 14m
MEXICO CITY 2309m
ARICA 29m
VALPARAISO 41m
WINNIPEG 240m
ST. LOUIS 173m
LOS ANGELES 95m
MANAUS 44m
LA PAZ 3658m
L. EVANGELISTOS 55m
BOSTON 38m
BIRMINGHAM 186m
CAYENNE 6m
RIO DE JANEIRO 61m
BUENOS AIRES 27m
BREST 17m
LISBON 95m
BERLIN 58m
MILAN 104m
ARCHANGEL 7m
MOSCOW 154m
KONYA 3370m

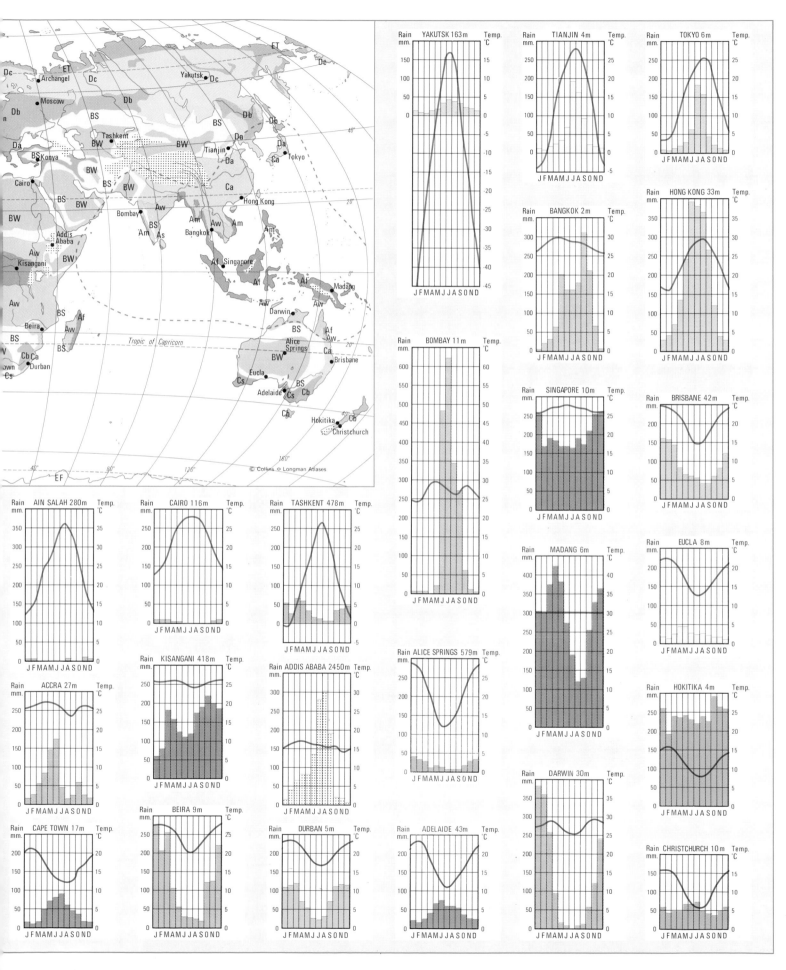

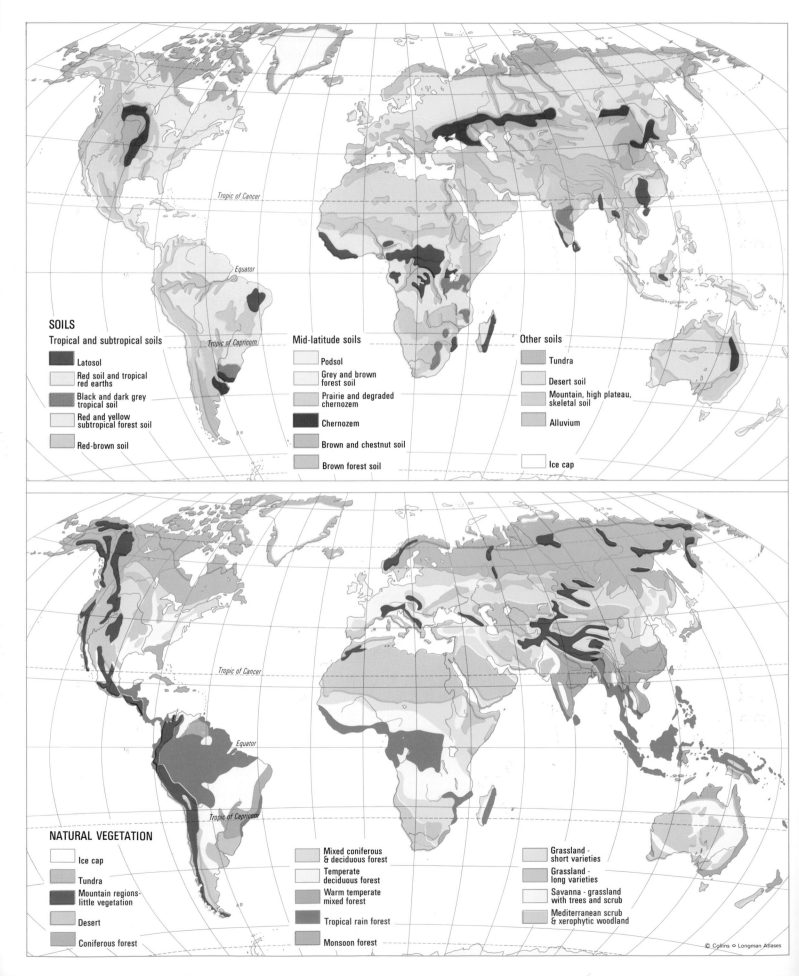

SOILS

Tropical and subtropical soils
- Latosol
- Red soil and tropical red earths
- Black and dark grey tropical soil
- Red and yellow subtropical forest soil
- Red-brown soil

Mid-latitude soils
- Podsol
- Grey and brown forest soil
- Prairie and degraded chernozem
- Chernozem
- Brown and chestnut soil
- Brown forest soil

Other soils
- Tundra
- Desert soil
- Mountain, high plateau, skeletal soil
- Alluvium
- Ice cap

NATURAL VEGETATION
- Ice cap
- Tundra
- Mountain regions-little vegetation
- Desert
- Coniferous forest
- Mixed coniferous & deciduous forest
- Temperate deciduous forest
- Warm temperate mixed forest
- Tropical rain forest
- Monsoon forest
- Grassland - short varieties
- Grassland - long varieties
- Savanna - grassland with trees and scrub
- Mediterranean scrub & xerophytic woodland

© Collins ○ Longman Atlases

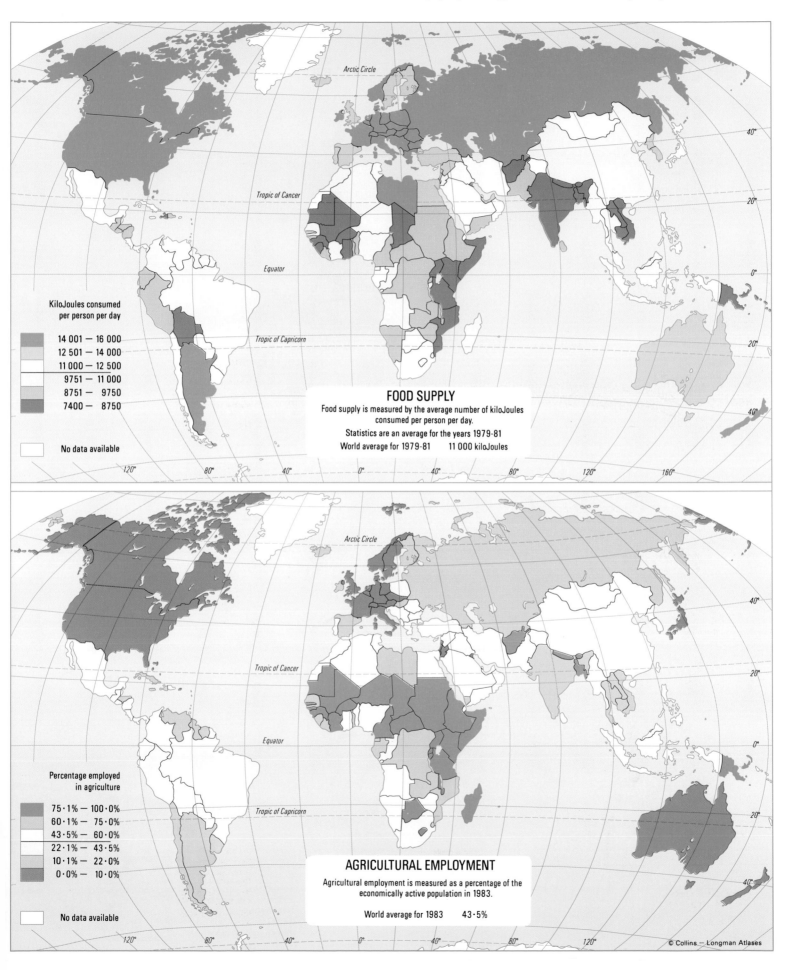

KiloJoules consumed
per person per day

14 001 — 16 000
12 501 — 14 000
11 000 — 12 500
9751 — 11 000
8751 — 9750
7400 — 8750

No data available

FOOD SUPPLY

Food supply is measured by the average number of kiloJoules
consumed per person per day.

Statistics are an average for the years 1979-81

World average for 1979-81   11 000 kiloJoules

Percentage employed
in agriculture

75·1% — 100·0%
60·1% — 75·0%
43·5% — 60·0%
22·1% — 43·5%
10·1% — 22·0%
0·0% — 10·0%

No data available

AGRICULTURAL EMPLOYMENT

Agricultural employment is measured as a percentage of the
economically active population in 1983.

World average for 1983   43·5%

© Collins — Longman Atlases

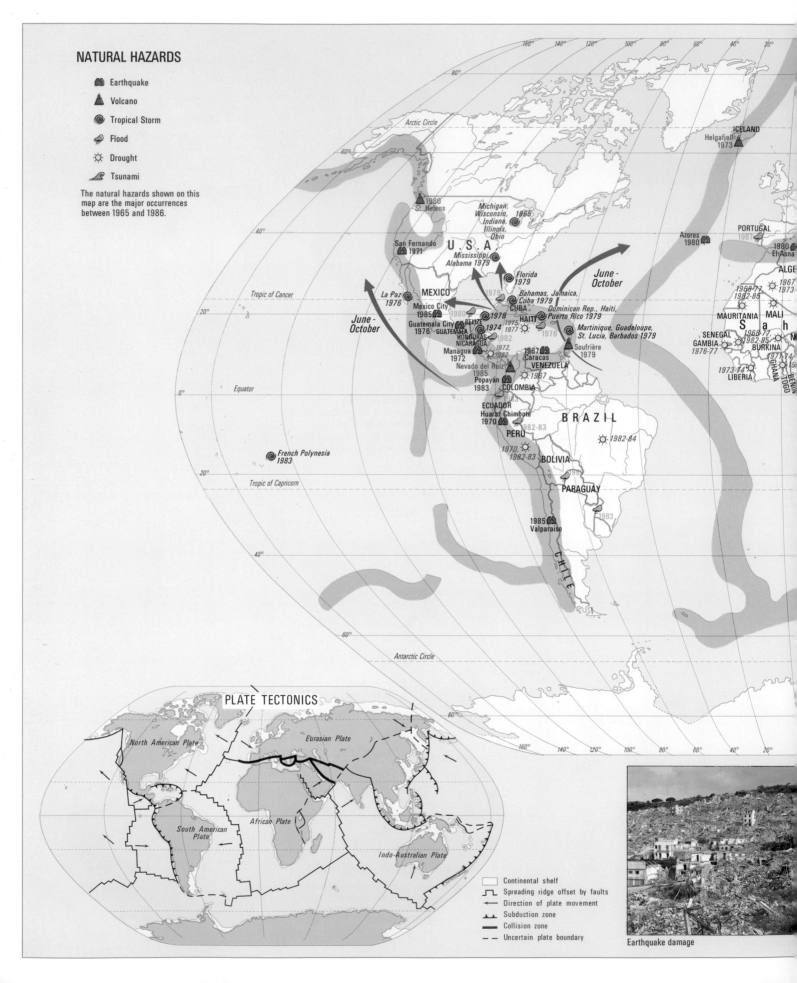

Earthquake damage

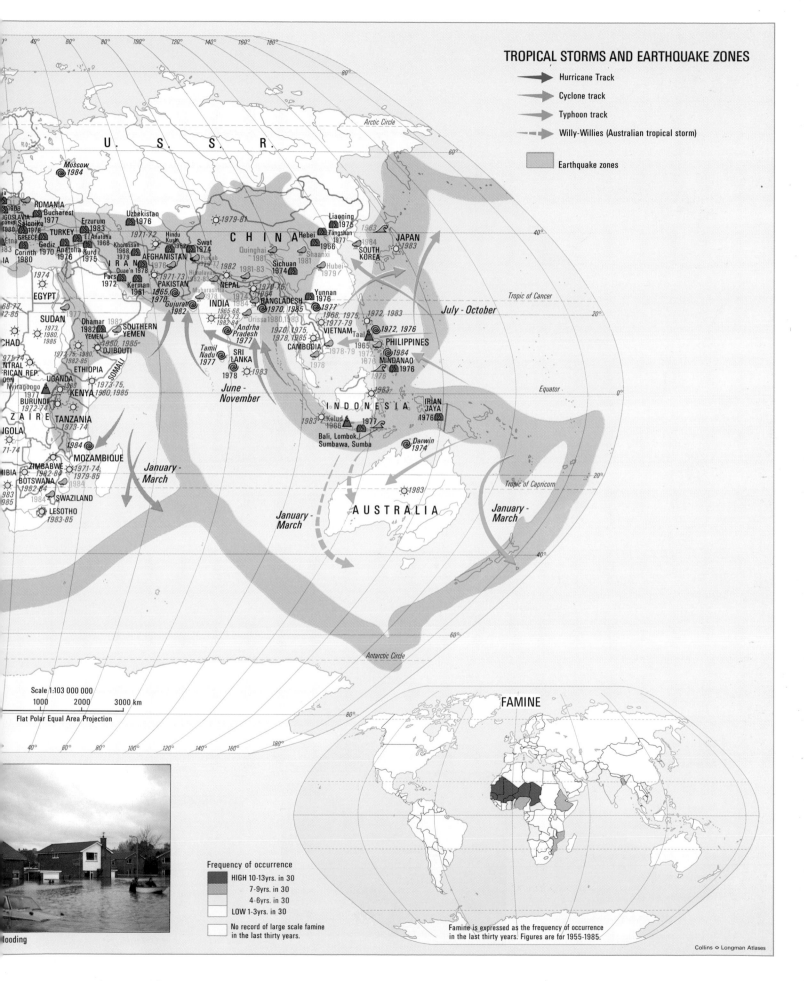

TROPICAL STORMS AND EARTHQUAKE ZONES

→ Hurricane Track
→ Cyclone track
→ Typhoon track
⇢ Willy-Willies (Australian tropical storm)

☐ Earthquake zones

Arctic Circle

U. S. S. R.

Moscow 1984

ROMANIA
Bucharest 1977
1968
IGOSLAVIA
pama Salonika
1980
GREECE 1978
Corinth 1970
IA 1980
1974
Etna 1983

Uzbekistan 1976

TURKEY
Erzurum 1983
El Anatolia
Gediz Anatolia 1966
1970 1976
Kurd 1975
IRAN
Quae'n 1978
Fars 1972
Kerman 1981

Hindu Kush
Khorassan 1968, 1979
1976
Swat 1974
Punjab 1982
Maharashtra 1978
AFGHANISTAN
1976

1979-81

CHINA

Liaoning 1975
Hebei 1966 Tangshan 1977
Quinghai 1981
Shaanxi 1981
Sichuan 1974
Hubei 1979

1963
1984 1983 JAPAN
SOUTH KOREA

Tropic of Cancer

July - October

60°
40°
20°

EGYPT
68-77
72-85
SUDAN
1973, 1980, 1985
CHAD
Dhamar 1982
YEMEN
SOUTHERN YEMEN
1980, 1985
DJIBOUTI
1973-75 1980
1982-85
ETHIOPIA
NTRAL RICAN REP. OON
UGANDA 1988
Nyiragongo 1977
ZAIRE
BURUNDI 1972-74
1973-74
IGOLA
71-74

PAKISTAN
1965 1970
Gujurat 1982

NEPAL
1982

Himalaya 82-83
Orissa 1980, 1983

INDIA
1965-68
1972-75
1982-84

Andhra Pradesh 1977
Tamil Nadu 1977
SRI LANKA
1978

BANGLADESH
1970, 1985
1978, 1985
1970, 1975,
1977-79
CAMBODIA 1978
1965 1979-79
1978

Yunnan 1976
1977
1968, 1975,
1972, 1983

VIETNAM
Taal
1972, 1976

PHILIPPINES
1965 1972
1876
MINDANAO 1984
1976
1976

Equator

June - November

1983

I N D O N E S I A
1983
Kelud 1966 1977
Bali, Lombok, Sumbawa, Sumba

IRIAN JAYA 1976

1983

Darwin 1974

TANZANIA 1973-74

1984
MOZAMBIQUE 1971-74,
1979-85
ZIMBABWE 1982-84
IBIA
BOTSWANA 1982-84
1984
983 1985
1984 SWAZILAND
LESOTHO 1983-85

January - March

January - March

AUSTRALIA

1983

Tropic of Capricorn

January - March

20°

40°

January - March

60°
Antarctic Circle

Scale 1:103 000 000
1000 2000 3000 km
Flat Polar Equal Area Projection

40° 60° 80° 100° 120° 140° 160° 180°

FAMINE

80°

Frequency of occurrence
- ☐ HIGH 10-13yrs. in 30
- ☐ 7-9yrs. in 30
- ☐ 4-6yrs. in 30
- ☐ LOW 1-3yrs. in 30
- ☐ No record of large scale famine in the last thirty years.

Famine is expressed as the frequency of occurrence in the last thirty years. Figures are for 1955-1985.

Flooding

Collins ◇ Longman Atlases

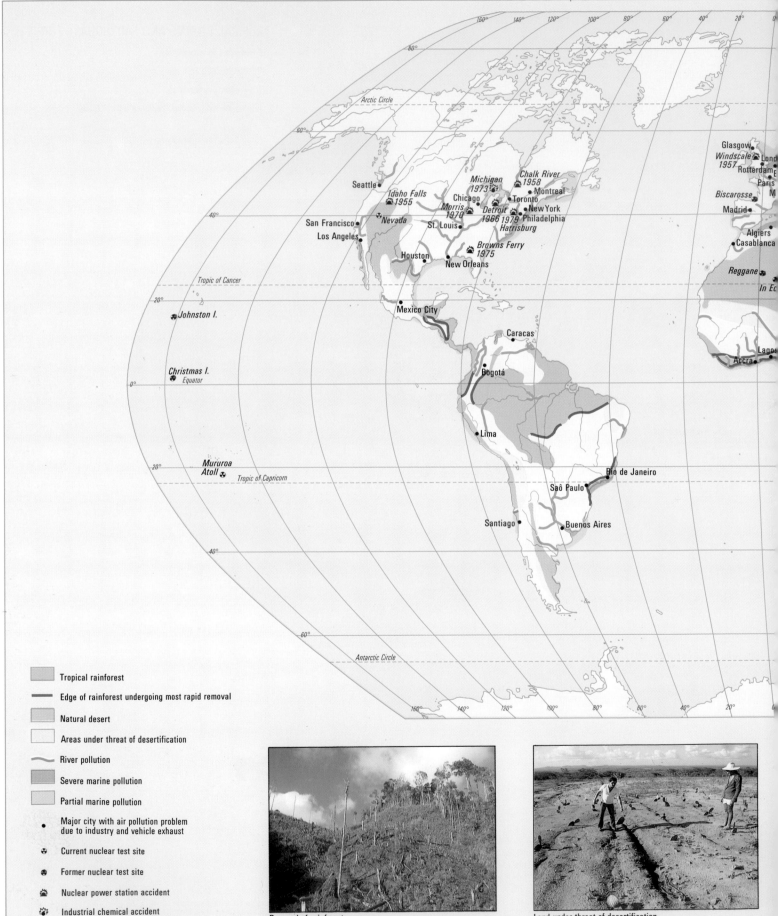

Arctic Circle

80°
60°
40°
20°
Tropic of Cancer
20°
Equator 0°
20°
Tropic of Capricorn
40°
60°
Antarctic Circle

Seattle
Idaho Falls 1955
San Francisco
Los Angeles
Nevada
Houston
New Orleans
Mexico City
Johnston I.
Christmas I.
Mururoa Atoll
Santiago

Michigan 1973
Chicago
Morris 1970
St. Louis
Browns Ferry 1975
Chalk River 1958
Montreal
Toronto
Detroit 1966 1979
Harrisburg
New York
Philadelphia

Caracas
Bogotá
Lima
Buenos Aires
Saô Paulo
Rio de Janeiro

Glasgow
Windscale 1957
Rotterdam
London
Paris
Biscarosse
Madrid
Algiers
Casablanca
Reggane
In Ec
Lagos
Accra

Legend:

- Tropical rainforest
- Edge of rainforest undergoing most rapid removal
- Natural desert
- Areas under threat of desertification
- River pollution
- Severe marine pollution
- Partial marine pollution
- Major city with air pollution problem due to industry and vehicle exhaust
- Current nuclear test site
- Former nuclear test site
- Nuclear power station accident
- Industrial chemical accident

Removal of rainforest

Land under threat of desertification

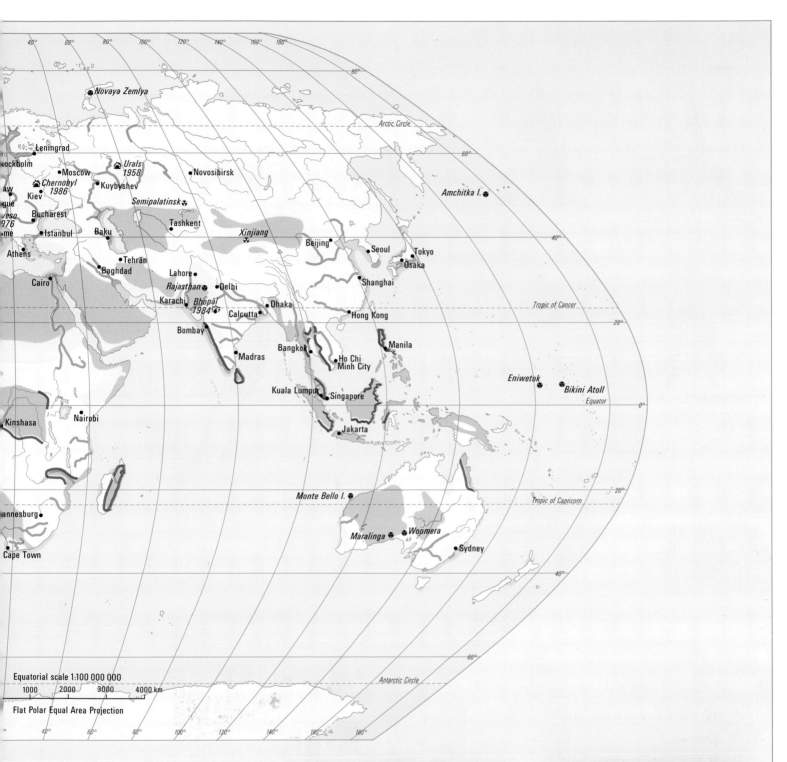

Novaya Zemlya

Arctic Circle

Leningrad
ockholm
Moscow
Urals 1958
Novosibirsk
Amchitka I.
Chernobyl 1986
Kuybyshev
aw
Kiev
Semipalatinsk
gue
Bucharest
eso 976
me
Istanbul
Baku
Tashkent
Xinjiang
Beijing
Seoul
Tokyo
Athens
Osaka
Tehrān
Shanghai
Cairo
Baghdad
Lahore
Rajasthan
Delhi
Karachi
Bhopāl 1984
Calcutta
Dhaka
Hong Kong
Tropic of Cancer
Bombay
Madras
Bangkok
Manila
Ho Chi Minh City
Eniwetok
Bikini Atoll
Kuala Lumpur
Singapore
Equator
Kinshasa
Nairobi
Jakarta
Monte Bello I.
Tropic of Capricorn
annesburg
Maralinga
Woomera
Sydney
Cape Town

Equatorial scale 1:100 000 000

1000   2000   3000   4000 km

Flat Polar Equal Area Projection

Antarctic Circle

Industrial air pollution

Effect of oil pollution on marine life

Air pollution from vehicle exhaust

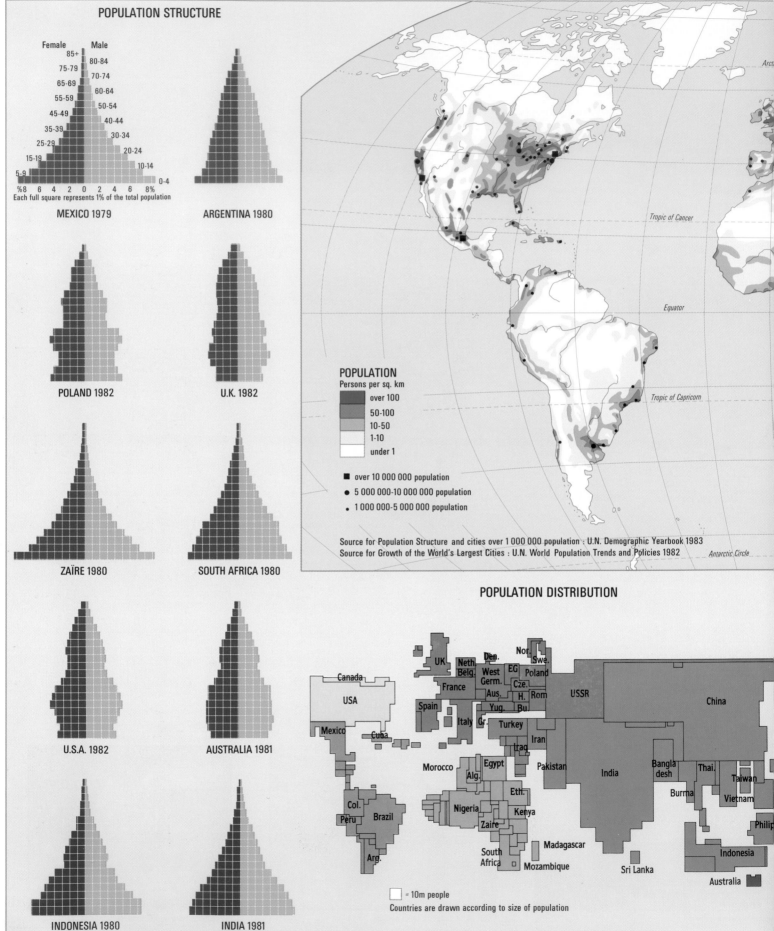

POPULATION STRUCTURE

Female   Male
85+
75-79   80-84
65-69   70-74
55-59   60-64
45-49   50-54
35-39   40-44
25-29   30-34
15-19   20-24
5-9   10-14
0-4
%8 6 4 2 0 2 4 6 8%
Each full square represents 1% of the total population

MEXICO 1979

ARGENTINA 1980

POLAND 1982

U.K. 1982

ZAÏRE 1980

SOUTH AFRICA 1980

U.S.A. 1982

AUSTRALIA 1981

INDONESIA 1980

INDIA 1981

POPULATION
Persons per sq. km
over 100
50-100
10-50
1-10
under 1

■ over 10 000 000 population
● 5 000 000-10 000 000 population
• 1 000 000-5 000 000 population

Source for Population Structure and cities over 1 000 000 population : U.N. Demographic Yearbook 1983
Source for Growth of the World's Largest Cities : U.N. World Population Trends and Policies 1982

Arctic Circle
Tropic of Cancer
Equator
Tropic of Capricorn
Antarctic Circle

POPULATION DISTRIBUTION

Canada
USA
Mexico
Cuba
UK
Neth.
Den.
Nor.
Belg.
Swe.
EG
Poland
France
West Germ.
Cze.
USSR
China
Spain
Aus.
H.
Rom
Italy
Gr.
Yug.
Bu.
Turkey
Iran
Morocco
Alg.
Egypt
Iraq
Pakistan
India
Bangla desh
Thai.
Taiwan
Burma
Vietnam
Nigeria
Eth.
Kenya
Col.
Peru
Brazil
Zaire
Philip
South Africa
Madagascar
Indonesia
Arg.
Mozambique
Sri Lanka
Australia

☐ = 10m people
Countries are drawn according to size of population

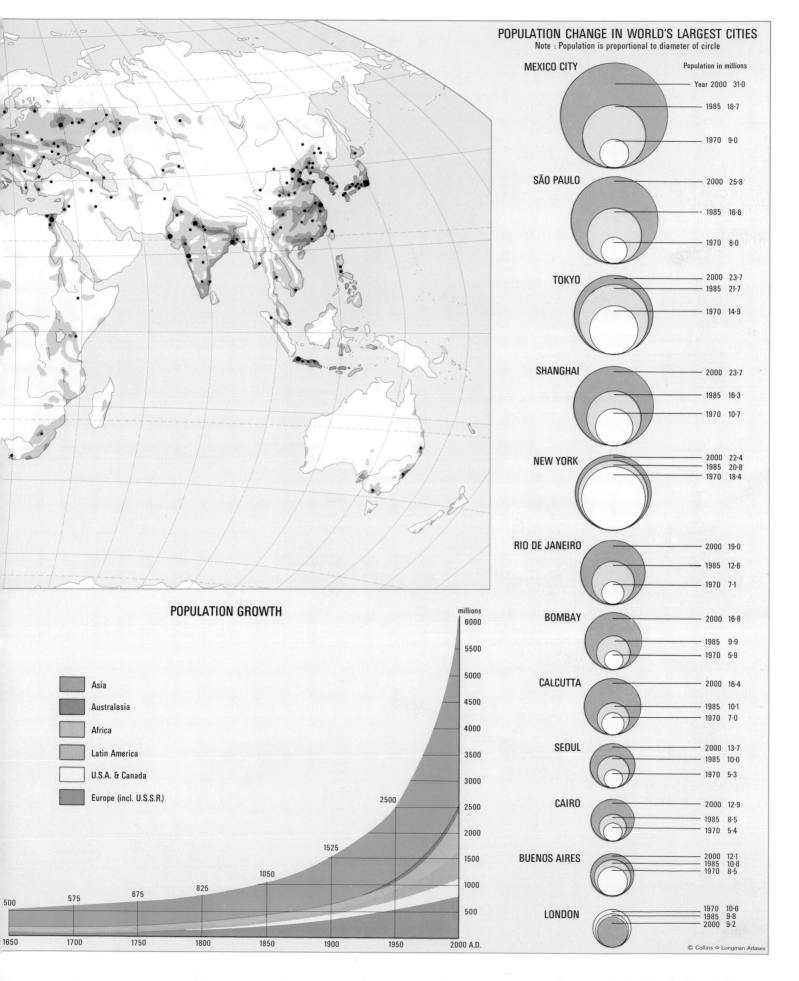

POPULATION CHANGE IN WORLD'S LARGEST CITIES
Note : Population is proportional to diameter of circle

MEXICO CITY
	Population in millions
Year 2000	31·0
1985	18·7
1970	9·0

SÃO PAULO
2000	25·8
1985	16·6
1970	8·0

TOKYO
2000	23·7
1985	21·7
1970	14·9

SHANGHAI
2000	23·7
1985	16·3
1970	10·7

NEW YORK
2000	22·4
1985	20·8
1970	18·4

RIO DE JANEIRO
2000	19·0
1985	12·6
1970	7·1

BOMBAY
2000	16·8
1985	9·9
1970	5·9

CALCUTTA
2000	16·4
1985	10·1
1970	7·0

SEOUL
2000	13·7
1985	10·0
1970	5·3

CAIRO
2000	12·9
1985	8·5
1970	5·4

BUENOS AIRES
2000	12·1
1985	10·8
1970	8·5

LONDON
1970	10·6
1985	9·8
2000	9·2

© Collins ◇ Longman Atlases

POPULATION GROWTH

Asia	
Australasia	
Africa	
Latin America	
U.S.A. & Canada	
Europe (incl. U.S.S.R.)	

millions
6000
5500
5000
4500
4000
3500
3000
2500
2000
1500
1000
500

2500
1525
1050
825
675
575
500

1650 1700 1750 1800 1850 1900 1950 2000 A.D.

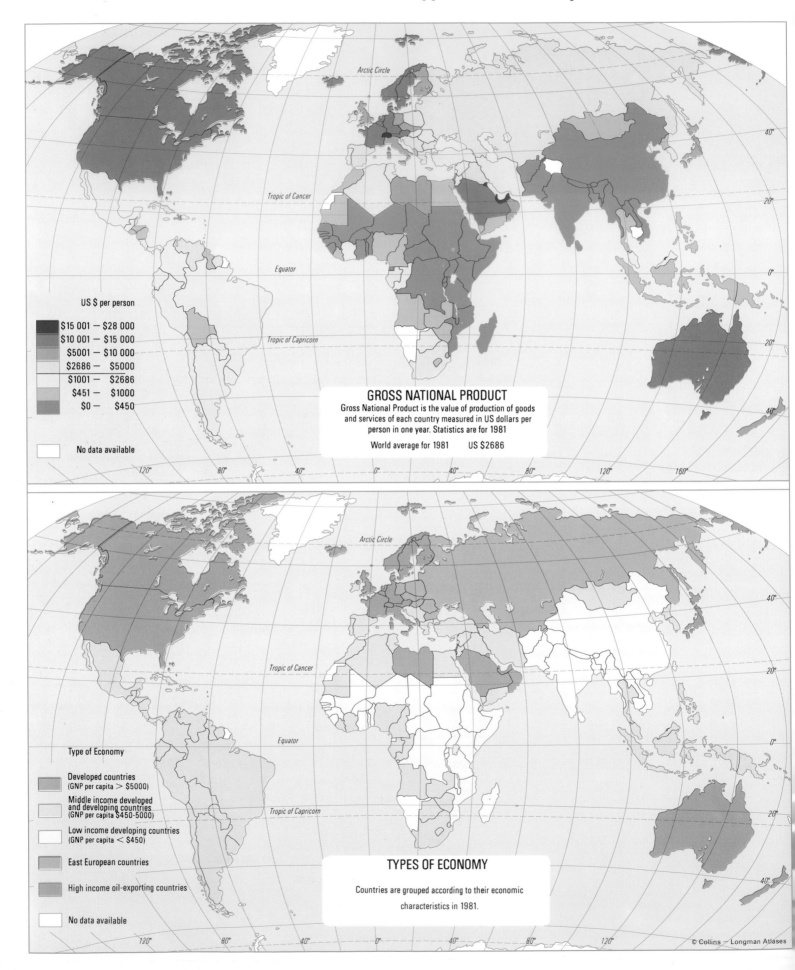

US $ per person

- $15 001 — $28 000
- $10 001 — $15 000
- $5001 — $10 000
- $2686 — $5000
- $1001 — $2686
- $451 — $1000
- $0 — $450

No data available

GROSS NATIONAL PRODUCT

Gross National Product is the value of production of goods and services of each country measured in US dollars per person in one year. Statistics are for 1981

World average for 1981   US $2686

Type of Economy

- Developed countries
  (GNP per capita > $5000)
- Middle income developed
  and developing countries
  (GNP per capita $450-5000)
- Low income developing countries
  (GNP per capita < $450)
- East European countries
- High income oil-exporting countries
- No data available

TYPES OF ECONOMY

Countries are grouped according to their economic characteristics in 1981.

© Collins – Longman Atlases

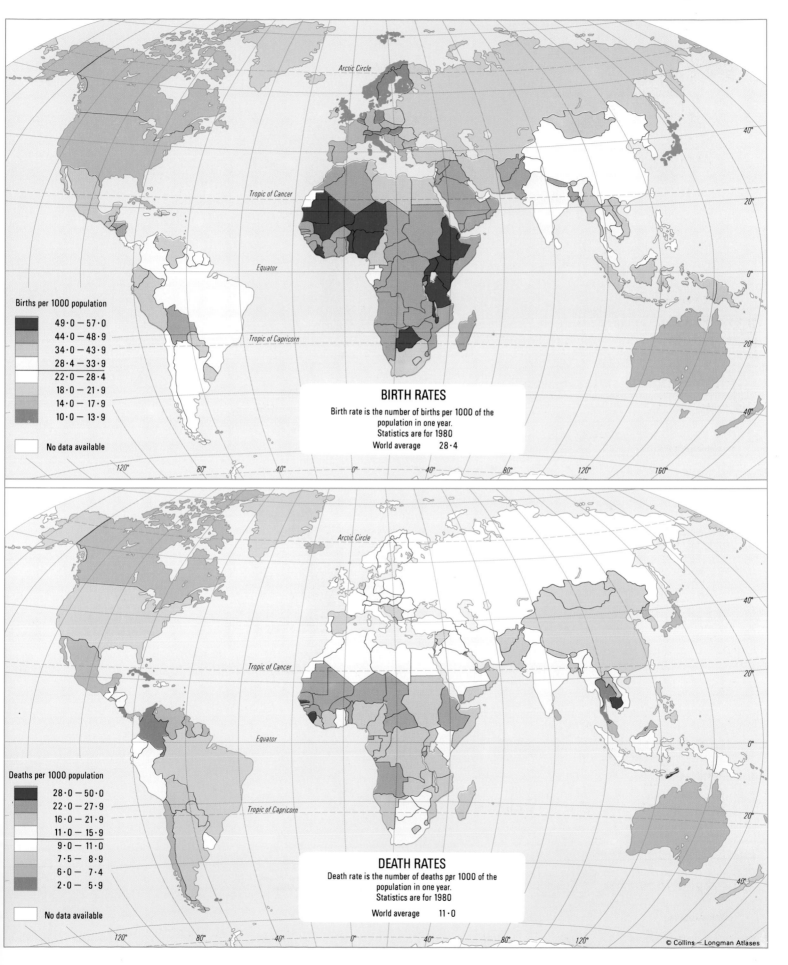

Births per 1000 population

49·0 — 57·0
44·0 — 48·9
34·0 — 43·9
28·4 — 33·9
22·0 — 28·4
18·0 — 21·9
14·0 — 17·9
10·0 — 13·9

No data available

BIRTH RATES

Birth rate is the number of births per 1000 of the
population in one year.
Statistics are for 1980
World average   28·4

Deaths per 1000 population

28·0 — 50·0
22·0 — 27·9
16·0 — 21·9
11·0 — 15·9
9·0 — 11·0
7·5 — 8·9
6·0 — 7·4
2·0 — 5·9

No data available

DEATH RATES

Death rate is the number of deaths per 1000 of the
population in one year.
Statistics are for 1980

World average   11·0

© Collins — Longman Atlases

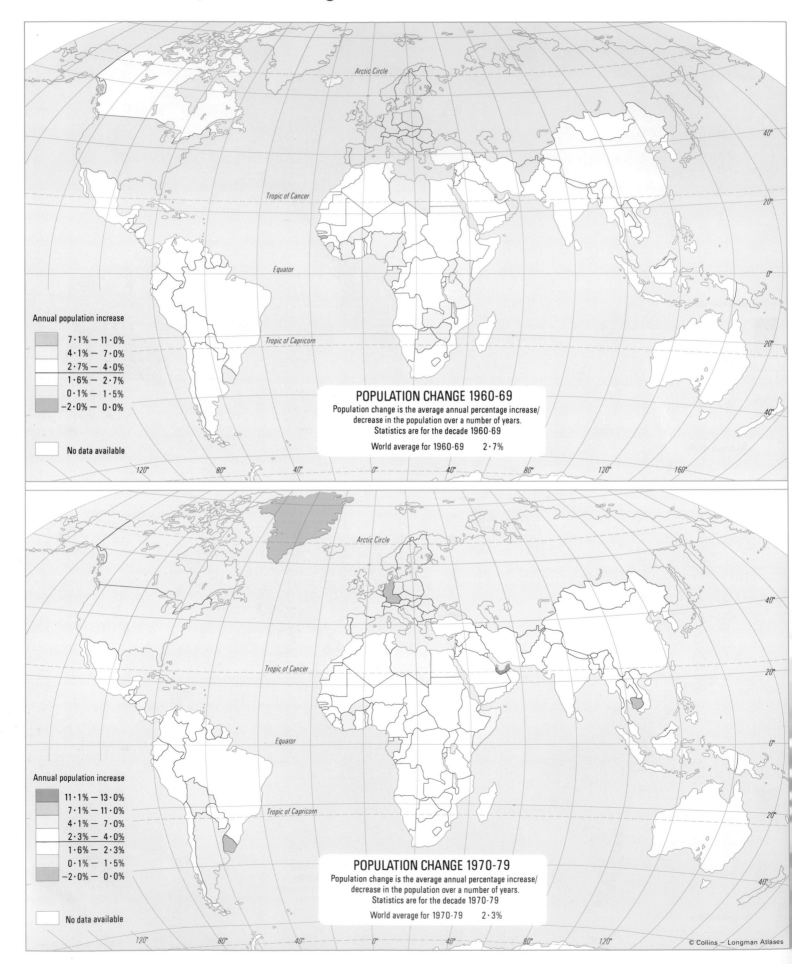

Annual population increase

7·1% — 11·0%
4·1% — 7·0%
2·7% — 4·0%
1·6% — 2·7%
0·1% — 1·5%
-2·0% — 0·0%

No data available

POPULATION CHANGE 1960-69

Population change is the average annual percentage increase/
decrease in the population over a number of years.
Statistics are for the decade 1960-69

World average for 1960-69   2·7%

Annual population increase

11·1% — 13·0%
7·1% — 11·0%
4·1% — 7·0%
2·3% — 4·0%
1·6% — 2·3%
0·1% — 1·5%
-2·0% — 0·0%

No data available

POPULATION CHANGE 1970-79

Population change is the average annual percentage increase/
decrease in the population over a number of years.
Statistics are for the decade 1970-79

World average for 1970-79   2·3%

© Collins – Longman Atlases

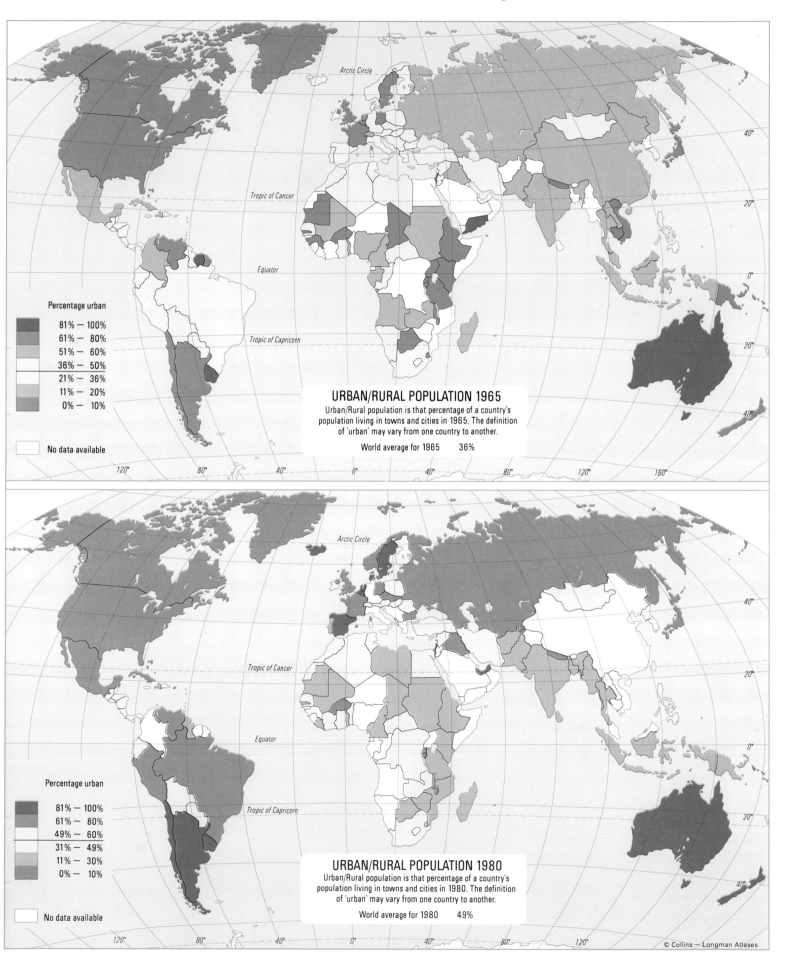

Percentage urban

81% — 100%
61% — 80%
51% — 60%
36% — 50%
21% — 36%
11% — 20%
0% — 10%

No data available

URBAN/RURAL POPULATION 1965
Urban/Rural population is that percentage of a country's
population living in towns and cities in 1965. The definition
of 'urban' may vary from one country to another.

World average for 1965   36%

Percentage urban

81% — 100%
61% — 80%
49% — 60%
31% — 49%
11% — 30%
0% — 10%

No data available

URBAN/RURAL POPULATION 1980
Urban/Rural population is that percentage of a country's
population living in towns and cities in 1980. The definition
of 'urban' may vary from one country to another.

World average for 1980   49%

© Collins – Longman Atlases

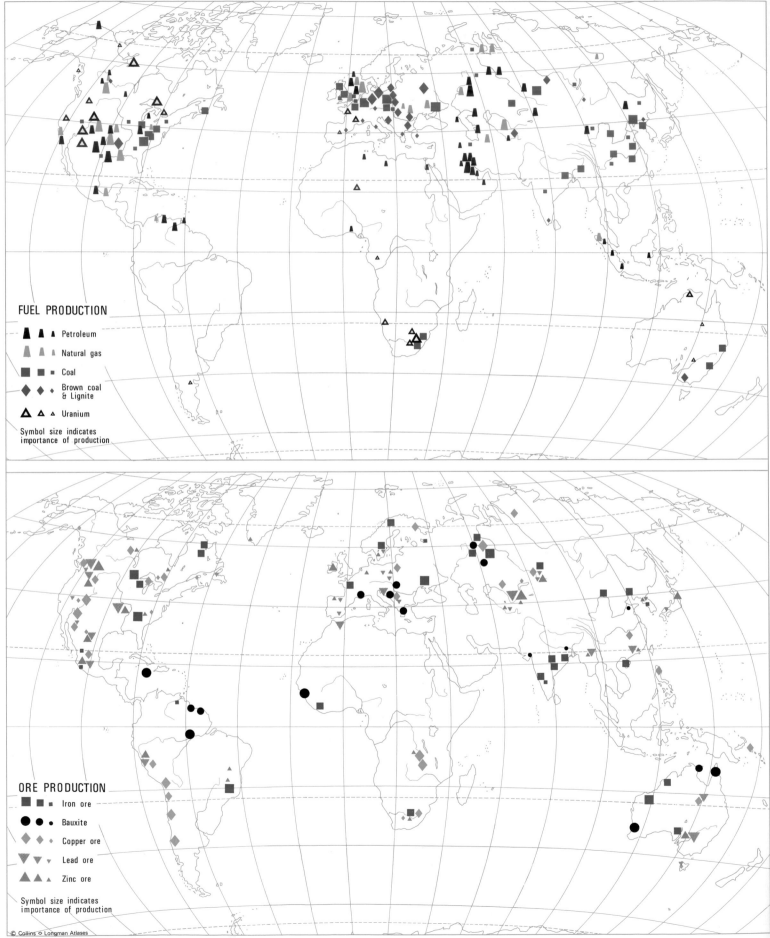

FUEL PRODUCTION

- ▲ ▲ ▴ Petroleum
- ▲ ▲ ▴ Natural gas
- ■ ■ ▪ Coal
- ◆ ◆ ◆ Brown coal & Lignite
- △ △ ▵ Uranium

Symbol size indicates importance of production

ORE PRODUCTION

- ■ ■ ▪ Iron ore
- ● ● • Bauxite
- ◆ ◆ ◆ Copper ore
- ▼ ▼ ▾ Lead ore
- ▲ ▲ ▴ Zinc ore

Symbol size indicates importance of production

© Collins ○ Longman Atlases

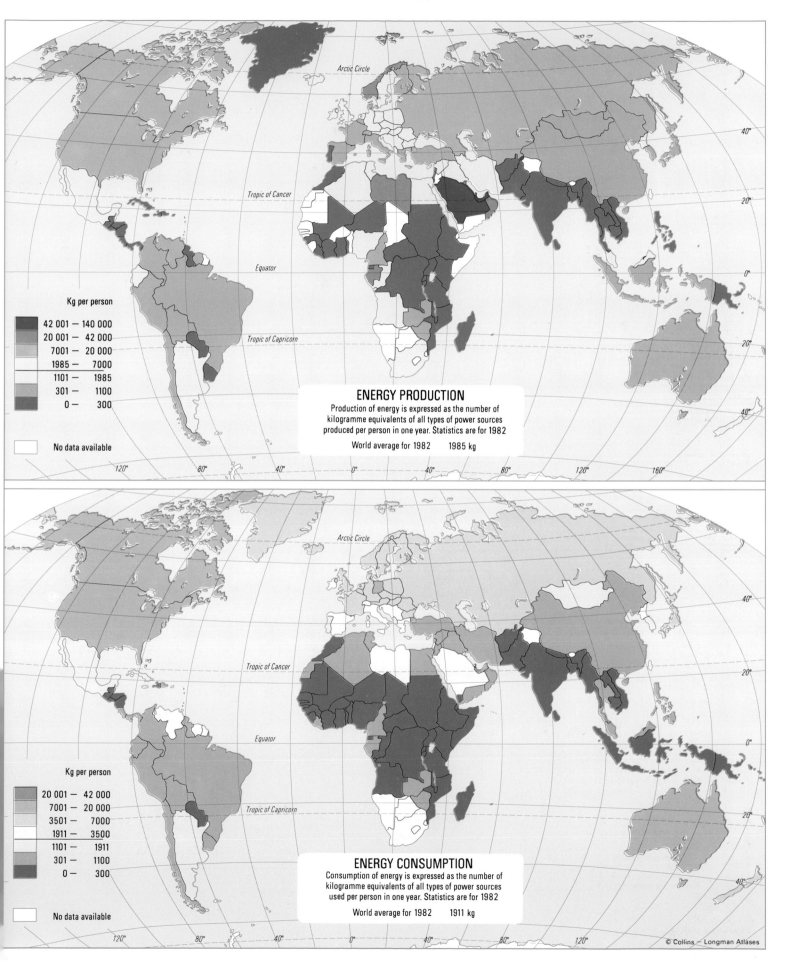

Kg per person

	42 001 — 140 000
	20 001 — 42 000
	7001 — 20 000
	1985 — 7000
	1101 — 1985
	301 — 1100
	0 — 300

No data available

ENERGY PRODUCTION

Production of energy is expressed as the number of kilogramme equivalents of all types of power sources produced per person in one year. Statistics are for 1982

World average for 1982   1985 kg

Kg per person

	20 001 — 42 000
	7001 — 20 000
	3501 — 7000
	1911 — 3500
	1101 — 1911
	301 — 1100
	0 — 300

No data available

ENERGY CONSUMPTION

Consumption of energy is expressed as the number of kilogramme equivalents of all types of power sources used per person in one year. Statistics are for 1982

World average for 1982   1911 kg

© Collins – Longman Atlases

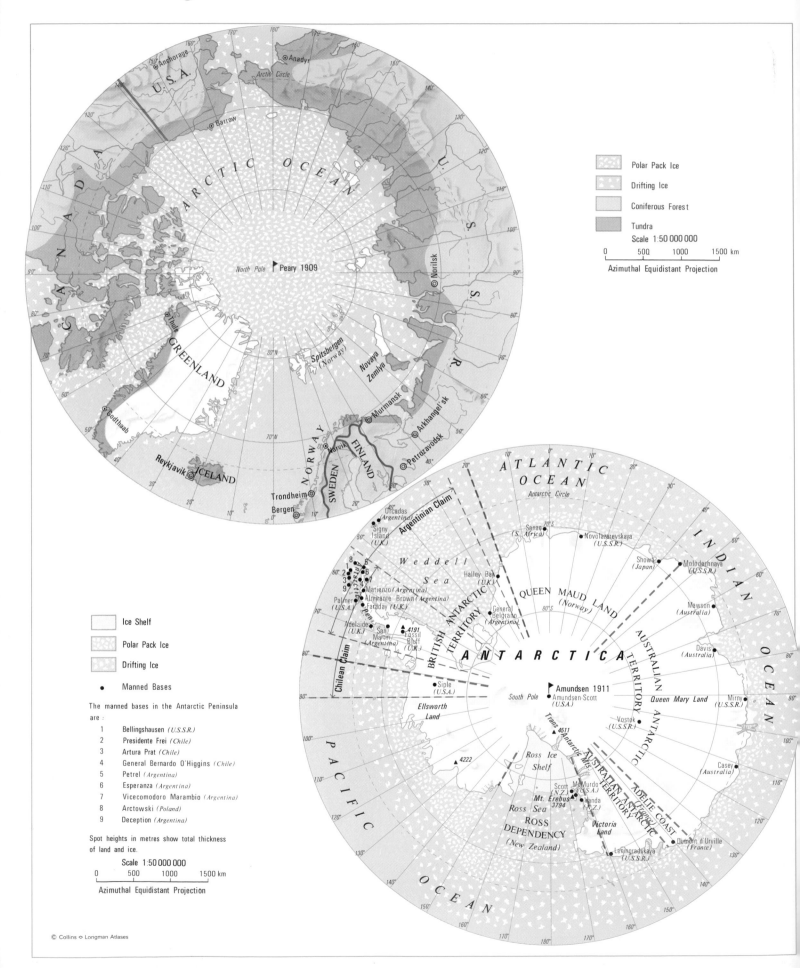

Legend (upper)

- Polar Pack Ice
- Drifting Ice
- Coniferous Forest
- Tundra

Scale 1:50 000 000

0 500 1000 1500 km

Azimuthal Equidistant Projection

Legend (lower)

- Ice Shelf
- Polar Pack Ice
- Drifting Ice
- • Manned Bases

The manned bases in the Antarctic Peninsula are :

1. Bellingshausen (U.S.S.R.)
2. Presidente Frei (Chile)
3. Artura Prat (Chile)
4. General Bernardo O'Higgins (Chile)
5. Petrel (Argentina)
6. Esperanza (Argentina)
7. Vicecomodoro Marambio (Argentina)
8. Arctowski (Poland)
9. Deception (Argentina)

Spot heights in metres show total thickness of land and ice.

Scale 1:50 000 000

0 500 1000 1500 km

Azimuthal Equidistant Projection

country	population	area in sq km	population density	exports	imports
EUROPE					
ALBANIA	2 841 000	28 748	99	non-ferrous metal ores	iron and steel
ANDORRA	34 000	453	75		food, instruments
AUSTRIA	7 549 000	83 849	90	machinery (non-electric)	machinery (non-electric), chemicals
BELGIUM	9 856 000	30 513	323	chemicals, motor vehicles, food	crude oil, food, motor vehicles
BULGARIA	8 939 000	110 912	81	transport equipment, machinery	transport equipment, machinery, crude oil
CZECHOSLOVAKIA	15 415 000	127 869	121	machinery (non-electric)	machinery (non-electric), crude oil and products
DENMARK	5 114 000	43 069	119	machinery (non-electric), food	machinery (non-electric), chemicals, crude oil and products
EAST GERMANY	16 699 000	108 178	154	machinery (non-electric)	crude oil and products and metals, machinery and transport equipment, food and other raw materials
FINLAND	4 863 000	337 032	14	paper, machinery	crude oil, machinery (non-electric)
FRANCE	58 652 000	547 026	100	food, chemicals, machinery (non-electric), motor vehicles	crude oil
GREECE	9 840 000	131 944	75	fruit and vegetables, textile yarns and fabrics	crude oil, food, machinery (non-electric), chemicals
HUNGARY	10 690 000	93 030	115	food, machinery (non-electric), checmicals, electrical machinery	machinery, chemicals, crude oil and products
ICELAND	237 000	103 000	2	fish, aluminium	petroleum products, machinery (non-electric)
IRELAND, REP. OF	3 508 000	70 283	50	chemicals, machinery (non-electric)	machinery, transport equipment, petroleum, chemicals
ITALY	56 559 000	301 225	188	machinery (non-electric)	crude oil, food
LIECHTENSTEIN	26 000	157	166	machinery and transport equipment, metal manufactures	
LUXEMBOURG	365 000	2 586	141	chemicals, steel and other metals	machinery, crude oil and products
MALTA	377 000	316	1 193	clothing, machinery	food, petroleum products, textile yarns and fabrics, machinery (non-electric)
MONACO	27 000	1.5	18 000		
NETHERLANDS	14 362 000	40 844	352	chemicals, petroleum products, food	crude oil, food
NORWAY	4 129 000	324 219	13	natural gas, crude oil	machinery (non-electric)
POLAND	36 571 000	312 677	117	machinery	machinery, food, crude oil
PORTUGAL	10 099 000	92 082	110	clothing, textile yarns and fabrics	petroleum, machinery, chemicals, transport equipment, cereals
ROMANIA	22 553 000	237 500	95	machinery and transport equipment, petroleum products, food, chemicals	machinery (non-electric)
SAN MARINO	22 000	61	361		
SPAIN	38 228 000	504 782	76	machinery (non-electric)	crude oil
SWEDEN	8 329 000	449 964	19	machinery, vehicles, paper, timber products, iron and steel	machinery, petroleum, chemical products
SWITZERLAND	6 505 000	41 288	158	machinery (non-electric), motor vehicles, paper	machinery (non-electric), petroleum products, crude oil
U.S.S.R.	272 500 000	22 402 200	12	crude oil and products	machinery
UNITED KINGDOM	55 610 000	244 046	228	machinery (non-electric), chemicals, crude oil	machinery (non-electric), food
WEST GERMANY	61 421 000	248 577	247	machinery (non-electric), vehicles, chemicals	crude oil, food
YUGOSLAVIA	22 855 000	255 804	89	machinery (non-electric), chemicals	chemicals, machinery (non-electric), iron and steel, petroleum and products, crude oil
ASIA					
AFGHANISTAN	17 222 000	647 497	27	natural gas, fruit and nuts, carpets	petroleum products, motor vehicles, textile yarns and fabrics
BAHRAIN	397 000	622	638	petroleum products, crude oil	crude oil
BANGLADESH	94 651 000	143 998	657	jute, jute products, leather	machinery, chemicals, crude oil and products
BHUTAN	1 360 000	47 000	29		food and raw materials, consumer manufactures
BRUNEI	260 000	5 765	45	natural gas, crude oil	machinery (non-electric), food, iron and steel
BURMA	37 553 000	676 552	55	rice, teak	machinery, textile yarns and fabrics, chemicals
CHINA	1 031 890 000	9 596 961	108	crude oil and products, food, textile yarns and fabrics, clothing	machinery, cereals, chemicals, iron and steel
CYPRUS	655 000	9 251	71	fruit and vegetables, clothing	machinery, crude oil, food
HONG KONG	5 313 000	1 045	5 084	clothing, electrical machinery	foodstuffs, textile yarns and fabrics, electrical machinery
INDIA	732 256 000	3 287 590	223	textile yarns and fabrics, foodstuffs	machinery, crude oil, petroleum products, chemicals
INDONESIA	159 434 000	1 904 569	84	crude oil, natural gas	chemicals, machinery (non-electric), crude oil and products, food

country	population	area in sq km	population density	exports	imports

ASIA *continued*

country	population	area in sq km	population density	exports	imports
IRAN	41 635 000	1 648 000	25	crude oil	foodstuffs, chemicals, motor vehicles, iron and steel, machinery (non-electric)
IRAQ	14 654 000	434 924	34	petroleum, dates, skins	machinery, vehicles, sugar, medicines
ISRAEL	4 097 000	20 770	197	crude oil	machinery (non-electric), electrical machinery, food
JAPAN	119 259 000	372 313	316	iron and steel, motor vehicles, electrical machinery, machinery (non-electric)	foodstuffs, crude oil
JORDAN	3 247 000	97 740	33	phosphates, chemicals	foodstuffs, crude oil
KAMPUCHEA (CAMBODIA)	6 888 000	181 035	38	rubber	machinery, chemicals, motor vehicles, iron and steel
KUWAIT	1 672 000	17 818	94	petroleum products, crude oil	foodstuffs, motor vehicles, electrical machinery
LAOS	4 209 000	236 800	18	timber, electricity, coffee	rice, petroleum products, electrical machinery
LEBANON	2 635 000	10 400	253	vegetables and fruit, financial paper and stamps, chemicals	machinery, food, gold
MALAYSIA	14 863 000	329 749	45	timber, crude oil, transistors, tubes etc.	machinery, foodstuffs, crude oil and products
MALDIVES	168 000	298	564	fresh fish, dried salt fish	foodstuffs
MONGOLIA	1 803 000	1 565 000	1	wool, meat, livestock	machinery
NEPAL	15 738 000	140 797	112	jute, goat and kid skins, fruit and vegetables, jute fabrics	manufactured goods, machinery and transport equipment, food, crude oil and products, chemicals
NORTH KOREA	19 185 000	120 538	159	metal and metal ores, raw materials (coal, cement, silk, tobacco), food	machinery and transport equipment, petroleum products, food
OMAN	1 131 000	212 457	5	crude oil	foodstuffs, motor vehicles, machinery (non-electric), petroleum products
PAKISTAN	89 729 000	803 943	113	rice, cotton, cotton cloth	machinery, crude oil, petroleum products
PHILIPPINES	51 956 000	300 000	173	electronic devices, clothing, metal ores	crude oil, machinery (non-electric), chemicals
QATAR	281 000	11 000	26	crude oil	foodstuffs, vehicles, machinery
SAUDI ARABIA	10 421 000	2 149 690	5	crude oil	foodstuffs, machinery (non-electric), electrical machinery, motor vehicles
SINGAPORE	2 502 000	581	4 306	petroleum products, electrical machinery	crude oil, machinery (non-electric), electrical machinery
SOUTH KOREA	39 951 000	98 484	406	clothing, textile yarns and fabrics, electrical machinery	crude oil, machinery (non-electric)
SOUTHERN YEMEN	2 158 000	332 968	6	petroleum products	food, crude oil
SRI LANKA	15 416 000	65 610	235	tea, rubber, clothing, petroleum products	machinery, crude oil, food
SYRIA	9 606 000	185 180	52	cotton, crude oil	crude oil, food, machinery (non-electric)
TAIWAN	18 458 000	35 961	513	clothing, electrical machinery	crude oil, electrical machinery, chemicals, machinery (non-electric)
THAILAND	49 459 000	514 000	96	rice, tapioca	crude oil, chemicals, machinery (non-electric), petroleum products
TURKEY	46 312 000	780 576	59	fruit and vegetables, textile yarns and fabrics	machinery, petroleum, medicines, transport equipment
U.A.E.	1 206 000	83 600	14	crude oil	machinery, foodstuffs, petroleum products
VIETNAM	57 181 000	329 556	174	coal, clothing	food and raw materials, manufactures, machinery and transport equipment
YEMEN	6 232 000	195 000	32	machinery, bakery products, sugar	foodstuffs, machinery, motor vehicles

AUSTRALASIA

country	population	area in sq km	population density	exports	imports
AUSTRALIA	15 369 000	7 686 848	2.1	metal ores, coal	machinery (non-electric), electrical machinery
FIJI	670 000	18 274	37	sugar, petroleum products	food, petroleum products
KIRIBATI	61 000	728	84	copra, fish	food, petroleum products, machinery
NAURU	8 000	21	381	phosphate	food, machinery and transport equipment
NEW CALEDONIA	149 000	19 058	8	ferro-alloys, nickel ore, nickel	machinery, food, petroleum products
NEW ZEALAND	3 203 000	268 676	12	meat, wool	chemicals, machinery (non-electric)
PAPUA NEW GUINEA	3 190 000	461 691	7	copper, coffee, gold	machinery, foodstuffs, petroleum products
SOLOMON ISLANDS	259 000	28 446	9	copra, fish, timber, palm oil	machinery, petroleum products, food
TONGA	104 000	699	149	coconut oil, vanilla beans	food, petroleum products, machinery
TUVALU	8 000	158	51	postage stamps	food, petroleum products
VANUATU	124 000	14 763	8	fish, copra	foodstuffs, petroleum products
WESTERN SAMOA	161 000	2 842	57	coconut oil, copra, taro	petroleum products, food, metal small manufactures

country	population	area in sq km	population density	exports	imports

NORTH AMERICA

country	population	area in sq km	population density	exports	imports
ANTIGUA AND BARBUDA	78 000	442	176	aircraft engines and machinery	foodstuffs, machinery
BAHAMAS	222 000	13 935	16	petroleum products, crude oil	crude oil
BARBADOS	252 000	431	584	sugar, clothing, electrical parts, petroleum products	foodstuffs, crude oil and products, chemicals
BELIZE	156 000	22 965	7	sugar, machinery, dairy products	food, petroleum products, machinery
BERMUDA	55 000	53	1 038	drugs and medicines, electronic supplies	petroleum products, machinery, food
CANADA	24 907 000	9 976 139	3	motor vehicles, machinery	transport equipment, manufactured goods, machinery, petroleum, machinery (non-electric), motor vehicles, crude oil
COSTA RICA	2 435 000	50 700	48	coffee, bananas	machinery (non-electric), chemicals, crude oil and products
CUBA	9 891 000	110 861	89	sugar	foodstuffs, chemicals
DOMINICA	76 000	751	101	bananas, soap	food, chemicals
DOMINICAN REPUBLIC	5 962 000	48 734	122	sugar, gold and alloys	foodstuffs, chemicals, crude oil, machinery
EL SALVADOR	5 232 000	21 041	249	coffee, cotton	machinery, chemicals, foodstuffs, crude oil
GREENLAND	52 000	2 175 600	0	zinc ore, fish and products	machinery, petroleum products, foodstuffs
GRENADA	110 000	344	320	nutmegs, cocoa, bananas	food, machinery and vehicles, petroleum products
GUATEMALA	7 932 000	108 889	73	coffee, bananas	machinery, chemicals, crude oil and products
HAITI	5 201 000	27 750	187	coffee, bauxite, toys and sports goods	foodstuffs, machinery, motor vehicles, petroleum products
HONDURAS	4 092 000	112 088	37	bananas, coffee	machinery (non-electric), chemicals, crude oil and products
JAMAICA	2 258 000	10 991	205	alumina, bauxite	foodstuffs, machinery, chemicals, crude oil and products
MEXICO	75 103 000	1 972 547	38	crude oil	machinery
NICARAGUA	3 058 000	130 000	24	cotton, coffee	machinery, chemicals, foodstuffs, crude oil and products
PANAMA	2 089 000	77 082	27	petroleum products, bananas, shrimps	machinery, chemicals, crude oil
PUERTO RICO	3 350 000	8 897	377	sugar	foodstuffs, machinery
ST KITTS - NEVIS	44 400	266	167	sugar	foodstuffs, machinery
ST LUCIA	125 000	616	203	bananas, cardboard boxes, clothing	food, machinery, petroleum products, chemicals
ST VINCENT	102 000	388	263	bananas	foodstuffs, machinery and vehicles, chemicals
U.S.A.	233 700 000	9 372 614	25	machinery (non-electric), electrical machinery	vehicles, crude oil, electrical machinery

SOUTH AMERICA

country	population	area in sq km	population density	exports	imports
ARGENTINA	29 627 000	2 766 889	11	meat and products, cereals	machinery (non-electric), chemicals, electrical machinery
BOLIVIA	6 082 000	1 098 581	6	tin, natural gas	machinery, vehicles, food
BRAZIL	129 660 000	8 511 965	15	machinery, animal feeding stuffs	machinery, crude oil
CHILE	11 682 000	756 945	15	copper	machinery (non-electric), foodstuffs, crude oil
COLOMBIA	27 515 000	1 138 914	24	coffee	machinery (non-electric), chemicals, vehicles, crude oil and products
ECUADOR	9 251 000	283 561	33	crude oil	machinery, chemicals, motor vehicles
FALKLAND ISLANDS	2 000	12 173	0	wool, postage stamps	metal small manufactures, food
GUIANA	70 000	91 000	1	timber, shellfish	foodstuffs, petroleum products, machinery
GUYANA	918 000	214 969	4	bauxite, sugar	petroleum products, machinery, chemicals, foodstuffs
PARAGUAY	3 473 000	406 752	9	cotton, timber, soyabeans	machinery, crude oil and products
PERU	18 707 000	1 285 216	15	copper, crude oil	machinery, chemicals, cereals
SURINAM	351 000	163 265	2	alumina, bauxite, aluminium	petroleum products, chemicals, machinery
TRINIDAD AND TOBAGO	1 149 000	5 130	224	petroleum products, crude oil	foodstuffs, machinery, crude oil
URUGUAY	2 968 000	176 215	17	wool, beef and veal	machinery, chemicals, crude oil, motor vehicles
VENEZUELA	16 394 000	912 050	18	petroleum products, crude oil	chemicals, machinery (non-electric), food, electrical machinery

AFRICA

country	population	area in sq km	population density	exports	imports
ALGERIA	20 500 000	2 381 741	9	crude oil	machinery (non-electric), food
ANGOLA	8 339 000	1 246 700	7	coffee, diamonds, crude oil	machinery and equipment, food, raw materials
BENIN	3 720 000	112 622	33	cotton, cocoa, palm kernel oil	machinery, textile yarns and fabrics, clothing

country	population	area in sq km	population density	exports	imports

AFRICA *continued*

country	population	area in sq km	population density	exports	imports
BOTSWANA	1 007 000	600 372	2	diamonds, meat and products, copper-nickel matte	foodstuffs, machinery, petroleum products, metals, motor vehicles
BURKINA	6 607 000	274 200	24	cotton, livestock, oil seeds and nuts	machinery, petroleum products, food, motor vehicles, chemicals
BURUNDI	4 421 000	27 834	159	coffee	food, machinery, motor vehicles
CAMEROON	9 165 000	475 442	19	coffee, cocoa, timber products, crude oil	chemicals, machinery (non-electric), petroleum products
CENTRAL AFRICAN REP	2 450 000	622 984	4	coffee, diamonds, timber	motor vehicles, chemicals, food, machinery
CHAD	4 789 000	1 284 000	4	cotton	machinery, petroleum products, chemicals, food
COMOROS	421 000	2 171	194	vanilla, essential oils, cloves	rice
CONGO	1 651 000	342 000	5	crude oil, veneers and plywood	machinery, food, chemicals
DJIBOUTI	330 000	22 000	15	special transactions	food
EGYPT	44 533 000	1 001 449	44	cotton, crude oil, petroleum products	machinery, food, motor vehicles
EQUATORIAL GUINEA	375 000	28 051	13	cocoa, timber	food, beverages and tobacco, crude oil and products, machinery and transport equipment
ETHIOPIA	33 680 000	1 221 900	28	coffee, skins and hides	chemicals, machinery, crude oil, motor vehicles
GABON	1 127 000	267 667	4	crude oil	machinery (non-electric), iron and steel, motor vehicles
GAMBIA	618 000	11 295	55	ground nuts, ground nut oil	foodstuffs, textile yarns and fabrics, machinery
GHANA	12 700 000	238 537	53	cocoa, gold	machinery, chemicals, crude oil and products, motor vehicles
GUINEA	5 177 000	245 857	21	bauxite, alumina	crude oil and products, textiles and clothing, rice
GUINEA BISSAU	863 000	36 125	24	groundnuts, fish	foodstuffs, machinery, petroleum products, textile yarns and fabrics
IVORY COAST	9 161 000	322 463	28	coffee, timber, cocoa	food, crude oil, machinery (non-electric)
KENYA	18 784 000	582 646	32	coffee, petroleum products, tea	machinery, crude oil, chemicals
LESOTHO	1 444 000	30 355	48	wool, diamonds, manufactures	foodstuffs, clothing
LIBERIA	2 057 000	111 369	18	iron ore, rubber	machinery, crude oil, food
LIBYA	3 342 000	1 759 540	2	crude oil	foodstuffs, electrical machinery, machinery (non-electric), motor vehicles
MADAGASCAR	9 400 000	587 041	16	coffee, spices	chemicals, machinery (non-electric), petroleum products
MALAWI	6 429 000	118 484	54	tobacco, tea, sugar	vehicles, petroleum products, chemicals, machinery (non-electric)
MALI	7 528 000	1 240 000	6	cotton, groundnuts, livestock	machinery, vehicles, petroleum products, medicines, chemicals, food
MAURITANIA	1 779 000	1 030 700	2	iron ore, fish	foodstuffs, vehicles, crude oil and products, machinery
MAURITIUS	993 000	2 045	486	sugar, clothing	machinery, food
MOROCCO	22 109 000	446 550	50	phosphates, fruit and vegetables	foodstuffs, crude oil, machinery (non-electric)
MOZAMBIQUE	13 311 000	801 590	17	cashew nuts, sugar	machinery, transport equipment, metals, chemicals
NAMIBIA	1 465 000	824 292	2	diamonds, uranium	
NIGER	5 772 000	1 267 000	5	uranium, livestock	petroleum products, food
NIGERIA	89 022 000	923 768	96	crude oil	vehicles, machinery, food
RWANDA	5 700 000	26 338	216	coffee, tea, metal ores	machinery, petroleum products, motor vehicles
SÃO TOMÉ AND PRÍNCIPE	92 000	964	95	cocoa	food, machinery, textiles, chemicals
SENEGAL	6 316 000	196 192	32	petroleum products, fish, phosphate fertiliser	machinery, food, crude oil, chemicals
SEYCHELLES	64 000	280	230	copra, fish	foodstuffs, petroleum products, machinery
SIERRA LEONE	3 472 000	71 740	48	diamonds, coffee, cocoa	machinery, foodstuffs, textile yarns and fabrics, crude oil
SOMALI REPUBLIC	5 269 000	637 657	8.1	livestock	motor vehicles, machinery, food
SOUTH AFRICA, REPUBLIC OF	30 802 000	1 221 037	25	gold	machinery, chemicals, crude oil and products, motor vehicles
SUDAN	20 362 000	2 505 813	8	cotton, groundnuts, sesame seed, cereals	machinery, food, chemicals, crude oil
SWAZILAND	605 000	17 363	35	sugar, wood pulp, chemicals	machinery and transport equipment, chemicals
TANZANIA	20 378 000	945 087	22	coffee, cotton	machinery, petroleum, manufactured goods
TOGO	2 756 000	56 785	49	phosphates, cocoa, coffee	machinery, crude oil, metal small manufactures, textile yarns and fabrics
TUNISIA	6 886 000	163 610	42	clothing, crude oil, chemicals	machinery, food, crude oil and products
UGANDA	14 625 000	236 036	62	coffee	machinery, motor vehicles, chemicals
WESTERN SAHARA	147 000	266 000	0.6		
ZAÏRE	31 151 000	2 345 409	13	copper, diamonds, coffee	foodstuffs, machinery, chemicals
ZAMBIA	6 242 000	752 614	8	copper	chemicals, crude oil and products
ZIMBABWE	7 740 000	390 580	20	tobacco, gold, nickel, asbestos, copper, meat	machinery, petroleum, chemical products

All the names on the maps in this atlas, except some of those on the special topic maps, are included in the index.

The names are arranged in **alphabetical order**. Where the name has more than one word the separate words are considered as one to decide the position of the name in the index:

Thetford
The Wash
The Weald
Thiers

Where there is more than one place with the same name, the country name is used to decide the order:

London Canada
London U.K.

If both places are in the same country, the county or state name is also used:

Avon *r.* Dorset U.K.
Avon *r.* Glos U.K.

Each entry in the index starts with the name of the place or feature, followed by the name of the country or region in which it is located. This is followed by the number of the most appropriate page on which the name appears, usually the largest scale map. Next comes the alphanumeric reference followed by the latitude and longitude.

Names of physical features such as rivers, capes, mountains etc are followed by a description. The descriptions are usually shortened to one or two letters, these abbreviations are keyed below. Town names are followed by a description only when the name may be confused with that of a physical feature:

Black River *town*

To help to distinguish the different parts of each entry, different styles of type are used:

place name	country name or region name	alphanumeric grid reference
description (if any)	page number	latitude/ longitude
Thames *r.*	U.K. **13**	**H3** 51.30N 0.05E

To use the **alphanumeric grid reference** to find a feature on the map, first find the correct page and then look at the letters printed in blue along the top and bottom of the map and the numbers printed in blue at the sides of the map. When you have found the correct letter and number follow the grid boxes up and along until you find the correct grid box in which the feature appears. You must then search the grid box until you find the name of the feature.

The **latitude and longitude reference** gives a more exact description of the position of the feature.

Page 6 of the atlas describes lines of latitude and lines of longitude, and explains how they are numbered and divided into degrees and minutes. Each name in the index has a different latitude and longitude reference, so the feature can be located accurately. The lines of latitude and lines of longitude shown on each map are numbered in degrees. These numbers are printed black along the top, bottom and sides of the map.

The drawing above shows part of the map on page 15 and the lines of latitude and lines of longitude.

The index entry for Wexford is given as follows

Wexford Rep. of Ire. **15 E2** 52.20N 6.25W

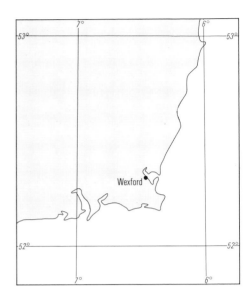

To locate Wexford, first find latitude 52N and estimate 20 minutes north from 52 degrees to find 52.20N, then find longitude 6W and estimate 25 minutes west from 6 degrees to find 6.25W. The symbol for the town of Wexford is where latitude 52.20N and longitude 6.25W meet.

On maps at a smaller scale than the map of Ireland, it is not possible to show every line of latitude and longitude. Only every 5 or 10 degrees of latitude and longitude may be shown. On these maps you must estimate the degrees and minutes to find the exact location of a feature.

Abbreviations

Afghan.	Afghanistan
Bangla.	Bangladesh
b., **B.**	bay, Bay
Beds.	Bedfordshire
Berks.	Berkshire
Bucks.	Buckinghamshire
Cambs.	Cambridgeshire
c., **C.**	cape, Cape
C.A.R.	Central African Republic
Czech.	Czechoslovakia
d.	internal division eg. county, state
Derbys.	Derbyshire
des.	desert
Dom. Rep.	Dominican Republic
D. and G.	Dumfries and Galloway
E. Germany	East Germany
E. Sussex	East Sussex
Equat. Guinea	Equatorial Guinea
est.	estuary
f.	physical feature eg. valley, plain, geographic district
Glos.	Gloucestershire
G.L.	Greater London
G.M.	Greater Manchester
g., **G.**	Gulf
Hants.	Hampshire
H. and W.	Hereford and Worcester
Herts.	Hertfordshire

Humber.	Humberside
i., I., is., Is.	island, Island, islands, Islands
I.o.M.	Isle of Man
I.o.W.	Isle of Wight
l., **L.**	lake, Lake
Lancs.	Lancashire
Leics.	Leicestershire
Liech.	Liechtenstein
Lincs.	Lincolnshire
Lux.	Luxembourg
Mersey.	Merseyside
M.G.	Mid Glamorgan
Mt.	Mount
mtn., **Mtn.**	mountain, Mountain
mts., **Mts.**	mountains, Mountains
Neth.	Netherlands
N. Ireland	Northern Ireland
Northants.	Northamptonshire
Northum.	Northumberland
N. Korea	North Korea
N. Yorks.	North Yorkshire
Notts.	Nottinghamshire
Oxon.	Oxfordshire
P.N.G.	Papua New Guinea
pen., **Pen.**	peninsula, Peninsula
Phil.	Philippines
Pt.	Point
r., **R.**	river, River
Rep. of Ire.	Republic of Ireland

R.S.A.	Republic of South Africa
Resr.	Reservoir
Somali Rep.	Somali Republic
Sd.	Sound
S. Yemen	Southern Yemen
S.G.	South Glamorgan
S. Korea	South Korea
S. Yorks.	South Yorkshire
Staffs.	Staffordshire
str., **Str.**	strait, Strait
Strath.	Strathclyde
Switz.	Switzerland
T. and W.	Tyne and Wear
U.A.E.	United Arab Emirates
U.S.S.R.	Union of Soviet Socialist Republics
U.K.	United Kingdom
U.S.A.	United States of America
Warwicks.	Warwickshire
W. Germany	West Germany
W.G.	West Glamorgan
W. Isles	Western Isles
W. Midlands	West Midlands
W. Sahara	Western Sahara
W. Sussex	West Sussex
W. Yorks.	West Yorkshire
Wilts.	Wiltshire
Yugo.	Yugoslavia

Boknafjorden *est.* Norway **50 A2** 59.15N 5.50E
Bolama Guinea Bissau **102 A3** 11.35N 15.30W
Bolangir India **63 E4** 20.41N 83.30E
Bolbec France **42 E5** 49.34N 0.28E
Bole Ghana **102 D2** 9.03N 2.23W
Bolgrad U.S.S.R. **49 N2** 45.42N 28.40E
Bolivia S. America **88 C6** 17.00S 65.00W
Bollnäs Sweden **50 D3** 61.20N 16.25E
Bolmen *l.* Sweden **50 C2** 57.00N 13.45E
Bologna Italy **46 E6** 44.30N 11.20E
Bolsena, L. Italy **46 E5** 42.36N 11.55E
Bolshevik *i.* U.S.S.R. **53 I5** 78.30N 102.00E
Bolshoi Lyakhovskiy *i.* U.S.S.R. **53 L4** 73.30N 142.00E
Bolsover U.K. **12 F5** 53.14N 1.18W
Bolton U.K. **12 E5** 53.35N 2.26W
Bolu Turkey **60 C6** 40.45N 31.38E
Bolus Hd. Rep. of Ire. **15 A1** 51.48N 10.21W
Bolvadin Turkey **60 C5** 38.43N 31.02E
Bolzano Italy **46 E7** 46.30N 11.20E
Boma Zaïre **99 B4** 5.50S 13.03E
Bombay India **63 D3** 18.56N 72.51E
Bomu *r.* C.A.R. **101 E2** 4.05N 22.27E
Bon, C. Tunisia **32 H2** 37.05N 11.03E
Bonaire *i.* Neth. Antilles **87 K2** 12.15N 68.27W
Bonar-Bridge U.K. **14 D4** 57.53N 4.22W
Bonavista Canada **81 M2** 48.38N 53.08W
Bondoukou Ivory Coast **102 D2** 8.03N 2.51W
Bone, G. of Indonesia **69 G3** 4.00S 120.50E
Bo'ness U.K. **14 E3** 56.01N 3.37W
Bonifacio France **46 D4** 41.23N 9.10E
Bonifacio, Str. of Med. Sea **46 D4** 41.18N 9.10E
Bonin Is. Japan **74 E10** 27.00N 142.10E
Bonn W. Germany **39 F2** 50.44N 7.06E
Bonny Nigeria **103 F1** 4.25N 7.10E
Bonny, Bight of Africa **103 F1** 2.58N 7.00E
Bontang Indonesia **68 F4** 0.05N 117.31E
Bonthain Indonesia **68 F2** 5.32S 119.58E
Boothia, G. of Canada **81 I5** 70.00N 90.00W
Boppard W. Germany **39 F2** 50.13N 7.35E
Borah Peak *mtn.* U.S.A. **82 D5** 44.09N 113.47W
Borås Sweden **50 C2** 57.44N 12.55E
Borāzjān Iran **61 H3** 29.14N 51.12E
Bordeaux France **42 D3** 44.50N 0.34W
Borden I. Canada **80 G5** 78.30N 111.00W
Borders *d.* U.K. **14 F2** 55.30N 2.53W
Bordesholm W. Germany **38 C2** 54.11N 10.00E
Bordö *i.* Faroe Is. **50 M9** 62.10N 7.13W
Borgå Finland **50 F3** 60.24N 25.40E
Börgefjell *mtn.* Norway **50 C4** 65.15N 13.50E
Borger U.S.A. **82 F4** 35.39N 101.24W
Borislav U.S.S.R. **49 K4** 49.18N 23.28E
Borisov U.S.S.R. **49 N7** 54.09N 28.30E
Borispol U.S.S.R. **49 O5** 50.21N 30.59E
Borken W. Germany **39 E3** 51.50N 6.52E
Borkum W. Germany **39 E5** 53.34N 6.41E
Borkum *i.* W. Germany **39 E5** 53.35N 6.45E
Borlänge Sweden **50 C3** 60.29N 15.25E
Borneo *i.* Asia **68 E4** 1.00N 114.00E
Bornholm *i.* Denmark **50 C1** 55.02N 15.00E
Borno *d.* Nigeria **103 G3** 12.20N 12.40E
Bornu, Plain of *f.* Nigeria **103 G3** 12.30N 13.00E
Borodyanka U.S.S.R. **49 N5** 50.38N 29.59E
Boroughbridge U.K. **12 F6** 54.05N 1.22W
Borth U.K. **13 C4** 52.30N 4.02W
Borzya U.S.S.R. **67 I7** 50.24N 116.35E
Bosa Italy **46 D4** 40.18N 8.29E
Boscastle U.K. **13 C2** 50.41N 4.43W
Bosna *r.* Yugo. **47 I6** 45.04N 18.27E
Bosnik Indonesia **69 J3** 1.09S 136.14E
Bosporus *str.* Turkey **47 N4** 41.07N 29.04E
Bosso Niger **103 G3** 13.43N 13.19E
Bosten Hu *l.* China **66 D5** 42.00N 87.00E
Boston U.K. **12 G4** 52.59N 0.02W
Boston U.S.A. **83 L5** 42.15N 71.05W
Botevgrad Bulgaria **47 K5** 42.55N 23.57E
Bothnia, G. of Europe **50 D3** 63.30N 20.30E
Botoşani Romania **49 M3** 47.44N 26.41E
Botrange *mtn.* Belgium **39 E2** 50.30N 6.04E
Botswana Africa **99 C2** 22.00S 24.00E
Bottrop W. Germany **39 E3** 51.31N 6.55E
Bouaflé Ivory Coast **102 C2** 7.01N 5.47W
Bouaké Ivory Coast **102 D2** 7.42N 5.00W
Bouar C.A.R. **103 H2** 5.58N 15.35E
Bou Craa Western Sahara **100 A4** 26.21N 12.57W
Bougainville *i.* P.N.G. **71 E5** 6.00S 155.00E
Bougouni Mali **102 C3** 11.25N 7.28W
Boulder U.S.A. **82 E5** 40.02N 105.16W
Boulogne France **42 E6** 50.43N 1.37E
Boumba *r.* Cameroon **103 H1** 2.00N 15.10E
Boumo Chad **103 H2** 9.01N 16.24E
Bouna Ivory Coast **102 D2** 9.19N 2.53W
Boundary Peak *mtn.* U.S.A. **82 C4** 37.51N 118.23W
Boundiali Ivory Coast **102 C2** 9.30N 6.31W
Bounty Is. Pacific Oc. **74 H3** 48.00S 178.30E
Bourem Mali **103 D4** 16.59N 0.20W
Bourg France **42 G4** 46.12N 5.13E
Bourganeuf France **42 E3** 45.57N 1.44E
Bourges France **42 F4** 47.05N 2.23E
Bourg Madame France **42 E2** 42.26N 1.55E
Bournemouth U.K. **13 F2** 50.43N 1.53W
Bo Xian China **67 I4** 33.40N 115.50E
Boxtel Neth. **39 D3** 51.36N 5.20E
Boyarka U.S.S.R. **49 O5** 50.20N 30.26E
Boyle Rep. of Ire. **15 C3** 53.58N 8.20W
Boyne *r.* Rep. of Ire. **15 E3** 53.43N 6.17W
Boyoma Falls *f.* Zaïre **99 C5** 0.18N 25.30E
Bozeman U.S.A. **82 D6** 45.40N 111.00W
Braband Denmark **38 D4** 56.09N 10.08E
Brabant *d.* Belgium **39 C2** 50.47N 4.30E
Brač *i.* Yugo. **47 H5** 43.20N 16.38E
Bracadale, L. U.K. **14 B4** 57.20N 6.32W
Bräcke Sweden **50 C3** 62.44N 15.30E
Brad Romania **47 K7** 46.06N 22.48E
Bradano *r.* Italy **47 H4** 40.23N 16.52E
Bradford U.K. **12 F5** 53.47N 1.45W
Bradworthy U.K. **13 C2** 50.55N 4.24W
Braemar U.K. **14 E3** 56.59N 3.27W
Braga Portugal **43 A4** 41.32N 8.26W
Bragança Portugal **43 B4** 41.47N 6.46W
Bragin U.S.S.R. **49 O5** 51.49N 30.16E
Brahmaputra *r.* Asia **63 F4** 23.50N 89.45E
Brăila Romania **49 N2** 45.18N 27.58E
Braintree U.K. **13 H3** 51.53N 0.31E
Bramming Denmark **38 B3** 55.28N 8.44E
Brampton U.K. **12 E6** 54.57N 2.42W
Branco *r.* Brazil **88 C7** 1.30S 62.00W
Brande Denmark **38 C3** 55.56N 9.09E
Brandenburg E. Germany **48 F6** 52.25N 12.34E
Brandon Canada **81 I2** 49.50N 99.57W
Brandon Mtn. Rep. of Ire. **15 A2** 52.14N 10.15W
Brandon Pt. Rep. of Ire. **15 A2** 52.17N 10.11W
Braniewo Poland **49 I7** 54.24N 19.50E
Brasília Brazil **88 E6** 15.54S 47.50W
Braşov Romania **49 L2** 45.40N 25.35E
Brass Nigeria **103 F1** 4.20N 6.15E
Bratislava Czech. **49 H4** 48.10N 17.10E
Bratsk U.S.S.R. **53 I3** 56.20N 101.15E
Bratsk Resr. U.S.S.R. **53 I3** 54.40N 103.00E
Braunschweig W. Germany **48 E6** 52.15N 10.30E
Braunton U.K. **13 C3** 51.06N 4.10W
Brawley U.S.A. **82 C3** 33.10N 115.30W
Bray Rep. of Ire. **15 E3** 53.12N 6.07W
Bray Hd. Rep. of Ire. **15 A1** 51.52N 10.28W
Brazil S. America **88 C7** 10.00S 52.00W
Brazilian Basin Atlantic Oc. **106 H3** 15.00S 25.00W
Brazilian Highlands Brazil **88 E6** 14.00S 45.00W
Brazos *r.* U.S.A. **83 G2** 28.55N 95.20W
Brazzaville Congo **99 B4** 4.14S 15.14E
Brda *r.* Poland **49 I6** 53.07N 18.08E
Breadalbane *f.* U.K. **14 D3** 56.30N 4.20W
Brechin U.K. **14 F3** 56.44N 2.39W
Breckland *f.* U.K. **13 H4** 52.30N 0.35E
Brecon U.K. **13 D3** 51.57N 3.23W
Brecon Beacons *mts.* U.K. **13 D3** 51.53N 3.27W
Breda Neth. **39 C3** 51.35N 4.46E
Bredstedt W. Germany **38 B2** 54.37N 8.58E
Bregenz Austria **48 D3** 47.31N 9.46E
Breidhafjördhur *est.* Iceland **50 I7** 65.15N 23.00W
Bremen W. Germany **48 D6** 53.05N 8.48E
Bremerhaven W. Germany **48 D6** 53.33N 8.35E
Brenner Pass Italy / Austria **48 E3** 47.00N 11.30E
Brenta *r.* Italy **46 F2** 45.25N 12.15E
Brentwood U.K. **13 H3** 51.39N 0.20E
Brescia Italy **46 E2** 45.33N 10.12E
Breskens Neth. **39 B3** 51.24N 3.34E
Bressay *i.* U.K. **14 G7** 60.08N 1.05W
Bressuire France **42 D4** 46.50N 0.28W
Brest France **42 B5** 48.23N 4.30W
Brest U.S.S.R. **49 K6** 52.08N 23.40E
Brewster, C. Greenland **76 R9** 70.00N 22.00W
Brezhnev U.S.S.R. **52 E3** 55.42N 52.20E
Briançon France **42 H3** 44.53N 6.39E
Bride U.K. **12 C6** 54.23N 4.22W
Bridgend U.K. **13 D3** 51.30N 3.33W
Bridgeport U.S.A. **83 L5** 41.12N 73.12W
Bridgetown Barbados **87 M2** 13.06N 59.37W
Bridgetown Rep. of Ire. **15 E2** 52.14N 6.32W
Bridgnorth U.K. **13 E4** 52.33N 2.24W
Bridgwater U.K. **13 D3** 51.08N 3.00W
Bridlington U.K. **12 G6** 54.04N 0.11W
Brienne-le-Château France **42 G5** 48.24N 4.32E
Brig Switz. **48 C3** 46.19N 8.00E
Brigg U.K. **12 G5** 53.33N 0.28W
Brighton U.K. **13 G2** 50.50N 0.09W
Brindisi Italy **47 H4** 40.38N 17.57E
Brisbane Australia **71 E3** 27.30S 153.00E
Bristol U.K. **13 E3** 51.26N 2.35W
Bristol B. U.S.A. **80 C3** 58.00N 158.50W
Bristol Channel U.K. **13 D3** 51.17N 3.20W
British Columbia *d.* Canada **80 F3** 55.00N 125.00W
British Isles Europe **8**
British Virgin Is. C. America **87 L3** 18.30N 64.30W
Brittany *f.* France **32 E4** 48.00N 3.00W
Brive France **42 E3** 45.09N 1.32E
Briviesca Spain **43 D5** 42.33N 3.19W
Brixham U.K. **13 D2** 50.23N 3.30W
Brno Czech. **48 H4** 49.11N 16.39E
Broad Bay U.K. **14 B5** 58.15N 6.15W
Broadway U.K. **13 F4** 52.02N 1.50W
Brod Yugo. **47 I6** 45.09N 18.02E
Brodick U.K. **14 C2** 55.35N 5.10W
Brody U.S.S.R. **49 L5** 50.05N 25.08E
Broken Hill *town* Australia **71 D2** 31.57S 141.30E
Bromley U.K. **13 H3** 51.23N 0.05E
Bromsgrove U.K. **13 E4** 52.20N 2.03W
Brönderslev Denmark **38 C5** 57.16N 9.58E
Brooke's Point *town* Phil. **68 F5** 8.50N 117.52E
Brooks Range *mts.* U.S.A. **80 C4** 68.50N 152.00W
Broom, L. U.K. **14 C4** 57.55N 5.15W
Broome Australia **71 B4** 17.58S 122.15E
Brora U.K. **14 E5** 58.01N 3.52W
Brora *r.* U.K. **14 E4** 57.59N 3.51W
Brosna *r.* Rep. of Ire. **15 D3** 53.12N 7.59W
Brough Shetland U.K. **14 G7** 60.29N 1.11W
Brough Cumbria U.K. **12 E6** 54.32N 2.17W
Broughton-in-Furness U.K. **12 D6** 54.17N 3.12W
Brovst Denmark **38 C5** 57.06N 9.31E
Bruay-en-Artois France **39 A2** 50.29N 2.36E
Bruges Belgium **39 B3** 51.13N 3.14E
Brühl W. Germany **39 E2** 50.50N 6.55E
Brunei Asia **68 E4** 4.56N 114.58E
Brunsbüttel W. Germany **38 C1** 53.54N 9.10E
Brunssun Neth. **39 D2** 50.57N 5.59E
Brunswick U.S.A. **83 J3** 31.09N 81.21W
Bruny I. Australia **74 E3** 43.15S 147.16E
Brussels Belgium **39 C2** 50.50N 4.23E
Bruton U.K. **13 E3** 51.06N 2.28W
Bryansk U.S.S.R. **52 C3** 53.15N 34.09E
Bubiyan I. Kuwait **61 H3** 29.45N 48.15E
Bucaramanga Colombia **88 B8** 7.08N 73.10W
Buchanan Liberia **102 B2** 5.57N 10.02W
Buchan Ness *c.* U.K. **14 G4** 57.28N 1.47W
Bucharest Romania **47 M6** 44.25N 26.06E
Buckhaven and Methil U.K. **14 E3** 56.10N 3.02W
Buckie U.K. **14 F4** 57.40N 2.58W
Buckingham U.K. **13 G4** 52.01N 0.59W
Buckinghamshire *d.* U.K. **13 G3** 51.50N 0.48W
Budapest Hungary **49 I3** 47.30N 19.03E
Bude U.K. **13 C2** 50.50N 4.32W
Bude Bay U.K. **13 C2** 50.50N 4.34W
Buea Cameroon **103 F1** 4.09N 9.13E
Buenaventura Colombia **88 B8** 3.54N 77.02W
Buenos Aires Argentina **89 D4** 34.40S 58.30W
Buffalo N.Y. U.S.A. **83 K5** 42.52N 78.55W
Buffalo Wyo. U.S.A. **82 E5** 44.21N 106.40W
Bug *r.* Poland **49 J6** 52.29N 21.11E
Bug *r.* U.S.S.R. **52 C2** 46.55N 31.59E
Buggs Island *l.* U.S.A. **83 K4** 36.35N 78.20W
Bugt China **67 J6** 48.45N 121.58E
Bugulma U.S.S.R. **52 E3** 54.32N 52.46E
Builth Wells U.K. **13 D4** 52.09N 3.25W
Buitenpost Neth. **39 E5** 53.15N 6.09E
Bujumbura Burundi **99 C4** 3.22S 29.21E
Bukavu Zaïre **99 C4** 2.30S 28.49E
Bukhara U.S.S.R. **52 F1** 39.47N 64.26E
Bukittinggi Indonesia **68 C3** 0.18S 100.20E
Bula Indonesia **69 I3** 3.07S 130.27E
Bulagan Mongolia **66 G6** 48.34N 103.12E
Bulan Phil. **69 G6** 12.40N 123.53E
Bulawayo Zimbabwe **99 C2** 20.10S 28.43E
Bulbjerg *mtn.* Denmark **38 C5** 57.09N 9.04E
Bulgaria Europe **47 L5** 42.30N 25.00E
Bulolo P.N.G. **69 L2** 7.13S 146.35E
Bulu, Gunung *mtn.* Indonesia **68 F4** 3.00N 116.00E
Bulun U.S.S.R. **53 K4** 70.50N 127.20E
Bunbury Australia **71 A2** 33.20S 115.34E
Buncrana Rep. of Ire. **15 D5** 55.08N 7.27W
Bundaberg Australia **71 E3** 24.50S 152.21E
Bunde W. Germany **39 F5** 53.12N 7.16E
Bundoran Rep. of Ire. **15 C4** 54.28N 8.20W
Bungay U.K. **13 I4** 52.28N 1.27E
Bungo suidō *str.* Japan **70 B3** 32.52N 132.30E
Bunguran *i.* Indonesia **68 D4** 4.00N 108.20E
Bunguran Selatan *i.* Indonesia **68 D4** 3.00N 108.50E
Buni Nigeria **103 G3** 11.20N 11.59E
Buol Indonesia **69 G4** 1.12N 121.28E
Buqbuq Egypt **60 B3** 31.30N 25.32E
Buraida Saudi Arabia **61 F2** 26.18N 43.58E
Buraimi U.A.E. **61 I2** 24.15N 55.45E
Burdur Turkey **60 C5** 37.44N 30.17E
Burdwān India **63 F4** 23.15N 87.52E
Burg E. Germany **48 E6** 52.17N 11.51E
Burgas Bulgaria **47 M5** 42.30N 27.29E
Burgess Hill *town* U.K. **13 G2** 50.56N 0.09W
Burgos Spain **43 D5** 42.21N 3.41W
Burgsteinfurt W. Germany **39 F4** 52.09N 7.21E
Burgsvik Sweden **50 D2** 57.03N 18.19E
Burhānpur India **63 D4** 21.18N 76.08E
Burias *i.* Phil. **69 G6** 12.50N 123.10E
Burica, Punta *c.* Panama **87 H1** 8.05N 82.50W
Burkina Africa **102 D3** 12.30N 2.00W
Burley U.S.A. **82 D5** 42.32N 113.48W
Burlington U.S.A. **83 L5** 44.25N 73.14W
Burma Asia **63 G4** 21.00N 96.30E
Burnham-on-Crouch U.K. **13 H3** 51.39N 0.50E
Burnham on Sea U.K. **13 E3** 51.14N 2.59W
Burnley U.K. **12 E5** 53.47N 2.15W
Burriana Spain **43 E3** 39.54N 0.05W
Burry Port U.K. **13 C3** 51.42N 4.17W
Bursa Turkey **47 N4** 40.11N 29.04E
Burton upon Trent U.K. **12 F4** 52.48N 1.39W
Buru *i.* Indonesia **69 H3** 3.30S 126.30E
Burujird Iran **61 H4** 33.54N 48.47E
Burullus, L. Egypt **60 C3** 31.30N 30.45E
Burundi Africa **99 C4** 3.30S 30.00E
Bury U.K. **12 E5** 53.34N 2.19W
Bury St. Edmunds U.K. **13 H4** 52.15N 0.42E
Būshehr Iran **61 H3** 28.57N 50.52E
Bussum Neth. **39 D4** 52.17N 5.10E
Büsum W. Germany **38 B2** 54.09N 8.52E
Buta Zaïre **99 C5** 2.49N 24.50E
Butaritari *i.* Kiribati **74 H8** 3.07N 172.48E
Bute *i.* U.K. **14 C2** 55.51N 5.07W
Bute, Sd. of U.K. **14 C2** 55.44N 5.10W
Butte U.S.A. **82 D6** 46.00N 112.31W
Butterworth Malaysia **68 C5** 5.24N 100.22E
Buttevant Rep. of Ire. **15 C2** 52.13N 8.40W
Butt of Lewis *c.* U.K. **14 B5** 58.31N 6.15W
Butuan Phil. **69 H5** 8.56N 125.31E
Butung *i.* Indonesia **69 G2** 5.00S 122.50E
Bützow E. Germany **38 E1** 53.52N 11.59E
Buxton U.K. **12 F5** 53.14N 1.51W
Buzău Romania **49 M2** 45.10N 26.49E
Buzău *r.* Romania **49 M2** 45.24N 27.48E
Bydgoszcz Poland **49 H6** 53.16N 18.00E
Bylot I. Canada **81 K5** 73.00N 78.30W
Byrranga Mts. U.S.S.R. **53 H4** 74.50N 101.00E
Byske *r.* Sweden **50 E4** 64.58N 21.10E
Bytom Poland **49 I5** 50.22N 18.54E

C

Cabanatuan Phil. **69 G7** 15.30N 120.58E
Cabimas Venezuela **88 B9** 10.26N 71.27W
Cabinda Angola **99 B4** 5.34S 12.12E
Cabot Str. Canada **81 M2** 47.00N 59.00W
Cabrera *i.* Spain **43 G3** 39.08N 2.56E
Cabrera, Sierra *mts.* Spain **43 B5** 42.10N 6.30W
Cabriel *r.* Spain **43 E3** 39.13N 1.07W
Cáceres Spain **43 B3** 39.29N 6.23W
Cacín *r.* Spain **43 C2** 37.10N 4.01W
Cader Idris *mtn.* U.K. **13 D4** 52.40N 3.53W
Cadí, Serra del *mts.* Spain **43 F5** 42.12N 1.35E
Cadillac U.S.A. **83 I5** 44.15N 85.23W
Cadiz Phil. **69 G6** 10.57N 123.18E
Cádiz Spain **43 B2** 36.32N 6.18W
Cádiz, G. of Spain **43 B2** 37.00N 7.10W
Caen France **42 D5** 49.11N 0.22W
Caernarfon U.K. **12 C5** 53.08N 4.17W
Caernarfon B. U.K. **12 C5** 53.05N 4.25W
Caerphilly U.K. **13 D3** 51.34N 3.13W
Cagayan de Oro Phil. **69 G5** 8.29N 124.40E
Cagliari Italy **46 D3** 39.14N 9.07E
Cagliari, G. of Med. Sea **46 D3** 39.07N 9.15E
Caguas Puerto Rico **87 K3** 18.08N 66.00W
Caha Mts. Rep. of Ire. **15 B1** 51.44N 9.45W
Caherciveen Rep. of Ire. **15 A1** 51.51N 10.14W
Cahir Rep. of Ire. **15 D2** 52.21N 7.56W
Cahora Bassa Dam Mozambique **99 D3** 15.33S 32.42E
Cahore Pt. Rep. of Ire. **15 E2** 52.33N 6.11W
Cahors France **42 E3** 44.28N 0.26E
Caibarién Cuba **87 I4** 22.31N 79.28W
Caicos Is. Turks & Caicos Is. **87 J4** 21.30N 72.00W
Cairngorms *mts.* U.K. **14 E4** 57.04N 3.30W
Cairns Australia **71 D4** 16.51S 145.43E
Cairo Egypt **60 C3** 30.03N 31.15E
Cairo U.S.A. **83 I4** 37.02N 89.02W
Cajamarca Peru **88 B7** 7.09S 78.32W
Calabar Nigeria **103 F1** 4.56N 8.22E
Calafat Romania **49 K1** 43.59N 22.57E
Calahorra Spain **43 D5** 42.18N 1.58W
Calamian Group *is.* Phil. **69 G6** 12.00N 120.05E
Calamocha Spain **43 E4** 40.54N 1.18W
Calapan Phil. **69 G6** 13.23N 121.10E
Călăraşi Romania **49 M2** 44.11N 27.21E
Calatayud Spain **43 E4** 41.21N 1.39W
Calbayog Phil. **69 G6** 12.04N 124.58E
Calcutta India **63 F4** 22.35N 88.21E
Caldas da Rainha Portugal **43 A3** 39.24N 9.08W
Calf of Man *i.* U.K. **12 C6** 54.03N 4.49W
Calgary Canada **80 G3** 51.05N 114.05W
Cali Colombia **88 B8** 3.24N 76.30W
Calicut India **63 D2** 11.15N 75.45E
Caliente U.S.A. **82 D4** 37.36N 114.31W
California *d.* U.S.A. **82 B4** 37.00N 120.00W
California, G. of Mexico **86 B5** 28.30N 112.30W
Callander U.K. **14 D3** 56.15N 4.13W
Callao Peru **88 B6** 12.05S 77.08W
Caloocan Phil. **69 G6** 14.38N 120.58E
Caltagirone Italy **46 G2** 37.14N 14.30E
Caltanissetta Italy **46 G2** 37.30N 14.05E
Calvi France **42 I2** 42.34N 8.44E
Calvinia R.S.A. **99 B1** 31.25S 19.47E
Cam *r.* U.K. **13 H4** 52.34N 0.21E
Camagüey Cuba **87 I4** 21.25N 77.55W
Camagüey, Archipiélago de Cuba **87 I4** 22.30N 78.00W
Camarón, C. Honduras **87 H3** 15.59N 85.00W
Ca Mau, Pointe de *c.* Vietnam **68 C5** 8.30N 104.35E
Cambay, G. of India **63 D4** 20.30N 72.00E
Camberley U.K. **13 G3** 51.20N 0.42W
Cambodia Asia **68 C6** 12.00N 105.00E
Camborne U.K. **13 B2** 50.12N 5.20W
Cambrai France **42 F6** 50.10N 3.14E
Cambrian Mts. U.K. **13 D4** 52.33N 3.33W
Cambridge U.K. **13 H4** 52.13N 0.08E
Cambridge Bay *town* Canada **80 H4** 69.09N 105.00W
Cambridgeshire *d.* U.K. **13 G4** 52.15N 0.05E
Camden U.K. **13 G3** 51.31N 0.15W
Camelford U.K. **13 C2** 50.38N 4.41W
Cameroon Africa **103 G2** 6.00N 12.30E
Cameroon, Mt. Cameroon **103 F1** 4.20N 9.05E
Campbell I. Pacific Oc. **74 G2** 52.30S 169.02E
Campbeltown U.K. **14 C2** 55.25N 5.36W
Campeche Mexico **86 F3** 19.50N 90.30W
Campeche *d.* Mexico **86 F3** 19.00N 90.00W
Campeche B. Mexico **86 F3** 19.30N 94.00W
Campina Grande Brazil **88 F7** 7.15S 35.53W
Campinas Brazil **89 E5** 22.54S 47.06W
Campine *f.* Belgium **39 C3** 51.05N 5.00E
Campo Cameroon **103 F1** 2.22N 9.50E
Campobasso Italy **46 G4** 41.34N 14.39E
Campo Grande Brazil **89 D5** 20.24S 54.35W
Campo Maior Portugal **43 B3** 39.01N 7.04W
Campos Brazil **89 E5** 21.46S 41.21W
Cam Ranh Vietnam **68 D6** 11.54N 109.14E
Camrose Canada **80 G3** 53.01N 112.48W
Canada N. America **80 F4** 60.00N 105.00W
Canadian *r.* U.S.A. **83 G4** 35.20N 95.40W
Canadian Shield *f.* N. America **76 K7** 50.00N 80.00W
Çanakkale Turkey **47 M4** 40.09N 26.26E
Canal du Midi France **42 E2** 43.18N 2.00E
Canary Is. Atlantic Oc. **100 A4** 29.00N 15.00W
Canaveral, C. U.S.A. **83 J2** 28.28N 80.28W
Canberra Australia **71 D2** 35.18S 149.08E
Candeleda Spain **43 C4** 40.10N 5.14W
Canea Greece **47 L1** 35.30N 24.02E
Çankiri Turkey **60 D6** 40.35N 33.37E
Canna *i.* U.K. **14 B4** 57.03N 6.30W
Cannes France **42 H2** 43.33N 7.00E
Cannich U.K. **14 D4** 57.21N 4.42W
Cannock U.K. **13 E4** 52.43N 2.00W
Canõas Brazil **89 D5** 29.55S 51.10W
Canon City U.S.A. **82 E4** 38.27N 105.14W
Cantabria, Sierra de *mts.* Spain **43 D5** 42.40N 2.30W
Cantabrian Mts. Spain **43 B5** 42.55N 5.10W
Canterbury U.K. **13 I3** 51.17N 1.05E
Can Tho Vietnam **68 D6** 10.03N 105.46E
Cao Bang Vietnam **68 D8** 22.40N 106.16E
Cape Basin Atlantic Oc. **106 J3** 38.00S 10.00E
Cape Breton I. Canada **81 L2** 46.00N 61.00W
Cape Coast *town* Ghana **103 D2** 5.10N 1.13W
Cape Johnson Depth Pacific Oc. **69 H6** 10.20N 127.20E

Dixmude Belgium **39 A3** 51.01N 2.52E
Dixon Entrance *str.* Canada / U.S.A. **80 E3** 54.10N133.30W
Diyālā *r.* Iraq **61 G4** 33.13N 44.33E
Diyarbakir Turkey **60 F5** 37.55N 40.14E
Djado Plateau *f.* Niger **100 D4** 22.00N 12.30E
Djelfa Algeria **100 C5** 34.43N 3.14E
Djénne Mali **102 D3** 13.55N 4.31W
Djibouti Africa **101 G3** 12.00N 42.50E
Djibouti *town* Djibouti **101 G3** 11.35N 43.11E
Djougou Benin **103 E2** 9.40N 1.47E
Dneprodzerzhinsk U.S.S.R. **52 C2** 48.30N 34.37E
Dnepropetrovsk U.S.S.R. **52 C2** 48.29N 35.00E
Dnestr *r.* U.S.S.R. **49 O3** 46.21N 30.20E
Dnieper *r.* U.S.S.R. **52 C2** 46.40N 32.10E
Doboj Yugo. **47 I6** 44.44N 18.02E
Docking U.K. **12 H4** 52.54N 0.40E
Dodecanese *is.* Greece **47 M2** 37.00N 27.00E
Dodge City U.S.A. **82 F4** 37.45N100.02W
Dodman Pt. U.K. **13 C2** 50.12N 4.48W
Dodoma Tanzania **99 D4** 6.10S 35.40E
Doetinchem Neth. **39 E3** 51.57N 6.17E
Dogai Coring *l.* China **63 F6** 34.30N 89.00E
Doha Qatar **61 H2** 25.15N 51.34E
Dokkedal Denmark **38 D4** 56.55N 10.16E
Dokkum Neth. **39 E5** 53.20N 6.00E
Dole France **42 G4** 47.05N 5.30E
Dolgellau U.K. **12 D4** 52.44N 3.53W
Dolina U.S.S.R. **49 K4** 49.00N 23.59E
Dollart *b.* W. Germany **39 F5** 53.20N 7.10E
Dolomites *mts.* Italy **46 E7** 46.25N 11.50E
Dolores Argentina **89 D4** 36.23S 57.44W
Dolphin and Union Str. Canada **80 G4** 69.20N118.00W
Dombås Norway **50 B3** 62.05N 9.07E
Dominica Windward Is. **87 L3** 15.30N 61.30W
Dominican Republic C. America **87 J3** 18.00N 70.00W
Dommel *r.* Neth. **39 D3** 51.44N 5.17E
Don *r.* England U.K. **12 G5** 53.41N 0.50W
Don *r.* Scotland U.K. **14 F4** 57.10N 2.05W
Don *r.* U.S.S.R. **52 D2** 47.06N 39.16E
Donaghadee U.K. **15 F4** 54.39N 5.33W
Donauwörth W. Germany **48 E4** 48.44N 10.48E
Don Benito Spain **43 C3** 38.57N 5.52W
Doncaster U.K. **12 F5** 53.31N 1.09W
Donegal Rep. of Ire. **15 C4** 54.39N 8.06W
Donegal *d.* Rep. of Ire. **15 C4** 54.52N 8.00W
Donegal B. Rep. of Ire. **15 C4** 54.32N 8.18W
Donegal Pt. Rep. of Ire. **15 B2** 52.42N 9.38W
Donets *r.* U.S.S.R. **33 N4** 47.50N 40.40E
Donetsk U.S.S.R. **52 D2** 48.00N 37.50E
Donga *r.* Nigeria **103 G2** 8.20N 10.00E
Dongfang China **67 H1** 19.04N108.39E
Donggala Indonesia **68 F3** 0.48S119.45E
Dong Hoi Vietnam **68 D7** 17.32N106.35E
Dongkala Indonesia **69 G4** 0.12N120.07E
Dongola Sudan **101 F3** 19.10N 30.27E
Dongting Hu *l.* China **67 H3** 29.40N113.00E
Donington U.K. **12 G4** 52.55N 0.10W
Doon, L. U.K. **14 D2** 55.15N 4.21W
Dorchester U.K. **13 E2** 50.52N 2.28W
Dordogne *r.* France **42 D3** 45.03N 0.34W
Dordrecht Neth. **39 C3** 51.48N 4.40E
Dore, Mont *mtn.* France **42 F3** 45.32N 2.49E
Dori Burkina **103 D3** 14.03N 0.02W
Dorking U.K. **13 G3** 51.14N 0.20W
Dornie U.K. **14 C4** 57.17N 5.30W
Dornoch U.K. **14 D4** 57.52N 4.02W
Dornoch Firth *est.* U.K. **14 E4** 57.50N 4.04W
Dornum W. Germany **39 F5** 53.39N 7.26E
Dörpen W. Germany **39 F4** 52.58N 7.20E
Dorset *d.* U.K. **13 E2** 50.48N 2.25W
Dorsten W. Germany **39 E3** 51.38N 6.58E
Dortmund W. Germany **39 F3** 51.32N 7.27E
Dortmund-Ems Canal W. Germany **39 F4** 52.20N 7.30E
Dosso Niger **103 E3** 13.03N 3.10E
Dothan U.S.A. **83 I3** 31.12N 85.25W
Douai France **39 B2** 50.22N 3.05E
Douala Cameroon **103 F1** 4.05N 9.43E
Douarnenez France **42 B5** 48.05N 4.20W
Doubs *r.* France **42 G4** 46.57N 5.03E
Douentza Mali **102 D3** 14.58N 2.48W
Douglas U.K. **12 C6** 54.09N 4.29W
Doumé Cameroon **103 G1** 4.13N 13.30E
Dounreay U.K. **14 E5** 58.33N 3.45W
Douro *r.* Portugal **43 A4** 41.10N 8.40W
Dove *r.* U.K. **12 F4** 52.50N 1.35W
Dover U.K. **13 I3** 51.07N 1.19E
Dover, Str. of U.K. **13 I2** 51.00N 1.30E
Dovey *r.* U.K. **13 D4** 52.33N 3.55W
Dovrefjell *mts.* Norway **50 B3** 62.05N 9.30E
Down *d.* U.K. **15 E4** 54.20N 6.00W
Downham Market U.K. **13 H4** 52.38N 0.35E
Downpatrick U.K. **15 F4** 54.21N 5.43W
Downpatrick Head Rep. of Ire. **15 B4** 54.20N 9.21W
Dowra Rep. of Ire. **15 C4** 54.10N 8.02W
Dra, Wadi *r.* Morocco **100 A4** 28.40N 11.06W
Drachten Neth. **39 E5** 53.05N 6.06E
Dragoman Pass Bulgaria / Yugo. **47 K5** 42.56N 22.52E
Draguignan France **42 H2** 43.32N 6.28E
Drakensberg *mts.* R.S.A. **99 C1** 30.00S 29.00E
Dráma Greece **47 L4** 41.09N 24.11E
Drammen Norway **50 B2** 59.45N 10.15E
Drau *r. see* **Drava** *r.* Austria **48**
Drava *r.* Yugo. **47 I6** 45.34N 18.56E
Drenthe *d.* Neth. **39 E4** 52.52N 6.30E
Dresden E. Germany **48 F5** 51.03N 13.45E
Dreux France **42 E5** 48.44N 1.23E
Drin *r.* Albania **47 I4** 41.45N 19.34E
Drina *r.* Yugo. **47 I6** 44.53N 19.20E
Drogheda Rep. of Ire. **15 E3** 53.42N 6.23W
Droitwich U.K. **13 E4** 52.16N 2.10W
Dronfield U.K. **12 F5** 53.18N 1.29W
Dronne *r.* France **42 D3** 45.02N 0.09W
Dronninglund Denmark **38 D5** 57.09N 10.20E
Drumheller Canada **80 G3** 51.28N112.40W
Drum Hills Rep. of Ire. **15 D2** 52.02N 7.45W
Drummore U.K. **14 D1** 54.42N 4.55W
Drut *r.* U.S.S.R. **49 O6** 53.03N 30.42E
Druz, Jebel ed *mts.* Syria **60 E4** 32.42N 36.42E
Drymen U.K. **14 D3** 56.04N 4.30W
Dschang Cameroon **103 G2** 5.28N 10.02E
Dubai U.A.E. **61 I2** 25.13N 55.17E
Dubawnt *r.* Canada **81 H4** 62.50N102.00W
Dubawnt L. Canada **81 H4** 62.50N102.00W
Dubica Yugo. **47 H6** 45.11N 16.48E
Dublin Rep. of Ire. **15 E3** 53.21N 6.18W
Dublin *d.* Rep. of Ire. **15 E3** 53.20N 6.18W
Dublin B. Rep. of Ire. **15 E3** 53.20N 6.09W
Dubno U.S.S.R. **49 L5** 50.28N 25.40E
Dubrovitsa U.S.S.R. **49 M5** 51.38N 26.40E
Dubrovnik Yugo. **47 I5** 42.40N 18.07E
Ducie I. Pacific Oc. **75 N5** 24.40S124.48W
Dudinka U.S.S.R. **53 H4** 69.27N 86.13E
Dudley U.K. **13 E4** 52.30N 2.05W
Duero *r. see* **Douro** *r.* Spain **43**
Dufftown U.K. **14 E4** 57.27N 3.11W
Dugi *i.* Yugo. **46 G6** 44.04N 15.00E
Duisburg W. Germany **39 E3** 51.26N 6.45E
Duiveland *i.* Neth. **39 C3** 51.39N 4.00E
Dukhan Qatar **61 H2** 25.24N 50.47E
Duleek Rep. of Ire. **15 E3** 53.39N 6.28W
Dülmen W. Germany **39 F3** 51.49N 7.17E
Duluth U.S.A. **83 H6** 46.50N 92.10W
Dumaguete Phil. **69 G5** 9.20N123.18E
Dumbarton U.K. **14 D2** 55.57N 4.35W
Dumfries U.K. **14 E2** 55.04N 3.37W
Dumfries and Galloway *d.* U.K. **14 E2** 55.05N 3.40W
Dumyât Egypt **60 C3** 31.26N 31.48E
Dunany Pt. Rep. of Ire. **15 E3** 53.51N 6.15W
Dunbar U.K. **14 F2** 55.59N 2.33W
Dunblane U.K. **14 E3** 56.12N 3.58W
Dunboyne Rep. of Ire. **15 E3** 53.25N 6.31W
Duncansby Head U.K. **14 E5** 58.39N 3.01W
Dundalk Rep. of Ire. **15 E4** 54.01N 6.25W
Dundalk B. Rep. of Ire. **15 E3** 53.55N 6.17W
Dundee U.K. **14 F3** 56.28N 3.00W
Dundrum U.K. **15 F4** 54.16N 5.51W
Dundrum Bay U.K. **15 F4** 54.10N 5.45W
Dunedin New Zealand **71 G1** 45.53S170.31E
Dunfermline U.K. **14 E3** 56.04N 3.29W
Dungannon U.K. **15 E4** 54.31N 6.47W
Dungarvan Rep. of Ire. **15 D2** 52.06N 7.39W
Dungeness U.K. **13 H2** 50.55N 0.58E
Dungiven U.K. **15 E4** 54.56N 6.58W
Dunhuang China **66 E5** 40.00N 94.40E
Dunkeld U.K. **14 E3** 56.35N 3.35W
Dunkirk France **48 A5** 51.02N 2.23E
Dunkwa Ghana **103 D2** 5.59N 1.45W
Dun Laoghaire Rep. of Ire. **15 E3** 53.17N 6.09W
Dunleer Rep. of Ire. **15 E3** 53.50N 6.23W
Dunmahon Rep. of Ire. **15 D2** 52.08N 7.23W
Dunmanus B. Rep. of Ire. **15 B1** 51.33N 9.40W
Dunnet Head U.K. **14 E5** 58.40N 3.23W
Dunoon U.K. **14 D2** 55.57N 4.57W
Duns U.K. **14 F2** 55.47N 2.20W
Dunshaughlin Rep. of Ire. **15 E3** 53.31N 6.34W
Dunstable U.K. **13 G3** 51.52N 0.30W
Durance *r.* France **42 G2** 43.55N 4.48E
Durango Mexico **86 D4** 24.01N104.00W
Durango *d.* Mexico **86 D4** 24.01N104.00W
Durban R.S.A. **99 D2** 29.53S 31.00E
Düren W. Germany **39 E2** 50.48N 6.30E
Durham U.K. **12 F6** 54.47N 1.34W
Durham *d.* U.K. **12 F6** 54.42N 1.45W
Durlston Head *c.* U.K. **13 F2** 50.35N 1.58W
Durmitor *mtn.* Yugo. **47 I5** 43.08N 19.03E
Durness U.K. **14 D5** 58.33N 4.45W
Durrës Albania **47 I4** 41.19N 19.27E
Durrow Rep. of Ire. **15 D2** 52.50N 7.25W
Dursey Head Rep. of Ire. **15 A1** 51.35N 10.15W
Dushanbe U.S.S.R. **66 A5** 38.38N 68.51E
Düsseldorf W. Germany **39 E3** 51.13N 6.47E
Duyun China **66 G3** 26.16N107.29E
Dvina *r.* U.S.S.R. **50 F2** 57.03N 24.00E
Dyatlovichi U.S.S.R. **49 O6** 52.08N 30.49E
Dyer, C. Canada **81 L4** 67.45N 61.45W
Dyérem *r.* Cameroon **103 G2** 6.36N 13.10E
Dyfed *d.* U.K. **13 C4** 52.00N 4.17W
Dyulty *mtn.* U.S.S.R. **61 G6** 41.55N 46.52E
Dzerzhinsk W.R.S.S.R. U.S.S.R. **49 M6** 53.40N 27.01E
Dzerzhinsk R.S.F.S.R. U.S.S.R. **52 D3** 56.15N 43.30E
Dzhambul U.S.S.R. **66 A5** 42.50N 71.25E
Dzhugdzhur Range *mts.* U.S.S.R. **53 L3** 57.30N138.00E

E

Eagle Pass *town* U.S.A. **82 F2** 28.44N100.31W
Ealing U.K. **13 G3** 51.32N 0.30W
Earn *r.* U.K. **14 E3** 56.21N 3.18W
Earn, L. U.K. **14 D3** 56.23N 4.12W
Easingwold U.K. **12 F6** 54.08N 1.10W
Easky Rep. of Ire. **15 C4** 54.18N 8.59W
East Anglian Heights *hills* U.K. **13 H4** 52.05N 0.20E
Eastbourne U.K. **13 H2** 50.46N 0.18E
East Cape U.S.S.R. **54 U9** 66.05N169.40W
East China Sea Asia **67 J3** 29.00N125.00E
Easter I. Pacific Oc. **75 Q5** 27.08S109.23W
Eastern Desert Egypt **60 C3** 28.15N 31.55E
Eastern Ghāts *mts.* India **63 E3** 16.30N 80.30E
Eastern Hajar *mts.* Oman **61 J1** 22.45N 58.45E
Eastern Indian-Antarctic Basin Indian Oc. **107 N2** 59.00S110.00E
Eastern Indian-Antarctic Ridge Indian Oc. **107 N2** 58.00S115.00E
Eastern Sayan *mts.* U.S.S.R. **53 H3** 53.30N 98.00E
East Flevoland *f.* Neth. **39 D4** 52.30N 5.40E
East Frisian Is. W. Germany **39 E5** 53.45N 7.00E
East Germany Europe **48 F6** 52.15N 12.30E
East Grinstead U.K. **13 H3** 51.08N 0.00
East Ilsley U.K. **13 F3** 51.32N 1.18W
East Kilbride U.K. **14 D2** 55.46N 4.09W
Eastleigh U.K. **13 F2** 50.58N 1.23W
East London R.S.A. **99 C1** 33.00S 27.54E
Eastmain Canada **81 K3** 52.10N 78.30W
Eastmain *r.* Canada **81 K3** 52.10N 78.30W
East Pacific Ridge Pacific Oc. **106 D3** 15.00S112.00W
East Retford U.K. **12 G5** 53.19N 0.55W
East Schelde *est.* Neth. **39 B3** 51.35N 3.57E
East Siberian Sea U.S.S.R. **53 N4** 73.00N160.00E
East Sussex *d.* U.K. **13 H2** 50.56N 0.12E
East Vlieland Neth. **39 D5** 53.18N 5.04E
Eauripik *i.* Caroline Is. **69 K5** 6.42N143.04E
Ebbw Vale *town* U.K. **13 D3** 51.48N 3.13W
Ebeltoft Denmark **38 D4** 56.12N 10.41E
Eberswalde E. Germany **48 F6** 52.50N 13.50E
Ebinur Hu *l.* China **66 C6** 45.00N 83.00E
Ebolowa Cameroon **103 G1** 2.56N 11.11E
Ebon *i.* Pacific Oc. **74 G8** 4.38N168.43E
Ebro *r.* Spain **43 F4** 40.43N 0.54E
Ebro Delta Spain **32 F3** 40.43N 0.54E
Ecclefechan U.K. **14 E2** 55.05N 3.17W
Echternach Lux. **39 E1** 49.49N 6.25E
Écija Spain **43 C2** 37.33N 5.04W
Eckernförde W. Germany **38 C2** 54.30N 9.50E
Ecuador S. America **88 B7** 2.00S 78.00W
Edam Neth. **39 D4** 52.30N 5.02E
Ed Damer Sudan **101 F3** 17.37N 33.59E
Eddrachillis Bay U.K. **14 C5** 58.18N 5.15W
Ede Neth. **39 D4** 52.03N 5.40E
Edea Cameroon **103 G1** 3.47N 10.13E
Eden *r.* U.K. **12 D6** 54.57N 3.02W
Edenderry Rep. of Ire. **15 D3** 53.21N 7.05W
Ederny U.K. **15 D4** 54.32N 7.40W
Edgeworthstown Rep. of Ire. **15 D3** 53.41N 7.39W
Édhessa Greece **47 K4** 40.47N 22.03E
Edinburgh U.K. **14 E2** 55.57N 3.13W
Edirne Turkey **47 M4** 41.40N 26.35E
Edmonton Canada **80 G3** 53.34N113.25W
Edmundston Canada **81 L2** 47.22N 68.20W
Edremit Turkey **47 M3** 39.35N 27.02E
Edward, L. Uganda / Zaïre **99 C4** 0.30S 29.30E
Edwards Plateau *f.* U.S.A. **82 F3** 30.30N100.30W
Eeklo Belgium **39 B3** 51.11N 3.34E
Egersund Norway **50 A2** 58.27N 6.01E
Eğridir Turkey **60 C5** 37.52N 30.51E
Eğridir L. Turkey **60 C5** 38.04N 30.55E
Egypt Africa **101 E4** 26.30N 29.30E
Éibar Spain **43 D5** 43.11N 2.28W
Eider *r.* W. Germany **38 B2** 54.18N 8.58E
Eifel *f.* W. Germany **39 E2** 50.10N 6.45E
Eigg *i.* U.K. **14 B3** 56.53N 6.09W
Eil, L. U.K. **14 C3** 56.51N 5.15W
Eindhoven Neth. **39 D3** 51.26N 5.30E
Eisenach E. Germany **48 E5** 50.59N 10.19E
Eisenhut *mtn.* Austria **48 F3** 47.00N 13.45E
Eisenhüttenstadt E. Germany **48 G6** 52.09N 14.41E
Eisleben E. Germany **48 E5** 51.32N 11.33E
Eitorf W. Germany **39 F2** 50.46N 7.27E
Eksjö Sweden **50 C2** 57.40N 15.00E
El Aaiún W. Sahara **100 A4** 27.10N 13.11W
El Agheila Libya **100 D5** 30.15N 19.12E
El Alamein Egypt **60 C3** 30.50N 28.57E
El 'Arîsh Egypt **60 D3** 31.08N 33.48E
El 'Arîsh, Wâdi *r.* Egypt **60 D3** 31.09N 33.49E
El Asnam Algeria **100 C5** 36.20N 1.30E
Elat Israel **60 D3** 29.33N 34.56E
Elâzig Turkey **60 E5** 38.41N 39.14E
Elba *i.* Italy **46 E5** 42.47N 10.17E
Elbasan Albania **47 J4** 41.07N 20.04E
Elbe *r.* W. Germany **48 E6** 53.33N 10.00E
Elbert, Mt. U.S.A. **82 E4** 39.05N106.27W
Elbeuf France **42 E5** 49.17N 1.01E
Elbistan Turkey **60 E5** 38.14N 37.11E
Elblag Poland **49 I7** 54.10N 19.25E
Elbrus *mtn.* U.S.S.R. **52 D2** 43.21N 42.29E
Elburg Neth. **39 D4** 52.27N 5.50E
Elburz Mts. Iran **101 H5** 36.00N 52.30E
Elche Spain **43 E3** 38.16N 0.41W
Elde *r.* E. Germany **48 E6** 53.17N 11.25E
El Djouf *des.* Africa **94 B7** 21.00N 8.00W
Eldoret Kenya **99 D5** 0.31N 35.17E
Elephant Butte Resr. U.S.A. **82 E3** 33.25N107.10W
Elephant I. Atlantic Oc. **89 D1** 61.00S 55.00W
El Escorial Spain **43 C4** 40.34N 4.08W
Eleuthera I. Bahamas **87 I5** 25.00N 76.00W
El Faiyûm Egypt **60 C3** 29.19N 30.50E
El Fasher Sudan **101 E3** 13.37N 25.22E
El Ferrol Spain **43 A5** 43.29N 8.14W
El Galâla, Gebel *mts.* Egypt **60 D3** 29.00N 32.10E
Elgin U.K. **14 E4** 57.39N 3.20W
El Gîza Egypt **60 C3** 30.01N 31.12E
El Golea Algeria **100 C5** 30.35N 2.51E
Elgon, Mt. Kenya / Uganda **99 D5** 1.07N 34.35E
El Hamad *des.* Asia **60 E3** 31.45N 39.00E
El Jadida Morocco **100 B5** 33.16N 8.30W
El Jauf Libya **101 E4** 24.09N 23.19E
Elk Poland **49 K6** 53.50N 22.22E
El Khârga Egypt **60 C2** 25.27N 30.32E
Elkhovo Bulgaria **47 M5** 42.10N 26.35E
Elko U.S.A. **82 C5** 40.50N115.46W
Ellen, Mt. U.S.A. **82 D4** 38.06N110.50W
Ellesmere I. Canada **81 J5** 78.00N 82.00W
Ellesmere Port U.K. **12 E5** 53.17N 2.50W
Ellon U.K. **14 F4** 57.22N 2.05W
El Mahalla el Kubra Egypt **60 C3** 30.59N 31.12E
Elmali Turkey **60 C5** 36.43N 29.56E
El Mansûra Egypt **60 C3** 31.03N 31.23E
El Minya Egypt **60 C3** 28.06N 30.45E
Elmshorn W. Germany **48 D6** 53.46N 9.40E
El Muglad Sudan **101 E3** 11.01N 27.50E
El Natrûn, Wâdi *f.* Egypt **60 C3** 30.25N 30.18E
El Obeid Sudan **101 F3** 13.11N 30.10E
Eloy U.S.A. **82 D3** 32.45N111.33W
El Paso U.S.A. **82 E3** 31.45N106.30W
El Qantara Egypt **60 D3** 30.52N 32.20E
El Qasr Egypt **60 C2** 25.43N 28.54E
El Qatrun Libya **100 D4** 24.55N 14.38E
El Real Panama **87 I1** 8.06N 77.42W
El Salvador C. America **87 G2** 13.30N 89.00W
El Tarfa, Wâdi *r.* Egypt **60 C3** 28.36N 30.50E
El Tigre Venezuela **88 C8** 8.44N 64.18W
El Tîh, Gebel *f.* Egypt **60 D3** 28.50N 34.00E
El Tûr Egypt **60 D3** 28.14N 33.37E
Elūru India **63 E3** 16.45N 81.10E
Elvas Portugal **43 B3** 38.53N 7.10W
Elverum Norway **50 B3** 60.54N 11.33E
Ely U.K. **13 H4** 52.25N 0.18E
Emba *r.* U.S.S.R. **52 E2** 46.40N 53.30E
Embleton U.K. **12 F7** 55.30N 1.37W
Emden W. Germany **39 F5** 53.23N 7.13E
Emi Koussi *mtn.* Chad **100 D3** 19.58N 18.30E
Emmeloord Neth. **39 D4** 52.43N 5.46E
Emmen Neth. **39 E4** 52.48N 6.55E
Emmerich W. Germany **39 E3** 51.49N 6.16E
Emory Peak *mtn.* U.S.A. **82 F2** 29.15N103.19W
Emporia U.S.A. **83 G4** 38.24N 96.10W
Ems *r.* W. Germany **39 F4** 53.14N 7.25E
Ems-Jade Canal W. Germany **39 F5** 53.28N 7.40E
Emyvale Rep. of Ire. **15 E4** 54.21N 6.59W
Enard Bay U.K. **14 C5** 58.09N 5.25W
Encarnación Paraguay **89 D5** 27.20S 55.50W
Enchi Ghana **102 D2** 5.53N 2.48W
Ende Indonesia **69 G2** 8.51S121.40E
Enderbury I. Kiribati **74 I7** 3.08S171.05W
Endicott Mts. U.S.A. **80 C4** 68.00N152.00W
Enewetak *i.* Pacific Oc. **74 G9** 11.30N162.15E
Enfield U.K. **13 G3** 51.40N 0.05W
Engaño, C. Phil. **69 G7** 18.30N122.20E
Engels U.S.S.R. **52 D2** 51.25N 46.07E
Enggano *i.* Indonesia **68 C2** 5.20S102.15E
Enghien Belgium **39 C2** 50.42N 4.02E
England U.K. **12 F4** 53.00N 2.00W
English Bāzār India **63 F4** 25.00N 88.12E
English Channel U.K. **13 F2** 50.15N 1.00W
Enkhuizen Neth. **39 D4** 52.42N 5.17E
Enköping Sweden **50 D2** 59.38N 17.07E
Enna Italy **46 G2** 37.34N 14.15E
En Nahud Sudan **101 E3** 12.41N 28.28E
Ennis Rep. of Ire. **15 B2** 52.51N 9.00W
Enniscorthy Rep. of Ire. **15 E2** 52.30N 6.35W
Enniskillen U.K. **15 D4** 54.21N 7.40W
Ennistymon Rep. of Ire. **15 B2** 52.56N 9.20W
Enns *r.* Austria **48 G4** 48.14N 14.22E
Enschede Neth. **39 E4** 52.13N 6.54E
Ensenada Mexico **86 A6** 31.53N116.35W
Entebbe Uganda **99 D5** 0.05N 32.29E
Enugu Nigeria **103 F2** 6.20N 7.29E
Epe Neth. **39 D4** 52.21N 5.59E
Epernay France **42 F5** 49.02N 3.58E
Épinal France **42 H5** 48.10N 6.28E
Epping U.K. **13 H3** 51.43N 0.08E
Epsom U.K. **13 G3** 51.20N 0.16W
Equatorial Guinea Africa **100 D2** 1.30N 10.30E
Erbil Iraq **61 G5** 36.12N 44.01E
Erciyaş, Mt. Turkey **60 D5** 38.33N 35.25E
Erdre *r.* France **42 D4** 47.27N 1.34W
Eregli Konya Turkey **60 D5** 37.30N 34.02E
Eregli Zonguldak Turkey **60 C6** 41.17N 31.26E
Erenhot China **67 H5** 43.50N112.00E
Erfde W. Germany **38 C2** 54.30N 9.20E
Erft *r.* W. Germany **39 E3** 51.12N 6.45E
Erfurt E. Germany **48 E5** 50.58N 11.02E
Ergani Turkey **60 E5** 38.17N 39.44E
Ergene *r.* Turkey **47 M4** 41.02N 26.22E
Ergig *r.* Chad **103 H3** 11.30N 15.30E
Erie U.S.A. **83 J5** 42.07N 80.05W
Erie, L. Canada / U.S.A. **83 J5** 42.15N 81.00W
Erigavo Somali Rep. **101 G3** 10.40N 47.20E
Erimo saki *c.* Japan **70 E7** 41.55N143.13E
Eriskay *i.* U.K. **14 A4** 57.04N 7.17W
Eritrea *f.* Ethiopia **101 F3** 15.30N 38.00E
Erkelenz W. Germany **39 E3** 51.05N 6.18E
Erlangen W. Germany **48 E4** 49.36N 11.02E
Ermelo Neth. **39 D4** 52.19N 5.38E
Erne *r.* Rep. of Ire. / U.K. **15 B4** 54.30N 8.15W
Erode India **63 D2** 11.21N 77.43E
Er Rahad Sudan **101 F3** 12.42N 30.33E
Errigal Mtn. Rep. of Ire. **15 C5** 55.02N 8.08W
Erris Head Rep. of Ire. **15 A4** 54.19N 10.00W
Er Roseires Sudan **101 F3** 11.52N 34.23E
Ertix He *r.* U.S.S.R. **66 D6** 48.00N 84.20E
Erzincan Turkey **60 E5** 39.44N 39.30E
Erzurum Turkey **60 F5** 39.57N 41.17E
Esbjerg Denmark **38 B3** 55.28N 8.28E
Escanaba U.S.A. **83 I6** 45.47N 87.04W
Esch Lux. **39 D1** 49.31N 5.59E
Eschweiler W. Germany **39 E2** 50.49N 6.16E
Escondido *r.* Nicaragua **87 H2** 11.58N 83.45W
Escuintla Guatemala **86 F2** 14.18N 90.47W
Esher U.K. **13 G3** 51.23N 0.22W
Esk *r.* U.K. **12 G6** 54.29N 0.35W
Eskilstuna Sweden **50 D2** 59.22N 16.31E
Eskimo Point *town* Canada **81 I4** 61.10N 94.15W
Eskişehir Turkey **60 C5** 39.46N 30.30E
Esla *r.* Spain **43 B4** 41.29N 6.03W
Eslāmābād Iran **61 G4** 34.08N 46.35E
Eslöv Sweden **38 G3** 55.50N 13.19E
Espírtu Santo I. Vanuatu **74 G6** 15.50S166.50E

Esquel Argentina **89 B3** 42.55S 71.20W
Essen W. Germany **39 E3** 51.27N 6.57E
Essequibo *r.* Guyana **88 D8** 6.48N 58.23W
Essex *d.* U.K. **13 H3** 51.46N 0.30E
Estepona Spain **43 C2** 36.26N 5.09W
Estevan Canada **80 H2** 49.09N103.00W
Eston U.K. **12 F6** 54.32N 1.10W
Estonia S.S.R. *d.* U.S.S.R. **52 C3** 58.45N 25.30E
Estrela, Serra da *mts.* Portugal **43 B4** 40.20N 7.40W
Estremoz Portugal **43 B3** 38.50N 7.35W
Étaples France **42 E6** 50.31N 1.39E
Ethiopia Africa **101 F3** 10.00N 39.00E
Ethiopian Highlands Ethiopia **101 F3** 10.00N 37.00E
Etive, L. U.K. **14 C3** 56.28N 5.20W
Etna, Mt. Italy **46 G2** 37.43N 14.59E
Etosha Pan *f.* Namibia **99 B3** 18.50S 16.30E
Ettelbrück Lux. **39 E1** 49.51N 6.06E
Et Tubeiq, Jebel *mts.* Saudi Arabia **60 E3** 29.30N 37.15E
Euboea *i.* Greece **47 L3** 38.30N 23.50E
Eufaula Resr. U.S.A. **83 G4** 35.15N 95.35W
Eugene U.S.A. **82 B5** 44.03N123.07W
Eugenia, Punta *c.* Mexico **86 A5** 27.50N115.50W
Eupen Belgium **39 E2** 50.38N 6.04E
Euphrates *r.* Asia **61 G3** 31.00N 47.27E
Eureka U.S.A. **82 B5** 40.49N124.10W
Europa, Picos de *mts.* Spain **43 C5** 43.10N 4.40W
Europe 32
Europoort Neth. **39 C3** 51.56N 4.08E
Euskirchen W. Germany **39 E2** 50.40N 6.47E
Eutin W. Germany **38 D2** 54.08N 10.38E
Evansville U.S.A. **83 I4** 38.02N 87.24W
Everest, Mt. Asia **63 F5** 27.59N 86.56E
Evesham U.K. **13 F4** 52.06N 1.57W
Evje Norway **50 A2** 58.36N 7.51E
Évora Portugal **43 B3** 38.34N 7.54W
Évreux France **42 E5** 49.03N 1.11E
Ewe, L. U.K. **14 C4** 57.52N 5.40W
Exe *r.* U.K. **13 D2** 50.40N 3.28W
Exeter U.K. **13 D2** 50.43N 3.31W
Exmoor Forest *hills* U.K. **13 D3** 51.08N 3.45W
Exmouth U.K. **13 D2** 50.38N 3.22W
Extremadura *d.* Spain **43 B3** 39.00N 6.00W
Exuma Is. Bahamas **87 I4** 24.00N 76.00W
Eyasi, L. Tanzania **99 D4** 3.40S 35.00E
Eye U.K. **13 I4** 52.20N 1.09E
Eyemouth U.K. **14 F2** 55.52N 2.05W
Eygurande France **42 F3** 45.40N 2.26E
Eyre, L. Australia **71 C3** 28.30S137.25E

F

Fåborg Denmark **38 D3** 55.06N 10.15E
Fada-N'Gourma Burkina **103 E3** 12.03N 0.22E
Faenza Italy **46 E6** 44.17N 11.52E
Fagernes Norway **50 B3** 60.59N 9.17E
Fagersta Sweden **50 C3** 59.59N 15.49E
Fairbanks U.S.A. **80 D4** 64.50N147.50W
Fair Head U.K. **15 E5** 55.13N 6.09W
Fair Isle U.K. **14 G6** 59.32N 1.38W
Fairweather, Mt. U.S.A. **80 E3** 59.00N137.30W
Faisalābād Pakistan **63 D5** 31.25N 73.09E
Faizābād India **63 E5** 26.46N 82.08E
Fajr, Wādī *r.* Saudi Arabia **60 E3** 30.00N 38.25E
Fakaofo Pacific Oc. **74 I7** 9.30S171.15W
Fakenham U.K. **12 H4** 52.51N 0.52E
Fakfak Indonesia **69 I3** 2.55S132.17E
Fakse Bugt *b.* Denmark **38 F3** 55.10N 12.20E
Falaise France **42 D5** 48.54N 0.11W
Falcarragh Rep. of Ire. **15 C5** 55.09N 8.09W
Falcone, C. Italy **46 D4** 40.57N 8.12E
Falémé *r.* Senegal **102 B3** 14.55N 12.00W
Falkenberg Sweden **50 C2** 56.55N 12.30E
Falkirk U.K. **14 E3** 56.00N 3.48W
Falkland Is. S. America **89 C2** 52.00S 60.00W
Falmouth U.K. **13 B2** 50.09N 5.05W
Falster *i.* Denmark **38 F2** 54.30N 12.00E
Falun Sweden **50 C3** 60.37N 15.40E
Famagusta Cyprus **60 D4** 35.07N 33.57E
Fannich, L. U.K. **14 D4** 57.38N 4.58W
Fanning I. Kiribati **75 K8** 3.52N159.20W
Fanö *i.* Denmark **38 B3** 55.25N 8.25E
Fao Iraq **61 H3** 29.57N 48.30E
Faradofay Madagascar **99 G6** 25.01S 47.00E
Farafra Oasis Egypt **60 C2** 27.00N 28.20E
Farâh Afghan. **62 B6** 32.23N 62.07E
Farâh *r.* Afghan. **62 B5** 31.25N 61.30E
Faranah Guinea **102 B3** 10.01N 10.47W
Fareham U.K. **13 F2** 50.51N 1.11W
Farewell, C. Greenland **81 N3** 60.00N 44.20W
Fargo U.S.A. **83 G6** 46.52N 96.59W
Farim Guinea Bissau **102 A3** 12.30N 15.09W
Farnborough U.K. **13 G3** 51.17N 0.46W
Farne Is. U.K. **12 F7** 55.38N 1.36W
Farnham U.K. **13 G3** 51.12N 0.49W
Faro Portugal **43 B2** 37.01N 7.56W
Faroe Is. Europe **50 L8** 62.00N 7.00W
Fårösund Sweden **50 D2** 57.51N 19.05E
Farrukhābād India **63 E5** 27.23N 79.35E
Fársala Greece **47 K3** 39.17N 22.22E
Farsö Denmark **38 C4** 56.47N 9.20E
Farsund Norway **50 A2** 58.05N 6.49E
Farum Denmark **38 F3** 55.49N 12.20E
Fasā Iran **61 I3** 28.55N 53.38E
Fastov U.S.S.R. **49 N5** 50.08N 29.59E
Făurei Romania **49 M2** 45.04N 27.15E
Fauske Norway **50 C4** 67.17N 15.25E
Favignana *i.* Italy **46 F2** 37.57N 12.19E
Faxaflói *b.* Iceland **50 I7** 64.30N 22.50W
Faxe *r.* Sweden **50 D3** 63.15N 17.15E
Fayetteville U.S.A. **83 K4** 35.03N 78.53W
Fdérik Mauritania **100 A4** 22.35N 12.30W
Feale *r.* Rep. of Ire. **15 B2** 52.28N 9.38W
Fear, C. U.S.A. **83 K3** 33.51N 77.59W
Fécamp France **42 E5** 49.45N 0.23E
Federal Capital Territory *d.* Nigeria **103 F2** 8.50N 7.00E
Feeagh, Lough Rep. of Ire. **15 B3** 53.55N 9.35W
Fehmarn *i.* W. Germany **48 E7** 54.30N 11.05E
Feira de Santana Brazil **88 F6** 12.17S 38.53W
Felanitx Spain **43 G3** 39.27N 3.08E
Feldkirch Austria **48 D3** 47.15N 9.38E
Felixstowe U.K. **13 I3** 51.58N 1.22E
Femer Baelt *str.* Denmark / W. Germany **38 E2** 54.35N 11.20E
Femunden *l.* Norway **50 B3** 62.05N 11.55E
Fengfeng China **67 I4** 36.34N114.19E
Fengjie China **67 H3** 31.00N109.30E
Fenyang China **67 H4** 37.14N111.43E
Fergana U.S.S.R. **52 F2** 40.23N 71.19E
Fergus Falls *town* U.S.A. **83 G6** 46.18N 96.00W
Ferkéssédougou Ivory Coast **102 C2** 9.30N 5.10W
Fermanagh *d.* U.K. **15 D4** 54.21N 7.40W
Fermoselle Spain **43 B4** 41.19N 6.24W
Fermoy Rep. of Ire. **15 C2** 52.08N 8.17W
Ferozepore India **63 D5** 30.55N 74.38E
Ferrara Italy **46 E6** 44.49N 11.38E
Ferret, Cap *c.* France **42 D3** 44.42N 1.16W
Fethiye Turkey **60 C5** 36.37N 29.06E
Fetlar *i.* U.K. **14 H7** 60.37N 0.52W
Fevzipaşa Turkey **60 E5** 37.07N 36.38E
Fez Morocco **100 B5** 34.05N 5.00W
Fianarantsoa Madagascar **99 G7** 21.27S 47.05E
Fife *d.* U.K. **14 E3** 56.10N 3.10W
Fife Ness *c.* U.K. **14 F3** 56.17N 2.36W
Figeac France **42 F3** 44.32N 2.01E
Figueira da Foz Portugal **43 A4** 40.09N 8.51W
Figueres Spain **43 G5** 42.16N 2.57E
Fiji Pacific Oc. **74 H6** 18.00S178.00E
Filey U.K. **12 G6** 54.12N 0.15W
Findhorn *r.* U.K. **14 E4** 57.37N 3.40W
Finisterre, C. Spain **43 A5** 42.54N 9.16W
Finland Europe **50 F3** 64.30N 27.00E
Finland, G. of Finland / U.S.S.R. **50 F2** 60.00N 26.50E
Finlay *r.* Canada **80 F3** 56.30N124.40W
Finn *r.* Rep. of Ire. **15 D4** 54.50N 7.30W
Finschhafen P.N.G. **69 L2** 6.35S147.51E
Firozābād India **63 E5** 27.09N 78.24E
Firth of Clyde *est.* U.K. **14 D2** 55.35N 4.53W
Firth of Forth *est.* U.K. **14 E3** 56.05N 3.00W
Firth of Lorn *est.* U.K. **14 C3** 56.20N 5.40W
Firth of Tay *est.* U.K. **14 F3** 56.24N 3.08W
Firūzābād Iran **61 I3** 28.50N 52.35E
Fisher Str. Canada **81 J4** 63.00N 84.00W
Fishguard U.K. **13 C3** 51.59N 4.59W
Flagstaff U.S.A. **82 D4** 35.12N111.38W
Flåm Norway **50 A3** 60.51N 7.08E
Flamborough Head U.K. **12 G6** 54.06N 0.05W
Flaming Gorge Resr. U.S.A. **82 E5** 41.10N109.30W
Flanders *f.* Belgium **39 B2** 50.52N 3.00E
Flanders East *d.* Belgium **39 B3** 51.00N 3.45E
Flanders West *d.* Belgium **39 A2** 51.00N 3.00E
Flannan Is. U.K. **14 A5** 58.16N 7.40W
Flathead L. U.S.A. **82 D6** 47.50N114.05W
Flattery, C. U.S.A. **82 B6** 48.23N124.43W
Fleetwood U.K. **12 D5** 53.55N 3.01W
Flekkefjord *town* Norway **50 A2** 58.17N 6.40E
Flen Sweden **50 D2** 59.04N 16.39E
Flensburg W. Germany **48 D7** 54.47N 9.27E
Flensburg Fjord *b.* Denmark / W. Germany **38 C2** 54.50N 9.50E
Flers France **42 D5** 48.45N 0.34W
Flinders *r.* Australia **71 D4** 17.30S140.45E
Flinders I. Australia **71 D2** 40.00S148.00E
Flinders Range *mts.* Australia **71 C2** 31.00S138.30E
Flin Flon Canada **81 H3** 54.47N101.51W
Flint U.K. **12 D5** 53.15N 3.10W
Flint U.S.A. **83 J5** 43.03N 83.40W
Flint *r.* U.S.A. **83 J3** 30.52N 84.35W
Flint I. Kiribati **75 K6** 11.26S151.48W
Florence Italy **46 E5** 43.46N 11.15E
Florence U.S.A. **83 K3** 34.12N 79.44W
Florenville Belgium **39 D1** 49.42N 5.19E
Flores *i.* Indonesia **69 G2** 8.40S121.20E
Flores Sea Indonesia **69 G2** 7.00S121.00E
Florianópolis Brazil **89 E5** 27.35S 48.31W
Florida *d.* U.S.A. **83 J2** 29.00N 82.00W
Florida, Straits of U.S.A. **76 L4** 24.00N 81.00W
Flórina Greece **47 J4** 40.48N 21.25E
Florö Norway **50 A3** 61.45N 4.55E
Flushing Neth. **39 B3** 51.27N 3.35E
Fly *r.* P.N.G. **69 K2** 8.22S142.23E
Focşani Romania **49 M2** 45.40N 27.12E
Foggia Italy **46 G4** 41.28N 15.33E
Föhr *i.* W. Germany **38 B2** 54.44N 8.30E
Foix France **42 E2** 42.57N 1.35E
Folda *est.* Norway **50 B4** 64.45N 11.20E
Foligno Italy **46 F5** 42.56N 12.43E
Folkestone U.K. **13 I3** 51.05N 1.11E
Fond du Lac Canada **80 H3** 59.20N107.09W
Fonseca, G. of Honduras **87 G2** 13.10N 87.30W
Fontainebleau France **42 F5** 48.24N 2.42E
Fontenay France **42 D4** 46.28N 0.48W
Forécariah Guinea **102 B2** 9.28N 13.06W
Forel, Mt. Greenland **81 O4** 67.00N 37.00W
Foreland Pt. U.K. **13 D3** 51.15N 3.50W
Forest of Atholl *f.* U.K. **14 E3** 56.53N 3.55W
Forest of Bowland *hills* U.K. **12 E5** 53.58N 2.30W
Forest of Dean *f.* U.K. **13 E3** 51.45N 2.35W
Forfar U.K. **14 F3** 56.38N 2.54W
Forlì Italy **46 F6** 44.13N 12.02E
Formby Pt. U.K. **12 D5** 53.33N 3.08W
Formentera *i.* Spain **43 F3** 38.41N 1.30E
Formosa Str. China / Taiwan **67 I2** 25.00N120.00E
Fornaes *c.* Denmark **38 D4** 56.28N 10.58E
Forres U.K. **14 E4** 57.37N 3.38W
Forssa Finland **50 E3** 60.49N 23.40E
Forst E. Germany **48 G5** 51.46N 14.39E
Fort Albany Canada **81 J3** 52.15N 81.35W
Fortaleza Brazil **88 F7** 3.45S 38.45W
Fort Augustus U.K. **14 D4** 57.09N 4.41W
Fort Chimo Canada **81 L3** 58.10N 68.15W
Fort Chipewyan Canada **80 G3** 58.46N111.09W
Fort Collins U.S.A. **82 E5** 40.35N105.05W
Fort-de-France Martinique **87 L2** 14.36N 61.05W
Fort Frances Canada **81 I2** 48.37N 93.23W
Fort George Canada **81 K3** 53.50N 79.01W
Fort Good Hope Canada **80 F4** 66.16N128.37W
Forth *r.* U.K. **14 E3** 56.06N 3.48W
Fort Lauderdale U.S.A. **83 J2** 26.08N 80.08W
Fort Liard Canada **80 F4** 60.14N123.28W
Fort McMurray Canada **80 G3** 56.45N111.27W
Fort McPherson Canada **80 E4** 67.29N134.50W
Fort Myers U.S.A. **83 J2** 26.39N 81.51W
Fort Nelson Canada **80 F3** 58.48N122.44W
Fort Norman Canada **80 F4** 64.55N125.29W
Fort Peck Dam U.S.A. **82 E6** 47.55N106.15W
Fort Peck Resr. U.S.A. **82 E6** 47.55N107.00W
Fort Randall U.S.A. **80 B3** 55.10N162.47W
Fort Reliance Canada **80 H4** 62.45N109.08W
Fort Resolution Canada **80 G4** 61.10N113.39W
Fortrose U.K. **14 D4** 57.34N 4.07W
Fort Rupert Canada **81 K3** 51.30N 79.45W
Fort St. John Canada **80 F3** 56.14N120.55W
Fort Scott U.S.A. **83 H4** 37.52N 94.43W
Fort Severn Canada **81 J3** 56.00N 87.40W
Fort Shevchenko U.S.S.R. **52 E2** 44.31N 50.15E
Fort Simpson Canada **80 F4** 61.46N121.15W
Fort Smith *d.* Canada **80 F4** 63.30N118.00W
Fort Smith U.S.A. **83 H4** 35.22N 94.27W
Fort Vermilion Canada **80 G3** 58.22N115.59W
Fort Wayne U.S.A. **83 I5** 41.05N 85.08W
Fort William U.K. **14 C3** 56.49N 5.07W
Fort Worth U.S.A. **83 G3** 32.45N 97.20W
Fort Yukon U.S.A. **80 D4** 66.35N145.20W
Foshan China **67 H2** 23.03N113.08E
Fougères France **42 D5** 48.21N 1.12W
Foula *i.* U.K. **14 F7** 60.08N 2.05W
Foulness I. U.K. **13 H3** 51.36N 0.52E
Foumban Cameroon **103 G2** 5.43N 10.50E
Fowey U.K. **13 C2** 50.20N 4.39W
Foxe Basin *b.* Canada **81 K4** 67.30N 79.00W
Foxe Channel Canada **81 J4** 65.00N 80.00W
Foyle *r.* U.K. **15 D4** 55.00N 7.20W
Foyle, Lough U.K. **15 D5** 55.05N 7.10W
France Europe **42 D4** 47.00N 2.00E
Francistown Botswana **99 C2** 21.11S 27.32E
Frankfort U.S.A. **83 J4** 38.11N 84.53W
Frankfurt E. Germany **48 G6** 52.20N 14.32E
Frankfurt W. Germany **48 D5** 50.06N 8.41E
Franklin D. Roosevelt L. U.S.A. **82 C6** 47.55N118.20W
Franz Josef Land *is.* U.S.S.R. **52 E5** 81.00N 54.00E
Fraser *r.* Canada **80 F2** 49.05N123.00W
Fraserburgh U.K. **14 G4** 57.42N 2.00W
Fredericia Denmark **38 C3** 55.34N 9.47E
Fredericksburg U.S.A. **83 K4** 38.18N 77.30W
Fredericton Canada **81 L2** 45.57N 66.40W
Frederiksborg *d.* Denmark **38 F3** 55.50N 12.10E
Frederikshåb Greenland **81 N4** 62.05N 49.30W
Frederikshavn Denmark **38 D5** 57.28N 10.33E
Frederikssund Denmark **38 F3** 55.51N 12.04E
Fredrikstad Norway **50 B2** 59.15N 10.55E
Freeport Bahamas **87 I5** 26.40N 78.30W
Freetown Sierra Leone **102 B2** 8.30N 13.17W
Freiberg E. Germany **48 F5** 50.54N 13.20E
Freiburg W. Germany **48 C3** 48.00N 7.52E
Freilingen W. Germany **39 F2** 50.33N 7.50E
Freising W. Germany **48 E4** 48.24N 11.45E
Fréjus France **42 H2** 43.26N 6.44E
Freshford Rep. of Ire. **15 D2** 52.43N 7.25W
Fresno U.S.A. **82 C4** 36.41N119.57W
Fribourg Switz. **48 C3** 46.50N 7.10E
Friedrichshafen W. Germany **48 D3** 47.39N 9.29E
Friedrichstadt W. Germany **38 C2** 54.23N 9.07E
Friesland *d.* Neth. **39 D5** 53.05N 5.45E
Friesoythe W. Germany **39 F5** 53.02N 7.52E
Frio, Cabo *c.* Brazil **89 E5** 22.50S 42.10W
Frisian Is. Europe **32 G5** 53.30N 6.00E
Frobisher B. Canada **81 L4** 63.00N 66.45W
Frobisher Bay *town* Canada **81 L4** 63.45N 68.30W
Frohavet *est.* Norway **50 B3** 63.55N 9.05E
Frome U.K. **13 E3** 51.14N 2.20W
Frome, L. Australia **71 C2** 30.45S139.45E
Frosinone Italy **46 F4** 41.36N 13.21E
Fröya *i.* Norway **50 B3** 63.45N 8.30E
Frunze U.S.S.R. **66 B5** 42.53N 74.46E
Frýdek-Místek Czech. **49 I4** 49.41N 18.22E
Fuerte *r.* Mexico **86 C5** 25.42N109.20W
Fuerteventura *i.* Canary Is. **100 A4** 28.20N 14.10W
Fujairah U.A.E. **61 J2** 25.10N 56.20E
Fujian *d.* China **67 I3** 26.30N118.00E
Fujin China **67 L6** 47.15N131.59E
Fujiyama *mtn.* Japan **70 D4** 35.23N138.42E
Fukui Japan **70 C5** 36.04N136.12E
Fukuoka Japan **70 A3** 33.39N130.21E
Fukushima Japan **70 D5** 37.44N140.28E
Fukuyama Japan **70 B4** 34.29N133.21E
Fulda W. Germany **48 D5** 50.35N 9.45E
Fumay France **39 C1** 49.59N 4.42E
Funabashi Japan **70 D4** 35.42N139.59E
Funafuti Tuvalu **74 H7** 8.31S179.13E
Funchal Madeira Is. **100 A5** 32.38N 16.54W
Fundy, B. of N. America **83 M5** 44.30N 66.30W
Funen *i.* Denmark **38 D3** 55.15N 10.30E
Furakawa Japan **70 D6** 38.30N140.50E
Fūrg Iran **61 I3** 28.19N 55.10E
Furnas Dam Brazil **89 E5** 20.40S 46.22W
Furneaux Group *is.* Australia **74 E3** 40.10S148.05E
Furnes Belgium **39 A3** 51.04N 2.40E
Fürstenau W. Germany **39 F4** 52.32N 7.41E
Fürstenwalde E. Germany **48 G6** 52.22N 14.04E
Fürth W. Germany **48 E4** 49.28N 11.00E
Fushun China **67 J5** 41.51N123.53E
Futa Jalon *f.* Guinea **102 B3** 11.30N 12.30W
Fuxin China **67 J5** 42.08N121.39E
Fuyu China **67 J6** 45.12N124.49E
Fuzhou Fujian China **67 I3** 26.01N119.20E
Fuzhou Jiangxi China **67 I3** 28.03N116.15E
Fyne, Loch U.K. **14 C2** 55.55N 5.23W
Fyns *d.* Denmark **38 D3** 55.10N 10.30E

G

Gabès Tunisia **100 D5** 33.52N 10.06E
Gabès, G. of Tunisia **100 D5** 34.00N 11.00E
Gabon Africa **99 B4** 0.00 12.00E
Gaborone Botswana **99 C2** 24.45S 25.55E
Gach Sārān Iran **61 H3** 30.13N 50.49E
Gadsden U.S.A. **83 I3** 34.00N 86.00W
Gaeta Italy **46 F4** 41.13N 13.35E
Gaeta, G. of Med. Sea **46 F4** 41.05N 13.30E
Gagnoa Ivory Coast **102 C2** 6.04N 5.55W
Gagnon Canada **81 L3** 51.56N 68.16W
Gaillac France **42 E2** 43.54N 1.53E
Gainesville U.S.A. **83 J2** 29.37N 82.31W
Gainsborough U.K. **12 G5** 53.25N 0.43W
Gairdner, L. Australia **71 C2** 31.30S136.00E
Gairloch *town* U.K. **14 C4** 57.43N 5.41W
Galapagos Is. Pacific Oc. **75 Q7** 0.30S 90.30W
Galashiels U.K. **14 F2** 55.37N 2.49W
Galaţi Romania **49 N2** 45.27N 28.03E
Galena U.S.A. **80 C4** 64.43N157.00W
Galicia *d.* Spain **43 A5** 43.00N 8.00W
Galle Sri Lanka **63 E1** 6.01N 80.13E
Gállego *r.* Spain **43 E4** 41.40N 0.55W
Galley Head Rep. of Ire. **15 C1** 51.31N 8.57W
Gallinas, C. Colombia **88 B9** 12.27N 71.44W
Gallipoli Italy **47 I4** 40.02N 18.01E
Gallipoli Turkey **47 M4** 40.25N 26.31E
Gällivare Sweden **50 E4** 67.10N 20.40E
Galloway *f.* U.K. **14 D2** 55.00N 4.28W
Gallup U.S.A. **82 E4** 35.32N108.46W
Galston U.K. **14 D2** 55.37N 4.21W
Galtby Finland **50 E3** 60.08N 21.33E
Galty Mts. Rep. of Ire. **15 C2** 52.20N 8.10W
Galveston U.S.A. **83 H2** 29.17N 94.48W
Galveston B. U.S.A. **83 H2** 29.40N 94.40W
Galway Rep. of Ire. **15 B3** 53.17N 9.04W
Galway *d.* Rep. of Ire. **15 B3** 53.25N 9.00W
Galway B. Rep. of Ire. **15 B3** 53.12N 9.07W
Gambia Africa **102 A3** 13.10N 16.00W
Gambia *r.* Gambia **102 A3** 13.28N 15.55W
Gambier, Îles *is.* Pacific Oc. **75 M5** 23.10S135.00W
Gander Canada **81 M2** 48.58N 54.34W
Gandía Spain **43 E3** 38.59N 0.11W
Ganges *r.* India **63 G4** 23.30N 90.25E
Ganges, Mouths of the India / Bangla. **63 F4** 22.00N 89.35E
Gangtok India **63 F5** 27.20N 88.39E
Gannat France **42 F4** 46.06N 3.11E
Gannett Peak *mtn.* U.S.A. **82 E5** 43.10N109.38W
Gansu *d.* China **66 F5** 36.00N103.00E
Ganzhou China **67 I2** 25.52N114.51E
Gao Mali **103 D4** 16.19N 0.09W
Gaoual Guinea **102 B3** 11.44N 13.14W
Gaoxiong Taiwan **67 J2** 22.36N120.17E
Gap France **42 H3** 44.33N 6.05E
Gar China **63 E6** 32.10N 79.59E
Gara, Lough Rep. of Ire. **15 C3** 53.56N 8.28W
Gard *r.* France **42 G2** 43.52N 4.40E
Garda, L. Italy **46 E6** 45.40N 10.40E
Garissa Kenya **99 D4** 0.27S 39.39E
Garmisch Partenkirchen W. Germany **48 E3** 47.30N 11.05E
Garonne *r.* France **42 D3** 45.00N 0.37W
Garoua Cameroon **103 G2** 9.17N 13.22E
Garrison Resr. U.S.A. **82 F6** 47.30N102.20W
Garron Pt. U.K. **15 F5** 55.04N 5.59W
Garry L. Canada **81 I4** 66.00N100.00W
Garut Indonesia **68 D2** 7.15S107.55E
Garvão Portugal **43 A2** 37.42N 8.21W
Garve U.K. **14 D4** 57.37N 4.41W
Gary U.S.A. **83 I5** 41.34N 87.20W
Garyarsa China **66 C3** 31.30N 80.40E
Gascony, G. of France **42 C3** 44.00N 2.40W
Gaspé Canada **81 L2** 48.50N 64.30W
Gata, C. Cyprus **60 D4** 34.33N 33.03E
Gata, Cabo de *c.* Spain **43 D2** 36.45N 2.11W
Gata, Sierra de *mts.* Spain **43 B4** 40.20N 6.30W
Gatehouse of Fleet U.K. **14 D1** 54.52N 4.13W
Gateshead U.K. **12 F6** 54.57N 1.34W
Gatun L. Panama **87 H1** 9.20N 80.00W
Gauhāti India **63 G5** 26.05N 91.55E
Gauja *r.* U.S.S.R. **50 F2** 57.10N 24.17E
Gavá Spain **43 F4** 41.18N 2.00E
Gävle Sweden **50 D3** 60.41N 17.10E
Gaya India **63 F4** 24.48N 85.00E
Gaya Niger **103 E3** 11.53N 3.31E
Gaza Egypt **60 D3** 31.30N 34.28E
Gaziantep Turkey **60 E5** 37.04N 37.21E
Gdańsk Poland **49 I7** 54.22N 18.38E
Gdańsk, G. of Poland **49 I7** 54.45N 19.15E
Gdov U.S.S.R. **50 F2** 58.48N 27.52E
Gdynia Poland **49 I7** 54.31N 18.30E
Gebze Turkey **60 C6** 40.48N 29.26E
Gediz *r.* Turkey **47 M3** 38.37N 26.47E
Gedser Denmark **38 E2** 54.35N 11.57E
Geel Belgium **39 D3** 51.10N 5.00E
Geelong Australia **71 D2** 38.10S144.26E
Geh Iran **61 K2** 26.14N 60.15E
Geidam Nigeria **103 G3** 12.55N 11.55E
Geilenkirchen W. Germany **39 E2** 50.58N 6.08E
Gejiu China **66 G2** 23.25N103.05E

Kárpathos *i.* Greece **47 M1** 35.35N 27.08E
Kars Turkey **60 F6** 40.35N 43.05E
Karsakpay U.S.S.R. **52 F2** 47.47N 66.43E
Kārūn *r.* Iran **61 H3** 30.25N 48.12E
Karup Denmark **38 C4** 56.18N 9.11E
Kasai *r.* Zaïre **99 B4** 3.10S 16.13E
Kasese Uganda **99 D5** 0.14N 30.08E
Kashi China **66 B5** 39.29N 76.02E
Kassalā Sudan **101 F3** 15.24N 36.30E
Kassel W. Germany **48 D5** 51.18N 9.30E
Kastamonu Turkey **60 D6** 41.22N 33.47E
Kastoría Greece **47 J4** 40.32N 21.15E
Kasūr Pakistan **63 D5** 31.07N 74.30E
Katha Burma **63 H4** 24.11N 96.20E
Katherîna, Gebel *mtn.* Egypt **60 D3** 28.30N 33.57E
Kathmandu Nepal **63 F5** 27.42N 85.19E
Kati Mali **102 C3** 12.41N 8.04W
Katowice Poland **49 I5** 50.15N 18.59E
Katrine, L. U.K. **14 D3** 56.25N 4.30W
Katrineholm Sweden **50 D2** 58.59N 16.15E
Katsina Nigeria **103 F3** 13.00N 7.32E
Katsina Ala Nigeria **103 F2** 7.10N 9.30E
Katsina Ala *r.* Nigeria **103 F2** 7.50N 8.58E
Kattegat *str.* Denmark / Sweden **50 B2** 57.00N 11.20E
Katwijk aan Zee Neth. **39 C4** 52.13N 4.27E
Kauai *i.* Hawaii U.S.A. **82 O9** 22.05N159.30W
Kaufbeuren W. Germany **48 E3** 47.53N 10.37E
Kauhajoki Finland **50 E3** 62.26N 22.10E
Kauhava Finland **50 E3** 63.06N 23.05E
Kaunas U.S.S.R. **50 E1** 54.52N 23.55E
Kaura Namoda Nigeria **103 F3** 12.39N 6.38E
Kāvali India **63 E3** 14.55N 80.01E
Kavála Greece **47 L4** 40.56N 24.24E
Kawagoe Japan **70 D4** 35.58N139.30E
Kawaguchi Japan **70 D4** 35.55N139.50E
Kawasaki Japan **70 D4** 35.30N139.45E
Kayan *r.* Indonesia **68 F4** 2.47N117.46E
Kayes Mali **102 B3** 14.26N 11.28W
Kayseri Turkey **60 D5** 38.42N 35.28E
Kazachye U.S.S.R. **53 L4** 70.46N136.15E
Kazakh Hills U.S.S.R. **54 J7** 49.00N 75.00E
Kazakhstan S.S.R. *d.* U.S.S.R. **52 E2** 49.00N 64.00E
Kazan U.S.S.R. **52 E3** 55.55N 49.10E
Kazanlŭk Bulgaria **47 L5** 42.38N 25.26E
Kazarun Iran **61 H3** 29.35N 51.39E
Kazatin U.S.S.R. **49 N4** 49.41N 28.49E
Kazbek *mtn.* U.S.S.R. **52 D2** 42.42N 44.30E
Kazincbarcika Hungary **49 J4** 48.16N 20.37E
Kéa *i.* Greece **47 L2** 37.36N 24.20E
Kearney U.S.A. **82 G5** 40.42N 99.04W
Kebnekaise *mtn.* Sweden **50 D4** 67.55N 18.30E
Kecskemét Hungary **49 I3** 46.54N 19.42E
Kediri Indonesia **68 E2** 7.55S112.01E
Kédougou Senegal **102 B3** 12.35N 12.09W
Keele Peak *mtn.* Canada **80 E4** 63.15N130.19W
Keetmanshoop Namibia **99 B2** 26.36S 18.08E
Keewatin *d.* Canada **81 I4** 65.00N 90.00W
Kefallinía *i.* Greece **47 J3** 38.15N 20.33E
Keflavík Iceland **50 I7** 64.01N 22.35W
Keighley U.K. **12 F5** 53.53N 1.51W
Keitele *l.* Finland **50 F3** 62.59N 26.00E
Keith U.K. **14 F4** 57.32N 2.57W
Kelang Malaysia **68 C4** 2.57N101.24E
Kelberg W. Germany **39 E2** 50.17N 6.56E
Kelkit *r.* Turkey **60 E6** 40.46N 36.32E
Kelloselkä Finland **50 G4** 66.55N 28.50E
Kells Rep. of Ire. **15 E3** 53.44N 6.53W
Kelowna Canada **80 G2** 49.50N119.29W
Kelso U.K. **14 F2** 55.36N 2.26W
Keluang Malaysia **68 C4** 2.01N103.18E
Kelvedon U.K. **13 H3** 51.51N 0.42E
Kemaliye Turkey **60 E5** 39.16N 38.29E
Kemerovo U.S.S.R. **52 H3** 55.25N 86.10E
Kemi Finland **50 F4** 65.45N 24.12E
Kemi *r.* Finland **50 F4** 65.47N 24.28E
Kemijärvi Finland **50 F4** 66.40N 27.21E
Kempten W. Germany **48 E3** 47.44N 10.19E
Kendal U.K. **12 E6** 54.19N 2.44W
Kendari Indonesia **69 G3** 3.57S122.36E
Kenema Sierra Leone **102 B2** 7.57N 11.11W
Kengtung Burma **66 F2** 21.16N 99.39E
Kenilworth U.K. **13 F4** 52.20N 1.34W
Kenitra Morocco **100 B5** 34.20N 6.34W
Kenmare Rep. of Ire. **15 B1** 51.53N 9.36W
Kennet *r.* U.K. **13 F3** 51.28N 0.57W
Keno Hill *town* Canada **80 E4** 63.58N135.22W
Kenora Canada **81 I2** 49.47N 94.26W
Kent *d.* U.K. **13 H3** 51.12N 0.40E
Kentucky *d.* U.S.A. **83 I4** 38.00N 85.00W
Kentucky L. U.S.A. **83 I4** 36.15N 88.00W
Kenya Africa **99 D5** 0.00 38.00E
Kenya, Mt. Kenya **99 D4** 0.10S 37.19E
Kerala *d.* India **63 D2** 10.30N 76.30E
Kerch U.S.S.R. **52 D2** 45.22N 36.27E
Kerema P.N.G. **69 L2** 7.59S145.46E
Kerguelen *i.* Indian Oc. **109 M2** 49.30S 69.30E
Kerguelen Basin Indian Oc. **107 M3** 35.00S 67.00E
Kerinci, Gunung *mtn.* Indonesia **68 C3** 1.45S101.20E
Kerkrade Neth. **39 E2** 50.52N 6.02E
Kermadec Is. Pacific Oc. **74 I5** 30.00S178.30W
Kermadec Trench Pacific Oc. **74 I4** 33.30S176.00W
Kermān Iran **101 H5** 30.18N 57.05E
Kermānshāh Iran **61 G4** 34.19N 47.04E
Kerme, G. of Turkey **47 M2** 36.52N 27.53E
Kerpen W. Germany **39 E2** 50.52N 6.42E
Kerry *d.* Rep. of Ire. **15 B2** 52.07N 9.35W
Kerry Head Rep. of Ire. **15 B2** 52.24N 9.56W
Kerteminde Denmark **38 D3** 55.27N 10.39E
Kerulen *r.* Mongolia **67 I6** 48.45N117.00E
Keşan Turkey **47 M4** 40.50N 26.39E
Keswick U.K. **12 D6** 54.37N 3.09W
Ketapang Indonesia **68 E3** 1.50S110.02E
Ketchikan U.S.A. **80 E3** 55.25N131.40W
Kete Krachi Ghana **103 D2** 7.50N 0.03W
Kettering U.K. **13 G4** 52.24N 0.44W
Keweenaw B. U.S.A. **83 I6** 47.00N 88.00W
Key, Lough Rep. of Ire. **15 C4** 54.00N 8.15W
Keynsham U.K. **13 E3** 51.25N 2.31W
Khabarovsk U.S.S.R. **67 L6** 48.32N135.08E
Khabur *r.* Syria **60 F4** 35.07N 40.30E
Khaburah Oman **61 J1** 23.58N 57.10E
Khairpur Pakistan **62 C5** 27.30N 68.50E
Khalkís Greece **47 K3** 38.27N 23.36E
Khanaqin Iraq **61 G4** 34.22N 45.22E
Khandwa India **63 D4** 21.49N 76.23E
Khangai Mts. Mongolia **54 L7** 49.00N 95.00E
Khanka, L. U.S.S.R. **67 L6** 45.00N132.30E
Khanty-Mansiysk U.S.S.R. **52 F3** 61.00N 69.00E
Khanu Iran **61 J2** 27.55N 57.45E
Kharagpur India **63 F4** 22.23N 87.22E
Khārān *r.* Iran **61 J2** 27.37N 58.48E
Kharga Oasis Egypt **60 C2** 25.00N 30.40E
Kharkov U.S.S.R. **52 D2** 50.00N 36.15E
Khartoum Sudan **101 F3** 15.33N 32.35E
Khartoum North Sudan **101 F3** 15.39N 32.34E
Khaskovo Bulgaria **47 L4** 41.57N 25.33E
Khatanga U.S.S.R. **53 I4** 71.50N102.31E
Khatangskiy G. U.S.S.R. **53 J4** 75.00N112.10E
Kherson U.S.S.R. **52 C2** 46.39N 32.38E
Khimki U.S.S.R. **52 D3** 55.53N 37.26E
Khíos *i.* Greece **47 L3** 38.23N 26.04E
Khirsan *r.* Iran **61 H3** 31.29N 50.23E
Khmelnitskiy U.S.S.R. **49 M4** 49.25N 26.49E
Khöbsögöl Dalai *l.* Mongolia **66 F7** 51.00N100.30E
Khodorov U.S.S.R. **49 L4** 49.20N 24.19E
Khoi Iran **61 G5** 38.32N 45.02E
Khoper *r.* U.S.S.R. **33 N4** 49.35N 42.17E
Khor Qatar **61 H2** 25.39N 51.32E
Khorramābād Iran **61 H4** 33.29N 48.21E
Khorramshahr Iran **61 H3** 30.26N 48.09E
Khotimsk U.S.S.R. **49 P6** 53.24N 32.36E
Khotin U.S.S.R. **49 M4** 48.30N 26.31E
Khouribga Morocco **100 B5** 32.54N 6.57W
Khulna Bangla. **63 F4** 22.49N 89.34E
Khurmuj Iran **61 H3** 28.40N 51.20E
Khwash Iran **61 K3** 28.14N 61.15E
Khyber Pass Asia **63 C6** 34.06N 71.05E
Kicking Horse Pass Canada **80 G3** 51.28N116.23W
Kidal Mali **100 C3** 18.27N 1.25E
Kidan *des.* Saudi Arabia **61 I1** 22.20N 54.20E
Kidderminster U.K. **13 E4** 52.23N 2.15W
Kidsgrove U.K. **12 E5** 53.07N 2.13W
Kiel W. Germany **48 E7** 54.20N 10.08E
Kiel Bay W. Germany **48 E7** 54.30N 10.30E
Kiel Canal W. Germany **48 D7** 53.54N 9.12E
Kielce Poland **49 J5** 50.52N 20.37E
Kieta P.N.G. **71 E5** 6.13S155.38E
Kiev U.S.S.R. **49 O5** 50.28N 30.50E
Kigali Rwanda **99 D4** 1.59S 30.05E
Kigoma Tanzania **99 C4** 4.52S 29.36E
Kii sanchi *mts.* Japan **70 C4** 34.00N135.20E
Kii suidō *str.* Japan **70 B3** 34.00N135.00E
Kikinda Yugo. **47 J6** 45.51N 20.30E
Kikori P.N.G. **69 K2** 7.25S144.13E
Kikwit Zaïre **99 B4** 5.02S 18.51E
Kil Sweden **50 C2** 59.30N 13.20E
Kila Kila P.N.G. **69 L2** 9.31S147.10E
Kilcullen Rep. of Ire. **15 E3** 53.08N 6.47W
Kildare Rep. of Ire. **15 E3** 53.10N 6.55W
Kildare *d.* Rep. of Ire. **15 E3** 53.10N 6.50W
Kilfinan U.K. **14 C2** 55.58N 5.19W
Kilimanjaro *mtn.* Tanzania **99 D4** 3.02S 37.20E
Kilis Turkey **60 E5** 36.43N 37.07E
Kilkee Rep. of Ire. **15 B2** 52.41N 9.40W
Kilkenny Rep. of Ire. **15 D2** 52.39N 7.16W
Kilkenny *d.* Rep. of Ire. **15 D2** 52.35N 7.15W
Kilkieran Bay Rep. of Ire. **15 B3** 53.18N 9.50W
Kilkís Greece **47 K4** 40.59N 22.51E
Killala B. Rep. of Ire. **15 B4** 54.15N 9.10W
Killard Pt. U.K. **15 F4** 54.18N 5.31W
Killarney Rep. of Ire. **15 B2** 52.04N 9.32W
Killary Harbour *b.* Rep. of Ire. **15 A3** 53.40N 10.00W
Killin U.K. **14 D3** 56.29N 4.20W
Killíni *mtn.* Greece **47 K2** 37.56N 22.22E
Killorglin Rep. of Ire. **15 B2** 52.05N 9.47W
Killybegs Rep. of Ire. **15 C4** 54.38N 8.29W
Killyleagh U.K. **15 F4** 54.23N 5.40W
Kilmarnock U.K. **14 D2** 55.37N 4.30W
Kilmichael Pt. Rep. of Ire. **15 E2** 52.43N 6.10W
Kilninver U.K. **14 C3** 56.20N 5.30W
Kilronan Rep. of Ire. **15 B3** 53.08N 9.42W
Kilrush Rep. of Ire. **15 B2** 52.39N 9.30W
Kilsyth U.K. **14 D3** 56.00N 4.04W
Kimberley R.S.A. **99 C2** 28.45S 24.46E
Kimito *i.* Finland **50 E3** 60.05N 22.30E
Kinabalu *mtn.* Malaysia **68 F5** 6.10N116.40E
Kindia Guinea **102 B3** 10.03N 12.49W
Kindu Zaïre **99 C4** 3.00S 25.56E
Kineshma U.S.S.R. **52 D3** 57.28N 42.08E
King Christian Ninth Land *f.* Greenland **81 O4** 68.20N 37.00W
King Frederik Sixth Coast *f.* Greenland **81 N4** 63.00N 44.00W
King I. Australia **71 D2** 39.50S144.00E
Kingissepp U.S.S.R. **50 E2** 58.12N 22.30E
King Leopold Ranges *mts.* Australia **71 B4** 17.00S125.30E
Kingman Reef Pacific Oc. **74 J8** 6.24N162.22W
Kingsbridge U.K. **13 D2** 50.17N 3.46W
Kingsclere U.K. **13 F3** 51.19N 1.13W
Kingsdown U.K. **13 H3** 51.20N 0.18E
Kingsley Dam U.S.A. **82 F5** 41.15N101.30W
King's Lynn U.K. **12 H4** 52.45N 0.25E
Kingsmill Group *is.* Kiribati **74 H7** 1.00S175.00E
Kingston Canada **81 K2** 44.14N 76.30W
Kingston Jamaica **87 I3** 17.58N 76.48W
Kingston upon Hull U.K. **12 G5** 53.45N 0.20W
Kingstown St. Vincent **87 L2** 13.12N 61.14W
Kingswood U.K. **13 E3** 51.28N 2.30W
Kings Worthy U.K. **13 F3** 51.06N 1.19W
Kington U.K. **13 D4** 52.12N 3.01W
Kingussie U.K. **14 D4** 57.05N 4.04W
Kinka zan *c.* Japan **70 E6** 38.20N141.32E
Kinki *d.* Japan **70 B4** 35.10N135.00E
Kinloch Rannoch U.K. **14 D3** 56.42N 4.11W
Kinnairds Hd. U.K. **14 G4** 57.42N 2.00W
Kinnegad Rep. of Ire. **15 D3** 53.28N 7.09W
Kinross U.K. **14 E3** 56.13N 3.27W
Kinsale Rep. of Ire. **15 C1** 51.41N 8.32W
Kinshasa Zaïre **99 B4** 4.18S 15.18E
Kintyre *pen.* U.K. **14 C2** 55.35N 5.35W
Kinvara Rep. of Ire. **15 C3** 53.08N 8.57W
Kiparissía Greece **47 J2** 37.15N 21.40E
Kippure *mtn.* Rep. of Ire. **15 E3** 53.10N 6.21W
Kirensk U.S.S.R. **53 J3** 57.45N108.00E
Kirghizstan S. S. R. *d.* U.S.S.R. **66 B5** 41.30N 75.00E
Kirgiz Steppe *f.* U.S.S.R. **52 E2** 49.28N 57.07E
Kiribati Pacific Oc. **74 H7** 4.00S175.00E
Kirikkale Turkey **60 D5** 39.51N 33.32E
Kirkby Lonsdale U.K. **12 E6** 54.11N 2.31W
Kirkby Stephen U.K. **12 E6** 54.27N 2.20W
Kirkcaldy U.K. **14 E3** 56.07N 3.10W
Kirkcudbright U.K. **14 D1** 54.50N 4.03W
Kirkenes Norway **50 G5** 69.44N 30.05E
Kirkland Lake *town* Canada **81 J2** 48.10N 80.02W
Kirklareli Turkey **47 M4** 41.44N 27.12E
Kirkūk Iraq **61 G4** 35.28N 44.26E
Kirkwall U.K. **14 F5** 58.59N 2.58W
Kirn W. Germany **39 F1** 49.47N 7.28E
Kirov U.S.S.R. **52 E3** 58.38N 49.38E
Kirovabad U.S.S.R. **61 G6** 40.39N 46.20E
Kirovakan U.S.S.R. **61 G6** 40.49N 44.30E
Kirovograd U.S.S.R. **52 C2** 48.31N 32.15E
Kirovsk U.S.S.R. **50 H4** 67.37N 33.39E
Kirriemuir U.K. **14 E3** 56.41N 3.01W
Kirşehir Turkey **60 D5** 39.09N 34.08E
Kiruna Sweden **50 E4** 67.53N 20.15E
Kiryu Japan **70 D5** 36.26N139.18E
Kisangani Zaïre **99 C5** 0.33N 25.14E
Kishinev U.S.S.R. **49 N3** 47.00N 28.50E
Kiskörös Hungary **49 I3** 46.38N 19.17E
Kismayu Somali Rep. **101 G1** 0.25S 42.31E
Kiso sammyaku *mts.* Japan **70 C4** 35.30N137.30E
Kissidougou Guinea **102 B2** 9.15N 10.08W
Kistna *r. see* Krishna *r.* India **63**
Kisumu Kenya **99 D4** 0.03S 34.47E
Kita Mali **102 C3** 13.04N 9.29W
Kitakyūshū Japan **70 A3** 33.50N130.50E
Kitchener Canada **81 J2** 43.27N 80.30W
Kíthira *i.* Greece **47 K2** 36.15N 23.00E
Kíthnos *i.* Greece **47 L2** 37.25N 24.25E
Kitikmeot *d.* Canada **80 G4** 70.00N105.00W
Kitimat Canada **80 F3** 54.05N128.38W
Kitinen *r.* Finland **50 F4** 67.16N 27.30E
Kitwe Zambia **99 C3** 12.48S 28.14E
Kivu, L. Rwanda / Zaïre **99 C4** 1.50S 29.10E
Kizil *r.* Turkey **60 D6** 41.45N 35.57E
Kjellerup Denmark **38 C4** 56.16N 9.28E
Kladno Czech. **48 G5** 50.10N 14.05E
Klagenfurt Austria **48 G3** 46.38N 14.20E
Klaipeda U.S.S.R. **50 E1** 55.43N 21.07E
Klamath Falls *town* U.S.A. **82 B5** 42.14N121.47W
Klamono Indonesia **69 I3** 1.08S131.28E
Klar *r.* Sweden **50 C2** 59.25N 13.25E
Kleve W. Germany **39 E3** 51.47N 6.11E
Klintehamn Sweden **50 D2** 57.24N 18.14E
Klintsy U.S.S.R. **49 P6** 52.45N 32.15E
Klöfta Norway **50 B3** 60.04N 11.06E
Knaresborough U.K. **12 F6** 54.01N 1.25W
Knighton U.K. **13 D4** 52.21N 3.02W
Knin Yugo. **46 H6** 44.02N 16.10E
Knockadoon Hd. Rep. of Ire. **15 D1** 51.52N 7.51W
Knockalongy *mtn.* Rep. of Ire. **15 C4** 54.12N 8.45W
Knockmealdown Mts. Rep. of Ire. **15 D2** 52.15N 7.55W
Knoxville U.S.A. **83 J4** 36.00N 83.57W
Knutsford U.K. **12 E5** 53.18N 2.22W
Kōbe Japan **70 C4** 34.42N135.15E
Koblenz W. Germany **39 F2** 50.21N 7.36E
Kobrin U.S.S.R. **49 L6** 52.16N 24.22E
Kobroör *i.* Indonesia **69 I2** 6.10S134.30E
Kočani Yugo. **47 K4** 41.55N 22.24E
Kōchi Japan **70 B3** 33.33N133.52E
Kodiak U.S.A. **80 C3** 57.49N152.30W
Kodiak I. U.S.A. **80 C3** 57.00N153.50W
Koforidua Ghana **103 D2** 6.01N 0.12W
Kōfu Japan **70 D4** 35.44N138.34E
Køge Denmark **38 F3** 55.28N 12.12E
Køge Bugt *b.* Denmark **38 F3** 55.30N 12.25E
Kohāt Pakistan **63 C6** 33.37N 71.30E
Kohīma India **63 G4** 25.40N 94.08E
Koidu Sierra Leone **102 B2** 8.41N 10.55W
Kokand U.S.S.R. **66 A5** 40.33N 70.55E
Kokas Indonesia **69 I3** 2.45S132.26E
Kokchetav U.S.S.R. **52 F3** 53.18N 69.25E
Kokenau Indonesia **69 J3** 4.42S136.25E
Kokkola Finland **50 E3** 63.50N 23.10E
Kokon Selka Finland **50 G3** 61.30N 29.30E
Kokpekty U.S.S.R. **66 C6** 48.45N 82.25E
Koksoak *r.* Canada **81 L3** 58.30N 68.15W
Kola U.S.S.R. **50 H5** 68.53N 33.01E
Kolaka Indonesia **69 G3** 4.04S121.38E
Kola Pen. U.S.S.R. **52 D4** 67.00N 38.00E
Kolār India **63 E2** 13.10N 78.10E
Kolari Finland **50 E4** 67.22N 23.50E
Kolarovgrad Bulgaria **47 M5** 43.15N 26.55E
Kolby Denmark **38 D3** 55.48N 10.33E
Kolding Denmark **38 C3** 55.29N 9.30E
Kolepom *i.* Indonesia **69 J2** 8.00S138.30E
Kolguyev *i.* U.S.S.R. **52 E4** 69.00N 49.00E
Kolhāpur India **63 D3** 16.43N 74.15E
Kolín Czech. **48 G5** 50.02N 15.10E
Köln *see* Cologne W. Germany **39**
Kolo Poland **49 I6** 52.12N 18.37E
Kołobrzeg Poland **48 G7** 54.10N 15.35E
Kolomyya U.S.S.R. **49 L4** 48.31N 25.00E
Kolpino U.S.S.R. **52 C3** 59.44N 30.39E
Kolwezi Zaïre **99 C3** 10.44S 25.28E
Kolyma *r.* U.S.S.R. **53 N4** 68.50N161.00E
Kolyma Range *mts.* U.S.S.R. **53 N3** 63.00N160.00E
Komadugu Gana *r.* Nigeria **103 G3** 13.06N 12.23E
Komatsu Japan **70 C5** 36.24N136.27E
Kommunizma, Peak *mtn.* U.S.S.R. **66 B5** 38.39N 72.01E
Komotiní Greece **47 L4** 41.07N 25.26E
Kompong Cham Cambodia **68 D6** 11.59N105.26E
Kompong Chhnang Cambodia **68 C6** 12.16N104.39E
Kompong Speu Cambodia **68 C6** 11.25N104.32E
Komsomolets *i.* U.S.S.R. **53 I5** 80.20N 96.00E
Komsomolsk-na-Amur U.S.S.R. **53 L2** 50.32N136.59E
Kongsberg Norway **50 B2** 59.42N 9.39E
Kongsvinger Norway **50 C3** 60.13N 11.59E
Kongur *mtn.* China **66 B5** 38.40N 75.30E
Konin Poland **49 I6** 52.13N 18.16E
Konkouré *r.* Guinea **102 B2** 9.55N 13.45W
Konstanz W. Germany **48 D3** 47.40N 9.10E
Kontagora Nigeria **103 F3** 10.24N 5.22E
Kontcha Cameroon **103 G2** 7.59N 12.15E
Kontum Vietnam **68 D6** 14.23N108.00E
Konya Turkey **60 D5** 37.51N 32.30E
Kopeysk U.S.S.R. **52 F3** 55.08N 61.39E
Köping Sweden **50 C2** 59.31N 16.01E
Korbach W. Germany **48 D5** 51.16N 8.53E
Korçë Albania **47 J4** 40.37N 20.45E
Korčula *i.* Yugo. **47 H5** 42.56N 16.53E
Korea B. Asia **67 J5** 39.00N124.00E
Korean Pen. Asia **54 O6** 37.00N127.00E
Korea Str. S. Korea / Japan **67 K4** 35.00N129.20E
Korhogo Ivory Coast **102 C2** 9.22N 5.31W
Kōriyama Japan **70 D5** 37.23N140.22E
Korma U.S.S.R. **49 O6** 53.08N 30.47E
Kornat *i.* Yugo. **46 G5** 43.48N 15.20E
Koror *i.* Belau **69 I5** 7.30N134.30E
Korosten U.S.S.R. **49 N5** 51.00N 28.30E
Korsör Denmark **38 E3** 55.19N 11.09E
Korsze Poland **49 J7** 54.10N 21.09E
Koryak Range *mts.* U.S.S.R. **53 N3** 62.20N171.00E
Kos *i.* Greece **47 M2** 36.48N 27.10E
Kościerzyna Poland **49 H7** 54.08N 18.00E
Kosciusko, Mt. Australia **71 D2** 36.28S148.17E
Košice Czech. **49 J4** 48.44N 21.15E
Kosovska-Mitrovica Yugo. **47 J5** 42.54N 20.51E
Kossovo U.S.S.R. **49 L6** 52.40N 25.18E
Kosti Sudan **101 F3** 13.11N 32.38E
Kostroma U.S.S.R. **52 D3** 57.46N 41.10E
Kostrzyn Poland **48 G6** 52.34N 14.41E
Kostyukovichi U.S.S.R. **49 P6** 53.20N 32.01E
Koszalin Poland **48 H7** 54.12N 16.09E
Kota India **63 D4** 25.11N 75.58E
Kota Bharu Malaysia **68 C5** 6.07N102.15E
Kotabumi Indonesia **68 C3** 4.52S104.59E
Kota Kinabalu Malaysia **68 F5** 5.59N116.04E
Kotelnyy *i.* U.S.S.R. **53 L5** 75.30N141.00E
Kotka Finland **50 F3** 60.26N 26.55E
Kotlas U.S.S.R. **52 D3** 61.15N 46.28E
Kotor Yugo. **47 I5** 42.28N 18.47E
Kotovsk U.S.S.R. **49 N3** 47.42N 29.30E
Kottagūdem India **63 E3** 17.32N 80.39E
Kotto *r.* C.A.R. **94 E5** 4.14N 22.02E
Kotuy *r.* U.S.S.R. **53 I4** 71.40N103.00E
Kotzebue U.S.A. **80 B4** 66.51N162.40W
Koulikoro Mali **102 C3** 12.55N 7.31W
Kouroussa Guinea **102 C3** 10.40N 9.50W
Koutiala Mali **102 C3** 12.20N 5.23W
Kouvola Finland **50 F3** 60.54N 26.45E
Kovel U.S.S.R. **49 L5** 51.12N 24.48E
Kowloon Hong Kong **67 I2** 22.20N114.15E
Koyukuk *r.* U.S.A. **80 C4** 64.50N157.30W
Kozan Turkey **60 D5** 37.27N 35.47E
Kozáni Greece **47 J4** 40.18N 21.48E
Krabi Thailand **68 B5** 8.04N 98.52E
Kragerö Norway **50 B2** 58.54N 9.25E
Kragujevac Yugo. **47 J6** 44.01N 20.55E
Kraljevo Yugo. **47 J5** 43.44N 20.41E
Kramfors Sweden **50 D3** 62.55N 17.50E
Krasnodar U.S.S.R. **52 D2** 45.02N 39.00E
Krasnovodsk U.S.S.R. **52 E2** 40.01N 53.00E
Krasnoyarsk U.S.S.R. **53 H3** 56.05N 92.46E
Kratie Cambodia **68 D6** 12.30N106.03E
Krefeld W. Germany **39 E3** 51.20N 6.32E
Krems Austria **48 G4** 48.25N 15.36E
Kribi Cameroon **103 F1** 2.56N 9.56E
Krichev U.S.S.R. **49 O6** 53.40N 31.44E
Krishna *r.* India **63 E3** 16.00N 81.00E
Kristiansand Norway **50 A2** 58.08N 7.59E
Kristianstad Sweden **50 C2** 56.02N 14.10E
Kristiansund Norway **50 A3** 63.15N 7.55E
Kristinehamn Sweden **50 C2** 59.17N 14.09E
Kristinestad Finland **50 E3** 62.16N 21.20E
Kristinovka U.S.S.R. **49 N4** 48.50N 29.58E
Krivoy Rog U.S.S.R. **52 C2** 47.55N 33.24E
Krk *i.* Yugo. **46 G6** 45.04N 14.36E
Kronshtadt U.S.S.R. **50 G3** 60.00N 29.40E
Kroonstad R.S.A. **99 C2** 27.40S 27.15E
Krosno Poland **49 J4** 49.42N 21.46E
Krugersdorp R.S.A. **99 C2** 26.06S 27.46E
Kruševac Yugo. **47 J5** 43.34N 21.20E
Kuala Lipis Malaysia **68 C4** 4.11N102.00E
Kuala Lumpur Malaysia **68 C4** 3.08N101.42E
Kuala Trengganu Malaysia **68 C5** 5.10N103.10E
Kuandang Indonesia **69 G4** 0.53N122.58E
Kuantan Malaysia **68 C4** 3.50N103.19E
Kuba U.S.S.R. **61 H6** 41.23N 48.33E

Morcenx France **42 D3** 44.02N 0.55W
Morden Canada **81 I2** 49.15N 98.10W
Morecambe U.K. **12 E6** 54.05N 2.51W
Morecambe B. U.K. **12 E6** 54.05N 3.00W
Morelia Mexico **86 D3** 19.40N101.11W
Morella Spain **43 E4** 40.37N 0.06W
Morelos *d.* Mexico **86 E3** 18.40N 99.00W
Morena, Sierra *mts.* Spain **43 C3** 38.10N 5.00W
Morez France **42 H4** 46.31N 6.02E
Morgan City U.S.A. **83 H2** 29.41N 91.13W
Morioka Japan **70 E6** 39.43N141.10E
Moriston *r.* U.K. **8 D5** 57.12N 4.38W
Morlaix France **42 C5** 48.35N 3.50W
Morocco Africa **100 B5** 31.00N 5.00W
Moro G. Phil. **69 G5** 6.30N123.20E
Morogoro Tanzania **99 D4** 6.49S 37.40E
Morón Cuba **87 I4** 22.08N 78.39W
Mörön Mongolia **66 F6** 49.36N100.08E
Morotai *i.* Indonesia **69 H4** 2.10N128.30E
Morpeth U.K. **12 F7** 55.09N 1.40W
Mors *i.* Denmark **38 B4** 56.50N 8.45E
Morsbach W. Germany **39 F2** 50.52N 7.44E
Mortagne France **42 E5** 48.32N 0.33E
Morvern *f.* U.K. **14 C3** 56.37N 5.45W
Morwell Australia **71 D2** 38.14S146.25E
Moscow U.S.S.R. **52 D3** 55.45N 37.42E
Mosel *r.* W. Germany **39 F2** 50.23N 7.37E
Moselle *r. see* Mosel *r.* France / Lux. **39**
Moshi Tanzania **99 D4** 3.20S 37.21E
Mosjöen Norway **50 C4** 65.50N 13.10E
Moskog Norway **50 A3** 61.30N 5.59E
Moskva *r.* U.S.S.R. **33 M6** 55.08N 38.50E
Mosquitia Plain Honduras **87 H3** 15.00N 84.00W
Mosquito Coast *f.* Nicaragua **87 H2** 13.00N 84.00W
Mosquitos, G. of Panama **87 H1** 9.00N 81.00W
Moss Norway **50 B2** 59.26N 10.41E
Mosso *l.* Denmark **38 C4** 56.02N 9.47E
Mossoró Brazil **88 F7** 5.10S 37.20W
Most Czech. **48 F5** 50.31N 13.39E
Mostar Yugo. **47 H5** 43.20N 17.50E
Mosul Iraq **60 F4** 36.21N 43.08E
Motagua *r.* Guatemala **87 G3** 15.56N 87.45W
Motala Sweden **50 C2** 58.34N 15.05E
Motherwell U.K. **14 E2** 55.48N 4.00W
Moulins France **42 F4** 46.34N 3.20E
Moulmein Burma **68 B7** 16.30N 97.40E
Mountain Ash *town* U.K. **13 D3** 51.42N 3.21W
Mount Bellew *town* Rep. of Ire. **15 C3** 53.29N 8.30W
Mount Gambier *town* Australia **71 D2** 37.51S140.50E
Mount Hagen *town* P.N.G. **69 K2** 5.54S144.13E
Mount Isa *town* Australia **71 C3** 20.50S139.29E
Mount Magnet *town* Australia **71 A3** 28.06S117.50E
Mountmellick Rep. of Ire. **15 D3** 53.08N 7.21W
Mount Newman *town* Australia **71 A3** 23.20S119.39E
Mount's Bay U.K. **13 B2** 50.02N 5.25W
Mourne *r.* U.K. **8 C4** 54.50N 7.28W
Mourne Mts. U.K. **15 E4** 54.10N 6.10W
Moussoro Chad **103 H3** 13.41N 16.31E
Moy *r.* Rep. of Ire. **15 B4** 54.10N 9.09W
Mozambique Africa **99 D3** 18.00S 35.00E
Mozambique Channel Indian Oc. **99 D3** 16.00S 42.30E
Mozyr U.S.S.R. **49 N6** 52.02N 29.10E
Mtwara Tanzania **99 E3** 10.17S 40.11E
Muang Chiang Rai Thailand **68 B7** 19.56N 99.51E
Muang Khon Kaen Thailand **68 C7** 16.25N102.50E
Muang Lampang Thailand **68 B7** 18.16N 99.30E
Muang Nakhon Phanom Thailand **68 C7** 17.22N104.45E
Muang Nakhon Sawan Thailand **68 C7** 15.35N100.10E
Muang Nan Thailand **68 C7** 18.52N100.42E
Muang Phitsanulok Thailand **68 C7** 16.50N100.15E
Muang Phrae Thailand **68 C7** 18.07N100.09E
Muar Malaysia **68 C4** 2.01N102.35E
Muara Brunei **68 F5** 5.01N115.01E
Muara Indonesia **68 C3** 0.32S101.20E
Mubi Nigeria **103 G3** 10.16N 13.17E
Muchinga Mts. Zambia **94 F3** 12.00S 31.00E
Muck *i.* U.K. **14 B3** 56.50N 6.14W
Mudanjiang China **67 K6** 44.36N129.42E
Mudhnib Saudi Arabia **61 G2** 25.52N 44.15E
Mugía Spain **43 A5** 43.06N 9.14W
Muğla Turkey **47 N2** 37.12N 28.22E
Muharraq Bahrain **61 H2** 26.16N 50.38E
Mühlhausen E. Germany **48 E5** 51.12N 10.27E
Muine Bheag Rep. of Ire. **15 E2** 52.41N 6.59W
Mukachevo U.S.S.R. **49 K4** 48.26N 22.45E
Mukah Malaysia **68 E4** 2.56N112.02E
Mukalla S. Yemen **101 G3** 14.34N 49.09E
Mukawa *r.* Japan **70 E8** 42.30N142.20E
Mulgrave I. Australia **69 K1** 10.05S142.00E
Mulhacén *mtn.* Spain **43 D2** 37.04N 3.22W
Mülheim N.-Westfalen W. Germany **39 E3** 51.25N 6.50E
Mülheim N.-Westfalen W. Germany **39 F2** 50.58N 7.00E
Mulhouse France **42 H4** 47.45N 7.21E
Mull *i.* U.K. **14 C3** 56.28N 5.56W
Mull, Sd. of U.K. **14 C3** 56.32N 5.55W
Mullaghanattin Rep. of Ire. **15 B1** 51.55N 9.52W
Mullaghareirk Mts. Rep. of Ire. **15 B2** 52.20N 9.10W
Mullaghmore *mtn.* U.K. **15 E4** 54.51N 6.51W
Mullet Pen. Rep. of Ire. **15 A4** 54.10N 10.05W
Mullingar Rep. of Ire. **15 D3** 53.31N 7.21W
Mull of Galloway *c.* U.K. **14 D1** 54.39N 4.52W
Mull of Kintyre *c.* U.K. **14 C2** 55.17N 5.45W
Multān Pakistan **63 C5** 30.10N 71.36E
Multyfarnham Rep. of Ire. **15 D3** 53.38N 7.24W
Muna *i.* Indonesia **69 G2** 5.00S122.30E
Mundo *r.* Spain **43 E3** 38.20N 1.50W
Munich W. Germany **48 E4** 48.08N 11.35E
Münster W. Germany **39 F3** 51.58N 7.37E
Muntok Indonesia **68 D3** 2.04S105.12E
Muonio Finland **50 E4** 67.52N 23.45E
Muonio *r.* Sweden / Finland **50 E4** 67.13N 23.30E
Murallón *mtn.* Argentina / Chile **89 B3** 49.48S 73.26W
Murat *r.* Turkey **33 M2** 38.40N 39.30E
Murchison *r.* Australia **71 A3** 27.30S114.10E
Murcia Spain **43 E2** 37.59N 1.08W
Murcia *d.* Spain **43 E3** 39.00N 2.00W
Mureş *r.* Romania **49 J3** 46.16N 20.10E
Muret France **42 E2** 43.28N 1.19E
Murghab *r.* Afghan. **62 B6** 36.50N 63.00E
Muria *mtn.* Indonesia **68 E2** 6.30S110.55E
Müritz, L. E. Germany **48 F6** 53.25N 12.45E
Murmansk U.S.S.R. **50 H5** 68.59N 33.08E
Murom U.S.S.R. **52 D3** 55.04N 42.04E
Muroran Japan **70 D8** 42.21N140.59E
Murray *r.* Australia **71 C2** 35.23S139.20E
Murrumbidgee *r.* Australia **71 D2** 34.38S143.10E
Murud *mtn.* Malaysia **68 F4** 3.45N115.30E
Murwāra India **63 E4** 23.49N 80.28E
Murzuq Libya **100 D4** 25.56N 13.57E
Muş Turkey **60 F5** 38.45N 41.30E
Musala *mtn.* Bulgaria **47 K5** 42.11N 23.35E
Muscat Oman **61 J1** 23.36N 58.37E
Musgrave Ranges *mts.* Australia **71 C3** 26.30S131.10E
Musi *r.* Indonesia **68 C3** 2.20S104.57E
Muskegon U.S.A. **83 I5** 43.13N 86.10W
Muskogee U.S.A. **83 G4** 35.45N 95.21W
Musselburgh U.K. **14 E2** 55.57N 3.04W
Mustang Nepal **63 E5** 29.10N 83.55E
Mustjala U.S.S.R. **50 E2** 58.30N 22.10E
Mut Turkey **60 D5** 36.38N 33.27E
Mutare Zimbabwe **99 D3** 18.58S 32.38E
Mutsu wan *b.* Japan **70 E7** 41.10N141.05E
Muwai Hakran Saudi Arabia **60 F1** 22.41N 41.37E
Muzaffarnagar India **63 D5** 29.28N 77.42E
Muzaffarpur India **63 F5** 26.07N 85.23E
Mwanza Tanzania **99 D4** 2.30S 32.54E
Mwene Ditu Zaïre **99 C4** 7.01S 23.27E
Mweru, L. Zambia / Zaïre **99 C4** 9.00S 28.40E
Myanaung Burma **63 G3** 18.25N 95.10E
Myingyan Burma **63 G4** 21.25N 95.20E
Myitkyinā Burma **63 H4** 25.24N 97.25E
Mymensingh Bangla. **63 G4** 24.45N 90.23E
Myrdal Norway **50 A3** 60.44N 7.08E
Mysore India **63 D2** 12.18N 76.37E
My Tho Vietnam **68 D6** 10.21N106.21E

N

Naas Rep. of Ire. **15 E3** 53.13N 6.41W
Nacala Mozambique **99 E3** 14.30S 40.37E
Nadiād India **63 D4** 22.42N 72.55E
Naestved Denmark **38 E3** 55.14N 11.47E
Naft Safid Iran **61 H3** 31.38N 49.20E
Naga Phil. **69 G6** 13.36N123.12E
Nāgāland *d.* India **63 G5** 26.10N 94.30E
Nagano Japan **70 D5** 36.39N138.10E
Nagaoka Japan **70 D5** 37.30N138.50E
Nāgappattinam India **63 E2** 10.45N 79.50E
Nagasaki Japan **70 A3** 32.45N129.52E
Nāgercoil India **63 D2** 8.11N 77.30E
Nag' Hammadi Egypt **60 D2** 26.04N 32.13E
Nagles Mts. Rep. of Ire. **15 C2** 52.05N 8.31W
Nagoya Japan **70 C4** 35.08N136.53E
Nāgpur India **63 E4** 21.10N 79.12E
Nagykanizsa Hungary **49 H3** 46.27N 17.01E
Naha Japan **67 K3** 26.10N127.40E
Nahāvand Iran **61 H4** 34.13N 48.23E
Nahe *r.* W. Germany **39 F1** 49.58N 7.54E
Nain Canada **81 L3** 56.30N 61.45W
Nairn U.K. **14 E4** 57.35N 3.52W
Nairobi Kenya **99 D4** 1.17S 36.50E
Nakaminato Japan **70 D5** 36.21N140.36E
Nakano shima *i.* Japan **70 A1** 29.55N129.55E
Nakatsu Japan **70 A3** 33.37N131.11E
Nakhichevan U.S.S.R. **61 G5** 39.12N 45.24E
Nakhodka U.S.S.R. **67 L5** 42.53N132.54E
Nakhon Pathom Thailand **68 B6** 13.50N100.01E
Nakhon Ratchasima Thailand **68 C7** 14.59N102.12E
Nakhon Si Thammarat Thailand **68 C5** 8.29N100.00E
Naknek U.S.A. **80 C3** 58.45N157.00W
Nakskov Denmark **38 E2** 54.50N 11.10E
Nakuru Kenya **99 D4** 0.16S 36.04E
Nalón *r.* Spain **43 B5** 43.35N 6.06W
Nālūt Libya **100 D5** 31.53N 10.59E
Namangan U.S.S.R. **66 A5** 40.59N 71.41E
Nam Co *l.* China **66 E3** 30.40N 90.30E
Nam Dinh Vietnam **68 D8** 20.25N106.12E
Namib Desert Namibia **99 B2** 22.50S 14.40E
Namibe Angola **99 B3** 15.10S 12.10E
Namibia Africa **99 B2** 22.00S 17.00E
Namlea Indonesia **69 H3** 3.15S127.07E
Namonuito *i.* Pacific Oc. **74 F8** 8.46N150.02E
Nampo N. Korea **67 J5** 38.40N125.30E
Nampula Mozambique **99 D3** 15.09S 39.14E
Namsos Norway **50 B4** 64.28N 11.30E
Namuchabawashan *mtn.* China **63 G5** 29.30N 95.10E
Namur Belgium **39 C2** 50.28N 4.52E
Namur *d.* Belgium **39 C2** 50.20N 4.45E
Nanaimo Canada **80 F2** 49.08N123.58W
Nanao Japan **70 C5** 37.03N136.58E
Nanchang China **67 I3** 28.38N115.56E
Nanchong China **66 G3** 30.54N106.06E
Nancy France **42 H5** 48.42N 6.12E
Nanda Devi *mtn.* India **63 E5** 30.21N 79.50E
Nander India **63 D3** 19.11N 77.21E
Nānga Parbat *mtn.* Jammu & Kashmir **63 D6** 35.10N 74.35E
Nanjing China **67 I4** 32.00N118.40E
Nan Ling *mts.* China **67 H2** 25.20N110.30E
Nanning China **67 H2** 22.50N108.19E
Nanping China **67 I3** 26.40N118.07E
Nanshan Is. S. China Sea **68 F6** 10.30N116.00E
Nantaise *r.* France **42 D4** 47.12N 1.35W
Nantes France **42 D4** 47.14N 1.35W
Nantong China **67 J4** 32.05N120.59E
Nantucket I. U.S.A. **83 M5** 41.16N 70.00W
Nantwich U.K. **12 E5** 53.03N 2.29W
Nanumea *i.* Tuvalu **74 H7** 5.40S176.10E
Nanyang China **67 H4** 33.06N112.31E
Napier New Zealand **71 G2** 39.30S176.54E
Naples Italy **46 G4** 40.50N 14.14E
Naples, G. of Med. Sea **46 G4** 40.42N 14.15E
Nara Mali **102 C4** 15.13N 7.20W
Nārāyanganj Bangla. **63 G4** 23.36N 90.28E
Narbada *r. see* Narmada *r.* India **63**
Narbonne France **42 F2** 43.11N 3.00E
Nares Str. Canada **81 K5** 78.30N 75.00W
Narmada *r.* India **63 D4** 21.40N 73.00E
Narodnaya *mtn.* U.S.S.R. **52 F4** 65.00N 61.00E
Narsimhapur India **63 E4** 22.58N 79.15E
Narva U.S.S.R. **50 G2** 59.22N 28.17E
Narva *r.* U.S.S.R. **50 F2** 59.30N 28.00E
Narvik Norway **50 D5** 68.26N 17.25E
Naryan Mar U.S.S.R. **52 E4** 67.37N 53.02E
Nasarawa Nigeria **103 F2** 8.35N 7.44E
Nashville U.S.A. **83 I4** 36.10N 86.50W
Näsijärvi *l.* Finland **50 E3** 61.30N 23.50E
Nāsik India **63 D4** 20.00N 73.52E
Nasratabad Iran **61 J3** 29.54N 59.58E
Nassau Bahamas **87 I5** 25.03N 77.20W
Nassau I. Cook Is. **74 J6** 11.33S165.25W
Nasser, L. Egypt **60 D1** 22.40N 32.00E
Nässjö Sweden **50 C2** 57.39N 14.40E
Natal Brazil **88 F7** 5.46S 35.15W
Natal Indonesia **68 B4** 0.35N 99.07E
Natchez U.S.A. **83 H3** 31.22N 91.24W
Natitingou Benin **103 E3** 10.17N 1.19E
Natron, L. Tanzania **99 D4** 2.18S 36.05E
Naumburg E. Germany **48 E5** 51.09N 11.48E
Nauru Pacific Oc. **74 G7** 0.32S166.55E
Navalmoral de la Mata Spain **43 C3** 39.54N 5.33W
Navan Rep. of Ire. **15 E3** 53.39N 6.42W
Naver *r.* U.K. **14 D5** 58.29N 4.12W
Navojoa Mexico **86 C5** 27.06N109.26W
Návpaktos Greece **47 J3** 38.24N 21.49E
Návplion Greece **47 K2** 37.33N 22.47E
Navrongo Ghana **103 D3** 10.51N 1.03W
Nawābshāh Pakistan **62 C5** 26.15N 68.26E
Náxos *i.* Greece **47 L2** 37.03N 25.30E
Nayarit *d.* Mexico **86 C4** 21.30N104.00W
Nazareth Israel **60 D4** 32.41N 35.16E
Nazas *r.* Mexico **86 D5** 25.34N103.25W
Nazilli Turkey **60 C5** 37.55N 28.20E
N'Djamena Chad **103 H3** 12.10N 14.59E
Ndola Zambia **99 C3** 13.00S 28.39E
Neagh, Lough U.K. **15 E4** 54.36N 6.25W
Neath U.K. **13 D3** 51.39N 3.48W
Nebraska *d.* U.S.A. **82 F5** 41.30N100.00W
Nebrodi Mts. Italy **46 G2** 37.53N 14.32E
Neches *r.* U.S.A. **83 H2** 29.55N 93.50W
Neckar *r.* W. Germany **48 D4** 49.32N 8.26E
Needles U.S.A. **82 D3** 34.51N114.36W
Neerpelt Belgium **39 D3** 51.13N 5.28E
Nefyn U.K. **12 C4** 52.58N 4.28W
Negev *des.* Israel **60 D3** 30.42N 34.55E
Negoiu *mtn.* Romania **49 L2** 45.36N 24.32E
Negotin Yugo. **47 K6** 44.14N 22.33E
Negra, C. Peru **88 A7** 6.06S 81.09W
Negrais, C. Burma **63 G3** 16.00N 94.30E
Negro *r.* Argentina **89 C3** 41.00S 62.48W
Negro *r.* Brazil **88 C7** 3.30S 60.00W
Negros *i.* Phil. **69 G6** 10.00N123.00E
Neijiang China **66 G3** 29.32N105.03E
Nei Monggol *d. see* Inner Mongolia *d.* China **67**
Neisse *r.* Poland / E. Germany **48 G6** 52.05N 14.42E
Neiva Colombia **88 B8** 2.58N 75.15W
Nejd *d.* Saudi Arabia **60 F2** 25.00N 42.00E
Neksö Denmark **50 C1** 55.04N 15.09E
Nellore India **63 E3** 14.29N 80.00E
Nelson Canada **80 G2** 49.29N117.17W
Nelson *r.* Canada **81 I3** 57.00N 93.20W
Nelson New Zealand **71 G1** 41.16S173.15E
Nelson U.K. **12 E5** 53.51N 2.11W
Nelson U.S.A. **82 D4** 35.30N113.16W
Neman *r.* U.S.S.R. **50 E1** 55.23N 21.15E
Nemours France **42 F5** 48.16N 2.41E
Nemuro Japan **70 F8** 43.22N145.36E
Nemuro kaikyō *str.* Japan **70 F8** 44.00N145.50E
Nenagh Rep. of Ire. **15 C2** 52.52N 8.13W
Nenana U.S.A. **80 D4** 64.35N149.20W
Nene *r.* U.K. **12 H4** 52.49N 0.12E
Nenjiang China **67 J6** 49.10N125.15E
Nepal Asia **63 E5** 28.00N 84.30E
Nephin Beg *mtn.* Rep. of Ire. **15 B4** 54.02N 9.38W
Nephin Beg Range *mts.* Rep. of Ire. **15 B4** 54.00N 9.40W
Nera *r.* Italy **46 F5** 42.33N 12.43E
Neretva *r.* Yugo. **47 H5** 43.02N 17.28E
Nes Neth. **39 D5** 53.27N 5.46E
Ness, Loch U.K. **14 D4** 57.16N 4.30W
Nesterov U.S.S.R. **49 L5** 50.04N 24.00E
Netherlands Europe **39 D4** 52.00N 5.30E
Netherlands Antilles S. America **87 K2** 12.30N 69.00W
Neto *r.* Italy **47 H3** 39.12N 17.08E
Neubrandenburg E. Germany **48 F6** 53.33N 13.16E
Neuchâtel Switz. **48 C3** 47.00N 6.56E
Neuchâtel, Lac de *l.* Switz. **48 C3** 46.55N 6.55E
Neuenhaus W. Germany **39 E4** 52.30N 6.58E
Neufchâteau Belgium **39 D1** 49.51N 5.26E
Neufchâtel France **42 E5** 49.44N 1.26E
Neukalen E. Germany **38 F1** 53.50N 12.47E
Neumünster W. Germany **48 D7** 54.06N 9.59E
Neuquén Argentina **89 C4** 38.55S 68.55W
Neuse *r.* U.S.A. **83 K4** 35.04N 77.04W
Neusiedler, L. Austria **48 H3** 47.52N 16.45E
Neuss W. Germany **39 E3** 51.12N 6.42E
Neustadt W. Germany **38 D2** 54.07N 10.49E
Neustrelitz E. Germany **48 F6** 53.22N 13.05E
Neuwied W. Germany **39 F2** 50.26N 7.28E
Nevada *d.* U.S.A. **82 C4** 39.00N117.00W
Nevada, Sierra *mts.* Spain **43 D2** 37.04N 3.20W
Nevada, Sierra *mts.* U.S.A. **82 C4** 37.30N119.00W
Nevers France **42 F4** 47.00N 3.09E
Nevşehir Turkey **60 D5** 38.38N 34.43E
New Amsterdam Guyana **88 D8** 6.18N 57.00W
Newark U.S.A. **83 L5** 40.44N 74.11W
Newark-on-Trent U.K. **12 G5** 53.05N 0.47W
New Bedford U.S.A. **83 L5** 41.38N 70.55W
New Bern U.S.A. **83 K4** 35.05N 77.04W
Newbiggin-by-the-Sea U.K. **12 F7** 55.10N 1.30W
New Britain *i.* P.N.G. **71 D5** 6.00S150.00E
New Brunswick *d.* Canada **81 L2** 47.00N 66.00W
Newbury U.K. **13 F3** 51.23N 1.20W
New Caledonia *i.* Pacific Oc. **71 F3** 22.00S165.00E
Newcastle Australia **71 E2** 32.55S151.46E
Newcastle U.K. **15 F4** 54.12N 5.54W
Newcastle U.S.A. **82 F5** 43.52N104.14W
Newcastle Emlyn U.K. **13 C4** 52.02N 4.27W
Newcastle-under-Lyme U.K. **12 E5** 53.01N 2.18W
Newcastle upon Tyne U.K. **12 F6** 54.58N 1.36W
Newcastle West Rep. of Ire. **15 B2** 52.27N 9.04W
New Delhi India **63 D5** 28.37N 77.13E
Newent U.K. **13 E3** 51.56N 2.25W
New Forest *f.* U.K. **13 F2** 50.52N 1.35W
Newfoundland *d.* Canada **81 L3** 55.00N 60.00W
Newfoundland *i.* Canada **81 M2** 48.30N 56.00W
New Galloway U.K. **14 D2** 55.04N 4.08W
New Guinea *i.* Austa. **69 J2** 5.00S140.00E
New Hampshire *d.* U.S.A. **83 L5** 44.00N 71.30W
Newhaven U.K. **13 H2** 50.48N 0.03E
New Haven U.S.A. **83 L5** 41.14N 72.50W
New Ireland *i.* P.N.G. **71 E5** 2.30S151.30E
New Jersey *d.* U.S.A. **83 L5** 40.00N 74.30W
Newmarket Rep. of Ire. **15 B2** 52.13N 9.01W
Newmarket U.K. **13 H4** 52.17N 0.26E
Newmarket on Fergus Rep. of Ire. **15 C2** 52.46N 8.55W
New Mexico *d.* U.S.A **82 E3** 34.00N106.00W
New Orleans U.S.A. **83 H3** 30.00N 90.03W
New Plymouth New Zealand **71 G2** 39.04S174.04E
Newport Tipperary Rep. of Ire. **15 C2** 52.42N 8.26W
Newport Mayo Rep. of Ire. **15 B3** 53.53N 9.35W
Newport Dyfed U.K. **13 C4** 52.01N 4.49W
Newport Essex U.K. **13 H3** 51.58N 0.15E
Newport Gwent U.K. **13 E3** 51.34N 2.59W
Newport Hants. U.K. **13 F2** 50.43N 1.18W
Newport News U.S.A. **83 K4** 36.59N 76.26W
New Providence *i.* Bahamas **87 I5** 25.03N 77.25W
Newquay U.K. **13 B2** 50.24N 5.06W
New Quay U.K. **13 C4** 52.13N 4.21W
New Radnor U.K. **13 D4** 52.13N 3.09W
New Romney U.K. **13 H2** 50.59N 0.58E
New Ross Rep. of Ire. **15 E2** 52.23N 6.59W
Newry U.K. **15 E4** 54.11N 6.21W
New Scone U.K. **14 E3** 56.26N 3.22W
New Siberian Is. U.S.S.R. **53 L4** 76.00N144.00E
New South Wales *d.* Australia **71 D2** 33.45S147.00E
Newton Abbot U.K. **13 D2** 50.33N 3.35W
Newton Aycliffe U.K. **12 F6** 54.36N 1.34W
Newtonmore U.K. **14 D4** 57.03N 4.10W
Newton Stewart U.K. **14 D1** 54.57N 4.29W
Newtown U.K. **13 D4** 52.31N 3.19W
Newtownabbey U.K. **15 F4** 54.39N 5.57W
Newtownards U.K. **15 F4** 54.35N 5.41W
Newtown Butler U.K. **15 D4** 54.11N 7.23W
Newtown St. Boswells U.K. **14 F2** 55.35N 2.40W
Newtownstewart U.K. **15 D4** 54.43N 7.26W
New York U.S.A. **83 L5** 40.40N 73.50W
New York *d.* U.S.A. **83 K5** 43.00N 75.00W
New Zealand Austa. **71 G1** 41.00S175.00E
Nezhin U.S.S.R. **49 O5** 51.03N 31.54E
Ngaoundéré Cameroon **103 G2** 7.20N 13.35E
Nguigmi Niger **103 G3** 14.00N 13.11E
Nguru Nigeria **103 G3** 12.53N 10.30E
Nha Trang Vietnam **68 D6** 12.15N109.10E
Niagara Falls *town* U.S.A. **83 K5** 43.06N 79.04W
Niamey Niger **103 E3** 13.32N 2.05E
Niangara Zaïre **99 C5** 3.45N 27.54E
Niapa, Gunung *mtn.* Indonesia **68 F4** 1.45N117.30E
Nias *i.* Indonesia **68 B4** 1.05N 97.30E
Nibe Denmark **38 C4** 56.59N 9.39E
Nicaragua C. America **87 G2** 13.00N 85.00W
Nicaragua, L. Nicaragua **87 G2** 11.30N 85.30W
Nicastro Italy **46 H3** 38.58N 16.16E
Nice France **42 H2** 43.42N 7.16E
Nicobar Is. India **63 G2** 8.00N 94.00E
Nicosia Cyprus **60 D4** 35.11N 33.23E
Nicoya, G. of Costa Rica **87 H1** 9.30N 85.00W
Nicoya Pen. Costa Rica **87 G2** 10.30N 85.30W
Nid *r.* Norway **50 B2** 58.26N 8.44E
Nidzica Poland **49 J6** 53.22N 20.26E
Niebüll W. Germany **38 B2** 54.47N 8.51E
Niers *r.* Neth. **39 D3** 51.43N 5.56E
Nieuwpoort Belgium **39 A3** 51.08N 2.45E
Nigde Turkey **60 D5** 37.58N 34.42E
Niger Africa **100 C3** 17.00N 9.30E
Niger *d.* Nigeria **103 F3** 9.50N 6.00E
Niger *r.* Nigeria **103 F1** 4.15N 6.05E
Niger Delta Nigeria **103 F1** 4.00N 6.10E
Nigeria Africa **103 F2** 9.00N 9.00E
Nihoa *i.* Hawaiian Is. **74 J10** 23.03N161.55W
Niigata Japan **70 D5** 37.58N139.02E
Niihama Japan **70 B3** 33.57N133.15E

Niiza Japan 70 D4 35.48N139.34E
Nijmegen Neth. 39 D3 51.50N 5.52E
Nikel U.S.S.R. 50 G5 69.20N 29.44E
Nikiniki Indonesia 69 G2 9.49S124.29E
Nikki Benin 103 E2 9.55N 3.18E
Nikolayev U.S.S.R. 52 C2 46.57N 32.00E
Nikolayevsk-na-Amur U.S.S.R. 53 L3 53.20N140.44E
Nikopol U.S.S.R. 52 C2 47.34N 34.25E
Niksar Turkey 60 E6 40.35N 36.59E
Nikšić Yugo. 47 I5 42.48N 18.56E
Nikumaroro *i.* Kiribati 74 I7 4.40S174.32W
Nila *i.* Indonesia 69 H2 6.45S129.30E
Nile *r.* Egypt 60 C3 31.30N 30.25E
Nile Delta Egypt 60 C3 31.00N 31.00E
Nilgiri Hills India 63 D2 11.30N 77.30E
Nimba, Mt. Guinea 102 C2 7.35N 8.28W
Nîmes France 42 G2 43.50N 4.21E
Nineveh *ruins* Iraq 60 F5 36.24N 43.08E
Ningbo China 67 J3 29.54N121.33E
Ningwu China 67 H5 39.00N112.19E
Ningxia Huizu *d.* China 66 G5 37.00N106.00E
Ninh Binh Vietnam 68 D8 20.14N106.00E
Ninove Belgium 39 C2 50.50N 4.02E
Niobrara *r.* U.S.A. 82 G5 42.45N 98.10W
Nioro Mali 102 C4 15.12N 9.35W
Niort France 42 D4 46.19N 0.27W
Nipigon Canada 81 J2 49.02N 88.26W
Nipigon, L. Canada 81 J2 49.50N 88.30W
Niriz Iran 61 I3 29.12N 54.17E
Niš Yugo. 47 J5 43.20N 21.54E
Nissum Bredning *b.* Denmark 38 B4 56.40N 8.20E
Nissum Fjord *b.* Denmark 38 B4 56.21N 8.11E
Niterói Brazil 89 E5 22.45S 43.06W
Nith *r.* U.K. 14 E2 55.00N 3.35W
Nitra Czech. 49 I4 48.20N 18.05E
Niue *i.* Cook Is. 74 J6 19.02S169.52W
Niut, Gunung *mtn.* Indonesia 68 D4 1.00N110.00E
Nivelles Belgium 39 C2 50.36N 4.20E
Nizāmābād India 63 E3 18.40N 78.05E
Nizhneudinsk U.S.S.R. 53 I3 54.55N 99.00E
Nizhnevartovsk U.S.S.R. 52 G3 60.57N 76.40E
Nizhniy Tagil U.S.S.R. 52 F3 58.00N 60.00E
Nkongsamba Cameroon 103 F1 4.59N 9.53E
Nobeoka Japan 70 A3 32.36N131.40E
Nogales Mexico 86 B6 31.20N111.00W
Nogent-le-Rotrou France 42 E5 48.19N 0.50E
Noguera Ribagorçana *r.* Spain 43 F4 41.27N 0.25E
Noirmoutier, Île de *i.* France 42 C4 47.00N 2.15W
Nokia Finland 50 E3 61.29N 23.31E
Nóla C.A.R. 103 H1 3.28N 16.08E
Nome U.S.A. 80 B4 64.30N165.30W
Nong Khai Thailand 68 C7 17.50N102.46E
Nonthaburi Thailand 68 C6 13.48N100.31E
Noord Brabant *d.* Neth. 39 D3 51.37N 5.00E
Noorvik U.S.A. 80 B4 66.50N161.14W
Nordborg Denmark 38 C3 55.04N 9.47E
Norddeich W. Germany 39 F5 53.35N 7.10E
Norden W. Germany 39 F5 53.34N 7.13E
Nordenham W. Germany 48 D6 53.30N 8.29E
Norderney *i.* W. Germany 39 F5 53.45N 7.15E
Nordfjord *est.* Norway 50 A3 61.50N 6.00E
Nordhausen E. Germany 48 E5 51.31N 10.48E
Nordhorn W. Germany 39 F4 52.27N 7.05E
Nord-Jyllands *d.* Denmark 38 C5 57.20N 10.00E
Nordstrand *i.* W. Germany 38 B2 54.30N 8.52E
Nordvik U.S.S.R. 53 J4 73.40N110.50E
Nore *r.* Rep. of Ire. 15 E2 52.25N 6.58W
Norfolk *d.* U.K. 13 H4 52.39N 1.00E
Norfolk U.S.A. 83 K4 36.54N 76.18W
Norfolk Broads *f.* U.K. 12 I4 52.45N 1.30E
Norfolk I. Pacific Oc. 71 F3 28.58S168.03E
Norfolk Island Ridge Pacific Oc. 74 G5 29.00S167.00E
Norilsk U.S.S.R. 53 H4 69.21N 88.02E
Normandie, Collines de *hills* France 42 D5 48.50N 0.40W
Norman Wells Canada 80 F4 65.19N126.46W
Nörresundby Denmark 38 C5 57.05N 9.52E
Norris L. U.S.A. 83 J4 36.20N 83.55W
Norrköping Sweden 50 D2 58.35N 16.10E
Norrtälje Sweden 50 D2 59.46N 18.43E
Norseman Australia 71 B2 32.15S121.47E
Northallerton U.K. 12 F6 54.20N 1.25W
North America 76
Northampton U.K. 13 G4 52.14N 0.54W
Northamptonshire *d.* U.K. 13 G4 52.18N 0.55W
North Battleford Canada 80 H3 52.47N108.19W
North Bay *town* Canada 81 K2 46.20N 79.28W
North Bend U.S.A. 82 B5 43.26N124.14W
North Berwick U.K. 14 F3 56.04N 2.43W
North Beveland *f.* Neth. 39 B3 51.35N 3.45E
North C. Norway 50 F5 71.10N 25.45E
North Canadian *r.* U.S.A. 83 G4 35.30N 95.45W
North Carolina *d.* U.S.A. 83 K4 35.30N 79.00W
North Channel U.K. 15 F5 55.15N 5.52W
North China Plain *f.* China 67 I4 34.30N117.00E
North Dakota *d.* U.S.A. 82 F6 47.00N100.00W
North Dorset Downs *hills* U.K. 13 E2 50.50N 2.30W
North Downs *hills* U.K. 13 G3 51.18N 0.10W
North Dvina *r.* U.S.S.R. 52 D4 64.40N 40.50E
North East Polder *f.* Neth. 39 D4 52.45N 5.45E
Northern Ireland *d.* U.K. 15 E4 54.40N 6.45W
Northern Territory *d.* Australia 71 C4 20.00S133.00E
North Esk *r.* U.K. 14 F3 56.45N 2.25W
North European Plain *f.* Europe 32 I5 56.00N 27.00E
North Fiji Basin Pacific Oc. 107 R4 17.00S173.00E
North Foreland *c.* U.K. 13 I3 51.21N 1.28E
North Frisian Is. W. Germany 48 D7 54.30N 8.00E
North Holland *d.* Neth. 39 C4 52.37N 4.50E
North I. New Zealand 71 G2 39.00S175.00E
Northiam U.K. 13 H2 50.59N 0.37E
North Korea Asia 67 K5 40.00N128.00E
North Platte U.S.A. 82 F5 41.09N100.45W
North Platte *r.* U.S.A. 82 F5 41.09N100.55W
North Ronaldsay *i.* U.K. 14 F6 59.23N 2.26W
North Sea Europe 32 F6 56.00N 3.00E
North Sporades *is.* Greece 47 K3 39.00N 24.00E
North Tawton U.K. 13 D2 50.48N 3.51W
North Truchas Peak *mtn.* U.S.A. 82 E4 35.58N105.48W
North Uist *i.* U.K. 14 A4 57.35N 7.20W
Northumberland *d.* U.K. 12 E7 55.12N 2.00W
North Walsham U.K. 12 I4 52.51N 1.38E
Northway U.S.A. 80 D4 62.58N142.00W
North Western Atlantic Basin Atlantic Oc. 106 F6 33.00N 55.00W
North West Highlands U.K. 14 C4 57.30N 5.15W
North West River *town* Canada 81 L3 53.30N 60.10W
Northwest Territories *d.* Canada 81 H4 66.00N 95.00W
Northwich U.K. 12 E5 53.16N 2.30W
North York Moors *hills* U.K. 12 G6 54.21N 0.50W
North Yorkshire *d.* U.K. 12 F6 54.14N 1.14W
Norton Sound *b.* U.S.A. 80 B4 63.50N164.00W
Norway Europe 50 B3 65.00N 13.00E
Norway House *town* Canada 81 I3 53.59N 97.50W
Norwegian Sea Europe 32 D8 66.00N 2.00E
Norwich U.K. 13 I4 52.38N 1.17E
Noss Head U.K. 14 E5 58.29N 3.02W
Nossob *r.* R.S.A./Botswana 99 C2 26.54S 20.39E
Noteć *r.* Poland 48 G6 52.44N 15.26E
Nottingham U.K. 12 F4 52.57N 1.10W
Nottinghamshire *d.* U.K. 12 G5 53.10N 1.00W
Nouadhibou Mauritania 100 A4 20.54N 17.01W
Nouakchott Mauritania 100 A3 18.09N 15.58W
Nouméa N. Cal. 71 G5 22.16S166.27E
Novara Italy 46 D6 45.27N 8.37E
Nova Scotia *d.* Canada 81 L2 45.00N 64.00W
Novaya Siberia *i.* U.S.S.R. 53 M4 75.20N148.00E
Novaya Zemlya *i.* U.S.S.R. 52 E4 74.00N 56.00E
Novelda Spain 43 E3 38.24N 0.45W
Nové Zámky Czech. 49 I3 47.59N 18.11E
Novgorod U.S.S.R. 52 C3 58.30N 31.20E
Novi Pazar Yugo. 47 J5 43.08N 20.28E
Novi Sad Yugo. 47 I6 45.16N 19.52E
Novo Arkhangel'sk U.S.S.R. 49 O4 48.34N 30.50E
Novograd Volynskiy U.S.S.R. 49 M5 50.34N 27.32E
Novogrudok U.S.S.R. 49 L6 53.35N 25.50E
Novokazalinsk U.S.S.R. 52 F2 45.48N 62.06E
Novokuybyshevsk U.S.S.R. 52 E3 53.05N 49.59E
Novokuznetsk U.S.S.R. 52 H3 53.45N 87.12E
Novorossiysk U.S.S.R. 52 D2 44.44N 37.46E
Novosibirsk U.S.S.R. 52 G3 55.04N 82.55E
Novozybkov U.S.S.R. 49 O6 52.31N 31.58E
Novy Port U.S.S.R. 52 G4 67.38N 72.33E
Nowa Sól Poland 48 G5 51.49N 15.41E
Nowgong India 63 G5 26.20N 92.41E
Nowy Korczyn Poland 49 J5 50.19N 20.48E
Nowy Sącz Poland 49 J4 49.39N 20.40E
Noyon France 39 A1 49.35N 3.00E
Nsukka Nigeria 103 F2 6.51N 7.29E
Nubian Desert Sudan 101 F4 21.00N 34.00E
Nueces *r.* U.S.A. 83 G2 27.55N 97.30W
Nueva Gerona Cuba 87 H4 21.53N 82.49W
Nuevitas Cuba 87 I4 21.34N 77.18W
Nuevo Laredo Mexico 86 E5 27.30N 99.30W
Nuevo León *d.* Mexico 86 D5 26.00N 99.00W
Nui *i.* Tuvalu 74 H7 7.12S177.10E
Nu Jiang *r. see* Salween *r.* China 66
Nukha U.S.S.R. 61 G6 41.12N 47.10E
Nuku'alofa Tonga 74 I5 21.07S175.12W
Nuku Hiva *i.* Marquesas Is. 75 L7 8.56S140.00W
Nukunono Pacific Oc. 74 I7 9.10S171.55W
Nukus U.S.S.R. 52 E2 42.28N 59.07E
Nullarbor Plain *f.* Australia 71 B2 31.30S128.00E
Numazu Japan 70 D4 35.08N138.50E
Nuneaton U.K. 13 F4 52.32N 1.29W
Nunivak I. U.S.A. 80 B4 60.00N166.30W
Nurmes Finland 50 G3 63.32N 29.10E
Nürnberg W. Germany 48 E4 49.27N 11.05E
Nusaybin Turkey 60 F5 37.05N 41.11E
Nuuk *see* Godthåb Greenland 81
Nyala Sudan 101 E3 12.01N 24.50E
Nyborg Denmark 38 D3 55.19N 10.49E
Nybro Sweden 50 C2 56.44N 15.55E
Nyíregyháza Hungary 49 J3 47.59N 21.43E
Nyköbing Vestjaellands Denmark 38 E3 55.55N 11.40E
Nyköbing Viborg Denmark 38 B4 56.49N 8.50E
Nyköbing Storstroms Denmark 38 E2 54.47N 11.53E
Nyköping Sweden 50 D2 58.45N 17.03E
Nynäshamn Sweden 50 D2 58.54N 17.55E
Nyong *r.* Cameroon 103 F1 3.15N 9.55E
Nyons France 42 G3 44.22N 5.08E
Nysa Poland 49 H5 50.29N 17.20E
N'zérékoré Guinea 102 C2 7.49N 8.48W

O

Oahe Resr. U.S.A. 82 F6 45.45N100.20W
Oahu *i.* Hawaiian Is. 75 K10 21.30N158.00W
Oakland U.S.A. 82 B4 37.50N122.15W
Oaxaca Mexico 86 E3 17.05N 96.41W
Oaxaca *d.* Mexico 86 E3 17.30N 97.00W
Ob *r.* U.S.S.R. 52 F4 66.50N 69.00E
Ob, G. of U.S.S.R. 52 G4 68.30N 74.00E
Oban U.K. 14 C3 56.26N 5.28W
Obbia Somali Rep. 101 G2 5.20N 48.30E
Oberhausen W. Germany 39 E3 51.28N 6.51E
Obi *i.* Indonesia 69 H3 1.45S127.30E
Obihiro Japan 70 E8 42.55N143.00E
Obuasi Ghana 103 D2 6.15N 1.36W
Ocaña Spain 43 D3 39.57N 3.30W
Occidental, Cordillera *mts.* Colombia 88 B8 6.00N 76.15W
Ocean I. *see* Banaba Kiribati 74
Ochil Hills U.K. 14 E3 56.18N 3.35W
Ocotlán Mexico 86 D4 20.21N102.42W
October Revolution *i.* U.S.S.R. 53 I5 79.30N 96.00E
Oda Ghana 103 D2 5.55N 0.56W
Odádhahraun *mts.* Iceland 50 J7 65.00N 17.30W
Odate Japan 70 D7 40.16N140.34E
Odawara Japan 70 D4 35.20N139.08E
Odda Norway 50 A3 60.03N 6.45E
Odder Denmark 38 D3 55.59N 10.11E
Ödemiş Turkey 47 N3 38.12N 28.00E
Odense Denmark 38 D3 55.24N 10.25E
Oder *r.* Poland 48 G6 53.30N 14.36E
Odessa U.S.A. 82 F3 31.50N102.23W
Odessa U.S.S.R. 49 O3 46.30N 30.46E
Odienné Ivory Coast 102 C2 9.36N 7.32W
Odorhei Romania 49 L3 46.18N 25.18E
Oeno I. Pacific Oc. 75 M5 23.55S130.45W
Ofanto *r.* Italy 46 H4 41.22N 16.12E
Offaly *d.* Rep. of Ire. 15 D3 53.15N 7.30W
Offenbach W. Germany 48 D5 50.06N 8.46E
Offenburg W. Germany 48 C4 48.29N 7.57E
Ōgaki Japan 70 C4 35.25N136.36E
Ogbomosho Nigeria 103 E2 8.05N 4.11E
Ogden U.S.A. 82 D5 41.14N111.59W
Ogeechee *r.* U.S.A. 83 J3 32.54N 81.05W
Ognon *r.* France 42 G4 47.20N 5.37E
Ogoja Nigeria 103 F2 6.40N 8.45E
Ogooué *r.* Gabon 99 A4 1.00S 9.05E
Ogosta *r.* Bulgaria 47 K5 43.44N 23.51E
Ogulin Yugo. 46 G6 45.17N 15.14E
Ogun *d.* Nigeria 103 E2 6.50N 3.20E
Ohio *d.* U.S.A. 83 J5 40.00N 83.00W
Ohio *r.* U.S.A. 83 I4 37.07N 89.10W
Ohře *r.* Czech. 48 G5 50.32N 14.08E
Ohrid Yugo. 47 J4 41.06N 20.48E
Ohridsko, L. Albania/Yugo. 47 J4 41.00N 20.43E
Oil City U.S.A. 83 K5 41.26N 79.30W
Oise *r.* France 42 F5 49.00N 2.10E
Oita Japan 70 A3 33.15N131.40E
Ojocaliente Mexico 86 D4 22.35N102.18W
Oka *r.* U.S.S.R. 33 N6 56.09N 43.00E
Okaba Indonesia 69 J2 8.06S139.46E
Okanogan *r.* U.S.A. 82 B6 47.45N120.05W
Okavango *r.* Botswana 99 C3 18.30S 22.04E
Okavango Basin *f.* Botswana 99 C3 19.30S 23.00E
Okayama Japan 70 B4 34.40N133.54E
Okazaki Japan 70 C4 34.58N137.10E
Okeechobee, L. U.S.A. 83 J2 27.00N 80.45W
Okefenokee Swamp *f.* U.S.A. 83 J3 30.40N 82.40W
Okehampton U.K. 13 C2 50.45N 4.00W
Okha U.S.S.R. 53 L3 53.35N142.50E
Okhotsk U.S.S.R. 53 L3 59.20N143.15E
Okhotsk, Sea of U.S.S.R. 53 M3 55.00N150.00E
Oki guntō *is.* Japan 70 B5 36.10N133.10E
Okinawa *i.* Japan 67 K3 26.30N128.00E
Okitipupa Nigeria 103 E2 6.31N 4.50E
Oklahoma *d.* U.S.A. 83 G4 35.00N 97.00W
Oklahoma City U.S.A. 83 G4 35.28N 97.33W
Oksby Denmark 38 B3 55.33N 8.11E
Oktyabrskiy U.S.S.R. 49 N6 52.35N 28.45E
Okushiri shima *i.* Japan 70 D8 42.00N139.50E
Öland *i.* Sweden 50 D2 56.50N 16.50E
Olbia Italy 46 D4 40.55N 9.29E
Old Crow Canada 80 E4 67.34N139.43W
Oldenburg W. Germany 39 G5 53.08N 8.13E
Oldenburg Sch.-Hol. W. Germany 48 E7 54.17N 10.52E
Oldenzaal Neth. 39 E4 52.19N 6.55E
Oldham U.K. 12 E5 53.33N 2.08W
Old Head of Kinsale *c.* Rep. of Ire. 15 C1 51.37N 8.33W
Old Rhine *r.* Neth. 39 C4 52.14N 4.26E
Olean U.S.A. 83 K5 42.05N 78.26W
Olekma *r.* U.S.S.R. 53 K3 60.20N120.30E
Olekminsk U.S.S.R. 53 K3 60.25N120.00E
Olenëk U.S.S.R. 53 J4 68.38N112.15E
Olenëk *r.* U.S.S.R. 53 K4 73.00N120.00E
Olenekskiy G. U.S.S.R. 53 J4 74.00N120.00E
Oléron, Île d' *i.* France 42 D3 45.55N 1.16W
Oleśnica Poland 49 H5 51.13N 17.23E
Olevsk U.S.S.R. 49 M5 51.12N 27.35E
Olga U.S.S.R. 67 L5 43.46N135.14E
Ölgod Denmark 38 B3 55.49N 8.39E
Olhão Portugal 43 B2 37.01N 7.50W
Olifants *r.* Namibia 99 B2 25.28S 19.23E
Olivares Spain 43 D3 39.45N 2.21W
Olney U.K. 13 G4 52.10N 0.41W
Ölögey Mongolia 66 E6 48.54N 90.00E
Olomouc Czech. 49 H4 49.36N 17.16E
Oloron France 42 D2 43.12N 0.35W
Olot Spain 43 G5 42.11N 2.30E
Olpe W. Germany 39 F3 51.02N 7.52E
Olsztyn Poland 49 J6 53.48N 20.29E
Oltenița Romania 49 M2 44.05N 26.31E
Olteț *r.* Romania 49 L2 44.13N 24.28E
Olympus, Mt. Cyprus 60 D4 34.55N 32.52E
Olympus, Mt. Greece 47 K4 40.04N 22.20E
Omagh U.K. 15 D4 54.36N 7.20W
Omaha U.S.A. 83 G5 41.15N 96.00W
Oman Asia 101 H3 22.30N 57.30E
Oman, G. of Asia 61 J2 25.00N 58.00E
Ombrone *r.* Italy 46 E5 42.40N 11.00E
Omdurman Sudan 101 F3 15.37N 32.59E
Ommen Neth. 39 E4 52.32N 6.25E
Omolon *r.* U.S.S.R. 53 N4 68.50N158.30E
Omono *r.* Japan 70 D6 39.44N140.05E
Omsk U.S.S.R. 52 G3 55.00N 73.22E
Omulew *r.* Poland 49 J6 53.05N 21.32E
Ōmuta Japan 70 A3 33.02N130.26E
Oña Spain 43 D5 42.44N 3.25W
Onda Spain 43 E3 39.58N 0.16W
Ondo *d.* Nigeria 103 F2 7.10N 5.20E
Onega, L. U.S.S.R. 52 D3 62.00N 35.30E
Onitsha Nigeria 103 F2 6.10N 6.47E
Onstwedde Neth. 39 F5 53.04N 7.02E
Ontaki san *mtn.* Japan 70 C4 35.55N137.29E
Ontario *d.* Canada 81 J3 52.00N 86.00W
Ontario, L. N. America 83 K5 43.40N 78.00W
Oosterhout Neth. 39 C3 51.38N 4.50E
Oosthuizen Neth. 39 C4 52.33N 5.00E
Oostmalle Belgium 39 C3 51.18N 4.45E
Opole Poland 49 H5 50.40N 17.56E
Oporto Portugal 43 A4 41.09N 8.37W
Oradea Romania 49 J3 47.03N 21.55E
Oran Algeria 100 B5 35.45N 0.38W
Orange Australia 71 D2 33.19S149.10E
Orange France 42 G3 44.08N 4.48E
Orange *r.* R.S.A. 99 B2 28.43S 16.30E
Orange, C. Brazil 88 D8 4.25N 51.32W
Orangeburg U.S.A. 83 J3 33.28N 80.53W
Orchies France 39 B2 50.28N 3.15E
Orchila *i.* Venezuela 87 K2 11.52N 66.10W
Ordu Turkey 60 E6 41.00N 37.52E
Orduña Spain 43 D5 43.00N 3.00W
Ordzhonikidze U.S.S.R. 52 D2 43.02N 44.43E
Örebro Sweden 50 C2 59.17N 15.13E
Oregon *d.* U.S.A. 82 B5 44.00N120.00W
Öregrund Sweden 50 D3 60.20N 18.30E
Orekhovo-Zuyevo U.S.S.R. 52 D3 55.47N 39.00E
Orel U.S.S.R. 52 D3 52.58N 36.00E
Ore Mts. Europe 32 H5 50.30N 12.50E
Orenburg U.S.S.R. 52 E2 51.50N 55.00E
Orense Spain 43 B5 42.20N 7.52W
Oressa *r.* U.S.S.R. 49 N6 52.33N 28.45E
Ore Sund *str.* Denmark 38 F3 56.00N 12.30E
Orford Ness *c.* U.K. 13 I4 52.05N 1.34E
Orgeyev U.S.S.R. 49 N3 47.24N 28.50E
Oriental, Cordillera *mts.* Colombia 88 B8 6.00N 74.00W
Orihuela Spain 43 E3 38.05N 0.56W
Orinoco *r.* Venezuela 88 C8 9.00N 61.30W
Orinoco Delta *f.* Venezuela 88 C8 9.00N 61.30W
Orissa *d.* India 63 E4 20.15N 84.00E
Oristano Italy 46 D3 39.53N 8.36E
Oristano, G. of Med. Sea 46 D3 39.50N 8.30E
Orivesi *l.* Finland 50 G3 62.20N 29.30E
Orizaba Mexico 86 E3 18.51N 97.08W
Orkney Is. *d.* U.K. 14 E5 59.00N 3.00W
Orlando U.S.A. 83 J2 28.33N 81.21W
Orléans France 42 E4 47.54N 1.54E
Ormskirk U.K. 12 E5 53.36N 2.51W
Orne *r.* France 42 D5 49.17N 0.10W
Örnsköldsvik Sweden 50 D3 63.19N 18.45E
Orona *i.* Kiribati 74 I7 4.29S172.10W
Orosei Italy 46 D4 40.23N 9.40E
Orosei, G. of Med. Sea 46 D4 40.15N 9.45E
Orosháza Hungary 49 J3 46.34N 20.40E
Oroville U.S.A. 82 C6 48.57N119.27W
Orsha U.S.S.R. 52 C3 54.30N 30.23E
Orsk U.S.S.R. 52 E2 51.13N 58.35E
Orşova Romania 49 K2 44.42N 22.22E
Orthez France 42 D2 43.29N 0.46W
Ørum Denmark 38 D4 56.27N 10.41E
Oruro Bolivia 88 C6 18.05S 67.00W
Orust *i.* Sweden 38 E6 58.08N 11.30E
Oryakhovo Bulgaria 47 K5 43.42N 23.58E
Ōsaka Japan 70 C4 34.40N135.30E
Osa Pen. Costa Rica 87 H1 8.20N 83.30W
Osh U.S.S.R. 52 G2 40.37N 72.49E
Oshawa Canada 81 K2 43.53N 78.51W
Ō shima *i.* Hokkaido Japan 70 D7 41.40N139.40E
Ō shima *i.* Tosan Japan 70 D4 34.40N139.28E
Oshogbo Nigeria 103 E2 7.50N 4.35E
Osijek Yugo. 47 I6 45.35N 18.43E
Oskarshamn Sweden 50 D2 57.16N 16.25E
Oslo Norway 50 B2 59.56N 10.45E
Oslofjorden *est.* Norway 50 B2 59.30N 10.30E
Osmancik Turkey 60 D6 40.58N 34.50E
Osmaniye Turkey 60 E5 37.04N 36.15E
Osnabrück W. Germany 39 G4 52.17N 8.03E
Osorno Spain 43 C5 42.24N 4.22W
Oss Neth. 39 D3 51.46N 5.31E
Ossa *mtn.* Greece 47 K3 39.47N 22.41E
Ossa, Mt. Australia 71 D1 41.52S146.04E
Osse *r.* Nigeria 103 F2 5.55N 5.15E
Ostend Belgium 39 A3 51.13N 2.55E
Oster *r.* U.S.S.R. 49 O5 50.50N 30.50E
Österdal *r.* Sweden 50 C3 61.03N 14.30E
Österö *i.* Faroe Is. 50 L9 62.10N 7.00W
Östersund Sweden 50 C3 63.10N 14.40E
Östhammar Sweden 50 D3 60.15N 18.25E
Ostrava Czech. 49 I4 49.50N 18.15E
Ostrołeka Poland 49 J6 53.06N 21.34E
Ostrov U.S.S.R. 50 G2 57.22N 28.22E
Ostrowiec-Świetokrzyski Poland 49 J5 50.57N 21.23E
Ostrów Mazowiecka Poland 49 J6 52.50N 21.51E
Ostrów Wielkopolski Poland 49 H5 51.39N 17.49E
Osŭm *r.* Bulgaria 47 L5 43.41N 24.51E
Osumi gunto *is.* Japan 70 A2 30.30N130.30E
Ōsumi kaikyō *str.* Japan 70 A2 31.30N131.00E
Osuna Spain 43 C2 37.14N 5.06W
Oswestry U.K. 12 D4 52.52N 3.03W
Otaru Japan 70 D8 43.14N140.59E
Oti *r.* Ghana 103 E2 8.43N 0.10E
Otra *r.* Norway 50 A2 58.10N 8.00E
Otranto Italy 47 I4 40.09N 18.30E
Otranto, Str. of Med. Sea 47 I4 40.10N 19.00E
Otta Norway 50 B3 61.46N 9.33E
Ottawa Canada 81 K2 45.25N 75.43W
Ottawa *r.* Canada 81 K2 45.23N 73.55W
Ottawa Is. Canada 81 J3 59.50N 80.00W
Otter *r.* U.K. 13 D2 50.40N 3.19W
Otterburn *town* U.K. 12 E7 55.13N 2.09W
Otterup Denmark 38 D3 55.31N 10.25E
Ouachita *r.* U.S.A. 83 H3 33.10N 92.10W

Ouachita Mts. U.S.A. **83 H3** 34.40N 94.30W
Ouagadougou Burkina **103 D3** 12.20N 1.40W
Ouahigouya Burkina **102 D3** 13.31N 2.21W
Ouargla Algeria **100 C5** 32.00N 5.16E
Oudenarde Belgium **39 B2** 50.50N 3.37E
Oudtshoorn R.S.A. **99 C1** 33.35S 22.12E
Ouessant, Île d' *i.* France **42 B5** 48.28N 5.05W
Oughter, L. Rep. of Ire. **15 D4** 54.00N 7.30W
Oujda Morocco **100 B5** 34.41N 1.45W
Oulu Finland **50 F4** 65.02N 25.27E
Oulu *r.* Finland **50 F4** 65.04N 25.23E
Oulujärvi *l.* Finland **50 F4** 64.30N 27.00E
Oum er Rbia *r.* Morocco **32 D1** 33.19N 8.21W
Ounas *r.* Finland **50 F4** 66.33N 25.37E
Oundle U.K. **13 G4** 52.30N 0.28W
Our *r.* Lux. **39 E1** 49.53N 6.16E
Ourthe *r.* Belgium **39 D2** 50.38N 5.36E
Ouse *r.* U.K. **12 G5** 53.51N 0.42W
Outer Hebrides *is.* U.K. **14 A4** 57.40N 7.35W
Overath W. Germany **39 F2** 50.56N 7.18E
Overflakkee *i.* Neth. **39 C3** 51.45N 4.08E
Overijssel *d.* Neth. **39 E4** 52.25N 6.30E
Overuman *l.* Sweden **50 C4** 66.06N 14.40E
Oviedo Spain **43 C5** 43.21N 5.50W
Ovruch U.S.S.R. **49 N5** 51.20N 28.50E
Owase Japan **70 C4** 34.04N136.12E
Owel, Lough Rep. of Ire. **15 D3** 53.34N 7.24W
Owen Falls Dam Uganda **99 D5** 0.30N 33.05E
Owen Sound *town* Canada **81 J2** 44.34N 80.56W
Owen Stanley Range *mts.* P.N.G. **71 D5** 9.30S148.00E
Owerri Nigeria **103 F2** 5.29N 7.02E
Owo Nigeria **103 F2** 7.10N 5.39E
Oxelösund Sweden **50 D2** 58.40N 17.10E
Oxford U.K. **13 F3** 51.45N 1.15W
Oxfordshire *d.* U.K. **13 F3** 51.46N 1.10W
Oykel *r.* U.K. **14 D4** 57.52N 4.22W
Oymyakon U.S.S.R. **53 L3** 63.30N142.44E
Oyo Nigeria **103 E2** 7.50N 3.55E
Oyo *d.* Nigeria **103 E2** 8.10N 3.40E
Ozamiz Phil. **69 G5** 8.09N123.59E
Ozark Plateau U.S.A. **83 H4** 36.00N 93.35W
Ozersk U.S.S.R. **49 K7** 54.26N 22.00E

P

Paamiut *see* Frederikshåb Greenland **81**
Pābna Bangla. **63 F4** 24.00N 89.15E
Pachuca Mexico **86 E4** 20.10N 98.44W
Pacific-Antarctic Basin Pacific Oc. **106 D1** 58.00S 98.00W
Pacific-Antarctic Ridge Pacific Oc. **106 A1** 57.00S145.00W
Pacific Ocean 75
Padang Indonesia **68 C3** 0.55S100.21E
Padangpanjang Indonesia **68 C3** 0.30S100.26E
Padangsidempuan Indonesia **68 B4** 1.20N 99.11E
Padborg Denmark **38 C2** 54.50N 9.22E
Paderborn W. Germany **48 D5** 51.43N 8.44E
Padre I. U.S.A. **83 G2** 27.00N 97.20W
Padstow U.K. **13 C2** 50.32N 4.56W
Padua Italy **46 E6** 45.27N 11.52E
Pag *i.* Yugo. **46 G6** 44.28N 15.00E
Pagadian Phil. **69 G5** 7.50N123.30E
Pagai Selatan *i.* Indonesia **68 C3** 3.00S100.18E
Pagai Utara *i.* Indonesia **68 C3** 2.42S100.05E
Pahala Hawaii U.S.A. **82 O8** 19.12N155.28W
Paible U.K. **14 A4** 57.35N 7.28W
Päijänne *l.* Finland **50 F3** 61.30N 25.30E
Paimboeuf France **42 C4** 47.14N 2.01W
Paisley U.K. **14 D2** 55.50N 4.26W
Pakanbaru Indonesia **68 C4** 0.33N101.20E
Pakistan Asia **62 B5** 30.00N 70.00E
Pak Lay Laos **68 C7** 18.10N101.24E
Pakse Laos **68 D7** 15.05N105.50E
Pakwach Uganda **99 D5** 2.17N 31.28E
Palana U.S.S.R. **53 N3** 59.05N159.59E
Palangkaraya Indonesia **68 E3** 2.16S113.56E
Palawan *i.* Phil. **68 F5** 9.30N118.30E
Palembang Indonesia **68 C3** 2.59S104.50E
Palencia Spain **43 C5** 42.01N 4.34W
Palenque Mexico **86 F3** 17.32N 91.59W
Palermo Italy **46 F3** 38.09N 13.22E
Palit, C. Albania **47 I4** 41.24N 19.23E
Palk Str. India / Sri Lanka **63 E2** 10.00N 79.40E
Palma Spain **43 G3** 39.36N 2.39E
Palma, B. of Spain **43 G3** 39.30N 2.40E
Palma del Río Spain **43 C2** 37.43N 5.17W
Palmas, C. Liberia **102 C1** 4.30N 7.55W
Palmas, G. of Med. Sea **46 D3** 39.00N 8.30E
Palmerston Atoll Cook Is. **74 J6** 18.04S163.10W
Palmerston North New Zealand **71 G1** 40.21S175.37E
Palmi Italy **46 G3** 38.22N 15.50E
Palmira Colombia **88 B8** 3.33N 76.17W
Palm Springs *town* U.S.A. **82 C3** 33.49N116.34W
Palmyra Syria **60 E4** 34.36N 38.15E
Palmyra I. Pacific Oc. **74 J6** 5.52N162.05W
Palmyras Pt. India **63 F4** 20.40N 87.00E
Paloh Indonesia **68 D4** 1.46N109.17E
Palopo Indonesia **69 G3** 3.01S120.12E
Palos, C. Spain **32 E2** 37.38N 0.41W
Pamekasan Indonesia **68 E2** 7.11S113.50E
Pamiers France **42 E2** 43.07N 1.36E
Pamirs *mts.* U.S.S.R. **66 B4** 37.50N 73.30E
Pampa U.S.A. **82 F4** 35.32N100.58W
Pampas *f.* Argentina **89 C4** 35.00S 63.00W
Pamplona Spain **43 E5** 42.49N 1.39W
Panama C. America **87 H1** 9.00N 80.00W
Panama, G. of Panama **87 I1** 8.30N 79.00W
Panama City Panama **87 I1** 8.57N 79.30W
Panama City U.S.A. **83 I3** 30.10N 85.41W
Panay *i.* Phil. **69 G6** 11.10N122.30E
Panevežys U.S.S.R. **50 F1** 55.44N 24.24E
Pangkalpinang Indonesia **68 D3** 2.05S106.09E
Pangnirtung Canada **81 L4** 66.05N 65.45W
Pantano del Esla *l.* Spain **43 C4** 41.40N 5.50W
Pantelleria *i.* Italy **46 F2** 36.48N 12.00E
Paola Italy **46 H3** 39.21N 16.03E
Pápa Hungary **49 H3** 47.19N 17.28E
Papeete Tahiti **75 L6** 17.32S149.34W
Papenburg W. Germany **39 F5** 53.05N 7.25E
Paphos Cyprus **60 D4** 34.45N 32.25E
Papua, G. of P.N.G. **69 K2** 8.50S145.00E
Papua New Guinea Austa. **71 D5** 6.00S143.00E
Papun Burma **68 B7** 18.05N 97.26E
Paracel Is. S. China Sea **68 E7** 16.20N112.00E
Paraguay *r.* Argentina **89 D5** 27.30S 58.50W
Paraguay S. America **89 D5** 23.00S 58.00W
Parakou Benin **103 E2** 9.23N 2.40E
Paramaribo Surinam **88 D8** 5.50N 55.14W
Paraná Argentina **89 C4** 31.45S 60.30W
Paraná *r.* Argentina **89 D4** 34.00S 58.30W
Parczew Poland **49 K5** 51.39N 22.54E
Pardubice Czech. **48 G5** 50.03N 15.45E
Parepare Indonesia **68 F3** 4.03S119.40E
Pariaman Indonesia **68 C3** 0.36S100.09E
Parigi Indonesia **69 G3** 0.49S120.10E
Paris France **42 F5** 48.52N 2.20E
Parkano Finland **50 E3** 62.03N 23.00E
Parker Dam U.S.A. **82 D3** 34.25N114.05W
Parma Italy **46 E6** 44.48N 10.18E
Parnaíba *r.* Brazil **88 E7** 3.00S 42.00W
Parnassós *mtn.* Greece **47 K3** 38.33N 22.35E
Pärnu U.S.S.R. **50 F2** 58.28N 24.30E
Pärnu *r.* U.S.S.R. **50 F2** 58.23N 24.32E
Páros *i.* Greece **47 L2** 37.04N 25.11E
Parral Mexico **86 C5** 26.58N105.40W
Parrett *r.* U.K. **13 E3** 51.10N 3.00W
Parry, C. Greenland **81 K5** 76.50N 71.00W
Parry Is. Canada **81 H5** 76.00N102.00W
Parseta *r.* Poland **48 G7** 54.12N 15.33E
Parthenay France **42 D4** 46.39N 0.14W
Partry Mts. Rep. of Ire. **15 B3** 53.40N 9.30W
Pasadena U.S.A. **82 C3** 34.10N118.09W
Pasay Phil. **69 G6** 14.33N121.00E
Paso de Bermejo *f.* Argentina **89 C4** 32.50S 70.00W
Paso Socompa *f.* Chile **89 C5** 24.27S 68.18W
Passage de la Déroute *str.* U.K. **13 E1** 49.30N 2.10W
Passau W. Germany **48 F4** 48.35N 13.28E
Passero, C. Italy **46 G2** 36.40N 15.08E
Pasto Colombia **88 B8** 1.12N 77.17W
Pasuruan Indonesia **68 E2** 7.38S112.44E
Pasvik *r.* Norway **50 G5** 69.45N 30.00E
Patagonia *f.* Argentina **89 C3** 45.00S 68.00W
Paterson U.S.A. **83 L5** 40.55N 74.10W
Pathfinder Resr. U.S.A. **82 E5** 42.25N106.55W
Patiāla India **63 D5** 30.21N 76.27E
Patkai Hills Burma **63 G5** 26.30N 95.40E
Patna India **63 F4** 25.37N 85.12E
Patos, L. Brazil **89 D4** 31.00S 51.10W
Pátras Greece **47 J3** 38.15N 21.45E
Patras, G. of Med. Sea **47 J3** 38.15N 21.35E
Patrickswell Rep. of Ire. **15 C2** 52.34N 8.42W
Patuca *r.* Honduras **87 H3** 15.50N 84.18W
Pau France **42 D2** 43.18N 0.22W
Pauillac France **42 D3** 45.12N 0.44W
Pavia Italy **46 D6** 45.10N 9.10E
Pavlodar U.S.S.R. **52 G3** 52.21N 76.59E
Pavlograd U.S.S.R. **52 C2** 48.34N 35.50E
Peace *r.* Canada **80 G3** 59.00N111.26W
Peace River *town* Canada **80 G3** 56.15N117.18W
Peale, Mt. U.S.A. **82 E4** 38.26N109.14W
Pearl *r.* U.S.A. **83 I3** 30.15N 89.25W
Peć Yugo. **47 J5** 42.40N 20.17E
Pechenga U.S.S.R. **50 G5** 69.28N 31.04E
Pechora *r.* U.S.S.R. **52 E4** 68.10N 54.00E
Pechora G. U.S.S.R. **52 E4** 69.00N 56.00E
Pecos U.S.A. **82 F3** 31.25N103.30W
Pecos *r.* U.S.A. **82 F2** 29.45N101.25W
Pécs Hungary **49 I3** 46.05N 18.14E
Peebles U.K. **14 E2** 55.39N 3.12W
Peel *r.* Canada **80 E4** 68.13N135.00W
Peel *f.* Neth. **39 D3** 51.30N 5.50E
Peel U.K. **12 C6** 54.12N 4.42W
Peene *r.* E. Germany **48 F6** 53.53N 13.49E
Pegu Burma **63 H3** 17.18N 96.31E
Pegu Yoma *mts.* Burma **63 G3** 18.40N 96.00E
Peipus, L. U.S.S.R. **50 F2** 58.30N 27.30E
Pekalongan Indonesia **68 D2** 6.54S109.37E
Pelat, Mont *mtn.* France **42 H3** 44.17N 6.41E
Peleng *i.* Indonesia **69 G3** 1.30S123.10E
Pelly *r.* Canada **80 E4** 62.50N137.35W
Pelotas Brazil **89 D4** 31.45S 52.20W
Pematangsiantar Indonesia **68 B4** 2.59N 99.01E
Pemba Mozambique **99 E3** 13.02S 40.30E
Pemba I. Tanzania **99 D4** 5.10S 39.45E
Pembroke U.K. **13 C3** 51.41N 4.57W
Peñaranda de Bracamonte Spain **43 C4** 40.54N 5.13W
Penarth U.K. **13 D3** 51.25N 3.10W
Peñas, Cabo de *c.* Spain **43 C5** 43.42N 5.52W
Pende *r.* Chad **103 H2** 7.30N 16.20E
Pendembu Sierra Leone **102 B2** 8.09N 10.42W
Pendine U.K. **13 C3** 51.45N 4.32W
Penganga *r.* India **63 E3** 18.52N 79.56E
Penicuik U.K. **14 E2** 55.50N 3.12W
Pennsylvania *d.* U.S.A. **83 K5** 41.00N 78.00W
Penny Highland *mtn.* Canada **81 L4** 67.10N 66.50W
Penonomé Panama **87 H1** 8.30N 80.20W
Penrhyn Atoll Cook Is. **75 K7** 9.00S158.00W
Penrith U.K. **12 E6** 54.40N 2.45W
Penryn U.K. **13 B2** 50.11N 5.08W
Pensacola U.S.A. **83 I3** 30.30N 87.12W
Penticton Canada **80 G2** 49.29N119.38W
Pentland Firth *str.* U.K. **14 E5** 58.40N 3.00W
Pentland Hills U.K. **14 E2** 55.45N 3.30W
Penza U.S.S.R. **52 D3** 53.11N 45.00E
Penzance U.K. **13 B2** 50.07N 5.32W
Penzhina, G. of U.S.S.R. **53 N3** 61.00N163.00E
Peoria U.S.A. **83 I5** 40.43N 89.38W
Perabumulih Indonesia **68 C3** 3.29S104.14E
Pereira Colombia **88 B8** 4.47N 75.46W
Péribonca *r.* Canada **81 K2** 48.50N 72.00W
Périgueux France **42 E3** 45.12N 0.44E
Perim *i.* S. Yemen **101 G3** 12.40N 43.24E
Perm U.S.S.R. **52 E3** 58.01N 56.10E
Pernik *see* Dimitrovo Bulgaria **47**
Péronne France **39 A1** 49.56N 2.57E
Perpignan France **42 F2** 42.42N 2.54E
Perranporth U.K. **13 B2** 50.20N 5.09W
Persepolis *ruins* Iran **61 I3** 29.55N 53.00E
Perth Australia **71 A2** 31.58S115.49E
Perth U.K. **14 E3** 56.24N 3.28W
Peru S. America **88 B7** 10.00S 75.00W
Peru Basin Pacific Oc. **106 E4** 19.00S 96.00W
Peru-Chile Trench Pacific Oc. **89 B5** 23.00S 71.30W
Perugia Italy **46 F5** 43.06N 12.24E
Péruwelz Belgium **39 B2** 50.32N 3.36E
Pervomaysk U.S.S.R. **49 O4** 48.03N 30.50E
Pervouralsk U.S.S.R. **52 E3** 56.59N 59.58E
Pesaro Italy **46 F5** 43.54N 12.54E
Pescara Italy **46 G5** 42.27N 14.13E
Pescara *r.* Italy **46 G5** 42.28N 14.13E
Peshāwar Pakistan **63 C6** 34.01N 71.40E
Petatlán Mexico **86 D3** 17.31N101.16W
Peterborough U.K. **13 G4** 52.35N 0.14W
Peterhead U.K. **14 G4** 57.30N 1.46W
Peterlee U.K. **12 F6** 54.45N 1.18W
Petersfield U.K. **13 G3** 51.01N 0.55W
Petra *ruins* Jordan **60 D3** 30.19N 35.26E
Petrich Bulgaria **47 K4** 41.25N 23.13E
Petropavlovsk U.S.S.R. **52 F3** 54.53N 69.13E
Petropavlovsk Kamchatskiy U.S.S.R. **53 N3** 53.03N158.43E
Petrópolis Brazil **89 E5** 22.30S 43.02W
Petrovsk Zabaykal'skiy U.S.S.R. **53 J2** 51.20N108.55E
Petrozavodsk U.S.S.R. **52 C3** 61.46N 34.19E
Pézenas France **42 F2** 43.28N 3.25E
Pforzheim W. Germany **48 D4** 48.53N 8.41E
Phangan, Ko *i.* Thailand **68 C5** 9.50N100.00E
Phangnga Thailand **68 B5** 8.29N 98.31E
Phan Rang Vietnam **68 D6** 11.35N109.00E
Phet Buri Thailand **68 B6** 13.01N 99.55E
Philadelphia U.S.A. **83 K5** 40.00N 75.10W
Philippeville Belgium **39 C2** 50.12N 4.32E
Philippines Asia **69 G6** 13.00N123.00E
Philippine Trench Pacific Oc. **69 H6** 8.45N127.20E
Phnom Penh Cambodia **68 C6** 11.35N104.55E
Phoenix U.S.A. **82 D3** 33.30N111.55W
Phoenix Is. Kiribati **74 I7** 4.00S172.00W
Phong Saly Laos **68 C8** 21.40N102.06E
Phuket Thailand **68 B5** 7.55N 98.23E
Phuket *i.* Thailand **68 B5** 8.10N 98.20E
Phu Quoc *i.* Cambodia **68 C6** 10.10N104.00E
Phu Tho Vietnam **68 D8** 21.23N105.13E
Piacenza Italy **46 D6** 45.03N 9.42E
Pianosa *i.* Italy **46 E5** 42.35N 10.05E
Piatra-Neamț Romania **49 M3** 46.56N 26.22E
Piave *r.* Italy **46 F6** 45.33N 12.45E
Picardy *f.* France **39 A1** 49.47N 2.45E
Pickering U.K. **12 G6** 54.14N 0.48W
Pickwick L. *resr.* U.S.A. **83 I4** 35.00N 88.10W
Piedras Negras Mexico **86 D5** 28.40N100.32W
Pieksämäki Finland **50 F3** 62.18N 27.10E
Pielinen *l.* Finland **50 G3** 63.20N 29.50E
Pierre U.S.A. **82 F5** 44.23N100.20W
Piešt'any Czech. **49 H4** 48.36N 17.50E
Pietermaritzburg R.S.A. **99 D2** 29.36S 30.24E
Pietersburg R.S.A. **99 C2** 23.54S 29.23E
Pietrosu *mtn.* Romania **49 L3** 47.36N 24.38E
Pietrosul *mtn.* Romania **49 L3** 47.08N 25.11E
Pikes Peak *mtn.* U.S.A. **82 E4** 38.50N105.03W
Piła Poland **48 H6** 53.09N 16.44E
Pilcomayo *r.* Argentina / Paraguay **89 D5** 25.15S 57.43W
Pilica *r.* Poland **49 J5** 51.52N 21.17E
Pílos Greece **47 J2** 36.55N 21.40E
Pinang, Pulau *i.* Malaysia **68 C5** 5.30N100.10E
Pinarbaşi Turkey **60 E5** 38.43N 36.23E
Pinar del Río Cuba **87 H4** 22.24N 83.42W
Pindus Mts. Albania / Greece **47 J4** 39.40N 21.00E
Pine Bluff *town* U.S.A. **83 H3** 34.13N 92.00W
Pinega *r.* U.S.S.R. **33 N7** 63.51N 42.00E
Pines, I. of Cuba **87 H4** 21.40N 82.40W
Ping *r.* Thailand **68 C7** 15.45N100.10E
Pingdingshan China **67 J5** 41.26N124.46E
Pingdong Taiwan **67 J2** 22.40N120.30E
Pingelap *i.* Pacific Oc. **74 G8** 6.15N160.40E
Pingliang China **66 G4** 35.25N107.14E
Pingxiang China **66 G2** 22.05N106.46E
Pini *i.* Indonesia **68 B4** 0.10N 98.30E
Piniós *r.* Greece **47 K3** 39.51N 22.37E
Pinrang Indonesia **68 F3** 3.48S119.41E
Pinsk U.S.S.R. **49 M6** 52.08N 26.01E
Piombino Italy **46 E5** 42.56N 10.30E
Piotrków Trybunalski Poland **49 I5** 51.25N 19.42E
Piracicaba Brazil **89 E5** 22.20S 47.40W
Piraeus Greece **47 K2** 37.56N 23.38E
Pírgos Greece **47 J2** 37.42N 21.27E
Pirna E. Germany **48 F5** 50.58N 13.58E
Pirot Yugo. **47 K5** 43.10N 22.32E
Pisa Italy **46 E5** 43.43N 10.24E
Pisciotta Italy **46 G4** 40.08N 15.12E
Písek Czech. **48 G4** 49.19N 14.10E
Pishan China **66 C4** 37.30N 78.20E
Pisuerga *r.* Spain **43 C4** 41.35N 5.40W
Pisz Poland **49 J6** 53.38N 21.49E
Pita Guinea **102 B3** 11.05N 12.15W
Pitcairn I. Pacific Oc. **75 M5** 25.04S130.06W
Piteå Sweden **50 E4** 65.19N 21.30E
Pitești Romania **49 L2** 44.52N 24.51E
Pitlochry U.K. **14 E3** 56.44N 3.47W
Pittsburgh U.S.A. **83 K5** 40.26N 79.58W
Piura Peru **88 A7** 5.15S 80.38W
Plana Cays *is.* Bahamas **87 J4** 22.31N 72.14W
Plasencia Spain **43 B4** 40.02N 6.05W
Platani *r.* Italy **46 F2** 37.24N 13.15E
Plateau *d.* Nigeria **103 F2** 8.50N 9.00E
Platí, C. Greece **47 K4** 40.26N 23.59E
Platinum U.S.A. **80 B3** 59.00N161.50W
Platte *r.* U.S.A. **83 G5** 41.05N 96.50W
Plauen E. Germany **48 F5** 50.29N 12.08E
Pleiku Vietnam **68 D6** 13.57N108.01E
Pleven Bulgaria **47 L5** 43.25N 24.39E
Pljevlja Yugo. **47 I5** 43.22N 19.22E
Płock Poland **49 I6** 52.33N 19.43E
Ploiești Romania **49 M2** 44.57N 26.02E
Plomb du Cantal *mtn.* France **42 F3** 45.04N 2.45E
Plombières France **42 H4** 47.58N 6.28E
Plön W. Germany **38 D2** 54.10N 10.26E
Plöner See *l.* W. Germany **38 D2** 54.06N 10.25E
Ploudalmézeau France **42 B5** 48.33N 4.39W
Plovdiv Bulgaria **47 L5** 42.09N 24.45E
Plymouth U.K. **13 C2** 50.23N 4.09W
Plzeň Czech. **48 F4** 49.45N 13.22E
Pô Burkina **103 D3** 11.11N 1.10W
Po *r.* Italy **46 F6** 44.51N 12.30E
Pobé Benin **103 E2** 7.00N 2.56E
Pobeda, Mt. U.S.S.R. **53 M4** 65.20N145.50E
Pobla de Segur Spain **43 F5** 42.15N 0.58E
Pocatello U.S.A. **82 D5** 42.53N112.26W
Pocklington U.K. **12 G5** 53.57N 0.47W
Podolsk U.S.S.R. **52 D3** 55.23N 37.32E
Podor Senegal **102 A4** 16.35N 15.02W
Poh Indonesia **69 G3** 1.00S122.50E
Pohnpei *i.* Pacific Oc. **74 F8** 6.55N158.15E
Pointe-à-Pitre Guadeloupe **87 L3** 16.14N 61.32W
Pointe Noire *town* Congo **99 B4** 4.46S 11.53E
Poitiers France **42 E4** 46.35N 0.20E
Pokhara Nepal **63 E5** 28.14N 83.58E
Poland Europe **49 I6** 52.30N 19.00E
Polatli Turkey **60 D5** 39.34N 32.08E
Policastro, G. of Med. Sea **46 G3** 40.00N 15.35E
Poligny France **42 G4** 46.50N 5.42E
Pollino *mtn.* Italy **46 H3** 39.53N 16.11E
Polperro U.K. **13 C2** 50.19N 4.31W
Poltava U.S.S.R. **52 C2** 49.35N 34.35E
Polynesia *is.* Pacific Oc. **74 I9** 4.00S165.00W
Pombal Portugal **43 A3** 39.55N 8.38W
Ponce Puerto Rico **87 K3** 18.00N 66.40W
Pondicherry India **63 E2** 11.59N 79.50E
Pond Inlet *str.* Canada **81 K5** 72.30N 75.00W
Ponferrada Spain **43 B5** 42.32N 6.31W
Ponta Grossa Brazil **89 D5** 25.07S 50.00W
Pont-à-Mousson France **42 H5** 48.55N 6.03E
Pontefract U.K. **12 F5** 53.42N 1.22W
Pontevedra Spain **43 A5** 42.25N 8.39W
Pontianak Indonesia **68 D3** 0.05S109.16E
Pontine Is. Italy **46 F4** 40.56N 12.58E
Pontine Mts. Turkey **60 E6** 40.32N 38.00E
Pontoise France **42 F5** 49.03N 2.05E
Pontrilas U.K. **13 E3** 51.56N 2.51W
Pontypool U.K. **13 D3** 51.43N 3.01W
Pontypridd U.K. **13 D3** 51.35N 3.19W
Poole U.K. **13 E2** 50.42N 2.02W
Poopó, L. Bolivia **89 C6** 19.00S 67.00W
Poperinge Belgium **39 A2** 50.51N 2.44E
Poplar Bluff *town* U.S.A. **83 H4** 36.40N 90.25W
Popocatépetl *mtn.* Mexico **86 E3** 19.02N 98.38W
Popondetta P.N.G. **69 L2** 8.45S148.15E
Poppholz W. Germany **38 C2** 54.37N 9.30E
Poprad Czech. **49 J4** 49.03N 20.18E
Porbandar India **63 C4** 21.40N 69.40E
Porcupine *r.* U.S.A. **80 D4** 66.25N145.20W
Pori Finland **50 E3** 61.28N 21.45E
Porkkala Finland **50 F3** 60.00N 24.25E
Pornic France **42 C4** 47.07N 2.05W
Poronaysk U.S.S.R. **53 L2** 49.13N142.55E
Porsangen *est.* Norway **50 F5** 70.30N 25.45E
Porsgrunn Norway **50 B2** 59.10N 9.40E
Porsuk *r.* Turkey **60 C5** 39.41N 31.56E
Portadown U.K. **15 E4** 54.25N 6.27W
Portaferry U.K. **15 F4** 54.23N 5.33W
Portage la Prairie *town* Canada **81 I2** 49.58N 98.20W
Portalegre Portugal **43 B3** 39.17N 7.25W
Port Angeles U.S.A. **82 B6** 48.06N123.26W
Port Antonio Jamaica **87 I3** 18.10N 76.27W
Port Arthur U.S.A. **83 H2** 29.55N 93.56W
Port Augusta Australia **71 C2** 32.30S137.46E
Port-au-Prince Haiti **87 J3** 18.33N 72.20W
Port Blair India **63 G2** 11.40N 92.30E
Port Bou Spain **43 G5** 42.25N 3.09E
Port Bouet Ivory Coast **102 D2** 5.14N 3.58W
Port Cartier Canada **81 L3** 50.03N 66.46W
Port Elizabeth R.S.A. **99 C1** 33.58S 25.36E
Port Ellen U.K. **14 B2** 55.39N 6.11W
Port Erin U.K. **12 C6** 54.05N 4.44W
Portglenone U.K. **15 E4** 54.51N 6.30W
Port Harcourt Nigeria **103 F1** 4.43N 7.05E
Porthcawl U.K. **13 D3** 51.29N 3.41W
Port Hedland Australia **71 A3** 20.24S118.36E
Porthmadog U.K. **12 C4** 52.56N 4.09W
Portimão Portugal **43 A2** 37.08N 8.32W
Port Isaac Bay U.K. **13 C2** 50.38N 4.50W
Portiței Mouth *f.* Romania **47 N6** 44.40N 29.00E
Portland Maine U.S.A. **83 L5** 43.41N 70.18W
Portland Oreg. U.S.A. **82 B6** 45.32N122.40W
Port Laoise Rep. of Ire. **15 D3** 53.03N 7.20W
Port Loko Sierra Leone **102 B2** 8.50N 12.50W
Portmarnock Rep. of Ire. **15 E3** 53.25N 6.10W
Port Moresby P.N.G. **69 L2** 9.30S147.07E
Portnaguiran U.K. **14 B5** 58.15N 16.11W
Port Nelson Canada **81 I3** 57.10N 92.35W

Ringwood U.K. **13 F2** 50.50N 1.49W
Riobamba Ecuador **88 B7** 1.44S 78.40W
Rio Branco Brazil **88 C7** 10.00S 67.49W
Rio de Janeiro Brazil **89 E5** 22.50S 43.17W
Río Gallegos Argentina **89 C2** 51.35S 69.15W
Rio Grande *town* Brazil **89 D4** 32.03S 52.18W
Rio Grande *r.* N. America **76 K4** 25.55N 97.08W
Río Grande *r.* Nicaragua **87 H2** 12.48N 83.30W
Ripon U.K. **12 F6** 54.08N 1.30W
Risha, Wadi *r.* Saudi Arabia **61 F2** 25.40N 44.08E
Rishiri jima *i.* Japan **70 E9** 45.11N141.15E
Risör Norway **50 B2** 58.44N 9.15E
Ristikent U.S.S.R. **50 G5** 68.40N 31.47E
Rivas Nicaragua **87 G2** 11.26N 85.50W
Rivers *d.* Nigeria **103 F1** 4.45N 6.35E
Riyadh Saudi Arabia **61 G2** 24.39N 46.44E
Rize Turkey **60 F6** 41.03N 40.31E
Rizzuto, C. Italy **47 H3** 38.53N 17.06E
Rjukan Norway **50 B2** 59.54N 8.33E
Roag, L. U.K. **14 B5** 58.17N 6.52W
Roanne France **42 G4** 46.02N 4.05E
Roanoke *r.* U.S.A. **83 K4** 36.00N 76.35W
Roberval Canada **81 K2** 48.31N 72.16W
Robin Hood's Bay *town* U.K. **12 G6** 54.27N 0.31W
Robson, Mt. Canada **80 G3** 53.00N119.09W
Roca, Cabo de Portugal **43 A3** 38.40N 9.31W
Roccella Italy **47 H3** 38.19N 16.24E
Rocha Uruguay **89 D4** 34.30S 54.22W
Rochdale U.K. **12 E5** 53.36N 2.10W
Rochechouart France **42 E3** 45.49N 0.50E
Rochefort Belgium **39 D2** 50.10N 5.13E
Rochefort France **42 D3** 45.57N 0.58W
Rochester U.K. **13 H3** 51.22N 0.30E
Rochester U.S.A. **83 K5** 43.12N 77.37W
Rochfort Bridge Rep. of Ire. **15 D3** 53.25N 7.20W
Rockford U.S.A. **83 I5** 42.16N 89.06W
Rockhampton Australia **71 E3** 23.22S150.32E
Rock Springs U.S.A. **82 E5** 41.35N109.13W
Rocky Mts. N. America **76 H7** 42.00N110.00W
Rocroi France **39 C1** 49.56N 4.31E
Rödby Denmark **38 E2** 54.42N 11.24E
Rodel U.K. **14 B4** 57.47N 6.58W
Rodez France **42 F3** 44.21N 2.34E
Rodonit, C. Albania **47 I4** 41.34N 19.25E
Rödvig Denmark **38 F3** 55.13N 12.20E
Roermond Neth. **39 D3** 51.12N 6.00E
Rohtak India **63 D5** 28.54N 76.35E
Rokan *r.* Indonesia **68 C4** 2.00N101.00E
Rokel *r.* Sierra Leone **102 B2** 8.36N 12.55W
Rolla U.S.A. **83 H4** 37.56N 91.55W
Roma *i.* Indonesia **69 H2** 7.45S127.20E
Romain, C. U.S.A. **83 K3** 33.01N 79.23W
Romaine *r.* Canada **81 L3** 50.20N 63.45W
Romania Europe **49 K3** 46.30N 24.00E
Romano, C. U.S.A. **83 J2** 25.50N 81.42W
Romans France **42 G3** 45.03N 5.03E
Rome Italy **46 F4** 41.54N 12.29E
Romilly France **42 F5** 48.31N 3.44E
Romney Marsh *f.* U.K. **13 H3** 51.05N 0.55E
Römö *i.* Denmark **38 B3** 55.10N 8.30E
Romorantin France **42 E4** 47.22N 1.44E
Rona *i.* U.K. **14 C4** 57.33N 5.59W
Ronda Spain **43 C2** 36.45N 5.10W
Rönde Denmark **38 D4** 56.18N 10.30E
Rönne Denmark **50 C1** 55.07N 14.43E
Roof Butte *mtn.* U.S.A. **82 E4** 36.29N109.05W
Roosendaal Neth. **39 C3** 51.32N 4.28E
Roosevelt *r.* Brazil **88 C7** 5.00S 60.30W
Roraima, Mt. Guyana **88 C8** 5.45N 61.00W
Röros Norway **50 B3** 62.35N 11.23E
Rosa, Mt. Italy / Switz. **48 C2** 45.56N 7.51E
Rosario Argentina **89 C4** 33.00S 60.40W
Roscommon Rep. of Ire. **15 C3** 53.38N 8.13W
Roscommon *d.* Rep. of Ire. **15 C3** 53.38N 8.11W
Roscrea Rep. of Ire. **15 D2** 52.57N 7.49W
Roseau Dominica **87 L3** 15.18N 61.23W
Roseburg U.S.A. **82 B5** 43.13N123.21W
Rosenheim W. Germany **48 F3** 47.51N 12.09E
Rosetown Canada **80 H3** 51.34N107.59W
Roshage *c.* Denmark **38 B5** 57.10N 8.30E
Rosières France **39 A1** 49.49N 2.43E
Roskilde Denmark **38 F3** 55.39N 12.07E
Roskilde *d.* Denmark **38 F3** 55.30N 12.05E
Roslags-Näsby Sweden **50 D2** 59.26N 18.02E
Rosslare Rep. of Ire. **15 E2** 52.17N 6.23W
Ross-on-Wye U.K. **13 E3** 51.55N 2.35W
Ross Sea Antarctica **107 R1** 73.00S179.00E
Rössvatnet *l.* Norway **50 C4** 65.50N 14.00E
Rostock E. Germany **48 F7** 54.06N 12.09E
Rostov U.S.S.R. **52 D2** 47.10N 39.45E
Rothbury U.K. **12 F7** 55.20N 1.54W
Rother *r.* U.K. **8 G2** 50.54N 0.48E
Rotherham U.K. **12 F5** 53.26N 1.21W
Rothes U.K. **14 E4** 57.31N 3.14W
Rothesay U.K. **14 C2** 55.50N 5.03W
Roti *i.* Indonesia **69 G1** 10.30S123.10E
Rotterdam Neth. **39 C3** 51.55N 4.29E
Roubaix France **39 B2** 50.42N 3.10E
Rouen France **42 E5** 49.26N 1.05E
Roulers Belgium **39 B2** 50.57N 3.06E
Roundup U.S.A. **82 E6** 46.27N108.34W
Rourkela India **63 F4** 22.16N 85.01E
Rousay *i.* U.K. **14 E6** 59.10N 3.02W
Rouyn Canada **81 K2** 48.15N 79.00W
Rovaniemi Finland **50 F4** 66.29N 25.40E
Rovinj Yugo. **46 F6** 45.06N 13.39E
Rovno U.S.S.R. **49 M5** 50.39N 26.10E
Royale, I. U.S.A. **83 I6** 48.00N 88.45W
Royal Leamington Spa U.K. **13 F4** 52.15N 1.32W
Royal Tunbridge Wells U.K. **13 H3** 51.07N 0.16E
Roye France **39 A1** 49.42N 2.48E
Royston U.K. **13 G4** 52.03N 0.01W
Rub al Khali *des.* Saudi Arabia **101 G3** 20.20N 52.30E
Rubtsovsk U.S.S.R. **52 G2** 51.29N 81.10E
Rūdān *r.* Iran **61 J2** 27.02N 56.53E
Rud-i-Pusht *r.* Iran **61 J3** 29.09N 58.09E
Rudolstadt E. Germany **48 E5** 50.44N 11.20E
Ruffec France **42 E4** 46.02N 0.12E
Rufiji *r.* Tanzania **99 D4** 8.02S 39.17E
Rufisque Senegal **102 A3** 14.43N 17.16W
Rugao China **67 J4** 32.27N120.35E
Rugby U.K. **13 F4** 52.23N 1.16W
Rugby U.S.A. **82 G6** 48.24N 99.59W
Rügen *i.* E. Germany **48 F7** 54.30N 13.30E
Ruhr *f.* W. Germany **39 F3** 51.22N 7.26E
Ruhr *r.* W. Germany **39 E3** 51.27N 6.41E
Rukwa, L. Tanzania **99 D4** 8.00S 32.20E
Ruma Yugo. **47 I6** 44.59N 19.51E
Rum Cay *i.* Bahamas **87 J4** 23.41N 74.53W
Rumoi Japan **70 E8** 43.56N141.39E
Runcorn U.K. **12 E5** 53.20N 2.42W
Ruoqiang China **66 D5** 39.00N 88.00E
Ruo Shui *r.* China **66 F5** 42.15N101.03E
Rur *r.* Neth. **39 D3** 51.12N 5.58E
Rurutu *i.* Pacific Oc. **75 K5** 22.25S151.20W
Ruse Bulgaria **47 L5** 43.50N 25.59E
Rushden U.K. **13 G4** 52.16N 0.33W
Russian S.F.S.R. *d.* U.S.S.R. **52 E3** 62.00N 80.00E
Rustavi U.S.S.R. **52 D2** 41.34N 45.03E
Rütenbrock W. Germany **39 F4** 52.51N 7.06E
Ruteng Indonesia **69 G2** 8.35S120.28E
Ruthin U.K. **12 D5** 53.07N 3.18W
Rutog China **66 C4** 33.30N 79.40E
Ruvuma *r.* Mozambique / Tanzania **99 E3** 10.30S 40.30E
Ruwandiz Iraq **61 G5** 36.38N 44.32E
Ruwenzori Range *mts.* Uganda / Zaïre **99 C5** 0.30N 30.00E
Rwanda Africa **99 C4** 2.00S 30.00E
Ryan, L. U.K. **14 C2** 55.00N 5.05W
Ryazan U.S.S.R. **52 D3** 54.37N 39.43E
Rybachi Pen. U.S.S.R. **50 H5** 69.45N 32.30E
Rybinsk Resr. U.S.S.R. **52 D3** 58.30N 38.25E
Rybnik Poland **49 I5** 50.06N 18.32E
Rybnitsa U.S.S.R. **49 N3** 47.42N 29.00E
Rye U.K. **13 H2** 50.57N 0.44E
Rye *r.* U.K. **12 G6** 54.09N 0.45W
Ryki Poland **49 J5** 51.39N 21.56E
Ryukyu Is. Japan **67 J2** 26.30N125.00E
Ryukyu Is. Trench Pacific Oc. **74 C10** 25.00N129.00E
Rzeszów Poland **49 J5** 50.04N 22.00E

S

Saale *r.* E. Germany **48 E5** 51.58N 11.53E
Saar *r.* W. Germany **39 E1** 49.43N 6.34E
Saarbrücken W. Germany **48 C4** 49.15N 6.58E
Saarburg W. Germany **39 E1** 49.36N 6.33E
Saaremaa *i.* U.S.S.R. **50 E2** 58.30N 22.30E
Saarijärvi Finland **50 F3** 62.44N 25.15E
Saba *i.* Leeward Is. **87 L3** 17.42N 63.26W
Šabac Yugo. **47 I6** 44.45N 19.41E
Sabadell Spain **43 G4** 41.33N 2.07E
Sabana, Archipiélago de Cuba **87 H4** 23.30N 80.00W
Sabinas Mexico **86 D5** 27.51N101.10W
Sabinas Hidalgo Mexico **86 D5** 26.33N100.10W
Sabine *r.* U.S.A. **83 H2** 29.40N 93.50W
Sable, C. Canada **81 L2** 43.30N 65.50W
Sable, C. U.S.A. **76 L4** 25.00N 81.20W
Sable I. Canada **81 M2** 44.00N 60.00W
Sacedón Spain **43 D4** 40.29N 2.44W
Sacramento U.S.A. **82 B4** 38.32N121.30W
Sacramento *r.* U.S.A. **82 B4** 38.05N122.00W
Sacramento Mts. U.S.A. **82 E3** 33.10N105.50W
Sádaba Spain **43 E5** 42.19N 1.10W
Sadiya India **63 G5** 27.49N 95.38E
Sado *i.* Japan **70 D6** 38.00N138.20E
Saeby Denmark **38 D5** 57.20N 10.30E
Safaha *des.* Saudi Arabia **60 E2** 26.30N 39.30E
Safaniya Saudi Arabia **61 H3** 28.00N 48.48E
Säffle Sweden **50 C2** 59.08N 12.55E
Saffron Walden U.K. **13 H4** 52.02N 0.19E
Safi Morocco **100 B5** 32.20N 9.17W
Saga Japan **70 A3** 33.08N130.30E
Sagaing Burma **63 G4** 22.00N 96.00E
Sagamihara Japan **70 D4** 35.35N139.30E
Sāgar India **63 E4** 23.50N 78.44E
Saglouc Canada **81 K4** 62.10N 75.40W
Sagua la Grande Cuba **87 H4** 22.55N 80.05W
Sagunto Spain **43 E3** 39.40N 0.17W
Sahagún Spain **43 C5** 42.23N 5.02W
Sahara *des.* Africa **100 B3** 18.00N 12.00E
Saharan Atlas *mts.* Algeria **100 C5** 34.20N 2.00E
Sahāranpur India **63 D5** 29.58N 77.33E
Sahba, Wadi *r.* Saudi Arabia **61 H1** 23.48N 49.50E
Sāhīwāl Pakistan **63 D5** 30.40N 73.06E
Saïda Lebanon **60 D4** 33.32N 35.22E
Sa'īdābād Iran **61 I3** 29.28N 55.43E
Saidpur Bangla. **63 F4** 25.48N 89.00E
Saimaa *l.* Finland **50 F3** 61.20N 28.00E
Saimbeyli Turkey **60 E5** 38.07N 36.08E
St. Abb's Head U.K. **14 F2** 55.54N 2.07W
St. Albans U.K. **13 G3** 51.47N 0.20W
St. Amand France **39 B2** 50.27N 3.26E
St. Amand-Mont-Rond *town* France **42 F4** 46.43N 2.29E
St. Andrews U.K. **14 F3** 56.20N 2.48W
St. Ann's Bay *town* Jamaica **87 I3** 18.26N 77.12W
St. Anthony Canada **81 M3** 51.24N 55.37W
St. Augustine U.S.A. **83 J2** 29.54N 81.19W
St. Austell U.K. **13 C2** 50.20N 4.48W
St. Barthélemy *i.* Leeward Is. **87 L3** 17.55N 62.50W
St. Bees Hd. U.K. **12 D6** 54.30N 3.40W
St. Boniface Canada **81 I2** 49.54N 97.07W
St. Brides Bay U.K. **13 B3** 51.50N 5.15W
St. Brieuc France **42 C5** 48.31N 2.45W
St. Catharines Canada **81 K2** 43.10N 79.15W
St. Catherine's Pt. U.K. **13 F2** 50.34N 1.20W
St. Céré France **42 E3** 44.52N 1.53E
St. Cloud U.S.A. **83 H6** 45.34N 94.10W
St. Croix *i.* U.S.V.Is. **87 L3** 17.45N 64.35W
St. David's U.K. **13 B3** 51.53N 5.16W
St. David's Head U.K. **13 B3** 51.55N 5.19W
St. Denis France **42 F5** 48.56N 2.21E
St. Dié France **42 H5** 48.17N 6.57E
St. Dizier France **42 G5** 48.38N 4.58E
St. Elias, Mt. U.S.A. **80 D4** 60.20N140.55W
Sainte Marie, Cap *c.* Madagascar **99 G6** 25.34S 45.10E
Saintes France **42 D3** 45.44N 0.38W
St. Étienne France **42 G3** 45.26N 4.26E
St. Feliu de Gixols Spain **43 G4** 41.47N 3.02E
Saintfield U.K. **15 F4** 54.29N 5.50W
St. Flour France **42 F3** 45.02N 3.05E
St. Gallen Switz. **48 D3** 47.25N 9.23E
St. Gaudens France **42 E2** 43.07N 0.44E
St. George's Grenada **87 L2** 12.04N 61.44W
St. George's Channel Rep. of Ire. / U.K. **15 E1** 51.30N 6.20W
St. Germain France **42 F5** 48.53N 2.04E
St. Gheorghe's Mouth *est.* Romania **47 N6** 44.51N 29.37E
St. Gilles-sur-Vie France **42 D4** 46.42N 1.56W
St. Girons France **42 E2** 42.59N 1.08E
St. Gotthard Pass Switz. **48 D3** 46.30N 8.55E
St. Govan's Head U.K. **13 C3** 51.36N 4.56W
St. Helena *i.* Atlantic Oc. **108 I4** 16.00S 6.00W
St. Helena B. R.S.A. **99 B1** 32.35S 18.00E
St. Helens U.K. **12 E5** 53.28N 2.43W
St. Helier U.K. **13 E1** 49.12N 2.07W
St. Hubert Belgium **39 D2** 50.02N 5.22E
St. Hyacinthe Canada **81 K2** 45.38N 72.57W
St. Ives U.K. **13 B2** 50.12N 5.30W
St. Jean Pied-de-Port France **42 D2** 43.10N 1.14W
St. John Canada **81 L2** 45.16N 66.03W
St. John *r.* Canada **81 L2** 45.30N 66.05W
St. John's Antigua **87 L3** 17.07N 61.51W
St. John's Canada **81 M2** 47.34N 52.41W
St. John's Pt. U.K. **15 F4** 54.13N 5.39W
St. Joseph U.S.A. **83 H4** 39.45N 94.51W
St. Kilda *i.* U.K. **8 B5** 57.55N 8.20W
St. Kitts-Nevis Leeward Is. **87 L3** 17.20N 62.45W
St. Lawrence *r.* Canada / U.S.A. **81 L2** 48.45N 68.30W
St. Lawrence, G. of Canada **81 L2** 48.00N 62.00W
St. Lawrence I. U.S.A. **80 A4** 63.00N170.00W
St. Lô France **42 D5** 49.07N 1.05W
St. Louis Senegal **102 A4** 16.01N 16.30W
St. Louis U.S.A. **83 H4** 38.40N 90.15W
St. Lucia Windward Is. **87 L2** 14.05N 61.00W
St. Maixent France **42 D4** 46.25N 0.12W
St. Malo France **42 C5** 48.39N 2.00W
St. Malo, Golfe de *g.* France **42 C5** 49.20N 2.00W
St.-Marc Haiti **87 J3** 19.08N 72.41W
St. Margaret's Hope U.K. **14 F5** 58.50N 2.57W
St. Martin *i.* Leeward Is. **87 L3** 18.05N 63.05W
St. Martin U.K. **13 E1** 49.26N 2.34W
St. Martin's *i.* U.K. **13 A1** 49.58N 6.17W
St. Mary U.K. **13 E1** 49.15N 2.09W
St. Mary's *i.* U.K. **13 A1** 49.55N 6.16W
St. Maurice *r.* Canada **81 K2** 46.20N 72.30W
St. Moritz Switz. **48 D3** 46.30N 9.51E
St. Nazaire France **42 C4** 47.17N 2.12W
St. Neots U.K. **13 G4** 52.13N 0.18W
St. Nicolas Belgium **39 C3** 51.10N 4.09E
St. Omer France **42 F6** 50.45N 2.15E
St. Paul France **42 F2** 42.49N 2.29E
St. Paul U.S.A. **83 H6** 45.00N 93.10W
St. Peter Port U.K. **13 E1** 49.27N 2.32W
St. Petersburg U.S.A. **83 J2** 27.45N 82.40W
St. Pierre and Miquelon *is.* N. America **81 M2** 47.00N 56.15W
St. Pölten Austria **48 G4** 48.13N 15.37E
St. Quentin France **39 B1** 49.51N 3.17E
St. Thomas *i.* U.S.V.Is. **87 L3** 18.22N 64.57W
St. Trond Belgium **39 D2** 50.49N 5.11E
St. Tropez France **42 H2** 43.16N 6.39E
St. Vallier France **42 G3** 45.11N 4.49E
St. Vincent, C. Portugal **43 A2** 37.01N 8.59W
St. Vincent and the Grenadines Windward Is. **87 L2** 13.00N 61.15W
St. Vith Belgium **39 E2** 50.15N 6.08E
St. Wendel W. Germany **39 F1** 49.27N 7.10E
St. Yrieix France **42 E3** 45.31N 1.12E
Sakai Japan **70 C4** 34.37N135.28E
Sakaka Saudi Arabia **60 F3** 29.59N 40.12E
Sakarya *r.* Turkey **60 C6** 41.08N 30.36E
Sakata Japan **70 D6** 38.55N139.51E
Sakété Benin **103 E2** 6.45N 2.45E
Sakhalin *i.* U.S.S.R. **53 L2** 50.00N143.00E
Sakskōbing Denmark **38 E2** 54.48N 11.42E
Sala Sweden **50 D2** 59.55N 16.38E
Salado *r.* La Pampa Argentina **89 C4** 36.15S 66.45W
Salado *r.* Santa Fé Argentina **89 C4** 32.40S 60.41W
Salado *r.* Mexico **86 E5** 26.46N 98.55W
Salala Oman **101 H3** 17.00N 54.04E
Salamanca Spain **43 C4** 40.58N 5.40W
Salar de Uyuni *l.* Bolivia **89 C5** 20.30S 67.45W
Salatiga Indonesia **68 E2** 7.15S110.34E
Salavat U.S.S.R. **52 E3** 53.22N 55.50E
Sala y Gomez *i.* Pacific Oc. **75 P5** 26.28S105.28W
Salbris France **42 F4** 47.26N 2.03E
Salcombe U.K. **13 D2** 50.13N 3.46W
Salekhard U.S.S.R. **52 F4** 66.33N 66.35E
Salem India **63 E2** 11.38N 78.08E
Salerno Italy **46 G4** 40.41N 14.45E
Salerno, G. of Med. Sea **46 G4** 40.30N 14.45E
Salford U.K. **12 E5** 53.30N 2.17W
Salgótarján Hungary **49 I4** 48.07N 19.48E
Salima Malaŵi **99 D3** 13.46S 34.26E
Salina Cruz Mexico **86 E3** 16.11N 95.12W
Salins France **42 G4** 46.56N 5.53E
Salisbury U.K. **13 F3** 51.04N 1.48W
Salisbury U.S.A. **83 K4** 38.22N 75.37W
Salisbury Plain *f.* U.K. **13 F3** 51.13N 1.55W
Salmās Iran **61 G5** 38.13N 44.50E
Salmon *r.* U.S.A. **82 C6** 45.50N116.50W
Salmon River Mts. U.S.A. **82 C5** 44.30N114.30W
Salo Finland **50 E3** 60.23N 23.10E
Salobreña Spain **43 D2** 36.45N 3.35W
Salon France **42 G2** 43.38N 5.06E
Salso *r.* Italy **46 F2** 37.07N 13.57E
Salt Jordan **60 D4** 32.03N 35.44E
Salta Argentina **89 C5** 24.46S 65.28W
Saltee Is. Rep. of Ire. **15 E2** 52.08N 6.36W
Saltfleet U.K. **12 H5** 53.24N 0.12E
Saltillo Mexico **86 D5** 25.30N101.00W
Salt Lake City U.S.A. **82 D5** 40.45N111.55W
Salton Sea *l.* U.S.A. **82 C3** 33.25N115.45W
Salûm Egypt **60 B3** 31.31N 25.09E
Salvador Brazil **88 F6** 12.58S 38.20W
Salwa Qatar **61 H2** 24.44N 50.50E
Salween *r.* Burma **66 F1** 16.30N 97.33E
Salyany U.S.S.R. **61 H5** 39.36N 48.59E
Salzach *r.* Austria **48 F4** 48.35N 13.30E
Salzburg Austria **48 F3** 47.54N 13.03E
Salzgitter W. Germany **48 E6** 52.02N 10.22E
Samaná Dom. Rep. **87 K3** 19.14N 69.20W
Samana Cay *i.* Bahamas **87 J4** 23.05N 73.45W
Samar *i.* Phil. **69 H6** 11.45N125.15E
Samarinda Indonesia **68 F3** 0.30S117.09E
Samarkand U.S.S.R. **52 F1** 39.40N 66.57E
Sāmarrā Iraq **61 F4** 34.13N 43.52E
Samawa Iraq **61 G3** 31.18N 45.18E
Sambalpur India **63 F4** 21.28N 84.04E
Sambor U.S.S.R. **49 K4** 49.31N 23.10E
Sambre *r.* Belgium **39 C2** 50.29N 4.52E
Sam Neua Laos **68 C8** 20.25N104.04E
Sámos *i.* Greece **47 M2** 37.44N 26.45E
Samothráki *i.* Greece **47 L4** 40.26N 25.35E
Sampit Indonesia **68 E3** 2.34S112.59E
Samrong Cambodia **68 C6** 14.12N103.31E
Samsö *i.* Denmark **38 D3** 55.50N 10.35E
Samsö Baelt *str.* Denmark **38 D3** 55.50N 10.50E
Samsun Turkey **60 E6** 41.17N 36.22E
Samui, Ko *i.* Thailand **68 C5** 9.30N100.00E
San Mali **102 D3** 13.21N 4.57W
Şan'ā' Yemen **101 G3** 15.23N 44.14E
Sana *r.* Yugo. **47 H6** 45.03N 16.23E
Sanaga *r.* Cameroon **103 F1** 3.35N 9.40E
San Ambrosio *i.* Chile **89 B5** 26.28S 79.53W
Sanandaj Iran **61 G4** 35.18N 47.01E
San Antonio U.S.A. **82 G2** 29.25N 98.30W
San Antonio, C. Cuba **87 H4** 21.50N 84.57W
San Antonio, Punta *c.* Mexico **86 A5** 29.45N115.41W
San Antonio Oeste Argentina **89 C3** 40.45S 64.58W
San Bernardino U.S.A. **82 C3** 34.07N117.18W
San Blas, C. U.S.A. **83 I2** 29.40N 85.25W
San Carlos Phil. **69 G7** 15.59N120.22E
San Carlos de Bariloche Argentina **89 B3** 41.11S 71.23W
San Cristóbal Dom. Rep. **87 J3** 18.27N 70.07W
San Cristóbal Venezuela **88 B8** 7.46N 72.15W
Sancti Spíritus Cuba **87 I4** 21.55N 79.28W
Sanda *i.* U.K. **14 C2** 55.17N 5.34W
Sandakan Malaysia **68 F5** 5.52N118.04E
Sanday *i.* U.K. **14 F6** 59.15N 2.33W
Sandbach U.K. **12 E5** 53.08N 2.20W
Sande W. Germany **38 B2** 54.44N 8.58E
San Diego U.S.A. **82 C3** 32.45N117.10W
Sandnes Norway **50 A2** 58.51N 5.45E
Sandness U.K. **14 G7** 60.19N 1.40W
Sandö *i.* Faroe Is. **50 M8** 61.50N 6.45W
Sandoway Burma **63 G3** 18.28N 94.20E
Sandown U.K. **13 F2** 50.40N 1.10W
Sandpoint *town* U.S.A. **82 C6** 48.17N116.34W
Sandringham U.K. **12 H4** 52.50N 0.30E
Sandviken Sweden **50 D3** 60.38N 16.50E
San Felipe Mexico **86 B6** 31.03N114.52W
San Félix *i.* Chile **89 A5** 26.23S 80.05W
San Fernando Phil. **69 G7** 16.39N120.19E
San Fernando Spain **43 B2** 36.28N 6.12W
San Fernando Trinidad **87 L2** 10.16N 61.28W
San Fernando de Apure Venezuela **88 C8** 7.53N 67.17W
San Francisco U.S.A. **82 B4** 37.45N122.27W
San Francisco, C. Ecuador **88 A8** 0.38N 80.08W
San Francisco de Macorís Dom. Rep. **87 J3** 19.19N 70.15W
Sanggan He *r.* China **67 I5** 40.23N115.18E
Sangha *r.* Congo **99 B4** 1.10S 16.47E
Sangi *i.* Indonesia **69 H4** 3.30N125.30E
Sangihe Is. Indonesia **69 H4** 2.45N125.20E
Sāngli India **63 D3** 16.55N 74.37E
Sangonera *r.* Spain **43 E2** 37.58N 1.04W
Sangre de Cristo Mts. U.S.A. **82 E4** 37.30N106.00W
Sanjo Japan **70 D5** 37.37N138.57E
San Jordi, G. of Spain **43 F4** 40.50N 1.10E
San Jorge, G. of Argentina **89 C3** 46.00S 66.00W
San José Costa Rica **87 H1** 9.59N 84.04W
San José Guatemala **86 F2** 13.58N 90.50W
San Jose U.S.A. **82 B4** 37.20N121.55W
San Juan Argentina **89 C4** 31.33S 68.31W
San Juan *r.* Costa Rica **87 H2** 10.50N 83.40W
San Juan Puerto Rico **87 K3** 18.29N 66.08W
San Juan *r.* U.S.A. **82 D4** 37.20N110.05W
San Juan del Norte Nicaragua **87 H2** 10.58N 83.40W
San Juan Mts. U.S.A. **82 E4** 37.30N107.00W
Sankt Peter W. Germany **38 B2** 54.19N 8.38E
San Lázaro, C. Mexico **86 B4** 24.50N112.18W
San Leonardo Spain **43 D4** 41.49N 3.04W

Sisak Yugo. **46 H6** 45.30N 16.21E
Sishen R.S.A. **99 C2** 27.48S 22.59E
Sisophon Cambodia **68 C6** 13.37N102.58E
Sisteron France **42 G3** 44.16N 5.56E
Sitka U.S.A. **80 E3** 57.05N135.20W
Sittang *r.* Burma **63 H3** 17.30N 96.53E
Sittard Neth. **39 D3** 51.00N 5.52E
Sivas Turkey **60 E5** 39.44N 37.01E
Sivrihisar Turkey **60 C5** 39.29N 31.32E
Siwa Egypt **60 B3** 29.11N 25.31E
Siwa Oasis Egypt **60 B3** 29.10N 25.45E
Sixmilecross U.K. **15 D4** 54.33N 7.09W
Sjöbo Sweden **38 G3** 55.39N 13.44E
Skaelskör Denmark **38 E3** 55.15N 11.18E
Skaerbaek Denmark **38 B3** 55.09N 8.47E
Skagen Denmark **38 D5** 57.44N 10.37E
Skagerrak *str.* Denmark / Norway **50 B2** 57.45N 8.55E
Skagway U.S.A. **80 E3** 59.23N135.20W
Skaill U.K. **14 F5** 58.57N 2.43W
Skälderviken *b.* Sweden **38 F4** 56.20N 12.40E
Skalintyy *mtn.* U.S.S.R. **53 K3** 56.00N130.40E
Skals Denmark **38 C4** 56.33N 9.23E
Skanderborg Denmark **38 C4** 56.01N 9.53E
Skanör Sweden **38 F3** 55.25N 12.50E
Skara Sweden **50 C2** 58.23N 13.25E
Skarżysko-Kamienna Poland **49 J5** 51.08N 20.53E
Skeena *r.* Canada **80 F3** 54.10N129.08W
Skegness U.K. **12 H5** 53.09N 0.20E
Skellefte *r.* Sweden **50 E4** 64.44N 21.07E
Skellefteå Sweden **50 E4** 64.45N 21.00E
Skelmersdale U.K. **12 E5** 53.34N 2.49W
Skene Sweden **50 C2** 57.30N 12.35E
Skerries Rep. of Ire. **15 E3** 53.34N 6.08W
Skhíza *i.* Greece **47 J2** 36.42N 21.45E
Ski Norway **50 B2** 59.43N 10.52E
Skiddaw *mtn.* U.K. **12 D6** 54.40N 3.09W
Skien Norway **50 B2** 59.14N 9.37E
Skikda Algeria **100 C5** 36.50N 6.58E
Skipness U.K. **14 C2** 55.46N 5.22W
Skipton U.K. **12 E5** 53.58N 2.03W
Skíros *i.* Greece **47 L3** 38.50N 24.33E
Skive Denmark **38 C4** 56.34N 9.03E
Skjálfanda Fljót *r.* Iceland **50 J7** 65.55N 17.30W
Skjern Denmark **38 B3** 55.57N 8.30E
Skjern *r.* Denmark **38 B3** 55.55N 8.22E
Skopje Yugo. **47 J4** 41.58N 21.27E
Skövde Sweden **50 C2** 58.24N 13.52E
Skovorodino U.S.S.R. **53 K3** 54.00N123.53E
Skreia Norway **50 B3** 60.38N 10.57E
Skull Rep. of Ire. **15 B1** 51.31N 9.33W
Skurup Sweden **38 G3** 55.30N 13.31E
Skye *i.* U.K. **14 B4** 57.20N 6.15W
Slagelse Denmark **38 E3** 55.24N 11.23E
Sľalowa Wola Poland **49 K5** 50.40N 22.05E
Slamet *mtn.* Indonesia **68 D2** 7.10S109.10E
Slaney *r.* Rep. of Ire. **15 E2** 52.21N 6.30W
Slantsy U.S.S.R. **50 G2** 59.09N 28.09E
Slatina Romania **47 L6** 44.26N 24.23E
Slave *r.* Canada **80 G4** 61.10N113.30W
Slavgorod W.R.S.S.R. U.S.S.R. **49 O6** 53.25N 31.00E
Slavgorod R.S.F.S.R. U.S.S.R. **52 G3** 53.01N 78.37E
Sleaford U.K. **12 G5** 53.01N 0.25W
Sleat, Sound of U.K. **14 C4** 57.07N 5.45W
Sledmere U.K. **12 G6** 54.03N 0.35W
Sleetmute U.S.A. **80 C4** 61.40N157.11W
Sliedrecht Neth. **39 C3** 51.48N 4.46E
Slieve Aughty Mts. Rep. of Ire. **15 C3** 53.05N 8.35W
Slieve Bloom Mts. Rep. of Ire. **15 D3** 53.05N 7.40W
Slieve Callan *mtn.* Rep. of Ire. **15 B2** 52.50N 9.20W
Slieve Donard *mtn.* U.K. **15 F4** 54.11N 5.56W
Slieve Gamph *mts.* Rep. of Ire. **15 C4** 54.08N 8.50W
Slievekimalta *mtn.* Rep. of Ire. **15 C2** 52.45N 8.19W
Slieve Mish *mts.* Rep. of Ire. **15 B2** 52.12N 9.50W
Slieve Miskish *mts.* Rep. of Ire. **15 B1** 51.40N 9.55W
Slievenamon Rep. of Ire. **15 D2** 52.26N 7.37W
Slieve Snaght *mtn.* Rep. of Ire. **15 D5** 55.12N 7.20W
Sligo Rep. of Ire. **15 C4** 54.17N 8.28W
Sligo *d.* Rep. of Ire. **15 C4** 54.10N 8.35W
Sligo B. Rep. of Ire. **15 C4** 54.18N 8.40W
Sliven Bulgaria **47 M5** 42.41N 26.19E
Slonim U.S.S.R. **49 L6** 53.05N 25.21E
Slough U.K. **13 G3** 51.30N 0.35W
Slovechna *r.* U.S.S.R. **49 N5** 51.41N 29.41E
Sluch *r.* U.S.S.R. **49 M6** 52.08N 27.31E
Sluis Neth. **39 B3** 51.18N 3.23E
Sľupsk Poland **49 H7** 54.28N 17.01E
Slutsk U.S.S.R. **49 M6** 53.02N 27.31E
Slyne Head Rep. of Ire. **15 A3** 53.25N 10.12W
Slyudyanka U.S.S.R. **66 G7** 51.40N103.40E
Smålandsfarvandet *str.* Denmark **38 E3** 55.05N 11.25E
Smöla *i.* Norway **50 A3** 63.20N 8.00E
Smolensk U.S.S.R. **52 C3** 54.49N 32.04E
Smólikas *mtn.* Greece **47 J4** 40.06N 20.55E
Smolyan Bulgaria **47 L4** 41.34N 24.45E
Smorgon U.S.S.R. **49 M7** 54.28N 26.20E
Snaefell *mtn.* Iceland **32 B7** 64.48N 15.34W
Snaefell *mtn.* U.K. **12 C6** 54.17N 4.29W
Snake *r.* U.S.A. **82 C6** 46.15N119.00W
Snåsa Norway **50 C4** 64.15N 12.23E
Snåsavatn *l.* Norway **50 B4** 64.10N 12.00E
Sneek Neth. **39 D5** 53.03N 5.40E
Sneem Rep. of Ire. **15 B1** 51.49N 9.55W
Snizort, L. U.K. **14 B4** 57.35N 6.30W
Snöhetta *mtn.* Norway **50 B3** 62.15N 9.05E
Snov *r.* U.S.S.R. **49 O5** 51.45N 31.45E
Snowdon *mtn.* U.K. **12 C5** 53.05N 4.05W
Soasiu Indonesia **69 H4** 0.40N127.25E
Sobat *r.* Sudan / Ethiopia **101 F2** 9.30N 31.30E
Sobernheim W. Germany **39 F1** 49.47N 7.40E
Sobral Brazil **88 E7** 3.45S 40.20W
Sochi U.S.S.R. **52 D2** 43.35N 39.46E
Society Is. Pacific Oc. **75 K6** 17.00S150.00W
Socorro I. Mexico **86 B3** 18.45N110.58W
Socotra *i.* S. Yemen **101 H3** 12.30N 54.00E
Sodankylä Finland **50 F2** 67.21N 26.31E
Söderhamn Sweden **50 D3** 61.19N 17.10E
Södertälje Sweden **50 D2** 59.11N 17.39E
Soest W. Germany **39 G3** 51.34N 8.06E
Sofia Bulgaria **47 K5** 42.41N 23.19E
Sognefjorden *est.* Norway **50 A3** 61.10N 5.50E
Sögüt Turkey **60 C5** 40.02N 30.10E
Sohag Egypt **60 C2** 26.33N 31.42E
Sohar Oman **61 J2** 24.23N 56.43E
Soignies Belgium **39 C2** 50.35N 4.04E
Soissons France **42 F5** 49.23N 3.20E
Söke Turkey **47 M2** 37.46N 27.26E
Sokodé Togo **103 E2** 8.59N 1.11E
Sokoľka Poland **49 K6** 53.25N 23.31E
Sokolo Mali **102 C3** 14.53N 6.11W
Sokoto Nigeria **103 F3** 13.02N 5.15E
Sokoto *d.* Nigeria **103 F3** 11.50N 5.05E
Sokoto *r.* Nigeria **103 E3** 11.23N 4.05E
Solikamsk U.S.S.R. **52 E3** 59.40N 56.45E
Solingen W. Germany **39 F3** 51.10N 7.05E
Sollefteå Sweden **50 D3** 63.09N 17.15E
Sóller Spain **43 G3** 39.47N 2.41E
Solomon Is. Pacific Oc. **71 E5** 8.00S160.00E
Šolta *i.* Yugo. **46 H5** 43.23N 16.17E
Solway Firth *est.* U.K. **12 D6** 54.50N 3.30W
Soma Turkey **47 M3** 39.11N 27.36E
Somali Republic Africa **101 G2** 5.30N 47.00E
Sombor Yugo. **47 I6** 45.48N 19.08E
Somerset *d.* U.K. **13 D3** 51.09N 3.00W
Somerset I. Canada **81 I5** 73.00N 93.30W
Somes *r.* Hungary **49 K4** 48.04N 22.30E
Somme *r.* France **42 E6** 50.01N 1.40E
Son *r.* India **63 F4** 25.55N 84.55E
Sönderborg Denmark **38 C2** 54.55N 9.48E
Sonderjyllands *d.* Denmark **38 C3** 55.10N 9.10E
Songhua Jiang *r.* China **67 L6** 47.46N132.30E
Songkhla Thailand **68 C5** 7.13N100.37E
Son La Vietnam **68 C8** 21.20N103.55E
Sonneberg E. Germany **48 E5** 50.22N 11.10E
Sonora *d.* Mexico **86 B5** 29.20N110.40W
Sonora *r.* Mexico **86 B5** 28.45N111.55W
Sonsorol *i.* Caroline Is. **69 I5** 5.20N132.13E
Son Tay Vietnam **68 D8** 21.06N105.32E
Sopron Hungary **48 H3** 47.41N 16.36E
Soria Spain **43 D4** 41.46N 2.28W
Sor Kvalöy *i.* Norway **50 D5** 69.45N 18.20E
Sorocaba Brazil **89 E5** 23.30S 47.32W
Soroki U.S.S.R. **49 N4** 48.08N 28.12E
Sorol *i.* Caroline Is. **69 K5** 8.09N140.25E
Sorong Indonesia **69 I3** 0.50S131.17E
Soroti Uganda **99 D5** 1.42N 33.37E
Söröya *i.* Norway **50 E5** 70.30N 22.30E
Sorraia *r.* Portugal **43 A3** 39.00N 8.51W
Sorsele Sweden **50 D4** 65.32N 17.34E
Sortavala U.S.S.R. **50 G3** 61.40N 30.40E
Sosnowiec Poland **49 I5** 50.18N 19.08E
Sotra *i.* Norway **50 A3** 60.20N 5.00E
Soure Portugal **43 A4** 40.04N 8.38W
Souris *r.* Canada **82 G6** 49.38N 99.35W
Sous le Vent, Îles *is.* Society Is. **75 K6** 16.30S151.30W
Sousse Tunisia **100 D5** 35.48N 10.38E
Soustons France **42 D2** 43.45N 1.19W
South America 88
Southampton U.K. **13 F2** 50.54N 1.23W
Southampton I. Canada **81 J4** 64.30N 84.00W
South Atlantic Ocean 89
South Australia *d.* Australia **71 C3** 29.00S135.00E
South Beveland *f.* Neth. **39 B3** 51.30N 3.50E
South Carolina *d.* U.S.A. **83 J3** 34.00N 81.00W
South Cerney U.K. **13 F3** 51.41N 1.54W
South China Sea Asia **68 E7** 12.30N115.00E
South Dakota *d.* U.S.A. **82 F5** 44.30N100.00W
South Dorset Downs *hills* U.K. **13 E2** 50.40N 2.20W
South Downs *hills* U.K. **13 G2** 50.54N 0.34W
South Eastern Atlantic Basin Atlantic Oc. **106 I3** 20.00S 0.00
Southend-on-Sea U.K. **13 H3** 51.32N 0.43E
Southern Alps *mts.* New Zealand **71 G1** 43.20S170.45E
Southern Uplands *hills* U.K. **14 E2** 55.30N 3.30W
Southern Yemen Asia **101 G3** 16.00N 49.30E
South Esk *r.* U.K. **14 F3** 56.43N 2.32W
South Fiji Basin Pacific Oc. **107 R3** 27.00S176.00E
South Flevoland *f.* Neth. **39 D4** 52.22N 5.22E
South Georgia *i.* Atlantic Oc. **89 F2** 54.00S 37.00W
South Glamorgan *d.* U.K. **13 D3** 51.27N 3.22W
South-haa U.K. **14 G7** 60.37N 1.19W
South Holland *d.* Neth. **39 C4** 52.00N 4.30E
South Honshu Ridge Pacific Oc. **74 E9** 22.00N141.00E
South I. New Zealand **71 G1** 43.00S171.00E
South Korea Asia **67 K4** 36.00N128.00E
South Molton U.K. **13 D3** 51.01N 3.50W
South Nahanni *r.* Canada **80 F4** 61.00N123.20W
South Orkney Is. Atlantic Oc. **89 E1** 60.50S 45.00W
Southport U.K. **12 D5** 53.38N 3.01W
South Ronaldsay *i.* U.K. **14 F5** 58.47N 2.56W
South Sandwich Is. Atlantic Oc. **89 G2** 58.00S 27.00W
South Sandwich Trench *f.* Atlantic Oc. **89 G2** 57.00S 25.00W
South Shetland Is. Antarctica **106 F1** 62.00S 60.00W
South Shields U.K. **12 F6** 54.59N 1.22W
South Tyne *r.* U.K. **12 E6** 54.59N 2.08W
South Uist *i.* U.K. **14 A4** 57.15N 7.20W
South Western Pacific Basin Pacific Oc. **106 A3** 39.00S148.00W
South West Peru Ridge Pacific Oc. **75 R5** 20.00S 82.00W
Southwold U.K. **13 I4** 52.19N 1.39E
South Yorkshire *d.* U.K. **12 F5** 53.28N 1.25W
Sovetsk U.S.S.R. **50 E1** 55.02N 21.50E
Sovetskaya Gavan U.S.S.R. **53 L2** 48.57N140.16E
Sozh *r.* U.S.S.R. **49 O5** 51.57N 30.48E
Spa Belgium **39 D2** 50.29N 5.52E
Spain Europe **43 B4** 40.00N 4.00W
Spalding U.K. **12 G4** 52.48N 0.10W
Spandau W. Germany **48 F6** 52.32N 13.13E
Spárti Greece **47 K2** 37.04N 22.28E
Spartivento, C. Calabria Italy **46 H2** 37.55N 16.04E
Spartivento, C. Sardinia Italy **46 D3** 38.53N 8.51E
Spátha, C. Greece **47 K1** 35.42N 23.43E
Spence Bay *town* Canada **81 I4** 69.30N 93.20W
Spencer G. Australia **71 C2** 34.30S136.10E
Sperrin Mts. U.K. **15 D4** 54.49N 7.06W
Spey *r.* U.K. **14 E4** 57.40N 3.06W
Spiekeroog *i.* W. Germany **39 F5** 53.48N 7.45E
Spilsby U.K. **12 H5** 53.11N 0.07E
Spithead *str.* U.K. **13 F2** 50.45N 1.05W
Spitsbergen *is.* Arctic Oc. **54 D10** 78.00N 19.00E
Spittal an der Drau Austria **48 F3** 46.48N 13.30E
Split Yugo. **47 H5** 43.32N 16.27E
Spodsbjerg Denmark **38 D2** 54.57N 10.50E
Spokane U.S.A. **82 C6** 47.40N117.25W
Spratly I. S. China Sea **68 E5** 8.45N111.54E
Spree *r.* E. Germany **48 F6** 52.32N 13.15E
Sprenge W. Germany **38 D2** 54.15N 10.04E
Springfield Ill. U.S.A. **83 I4** 39.49N 89.39W
Springfield Miss. U.S.A. **83 H4** 37.11N 93.19W
Springs *town* R.S.A. **99 C2** 26.15S 28.26E
Spurn Head U.K. **12 H5** 53.35N 0.08E
Sredne Kolymskaya U.S.S.R. **53 M4** 67.27N153.35E
Sri Lanka Asia **63 E1** 7.30N 80.50E
Srinagar Jammu & Kashmir **63 D6** 34.08N 74.50E
Stadskanaal Neth. **39 E5** 53.02N 6.55E
Stadtkyll W. Germany **39 E2** 50.21N 6.32E
Staffa *i.* U.K. **14 B3** 56.26N 6.21W
Stafford U.K. **12 E4** 52.49N 2.09W
Staffordshire *d.* U.K. **12 E4** 52.40N 1.57W
Staines U.K. **13 G3** 51.26N 0.31W
Stainforth U.K. **12 F5** 53.37N 1.01W
Stamford U.K. **13 G4** 52.40N 0.28W
Stanley Falkland Is. **89 D2** 51.45S 57.56W
Stanley U.K. **12 F6** 54.53N 1.43W
Stanley, Mt. Uganda / Zaïre **94 E5** 0.20N 30.50E
Stanovoy Range *mts.* U.S.S.R. **53 K3** 56.00N125.40E
Stara Zagora Bulgaria **47 L5** 42.26N 25.37E
Starbuck I. Kiribati **75 K7** 5.37S155.55W
Stargard Poland **48 G6** 53.21N 15.01E
Starogard Gdański Poland **49 I6** 53.59N 18.33E
Starokonstantinov U.S.S.R. **49 M4** 49.48N 27.10E
Start Pt. U.K. **13 D2** 50.13N 3.38W
Staryy Oskol U.S.S.R. **52 D2** 51.20N 37.50E
Stavanger Norway **50 A2** 58.58N 5.45E
Stavelot Belgium **39 D2** 50.23N 5.54E
Staveren Neth. **39 D4** 52.53N 5.21E
Stavropol' U.S.S.R. **52 D2** 45.03N 41.59E
Steenbergen Neth. **39 C3** 51.36N 4.19E
Steenvorde France **39 A2** 50.49N 2.35E
Steenwijk Neth. **39 E4** 52.47N 6.07E
Steinkjer Norway **50 B3** 64.00N 11.30E
Stenay France **39 D1** 49.29N 5.12E
Stendal E. Germany **48 E6** 52.36N 11.52E
Stepanakert U.S.S.R. **61 G5** 39.48N 46.45E
Sterling U.S.A. **82 F5** 40.37N103.13W
Sterlitamak U.S.S.R. **52 E3** 53.40N 55.59E
Stevenage U.K. **13 G3** 51.54N 0.11W
Stevenston U.K. **14 D2** 55.39N 4.43W
Stewart Canada **80 F3** 55.56N129.59W
Stewart I. New Zealand **71 F1** 47.02S167.51E
Steyr Austria **48 G4** 48.04N 14.25E
Stikine *r.* Canada **80 E3** 56.45N132.30W
Stikine Mts. Canada **80 E4** 59.00N129.00W
Stilton U.K. **13 G4** 52.31N 0.18W
Stinchar *r.* U.K. **14 C2** 55.06N 5.01W
Stirling U.K. **14 E3** 56.07N 3.57W
Stjördalshalsen Norway **50 B3** 63.30N 10.59E
Stockbridge U.K. **13 F3** 51.07N 1.29W
Stockholm Sweden **50 D2** 59.20N 18.05E
Stockport U.K. **12 E5** 53.25N 2.11W
Stocksbridge U.K. **12 F5** 53.29N 1.35W
Stockton U.S.A. **82 B4** 37.59N121.20W
Stockton-on-Tees U.K. **12 F6** 54.33N 1.20W
Stoke-on-Trent U.K. **12 E5** 53.01N 2.11W
Stolin U.S.S.R. **49 M5** 51.52N 26.51E
Stone U.K. **12 E4** 52.55N 2.10W
Stonehaven U.K. **14 F3** 56.58N 2.13W
Stony Tunguska *r.* U.S.S.R. **53 H3** 61.40N 90.00E
Storå *r.* Denmark **38 B4** 56.20N 8.19E
Stora Lulevatten *l.* Sweden **50 D4** 67.00N 19.30E
Storavan *l.* Sweden **50 D4** 65.45N 18.10E
Storby Finland **50 D3** 60.14N 19.36E
Stord *i.* Norway **50 A2** 59.50N 5.25E
Store Baelt *str.* Denmark **38 D3** 55.30N 11.00E
Stören Norway **50 B3** 63.03N 10.16E
Stornoway U.K. **14 B5** 58.12N 6.23W
Storsjön *l.* Sweden **50 C3** 63.10N 14.20E
Storstroms *d.* Denmark **38 E2** 55.00N 11.30E
Storuman Sweden **50 D4** 65.05N 17.10E
Storuman *l.* Sweden **50 D4** 65.14N 16.50E
Stour *r.* Dorset U.K. **13 F2** 50.43N 1.47W
Stour *r.* Kent U.K. **13 I3** 51.19N 1.25E
Stour *r.* Suffolk U.K. **13 I3** 51.56N 1.03E
Stourport-on-Severn U.K. **13 E4** 52.20N 2.18W
Stövring Denmark **38 C4** 56.53N 9.53E
Stow in the Wold U.K. **13 F3** 51.56N 1.41W
Stowmarket U.K. **13 H4** 52.11N 0.59E
Strabane U.K. **15 D4** 54.50N 7.30W
Stradbally Rep. of Ire. **15 D3** 53.01N 7.11W
Stralsund E. Germany **48 F7** 54.18N 13.06E
Strangford Lough U.K. **15 F4** 54.28N 5.35W
Stranraer U.K. **14 C1** 54.54N 5.02W
Strasbourg France **42 H5** 48.35N 7.45E
Stratford-upon-Avon U.K. **13 F4** 52.12N 1.42W
Strathclyde *d.* U.K. **14 D2** 55.45N 4.45W
Strathmore *f.* U.K. **14 E3** 56.44N 3.15W
Strathspey *f.* U.K. **14 E4** 57.25N 3.25W
Straubing W. Germany **48 F4** 48.53N 12.35E
Straumnes *c.* Iceland **50 I7** 66.30N 23.05W
Street U.K. **13 E3** 51.07N 2.45W
Stromboli *i.* Italy **46 G3** 38.48N 15.14E
Stromeferry U.K. **14 C4** 57.20N 5.34W
Stromness U.K. **14 E5** 58.58N 3.19W
Strömö *i.* Faroe Is. **50 L9** 62.08N 7.00W
Strömstad Sweden **50 B2** 58.56N 11.11E
Ströms Vattudal *l.* Sweden **50 C3** 63.55N 15.30E
Stronsay *i.* U.K. **14 F6** 59.07N 2.36W
Stroud U.K. **13 E3** 51.44N 2.13W
Struer Denmark **38 B4** 56.30N 8.37E
Struma *r.* Greece **47 K4** 40.45N 23.51E
Strumica Yugo. **47 K4** 41.26N 22.39E
Stryn Norway **50 A3** 61.55N 6.47E
Stryy U.S.S.R. **49 K4** 49.16N 23.51E
Stubbeköbing Denmark **38 F2** 54.53N 12.04E
Sturminster Newton U.K. **13 E2** 50.57N 2.28W
Stuttgart W. Germany **48 D4** 48.47N 9.12E
Styr *r.* U.S.S.R. **49 M6** 52.07N 26.35E
Suakin Sudan **101 F3** 19.04N 37.22E
Subotica Yugo. **47 I7** 46.04N 19.41E
Suceava Romania **49 M3** 47.39N 26.19E
Suck *r.* Rep. of Ire. **15 C3** 53.16N 8.03W
Sucre Bolivia **89 C6** 19.05S 65.15W
Sudan Africa **101 E3** 14.00N 30.00E
Sudbury Canada **81 J2** 46.30N 81.01W
Sudbury U.K. **13 H4** 52.03N 0.43E
Sudd *f.* Sudan **101 E2** 7.50N 30.00E
Sudeten Mountains Czech. / Poland **48 H5** 50.30N 16.30E
Sudirman Mts. Indonesia **69 J3** 3.50S136.30E
Suez Egypt **60 D3** 29.59N 32.33E
Suez, G. of Egypt **60 D3** 28.48N 33.00E
Suez Canal Egypt **60 D3** 30.40N 32.20E
Suffolk *d.* U.K. **13 H4** 52.16N 1.00E
Suhl E. Germany **48 E5** 50.37N 10.43E
Suir *r.* Rep. of Ire. **15 D2** 52.17N 7.00W
Sukabumi Indonesia **68 D2** 6.55S106.50E
Sukadana Indonesia **68 E3** 1.15S110.00E
Sukaraja Indonesia **68 E3** 2.23S110.35E
Sukhona *r.* U.S.S.R. **52 D3** 61.30N 46.28E
Sukhumi U.S.S.R. **52 D2** 43.01N 41.01E
Sukkertoppen Greenland **81 M4** 65.40N 53.00W
Sukkur Pakistan **62 C5** 27.42N 68.54E
Sulaimaniya Iraq **61 G4** 35.32N 45.27E
Sulaimān Range *mts.* Pakistan **63 C5** 30.50N 70.20E
Sulaimiya Saudi Arabia **61 G2** 24.10N 47.20E
Sula Is. Indonesia **69 H3** 1.50S125.10E
Sulawesi *d.* Indonesia **69 G3** 2.00S120.30E
Sulina Romania **47 N6** 45.08N 29.40E
Sullana Peru **88 A7** 4.52S 80.39W
Sulmona Italy **46 F5** 42.04N 13.57E
Sulu Archipelago Phil. **69 G5** 5.30N121.00E
Sulu Sea Pacific Oc. **69 G5** 8.00N120.00E
Sumatra *i.* Indonesia **68 B4** 2.00S102.00E
Sumba *i.* Indonesia **68 F2** 9.30S119.55E
Sumbawa *i.* Indonesia **68 F2** 8.45S117.50E
Sumburgh Head U.K. **14 G6** 59.51N 1.16W
Sumgait U.S.S.R. **61 H6** 40.35N 49.38E
Summan *f.* Saudi Arabia **61 G2** 27.00N 47.00E
Sumy U.S.S.R. **52 C2** 50.55N 34.49E
Sunagawa Japan **70 E8** 43.30N141.55E
Sunart, L. U.K. **14 C3** 56.42N 5.45W
Sundarbans *f.* India / Bangla. **63 F4** 22.00N 89.00E
Sunda Str. Indonesia **68 D2** 6.00S105.50E
Sunderland U.K. **12 F6** 54.55N 1.22W
Sundsvall Sweden **50 D3** 62.22N 17.20E
Sungaipenuh Indonesia **68 C6** 2.00S101.28E
Sungguminasa Indonesia **68 F2** 5.14S119.27E
Sungurlu Turkey **60 D6** 40.10N 34.23E
Sunwu China **67 K6** 49.40N127.10E
Sunyani Ghana **102 D2** 7.22N 2.18W
Suomussalmi Finland **50 G4** 64.52N 29.10E
Suō nada *str.* Japan **70 A3** 33.45N131.30E
Suonenjoki Finland **50 F3** 62.40N 27.06E
Superior U.S.A. **83 H6** 46.42N 92.05W
Superior, L. N. America **83 I6** 48.00N 88.00W
Süphan Dagları *mtn.* Turkey **60 F5** 38.55N 42.55E
Şūr Oman **61 J1** 22.23N 59.32E
Sura *r.* U.S.S.R. **33 O6** 56.10N 46.00E
Surabaya Indonesia **68 E2** 7.14S112.45E
Surakarta Indonesia **68 E2** 7.32S110.50E
Surat India **63 D4** 21.10N 72.54E
Sûre *r.* Lux. **39 E1** 49.43N 6.31E
Surgut U.S.S.R. **52 G3** 61.13N 73.20E
Surigao Phil. **69 H5** 9.47N125.29E
Surin Thailand **68 C6** 14.50N103.34E
Surinam S. America **88 D8** 4.30N 56.00W
Surrey *d.* U.K. **13 G3** 51.16N 0.30W
Surtsey *i.* Iceland **50 I6** 63.18N 20.37W
Sutlej *r.* Pakistan **63 C5** 29.26N 71.09E
Sutton U.K. **13 G3** 51.21N 0.10W
Sutton in Ashfield U.K. **12 F5** 53.08N 1.16W
Suva Fiji **74 H6** 18.08S178.25E
Suwaľki Poland **49 K7** 54.07N 22.56E
Suwon S. Korea **67 K4** 37.16N126.59E
Suzhou China **67 J3** 31.21N120.40E
Suzu misaki *c.* Japan **70 C5** 37.30N137.21E
Svartisen *mtn.* Norway **50 C4** 66.30N 14.00E
Svedala Sweden **38 G3** 55.30N 13.11E
Sveg Sweden **50 C3** 62.02N 14.20E
Svendborg Denmark **38 D3** 55.04N 10.38E
Svenstrup Denmark **38 C4** 56.58N 9.52E
Sverdlovsk U.S.S.R. **52 F3** 56.52N 60.35E
Svetogorsk U.S.S.R. **50 G3** 61.07N 28.50E
Svishtov Bulgaria **47 L5** 43.36N 25.23E

Svitavy Czech. **48 H4** 49.45N 16.27E
Svobodnyy U.S.S.R. **67 K7** 51.24N128.05E
Svolvaer Norway **50 C5** 68.15N 14.40E
Swaffham U.K. **13 H4** 52.40N 0.40E
Swains I. Samoa **74 I6** 11.03S171.06W
Swale *r.* U.K. **12 F6** 54.05N 1.20W
Swanage U.K. **13 F2** 50.36N 1.58W
Swansea U.K. **13 D3** 51.37N 3.57W
Swaziland Africa **99 D2** 26.30S 31.30E
Sweden Europe **50 C2** 63.00N 16.00E
Sweetwater U.S.A. **82 F3** 32.37N100.25W
Swift Current *town* Canada **80 H3** 50.17N107.49W
Swilly, Lough Rep. of Ire. **15 D5** 55.10N 7.32W
Swindon U.K. **13 F3** 51.33N 1.47W
Świnoujście Poland **48 G6** 53.55N 14.18E
Switzerland Europe **48 C3** 47.00N 8.00E
Syderö *i.* Faroe Is. **50 M8** 61.30N 6.50W
Sydney Australia **71 E2** 33.55S151.10E
Sydney Canada **81 L2** 46.10N 60.10W
Syktyvkar U.S.S.R. **52 E3** 61.42N 50.45E
Sylhet Bangla. **63 G4** 24.53N 91.51E
Sylt *i.* W. Germany **48 D7** 54.50N 8.20E
Syracuse U.S.A. **83 K5** 43.03N 76.10W
Syr Darya *r.* U.S.S.R. **52 F2** 46.00N 61.12E
Syria Asia **60 E4** 35.00N 38.00E
Syriam Burma **68 B7** 16.45N 96.17E
Syrian Desert Asia **60 E4** 32.00N 39.00E
Syzran U.S.S.R. **52 E3** 53.10N 48.29E
Szczecin Poland **48 G6** 53.25N 14.32E
Szczecinek Poland **48 H6** 53.42N 16.41E
Szeged Hungary **47 J7** 46.16N 20.08E
Székesfehérvár Hungary **49 I3** 47.12N 18.25E
Szekszárd Hungary **47 I7** 46.22N 18.44E
Szombathely Hungary **48 H3** 47.12N 16.38E

T

Tabasco *d.* Mexico **86 F3** 18.30N 93.00W
Tábor Czech. **48 G4** 49.25N 14.41E
Tabora Tanzania **99 D4** 5.02S 32.50E
Tabou Ivory Coast **102 C1** 4.28N 7.20W
Tabrīz Iran **61 G5** 38.05N 46.18E
Tabūk Saudi Arabia **60 E3** 28.25N 36.35E
Tacloban Phil. **69 G6** 11.15N124.59E
Tacoma U.S.A. **82 B6** 47.16N122.30W
Tacuarembó Uruguay **89 D4** 31.42S 56.00W
Tademait Plateau Algeria **100 C4** 28.45N 2.10E
Tadzhikistan S.S.R. *d.* U.S.S.R. **66 A5** 39.00N 70.30E
Taegu S. Korea **67 K4** 35.52N128.36E
Taejon S. Korea **67 K4** 36.20N127.26E
Taganrog U.S.S.R. **52 D2** 47.14N 38.55E
Tagaytay City Phil. **69 G6** 14.07N120.58E
Tagbilaran Phil. **69 G5** 9.38N123.53E
Tagus *r.* Portugal **43 A3** 39.00N 8.57W
Tahat, Mt. Algeria **100 C4** 23.20N 5.40E
Tahiti *i.* Society Is. **75 L6** 17.37S149.27W
Taibei Taiwan **67 J2** 25.05N121.32E
Taidong Taiwan **67 J2** 22.49N121.10E
Taima Saudi Arabia **60 E2** 27.37N 38.30E
Tain U.K. **14 D4** 57.49N 4.02W
Tainan Taiwan **67 J2** 23.01N120.14E
Taiping Malaysia **68 C4** 4.54N100.42E
Taivalkoski Finland **50 G4** 65.35N 28.20E
Taiwan Asia **67 J2** 23.30N121.00E
Taiyuan China **67 H4** 37.50N112.30E
Taizhong Taiwan **67 J2** 24.09N120.40E
Taizhou China **67 I4** 32.30N119.50E
Ta'izz Yemen **101 G3** 13.35N 44.02E
Tajan Indonesia **68 E3** 0.02S110.05E
Tajrīsh Iran **61 H4** 35.48N 51.20E
Tajuna *r.* Spain **43 D4** 40.10N 3.35W
Tak Thailand **68 B7** 16.47N 99.10E
Takalar Indonesia **68 F2** 5.29S119.26E
Takamatsu Japan **70 B4** 34.28N134.05E
Takaoka Japan **70 C5** 36.47N137.00E
Takasaki Japan **70 D5** 36.20N139.00E
Tākestān Iran **61 H5** 36.02N 49.40E
Taklimakan Shamo *des.* China **66 C5** 38.10N 82.00E
Talasskiy Alatau *mts.* U.S.S.R. **66 B5** 42.20N 73.20E
Talaud Is. Indonesia **69 H4** 4.20N126.50E
Talavera de la Reina Spain **43 C3** 39.58N 4.50W
Talca Chile **89 B4** 35.28S 71.40W
Talcahuano Chile **89 B4** 36.40S 73.10W
Taliabu *i.* Indonesia **69 G3** 1.50S124.55E
Talkeetna U.S.A. **80 C4** 62.20N150.09W
Tallahassee U.S.A. **83 J3** 30.28N 84.19W
Tallinn U.S.S.R. **50 F2** 59.22N 24.48E
Talnoye U.S.S.R. **49 O4** 48.55N 30.40E
Tamale Ghana **103 D2** 9.26N 0.49W
Tamanrasset Algeria **100 C4** 22.50N 5.31E
Tamar *r.* U.K. **13 C2** 50.28N 4.13W
Tamaulipas *d.* Mexico **86 E4** 24.00N 98.20W
Tambacounda Senegal **102 B3** 13.45N 13.40W
Tambov U.S.S.R. **52 D3** 52.44N 41.28E
Tambre *r.* Spain **43 A5** 42.50N 8.55W
Tâmega *r.* Portugal **43 A4** 41.04N 8.17W
Tamil Nadu *d.* India **63 E2** 11.15N 79.00E
Tampa U.S.A. **83 J2** 27.58N 82.38W
Tampere Finland **50 E3** 61.32N 23.45E
Tampico Mexico **86 E4** 22.18N 97.52W
Tamsagbulag Mongolia **67 I6** 47.10N117.21E
Tamworth Australia **71 E2** 31.07S150.57E
Tamworth U.K. **13 F4** 52.39N 1.40W
Tana *r.* Kenya **99 E4** 2.32S 40.32E
Tana Norway **50 G5** 70.26N 28.14E
Tana *r.* Norway **50 G5** 69.45N 28.15E
Tana *i.* Vanuatu **74 G6** 19.30S169.20E
Tana, L. Ethiopia **101 F3** 12.00N 37.20E
Tanacross U.S.A. **80 D4** 63.12N143.30W
Tanahmerah Indonesia **69 K2** 6.08S140.18E
Tanana U.S.A. **80 C4** 65.11N152.10W
Tanaro *r.* Italy **46 D6** 45.01N 8.46E
Tanega shima *i.* Japan **70 A2** 30.32N131.00E
Tanga Tanzania **99 D4** 5.07S 39.05E
Tanganyika, L. Africa **99 C4** 5.37S 29.30E
Tanggula Shan *mts.* China **66 E4** 32.40N 92.30E
Tangier Morocco **100 B5** 35.48N 5.45W
Tangra Yumco *l.* China **63 F5** 31.00N 86.30E
Tangshan China **67 I5** 39.37N118.05E
Tanimbar Is. Indonesia **69 I2** 7.50S131.30E
Tanjay Phil. **69 G5** 9.31N123.10E
Tanjungbalai Indonesia **68 B4** 2.59N 99.46E
Tanjungkarang Indonesia **68 D2** 5.28S105.16E
Tanjungpandan Indonesia **68 D3** 2.44S107.36E
Tanjungredeb Indonesia **68 F4** 2.09N117.29E
Tannis Bugt *b.* Denmark **38 D5** 57.40N 10.10E
Tannu Ola Range *mts.* U.S.S.R. **53 H2** 51.00N 93.30E
Tano *r.* Ghana **102 D2** 5.07N 2.54W
Tanout Niger **103 F3** 14.55N 8.49E
Ṭanṭā Egypt **60 C3** 30.48N 31.00E
Tanzania Africa **99 D4** 5.00S 35.00E
Tao'an China **67 J6** 45.25N122.46E
Tapachula Mexico **86 F2** 14.54N 92.15W
Tapajós *r.* Brazil **88 D7** 2.40S 55.30W
Tāpti *r.* India **63 D4** 21.05N 72.45E
Tara *r.* U.S.S.R. **52 G3** 56.30N 74.40E
Tara *r.* Yugo. **47 I5** 43.23N 18.47E
Tarakan Indonesia **68 F4** 3.20N117.38E
Tarancón Spain **43 D4** 40.01N 3.01W
Taranto Italy **47 H4** 40.28N 17.14E
Taranto, G. of Italy **47 H4** 40.00N 17.20E
Tarawa *i.* Kiribati **74 H8** 1.25N173.00E
Tarbagatay Range *mts.* U.S.S.R. **66 C6** 47.00N 83.00E
Tarbat Ness *c.* U.K. **14 E4** 57.52N 3.46W
Tarbert Rep. of Ire. **15 B2** 52.33N 9.24W
Tarbert Strath. U.K. **14 C2** 55.52N 5.26W
Tarbert W. Isles U.K. **14 B4** 57.55N 6.50W
Tarbes France **42 E2** 43.14N 0.05E
Tardoire *r.* France **42 D3** 45.57N 1.00W
Tarifa Spain **43 C2** 36.01N 5.36W
Tarija Bolivia **89 C5** 21.33S 64.45W
Tarim He *r.* China **66 C5** 41.00N 83.30E
Tarkwa Ghana **103 D2** 5.16N 1.59W
Tarlac Phil. **69 G7** 15.29N120.35E
Tarm Denmark **38 B3** 55.54N 8.31E
Tarn *r.* France **42 E3** 44.15N 1.15E
Tarnica *mtn.* Poland **49 K4** 49.05N 22.44E
Tarnów Poland **49 J5** 50.01N 20.59E
Tarragona Spain **43 F4** 41.07N 1.15E
Tarsus Turkey **60 D5** 36.52N 34.52E
Tartary, G. of U.S.S.R. **53 L2** 47.40N141.00E
Tartu U.S.S.R. **50 F2** 58.20N 26.44E
Tarutino U.S.S.R. **49 N3** 46.09N 29.04E
Tarutung Indonesia **68 B4** 2.01N 98.54E
Tashkent U.S.S.R. **66 A5** 41.16N 69.13E
Tasiilaq *see* Ammassalik Greenland **81**
Tasikmalaya Indonesia **68 D2** 7.20S108.16E
Tasinge *i.* Denmark **38 D2** 54.58N 10.38E
Tasmania *d.* Australia **71 D1** 42.00S147.00E
Tasman Sea Pacific Oc. **71 E2** 38.00S162.00E
Tåstrup Denmark **38 F3** 55.39N 12.28E
Tatarsk U.S.S.R. **52 G3** 55.14N 76.00E
Tatnam, C. Canada **81 I3** 57.00N 91.00W
Tatvan Turkey **60 F5** 38.31N 42.15E
Taung-gyi Burma **63 H4** 20.49N 97.01E
Taunton U.K. **13 D3** 51.01N 3.07W
Taunus *mts.* W. Germany **48 D5** 50.07N 7.48E
Taurus Mts. Turkey **60 D5** 37.15N 34.15E
Tavira Portugal **43 B2** 37.07N 7.39W
Tavistock U.K. **13 C2** 50.32N 4.08W
Tavoy Burma **68 B6** 14.07N 98.18E
Taw *r.* U.K. **13 C3** 51.05N 4.04W
Tawau Malaysia **68 F4** 4.16N117.54E
Tay *r.* U.K. **14 E3** 56.21N 3.18W
Tay, Loch U.K. **14 D3** 56.32N 4.08W
Taylor, Mt. U.S.A. **82 E4** 35.14N107.36W
Taymyr, L. U.S.S.R. **53 I4** 74.20N101.00E
Taymyr Pen. U.S.S.R. **53 I4** 75.30N 99.00E
Tayport U.K. **14 F3** 56.26N 2.52W
Tayshet U.S.S.R. **53 I3** 55.56N 98.01E
Tayside *d.* U.K. **14 E3** 56.35N 3.28W
Taytay Phil. **68 F6** 10.47N119.32E
Taz *r.* U.S.S.R. **52 G4** 67.30N 78.50E
Tbilisi U.S.S.R. **61 G6** 41.43N 44.48E
Tebingtinggi Indonesia **68 C3** 3.37S103.09E
Tebingtinggi Indonesia **68 B4** 3.20N 99.08E
Tecuci Romania **49 M2** 45.49N 27.27E
Tees *r.* U.K. **12 F6** 54.35N 1.11W
Tegal Indonesia **68 D2** 6.52S109.07E
Tegucigalpa Honduras **87 G2** 14.05N 87.14W
Tehrān Iran **61 H4** 35.40N 51.26E
Tehuacán Mexico **86 E3** 18.30N 97.26W
Tehuantepec Mexico **86 E3** 16.21N 95.13W
Tehuantepec, G. of Mexico **86 F3** 16.00N 95.00W
Teifi *r.* U.K. **13 C4** 52.05N 4.41W
Teignmouth U.K. **13 D2** 50.33N 3.30W
Tekirdag Turkey **47 M4** 40.59N 27.30E
Tela Honduras **87 G3** 15.56N 87.25W
Telavi U.S.S.R. **61 G6** 41.56N 45.30E
Tel Aviv-Yafo Israel **60 D4** 32.05N 34.46E
Telford U.K. **13 E4** 52.42N 2.30W
Telgte W. Germany **39 F3** 51.59N 7.46E
Télimélé Guinea **102 B3** 10.54N 13.02W
Tel Kotchek Syria **60 F5** 36.48N 42.04E
Tell Atlas *mts.* Algeria **100 C5** 36.10N 4.00E
Telok Anson Malaysia **68 C4** 4.00N101.00E
Telukbetung Indonesia **68 D2** 5.28S105.16E
Tema Ghana **103 D2** 5.41N 0.01W
Teme *r.* U.K. **13 E4** 52.10N 2.13W
Temirtau U.S.S.R. **52 G2** 50.05N 72.55E
Tempio Italy **46 D4** 40.54N 9.06E
Temple U.S.A. **83 G3** 31.06N 97.22W
Templemore Rep. of Ire. **15 D2** 52.48N 7.51W
Temuco Chile **89 B4** 38.45S 72.40W
Tenasserim Burma **68 B6** 12.05N 99.00E
Tenby U.K. **13 C3** 51.41N 4.42W
Ten Degree Channel Indian Oc. **68 A5** 10.00N 92.30E
Tenerife *i.* Canary Is. **100 A4** 28.10N 16.30W
Tengchong China **66 F2** 25.02N 98.28E
Tengiz, L. U.S.S.R. **52 F2** 50.30N 69.00E
Teng Xian China **67 I4** 35.10N117.14E
Tenke Zaïre **99 C3** 10.34S 26.12E
Tennessee *d.* U.S.A. **83 I4** 36.00N 86.00W
Tennessee *r.* U.S.A. **83 I4** 37.10N 88.25W
Teófilo Otoni Brazil **89 E6** 17.52S 41.31W
Tepic Mexico **86 D4** 21.30N104.51W
Teplice Czech. **48 F5** 50.40N 13.50E
Ter *r.* Spain **43 G5** 42.02N 3.10E
Tera *r.* Portugal **43 A3** 38.55N 8.01W
Teramo Italy **46 F5** 42.40N 13.43E
Terassa Spain **43 F4** 41.34N 2.00E
Terebovlya U.S.S.R. **49 L4** 49.18N 25.44E
Terekhova U.S.S.R. **49 O6** 52.13N 31.28E
Teresina Brazil **88 E7** 4.50S 42.50W
Termez U.S.S.R. **52 F1** 37.15N 67.15E
Termini Italy **46 F2** 37.59N 13.42E
Terminos Lagoon Mexico **86 F3** 18.30N 91.30W
Termoli Italy **46 G4** 41.58N 14.59E
Ternate Indonesia **69 H4** 0.48N127.23E
Terneuzen Neth. **39 B3** 51.20N 3.50E
Terni Italy **46 F5** 42.34N 12.44E
Ternopol U.S.S.R. **49 L4** 49.35N 25.39E
Terre Haute U.S.A. **83 I4** 39.27N 87.24W
Terschelling *i.* Neth. **39 D5** 53.25N 5.25E
Teruel Spain **43 E4** 40.21N 1.06W
Teslin *r.* Canada **80 E4** 62.00N135.00W
Tessaoua Niger **103 F3** 13.46N 7.55E
Test *r.* U.K. **13 F2** 50.55N 1.29W
Têt *r.* France **42 F2** 42.43N 3.00E
Teterev *r.* U.S.S.R. **49 O5** 51.03N 30.30E
Tetiyev U.S.S.R. **49 N4** 49.22N 29.40E
Tetuan Morocco **100 B5** 35.34N 5.22W
Teviot *r.* U.K. **14 F2** 55.36N 2.27W
Teviothead U.K. **14 F2** 55.20N 2.55W
Tewkesbury U.K. **13 E3** 52.00N 2.10W
Texarkana U.S.A. **83 H3** 33.28N 94.02W
Texas *d.* U.S.A. **82 F3** 32.00N100.00W
Texel *i.* Neth. **39 C5** 53.05N 4.47E
Texoma, L. U.S.A. **83 G3** 34.00N 96.40W
Tezpur India **63 G5** 26.38N 92.49E
Thabana Ntlenyana *mtn.* Lesotho **94 E2** 29.30S 29.10E
Thailand Asia **68 C7** 16.00N102.00E
Thailand, G. of Asia **68 C6** 11.00N101.00E
Thai Nguyen Vietnam **68 D8** 21.31N105.55E
Thakhek Laos **68 C7** 17.25N104.45E
Thale Luang *l.* Thailand **68 C5** 7.30N100.20E
Thame *r.* U.K. **13 F3** 51.38N 1.11W
Thames *r.* U.K. **13 H3** 51.30N 0.05E
Thāna India **63 D3** 19.14N 73.02E
Thanh Hóa Vietnam **68 D7** 19.50N105.48E
Thanjāvūr India **63 E2** 10.46N 79.09E
Thar Desert India **63 C5** 28.00N 72.00E
Tharrawaddy Burma **66 E1** 17.37N 95.48E
Tharthar, Wadi *r.* Iraq **60 F4** 34.18N 43.07E
Tharthar Basin *f.* Iraq **60 F4** 33.56N 43.16E
Thásos *i.* Greece **47 L4** 40.40N 24.39E
Thaton Burma **68 B7** 17.00N 97.39E
Thaungdut Burma **63 G4** 24.26N 94.45E
Thayetmyo Burma **63 G3** 19.20N 95.18E
Thebes *ruins* Egypt **60 D2** 25.41N 32.40E
The Cherokees, L. O' U.S.A. **83 H4** 36.45N 94.50W
The Cheviot *mtn.* U.K. **12 E7** 55.29N 2.10W
The Cheviot Hills U.K. **12 E7** 55.22N 2.24W
The Everglades *f.* U.S.A. **83 J2** 26.00N 80.30W
The Fens *f.* U.K. **13 H4** 52.40N 0.07E
The Gulf Asia **61 H2** 27.00N 50.00E
The Hague Neth. **39 C4** 52.05N 4.16E
The Little Minch *str.* U.K. **14 B4** 57.40N 6.45W
Thelon *r.* Canada **81 I4** 64.23N 96.15W
The Machers *f.* U.K. **14 D1** 54.45N 4.28W
The Minch *str.* U.K. **14 C5** 58.10N 5.50W
The Needles U.K. **13 F2** 50.40N 1.35W
Theodore Roosevelt L. U.S.A. **82 D3** 33.30N111.10W
The Pas Canada **81 H3** 53.50N101.15W
The Pennines *hills* U.K. **12 E6** 54.40N 2.20W
The Rhinns *f.* U.K. **14 C1** 54.50N 5.02W
Thermopylae, Pass of Greece **47 K3** 38.47N 22.34E
The Snares *is.* New Zealand **74 G3** 48.00S166.30E
The Solent *str.* U.K. **13 F2** 50.45N 1.20W
Thessaloniki Greece **47 K4** 40.38N 22.56E
Thessaloniki, G. of Med. Sea **47 K4** 40.10N 23.00E
Thetford U.K. **13 H4** 52.25N 0.44E
The Wash *b.* U.K. **12 H4** 52.55N 0.15E
The Weald *f.* U.K. **13 H3** 51.05N 0.20E
Thiers France **42 F3** 45.51N 3.33E
Thiès Senegal **102 A3** 14.50N 16.55W
Thimbu Bhutan **63 F5** 27.29N 89.40E
Thionville France **42 H5** 49.22N 6.11E
Thíra *i.* Greece **47 L2** 36.24N 25.27E
Thirsk U.K. **12 F6** 54.15N 1.20W
Thisted Denmark **38 B4** 56.58N 8.42E
Thitu Is. S. China Sea **68 E6** 10.50N114.20E
Thjórsá *r.* Iceland **50 I6** 63.53N 20.38W
Tholen *i.* Neth. **39 C3** 51.34N 4.07E
Thomasville U.S.A. **83 J3** 30.50N 83.59W
Thonburi Thailand **68 C6** 13.43N100.27E
Thorshavn Faroe Is. **50 M9** 62.02N 6.47W
Thouars France **42 D4** 46.59N 0.13W
Thrapston U.K. **13 G4** 52.23N 0.30W
Three Kings Is. New Zealand **74 H4** 34.09S172.09E
Thuin Belgium **39 C2** 50.21N 4.20E
Thule Greenland **81 L5** 77.30N 69.29W
Thun Switz. **48 C3** 46.46N 7.38E
Thunder Bay *town* Canada **81 J2** 48.25N 89.14W
Thuringian Forest *mts.* E. Germany **48 E5** 50.40N 10.50E
Thurles Rep. of Ire. **15 D2** 52.41N 7.50W
Thurso U.K. **14 E5** 58.35N 3.32W
Thurso *r.* U.K. **8 E6** 58.35N 3.32W
Thyborön Denmark **38 B4** 56.42N 8.12E
Tianjin China **67 I5** 39.08N117.12E
Tian Shan *mts.* Asia **66 C5** 42.00N 80.30E
Tianshui China **66 G4** 34.25N105.58E
Tibati Cameroon **103 G2** 6.25N 12.33E
Tiber *r.* Italy **46 F4** 41.45N 12.16E
Tiberias, L. Israel **60 D4** 32.49N 35.36E
Tibesti Mountains Chad **100 D4** 21.00N 17.30E
Tibet *d.* China **66 D4** 32.20N 86.00E
Tibetan Plateau *f.* China **66 D4** 34.00N 86.15E
Tiburon I. Mexico **86 B5** 29.00N112.25W
Ticino *r.* Italy **46 D6** 45.09N 9.12E
Tidjikdja Mauritania **100 A3** 18.29N 11.31W
Tiel Neth. **39 D3** 51.53N 5.26E
Tielt Belgium **39 B3** 51.00N 3.20E
Tierra Blanca Mexico **86 E3** 18.28N 96.12W
Tierra del Fuego *i.* S. America **89 C2** 54.00S 68.30W
Tietar *r.* Spain **43 C3** 39.50N 6.00W
Tigris *r.* Asia **61 G3** 31.00N 47.27E
Tihama *f.* Saudi Arabia **101 F4** 20.30N 40.30E
Tijuana Mexico **86 A6** 32.29N117.10W
Tiksi U.S.S.R. **53 K4** 71.40N128.45E
Tilburg Neth. **39 D3** 51.34N 5.05E
Tilbury U.K. **13 H3** 51.28N 0.25E
Till *r.* U.K. **12 E7** 55.41N 2.11W
Tillabéri Niger **103 E3** 14.28N 1.27E
Timbuktu Mali **102 D4** 16.49N 2.59W
Timiş *r.* Yugo./Romania **49 J2** 44.49N 20.28E
Timişoara Romania **49 J2** 45.47N 21.15E
Timmins Canada **81 J2** 48.30N 81.20W
Timok *r.* Yugo. **47 K6** 44.13N 22.40E
Timor *i.* Indonesia **69 H2** 9.30S125.00E
Timor Sea Austa. **71 B4** 13.00S122.00E
Tinahely Rep. of Ire. **15 E2** 52.48N 6.30W
Tinglev Denmark **38 C2** 54.57N 9.15E
Tingsryd Sweden **50 C2** 56.31N 15.00E
Tinkisso *r.* Guinea **102 C3** 11.25N 9.05W
Tinne *r.* Norway **50 B2** 59.05N 9.43E
Tínos *i.* Greece **47 L2** 37.36N 25.08E
Tioman, Pulau *i.* Malaysia **68 C4** 2.45N104.10E
Tipperary Rep. of Ire. **15 C2** 52.29N 8.10W
Tipperary *d.* Rep. of Ire. **15 D2** 52.37N 7.55W
Tiranë Albania **47 I4** 41.20N 19.48E
Tirano Italy **46 E7** 46.12N 10.10E
Tiraspol U.S.S.R. **49 N3** 46.50N 29.38E
Tirebolu Turkey **60 E6** 41.02N 38.49E
Tiree *i.* U.K. **14 B3** 56.30N 6.50W
Tîrgu-Jiu Romania **49 K2** 45.03N 23.17E
Tîrgu-Lăpuş Romania **49 K3** 47.27N 23.52E
Tîrgu Mureş Romania **49 L3** 46.33N 24.34E
Tirlemont Belgium **39 C2** 50.49N 4.56E
Tirso *r.* Italy **46 D3** 39.52N 8.33E
Tiruchirapalli India **63 E2** 10.50N 78.43E
Tirunelveli India **63 D2** 8.45N 77.43E
Tiruppur India **63 D2** 11.05N 77.20E
Tisa *r.* Yugo. **49 J2** 45.09N 20.16E
Tisza *r. see* Tisa *r* Hungary **49**
Titicaca, L. Bolivia/Peru **88 C6** 16.00S 69.00W
Titograd Yugo. **47 I5** 42.30N 19.16E
Titovo Užice Yugo. **47 I5** 43.52N 19.51E
Titov Veles Yugo. **47 J4** 41.43N 21.49E
Tiverton U.K. **13 D2** 50.55N 3.29W
Tizimín Mexico **87 G4** 21.10N 88.09W
Tizi Ouzou Algeria **100 C5** 36.44N 4.05E
Tjörn *i.* Sweden **38 E5** 58.00N 11.30E
Tlaxcala *d.* Mexico **86 E3** 19.45N 98.20W
Tlemcen Algeria **100 B5** 34.53N 1.21W
Toab U.K. **14 G6** 59.53N 1.18W
Toamasina Madagascar **99 G8** 18.10S 49.23E
Toba, L. Indonesia **68 B4** 2.45N 98.50E
Tobelo Indonesia **69 H4** 1.45N127.59E
Tobermory U.K. **14 B3** 56.37N 6.04W
Tobi *i.* Caroline Is. **69 I4** 3.01N131.10E
Tobi shima *i.* Japan **70 D6** 39.12N139.32E
Toboali Indonesia **68 D3** 3.00S106.30E
Tobol *r.* U.S.S.R. **52 F3** 58.15N 68.12E
Tobolsk U.S.S.R. **52 F3** 58.15N 68.12E
Tobruk Libya **101 E5** 32.06N 23.58E
Tocantins *r.* Brazil **88 E7** 2.40S 49.20W
Tocorpuri *mtn.* Bolivia **89 C5** 22.26S 67.53W
Tofuku *d.* Japan **70 D6** 39.00N139.50E
Togian Is. Indonesia **69 G3** 0.20S122.00E
Togo Africa **103 E2** 8.00N 1.00E
Tokai *d.* Japan **70 C4** 35.00N137.00E
Tokat Turkey **60 E6** 40.20N 36.35E
Tokelau Is. Pacific Oc. **74 I7** 9.00S171.45W
Tokuno *i.* Japan **67 K3** 27.40N129.00E
Tokushima Japan **70 B4** 34.03N134.34E
Tokuyama Japan **70 A4** 34.04N131.48E
Tōkyō Japan **70 D4** 35.40N139.45E
Tolbukhin Bulgaria **47 M5** 43.34N 27.52E
Toledo Spain **43 C3** 39.52N 4.02W
Toledo U.S.A. **83 J5** 41.40N 83.35W
Toledo, Montes de *mts.* Spain **43 C3** 39.35N 4.30W
Toliara Madagascar **99 F7** 23.20S 43.41E
Tolo, G. of Indonesia **69 G3** 2.00S122.30E
Tolosa Spain **43 D5** 43.09N 2.04W
Toluca Mexico **86 E3** 19.20N 99.40W
Toluca *mtn.* Mexico **86 E3** 19.10N 99.40W
Tol'yatti U.S.S.R. **52 E3** 53.32N 49.24E
Tomakomai Japan **70 E8** 42.39N141.33E
Tomaszów Mazowiecki Poland **49 J5** 51.32N 20.01E
Tombigbee *r.* U.S.A. **83 I3** 31.05N 87.55W
Tomelloso Spain **43 D3** 39.09N 3.01W
Tomini Indonesia **69 G4** 0.31N120.30E
Tomini G. Indonesia **69 G3** 0.30S120.45E
Tomintoul U.K. **14 E4** 57.17N 3.22W
Tom Price Australia **71 A3** 22.49S117.51E

U

V